France FDI Screening

Legal and Strategic Framework

Collection
By the same author

Le guide des investissements étrangers dans les secteurs stratégiques, ed. Ellipses, 2011
(The Guide to Foreign Investment in Strategic Sectors)

Mondialisation et patriotisme économique, preface by Nicolas Dufourcq, Chairman and CEO of Bpifrance, ed. JM Laffont, 2014
(Globalization and Economic Patriotism)

Lobbying, du déni au défi, with Grégory Houillon, preface by Bernard Accoyer, former President of the National Assembly, ed. PresseLittéraire, 2016
(Lobbying: From Denial to Challenge)

Sécurité économique et souverainetés industrielles, preface by Bruno Le Maire, former Minister of the Economy, ed. Presses Universitaires de France (PUF), 2020
(Economic Security and Industrial Sovereignties)

CFIUS, Le contrôle des investissements étrangers aux États-Unis, ed. Relians, 2022
(CFIUS – Foreign Investment Screening in the United States)

IEF, Le contrôle des investissements étrangers en France, 1st ed., ed. Relians, 2024
(IEF – Foreign Investment Screening in France)

IEF, Le contrôle des investissements étrangers en France – 2eme édition, 2nd ed., ed. Relians, 2025
(IEF – Foreign Investment Screening in France)

France FDI Screening

Legal and Strategic Framework

Expanded and Updated English Edition

Pascal DUPEYRAT

First English edition: January 2026
ISBN (Paperback): 978-2-9584520-4-9
ISBN (eBook): 978-2-9584520-6-3

Published by Relians Publishing
Paris, France
www.relians.fr

Print-on-demand printing by IngramSpark (Ingram Content Group).

Cover image: 123RF

ISBN 978-2-9584520-4-9

This book is the expanded and updated English edition of the second French edition of the original work, revised in September 2025 and first published in French in 2024 under the title "IEF : Le contrôle des investissements étrangers en France", by Relians Publishing.

Table of contents

This English version was produced with the assistance of ChatGPT (OpenAI), under the supervision of the author, based on the original second French edition published in 2025.

It has been carefully adapted for an international readership with legal interest in the French regulatory framework for foreign direct investment (FDI). The present edition incorporates new commentary, updated figures, and legal developments as of mid-2025. All translations of French legal texts and references are unofficial unless otherwise stated.

Introduction

This first English edition of the second French version of a book devoted to the screening of foreign direct investment (FDI) in France is published against the backdrop of a renewed role of States in regulating business activity. Following the wave of liberalization in the 1990s, which enshrined the free movement of capital as a cornerstone of market economies, the 2020s mark a turning point: the freedom to invest remains intact, but it is now counterbalanced by heightened governmental vigilance aimed at protecting strategic sectors and the sovereign interests of nations.

France provides a particularly telling example of this evolution. In an international environment defined by persistent geopolitical tensions and intensifying economic competition, the protection of sensitive technologies and enterprises essential to national security has become a priority. As France's Minister of the Economy, Éric Lombard, emphasized[1]: "*Current geopolitical tensions highlight the urgent need to secure and develop strategic sectors that safeguard our national interests. The Government's action in this regard is more necessary than ever, requiring us to preserve, within our national territory, our industrial capacities, know-how, and technologies, and to prevent their capture.*"

At the heart of this strategy lies the French FDI screening regime also known as the IEF regime. The State plays an active role, endowed with powers to authorize, block, or impose modifications on contemplated transactions, reinforced by economic police prerogatives (injunctions, sanctions, and even forced divestments). Once regarded as marginal, this screening mechanism has now become a mandatory step in transactions involving foreign investors and sensitive activities.

This new edition addresses a dual necessity. First, it incorporates recent legislative and regulatory developments, most notably the 2025 Guidelines, which represent a decisive milestone in the consolidation of the regime. It also takes into account the broader institutional and political context in which the screening mechanism now operates, shaped by the strengthening of parliamentary oversight, the adoption of a new law on foreign interference, the ongoing reform of the European Union's FDI screening framework, and the publication of the guidelines of the High Authority for Transparency in Public Life (HATVP) regarding influence activities. Second, it reflects the experience accumulated by both practitioners and authorities over recent years, illustrated by concrete cases, landmark decisions, and the statistical data provided in annual reports.

Structured in four main parts, the book offers a comprehensive analysis of the French FDI screening regime . The first part sets out its foundational principles and

1. France, Ministry of the Economy, Finance and Industrial and Digital Sovereignty, Directorate General of the Treasury, Annual Report 2025, "Foreign Direct Investment Screening in France," published July 30, 2025, last accessed July 31, 2025, available at https://www.tresor.economie.gouv.fr/Articles/2025/07/30/publication-du-rapport-annuel-sur-le-controle-ief-en-2024

possible exemptions. The second details the eligibility criteria and strategic considerations guiding the review. The third examines the procedural framework, from the initial filing to the final decision. The fourth part explores available remedies and litigation avenues.

Beyond the technicalities of the procedure, this book seeks to demonstrate that FDI screening is not merely an administrative formality but a strategic instrument of economic sovereignty. It serves to preserve the Nation's fundamental interests, while ensuring that France remains both open and attractive to investment.

Part One

The IEF Framework

Since 1966, the freedom to invest has constituted a fundamental principle of the French economy. It governs and structures economic exchanges, particularly financial relations with foreign entities.

Sixty years after the establishment of this political commitment to engage with the world, it is clear that France has undergone a profound transformation of its economy, notably by dismantling the screening regimes that had been implemented during the crises of the 20th century. This commitment to economic openness was further reinforced through France's participation in the Common Market and subsequently within the European Union.

In 2024 [2], despite a persistently uncertain economic and geopolitical environment, France remained, for the sixth consecutive year, the leading destination for foreign direct investment (FDI) in Europe. According to the EY Attractiveness Barometer 2025, the country attracted 1,025 projects, maintaining its position ahead of its historical competitors: the United Kingdom, with 853 projects (–13%), and Germany, with 608 projects (–17%).

Although this performance reflects a 14% decline compared to 2023 (1,194 projects), it nevertheless demonstrates the resilience of France's investment appeal in a global context of slowing FDI flows. At the European level, foreign investment projects fell to 5,383, their lowest level in nine years, representing an average decrease of 5% compared to 2023.

France thus consolidates its status as a prime destination for foreign investors, supported by its industrial capacity, innovation ecosystem, and the steady establishment of high–value-added projects, despite ongoing challenges related to energy costs, competitiveness, and regulatory complexity.

This leading position is all the more remarkable given the vigorous domestic debates concerning the appropriate balance to be struck between openness to foreign investment on one hand, and the necessity to protect, or even adopt a degree of protectionism, on the other.

2. Ernst & Young Advisory, "New Shocks, New Challenges for France and Europe," published May 15, 2025, accessed July 31, 2025, available at https://www.ey.com/content/dam/ey-unified-site/ey-com/fr-fr/campaigns/foreign-direct-investment-surveys/documents/ey-barometre-ey-attractivite-france-2025.pdf

In this context, following an international trend initiated by the United States in 2018 to strengthen foreign investment screening [3], France adjusted its policy to better align with its national security interests. This culminated in the adoption in 2019 of the PACTE law [4], which reinforced the foreign direct investment screening framework in France, commonly referred to by its acronym, the IEF system.

The rationale for this reinforcement became fully evident during the 2020 Covid crisis, which underscored the absolute necessity to safeguard the French economy, particularly its strategic sectors, in the event of stock market turmoil and severe depreciation of the CAC 40 index. One year later, the war in Ukraine reaffirmed fundamental concerns relating to control of the value chain, securing the supply of strategic resources, and protecting critical infrastructure of vital importance.

Emerging from this profound reassessment, the issue of sovereignty returned to the forefront, now recognized as a matter of public policy, reflected in the 2022 assignment [5] of responsibility for "industrial and digital sovereignty". to the Minister of the Economy, the government's second-ranking official.

It is against this backdrop that foreign investment operations, including mergers and acquisitions, in strategic sectors are now conducted.

The State has thus become a fully-fledged actor in foreign investment transactions: it may authorize, refuse, or conditionally approve an investment, impose sanctions for non-compliance with commitments, and, where appropriate, demand divestment of a completed transaction. These considerations have significant consequences on the practice of mergers and acquisitions in France.

Understanding the IEF framework has become imperative for all market participants. Accordingly, this first part will examine the principles and exemptions of foreign investment screening in France (Chapter 1), then analyze the legal texts organizing the screening regime (Chapter 2) and their regulation through official guidelines (Chapter 3). It will also address the respective roles of the Minister of the Economy responsible for the framework (Chapter 4), as well as Parliament's oversight function (Chapter 5). Furthermore, it will consider how the IEF system interacts with European screening mechanisms (Chapter 6) and other safeguards designed to protect national interests (Chapter 7). This section will also address the cost-free nature of the French FDI screening procedure (Chapter 8). Finally, it will examine the issue of transparency regarding foreign influence and interference activities in connection with the screening framework, in light of the rules laid down by the High Authority for the Transparency of Public Life (HATVP) (Chapter 9).

3. United States, U.S. Government Publishing Office, 115th Congress, Public Law 115-232, John S. McCain National Defense Authorization Act for Fiscal Year 2019, August 13, 2018, p. 132, STAT. 1636, legislative history H.R. 5515, 538, Foreign Investment Risk Review Modernization Act of 2018, available at https://www.govinfo.gov/app/details/PLAW-115publ232 (last accessed September 1, 2025)
4. France, Law No. 2019-486 of May 22, 2019, on Business Growth and Transformation, Official Journal of the French Republic, No. 0119, May 23, 2019, NOR: ECOT1810669L
5. France, Decree of May 20, 2022, concerning the composition of the Government, Official Journal of the French Republic, No. 0118, May 21, 2022, NOR: HRUX2213743D

Chapter 1

Principle and Exception Underpinning the Foreign Direct Investment Screening in France

The freedom of foreign nationals to invest in France is a cornerstone of the country's economic model, which aims to remain open and attractive. This fundamental freedom enables foreign investors to contribute meaningfully to France's economic development.

However, this freedom is subject to limitations aimed at safeguarding national interests. The exception to the freedom of foreign investment is grounded in the State's legitimate objective to protect strategic sectors and vital national interests. To this end, France has established a screening mechanism designed to ensure the preservation of national sovereignty. This mechanism is commonly referred to as the foreign investment screening mechanism in France, or by its French acronym, IEF (Investissements Étrangers en France).

The notion of the «National:interest," which lies at the heart of this derogation, remains a context-dependent and evolving concept. Accordingly, this chapter – and the ones that follow – will examine the criteria and developments that have shaped this notion, thereby underscoring the need for constant adaptation to shifting economic and geopolitical realities.

The Freedom to Invest in France Is the Governing Principle

France is a country built upon the rule of law and individual liberties. It therefore enshrines the principle of investment freedom within its economic framework and attaches particular importance to the freedom of foreign nationals to invest. This principle constitutes the legal and policy foundation of France's financial relations with the rest of the world.

Historically [6], up until 1966, the French regulatory regime governing financial relations with foreign countries consisted largely of emergency measures adopted during the two World Wars. These included a patchwork of legislative instruments, laws,

6. France, DUPEYRAT, Pascal, *"Sécurité économique et souverainetés industrielles"*, 2020, PUF Publishing, foreword by LE MAIRE, Bruno, pp. 81–85

decrees, ordinances, and even "décrets-lois" (a now-defunct form of delegated legislation), all sharing the common objective of subjecting cross-border financial activity to prior authorization. During this period, the French economy was characterized by a highly centralized model with numerous authorization regimes in place. However, it is worth noting that most of these measures focused on controlling foreign exchange rather than regulating foreign investment per se.

Between 1945 and 1966, as France's economy recovered and became increasingly integrated into international markets, the regulatory framework for foreign investment began to liberalize gradually. Notable among these liberalizing measures was the Act [7] of February 2, 1948, which restored freedom of trade, as well as the decree of January 21, 1959, which introduced a more liberal regime [8] for foreign investments in France.

The full recognition of foreign investment freedom came in 1966, under the leadership of General de Gaulle. At that time, the French Government , observing the progressive liberalization of cross-border financial relations, proposed the repeal of the various regulations still in force. The stated objective was to eliminate non-tariff barriers to foreign investment. More fundamentally, the Government sought to bring legal doctrine into alignment with actual practice: freedom would henceforth be the rule, and authorization the exception [9]. This shift is clearly articulated in the official explanatory memorandum [10] accompanying the 1966 draft law, which stated: "*It is not acceptable that the principle should be prohibition while practice reflects freedom.*"

Since 1966, financial relations with foreign countries have been governed by the principle of freedom. Article 1 of the Act [11] of December 25, 1966, now codified in Article L.151-1 of the Monetary and Financial Code, provides that: "*Financial relations between France and foreign countries are unrestricted. This freedom is exercised in accordance with the provisions of this Act and subject to France's international commitments.*"

The reform introduced by the 1966 law was not merely legal; it also reflected broader economic and political considerations. The freedom to invest must be understood in the context of the Cold War, when the free-market model stood in direct contrast, and often opposition, to the centrally planned economies of the communist bloc. As such, the French Minister of the Economy and Finance could assert, during

7. France, Law No. 48-178 of February 2, 1948, amending certain provisions of the foreign exchange regulations, Official Journal of the French Republic, February 3, 1948, p. 1114
8. France, Ministry of Finance and Economic Affairs, Office of Foreign Exchange, Opinion No. 669 on the regime applicable to foreign investments in the Franc Zone, Official Journal of the French Republic, No. 0017, January 21, 1959, p. 1130
9. This principle/exception framework is also reflected, in reverse, in Articles 63 and 65 of the TFEU (see supra).
10. France, National Assembly, Report, Annex No. 2253, VALLON, Louis, Deputy, Official Journal of the National Assembly, December 14, 1966, p. 1117, submitted on behalf of the Finance Committee on Bill No. 2183, National Assembly Documents, preparatory works, discussed and adopted following a declaration of urgency, sitting of December 13, 1966. See also National Assembly Documents, sitting of November 29, 1966, Annex No. 2183, p. 951
11. France, Law No. 66-1008 of December 28, 1966, on financial relations with foreign countries, Official Journal of the French Republic, No. 0299, December 29, 1966, p. 11621

the presentation of the 1966 bill on financial relations with foreign countries [12] : *"Freedom is the principle... a principle that is consistent not only with our political tradition, but also with our conception of international relations and, I would even say, of economic relations between individuals around the world."*

From Liberalization to Regulation: The Gradual Structuring of France's Foreign Investment Control Framework (1966–1996)

Between 1966 and 1996, France undertook a sweeping liberalization of its financial relations with foreign countries. This liberalization was driven both by economic theory and by European integration within the broader context of globalization. These motivations are clearly reflected in the legislative history of the 1996 Law [13] (discussed below), which reframed foreign investment flows not as a loss of control over national assets, but as a net benefit to economic activity and employment [14].

Throughout this period, reform initiatives were primarily aimed at aligning France's foreign direct investment screening regime with its international commitments. On the one hand, within the framework of the Organisation for Economic Co-operation and Development [15] (OECD), France pledged to gradually eliminate restrictions on capital movements. On the other hand, European law, particularly the Treaty [16] of Rome as amended by the Maastricht Treaty [17] (ratified on September 20, 1992), established the principle of full liberalization of capital movements between Member States and third countries. More broadly, this liberalization was reinforced by a growing network of bilateral investment treaties (BITs).).

It was during this same period that France's legal framework for foreign investment began to take shape. However, it must be acknowledged that this process was largely empirical, evolving by trial and error, and resulting in a legal architecture that may appear fragmented or inconsistent when assessed retrospectively.

12. France, National Assembly, Debates, Official Report, 1st sitting of December 14, 1966, Financial Relations with Foreign Countries, discussion following a declaration of urgency on a draft bill, DEBRE, Michel, Minister of the Economy and Finance, Official Journal of the National Assembly, December 14, 1966, p. 5515
13. France, Law No. 96-109 of February 14, 1996, on financial relations with foreign countries with respect to foreign investments in France, Official Journal of the French Republic, No. 39, February 15, 1996, p. 2385, NOR: ECOX9500155L
14. France, National Assembly, Report No. 2492 of January 18, 1996, MENUEL, Georges, Deputy, submitted on behalf of the Finance, General Economy and Planning Committee on Bill No. 2347 supplementing Law No. 66-1008 of December 28, 1966, on financial relations with foreign countries with respect to foreign investments, National Assembly Document, distributed January 22, 1996
15. Organisation for Economic Co-operation and Development (OECD), Code of Liberalisation of Capital Movements, OECD Council Decision of December 12, 1961 (OECD/C(61)96), available at www.oecd.org/investment/codes.htm (last accessed September 1, 2025)
16. European Union, Treaty establishing the European Economic Community, March 25, 1957, Document 11957E/TXT, ELI: http://data.europa.eu/eli/treaty/teec/sign, Articles 73 B and 73 C
17. European Union, Treaty establishing the European Community, codified version of the Treaty establishing the European Community, August 31, 1992, consolidated version, ELI: http://data.europa.eu/eli/treaty/tec_1992/oj, Articles 56 (ex-Article 73 B) and 57 (ex-Article 73 C)

To grasp the evolution of France's foreign direct investment screening system, one must engage in a kind of legal archaeology, identifying and analyzing the successive layers of regulatory instruments that gradually structured the regime.

The first notable step was the Circular [18] of May 21, 1987 on French direct investment abroad and foreign direct investment in France. This Circular relaxed the applicable rules by subjecting intra-Community investors to a simplified regime of prior notification, while maintaining a system of prior authorization for non-Community investors.

Following this development, the French government adopted the Decree [19] of December 29, 1989 regulating financial relations with foreign countries, which was quickly amended and supplemented by the Decree [20] of January 15, 1990. This 1990 Decree marked a turning point by exempting European investors, permanently established and formally recognized as such, from any prior notification requirement, except for investments falling within specific sensitive sectors (see below).

On February 11, 1992, the government adopted a new Decree [21] further relaxing the regime by exempting certain lower-value transactions originating from non-EU countries from prior authorization. At the same time, the regime applicable to European investors was extended to include investors from countries party to the Agreement on the European Economic Area (EEA).

The year 1996 represented a major milestone in the liberalization process that had begun three decades earlier with the foundational law of December 28, 1966. The Law [22] of February 14, 1996 on financial relations with foreign countries as regards foreign investment in France, together with its implementing Decree [23] of the same date, formally abolished the requirement for prior authorization or notification for most categories of foreign direct investment (FDI) in France. Henceforth, FDI became subject only to a statistical reporting obligation, as provided by Article 11 of the implementing Decree.

This 1996 reform eliminated the dual-track system, notification versus authorization, based on the origin of the investment (Community or non-Community), in favor

18. France, Ministry of the Economy, Finance and Privatization, Circular of May 21, 1987, on French direct investments abroad and foreign direct investments in France, Official Journal of the French Republic, No. 119, May 23, 1987, p. 5656, NOR: ECOT8770005C
19. France, Decree No. 89-938 of December 29, 1989, regulating financial relations with foreign countries, Official Journal of the French Republic, No. 0303, December 30, 1989, p. 16411, NOR: ECOX8910405D
20. France, Decree No. 90-58 of January 15, 1990, amending and supplementing Decree No. 89-938 of December 29, 1989, regulating financial relations with foreign countries, Official Journal of the French Republic, No. 13, January 16, 1990, p. 650, NOR: ECOX9010021D
21. France, Decree No. 92-134 of February 11, 1992, amending Decree No. 89-938 of December 29, 1989, as amended, regulating financial relations with foreign countries, Official Journal of the French Republic, No. 36, February 12, 1992, p. 2271, NOR: ECOX9210017D
22. France, Law No. 96-109 of February 14, 1996, on financial relations with foreign countries with respect to foreign investments in France, Official Journal of the French Republic, No. 39, February 15, 1996, p. 2385, NOR: ECOX9500155L
23. France, Decree No. 96-117 of February 14, 1996, amending Decree No. 89-938 of December 29, 1989, regulating financial relations with foreign countries, Official Journal of the French Republic, No. 39, February 15, 1996, p. 2408, NOR: ECOT9640306D

of a more streamlined and liberalized approach [24]. This transformation was subsequently codified in Article L.151-1 of the French Monetary and Financial Code, which provides: "Financial relations between France and foreign countries are free. This freedom is exercised under the conditions laid down in this Chapter, in compliance with France's international commitments."

Since the enactment of the 1996 Law, the overarching principle of the freedom of foreign investment in France has not been challenged. More recently, this principle was reaffirmed in the legislative memorandum accompanying the 2019 PACTE Law [25], the first piece of legislation since 1996 to directly address the protection of strategic sectors. That memorandum emphasized that "financial relations with foreign countries are in principle free; France fully encourages such relations and seeks to remain attractive to both foreign and domestic investors who wish to contribute to the country's economic development."

This commitment to openness is regularly highlighted in governmental communications on the Choose France summits, an initiative aimed at promoting France as a top-tier destination for foreign direct investment. These events underscore [26] the importance French public authorities attach to international investment in sustaining national competitiveness and innovation.

In conclusion, this legal archaeology of France's foreign investment framework reveals a progressive trajectory from stringent regulation toward liberalization, underpinned by the guiding principle of freedom to invest. Yet, this liberal framework coexists with a derogatory regime applicable to sensitive sectors. This regime, grounded in public order and national security considerations, falls within the regulatory domain and empowers the French authorities to subject certain transactions to prior review and approval where strategic interests are at stake.

The Protection of National Interests as a Justification for the Derogation from the Freedom to Invest

In French legislation, the existence of a derogation from the principle of freedom of foreign investment is concomitant with the establishment of that very principle. This derogation is primarily grounded in the protection of national interests.

Indeed, the Law [27] of December 28, 1966, on financial relations with foreign countries provides that "the Government may, in order to safeguard national interests and by decree adopted upon the recommendation of the Minister of the Economy and

24. France, CARREAU, Dominique and HURSTEL, Daniel, " La Nouvelle Liberté des investissements directs étrangers en France " Dalloz, 1996, Chroniques, p. 239
25. France, Law No. 2019-486 of May 22, 2019, on Business Growth and Transformation, Official Journal of the French Republic, No. 0119, May 23, 2019, NOR: ECOT1810669L
26. France, Senate, Oral Question No. 2235G to the Prime Minister, January 19, 2022, Official Journal of the Senate, January 20, 2022, p. 665, PATRIAT, François, Senator, RDPI Group, Ministerial Reply, January 19, 2022, Official Journal of the Senate, January 20, 2022, p. 665
27. France, Law No. 66-1008 of December 28, 1966, on financial relations with foreign countries, Official Journal of the French Republic, No. 0299, December 29, 1966, p. 11621

Finance, subject the formation or liquidation of foreign investments in France to a declaration, prior authorization, or control." From the outset, the legislator established an exception to the freedom of foreign investment, an exception rooted in public policy and thus binding upon the parties regardless of their individual intent.

The explanatory memorandum of the 1966 bill clarifies the rationale behind this derogation: "The public authorities of an independent Nation must at all times possess broad powers of action in this field in order to ensure a necessary degree of autonomy for the pursuit of our economic, financial, or social policy." The report of the French Senate on the 1966 draft legislation further illuminates the broader philosophy of the reform, justifying the derogation provided under Article 3 by pointing to the risk of "colonization of the vital sectors of our economy."

Another notable aspect of the 1966 reform is that the legislator vested the executive branch, at that time, exclusively, with the authority to assess and determine the measures necessary to protect national interests. In other words, the legislature delegated to the Government the power to define the derogation regime by decree. Parliamentary debates offer little clarification regarding the precise nature of the «National:interests" to be protected. The minister's explanation of the derogation merely invoked a statistical concern, a need to track foreign investments in France, an argument that failed to convince. It is more likely that the lack of a clear definition of "national interest" reflects a deliberate governmental strategy to avoid being constrained by an overly rigid legal framework.

In much the same spirit as the 1966 legislation, the PACTE Act [28] of 2019 reiterates that when foreign investments are "likely to affect public order, public security, or national defense interests," such investments are subject to prior authorization by the Minister of the Economy.

More specifically, the Monetary and Financial Code [29] defines the relevant notion as encompassing any activity that, even on an occasional basis, contributes to the exercise of public authority or is likely to impair public order, public safety, or national defense interests, as well as activities related to the research, production, or marketing of arms, munitions, gunpowder, and explosive substances.

While this definition may appear somewhat eclectic or piecemeal, akin to a "laundry list", this is largely because the concept of protecting national interests in France has developed empirically over time, without the benefit of a comprehensive theoretical framework or alignment with broader conceptual evolutions such as the notion of national security. To be more precise, national security could arguably be understood as encompassing both internal and external security. On this basis, internal security would relate primarily to public order and the exercise of public authority, whereas external security would concern national defense.

That said, the French legislature has not yet taken the step of formally adopting such an integrated framework.

---

28. France, Law No. 2019-486 of May 22, 2019, on Business Growth and Transformation, Official Journal of the French Republic, No. 0119, May 23, 2019, NOR: ECOT1810669L
29. France, Monetary and Financial Code, Article L. 151-3

The Notion of National Interest Remains Contextual and Evolving

France's definition of its national interests, its strategic sectors, and other sensitive areas has emerged gradually over time. A plausible explanation for this evolution is that French authorities long refrained from adopting a detailed or rigid approach to defining these interests, likely in order to preserve maximum discretion in the exercise of sovereign control. This explains the multitude of legislative and regulatory amendments enacted over a fifty-year period, from 1966 to 2019, relating to the definition of what France considers to fall within the scope of national interest in the context of foreign direct investment (FDI) screening.

The starting point of this legal construction can be traced back to the 1966 reform, which confined the protected sectors to those deemed to affect the «National:interest." However, neither the Decree [30] of January 27, 1967, which implemented the 1966 law, nor the Decree [31] of December 29, 1989, on financial relations with foreign countries provided further clarification on the specific sectors subject to control under this framework. Article 3(1)(c) of the 1966 Law [32] stipulated that "the Government may, in order to protect national interests and by decree issued upon the report of the Minister of the Economy and Finance, subject the establishment or liquidation of foreign investments in France to prior notification, prior authorization, or control." Accordingly, the concept of national interest was the sole criterion against which public authorities were to assess foreign investments.

By comparison, entrusting the executive branch alone with the power to define «National:interest" echoes the U.S. model, under which US Congress has delegated to the President the authority to define the concept of «National:security."

It was only with the Decree [33] of January 15, 1990, amending and supplementing the 1989 Decree, that a formal list of sectors derogating from the principle of investment freedom for foreign investors was introduced for the first time. This text identified activities exempt from the general principle of free foreign investment. Specifically, it referred to (i) activities contributing, even occasionally, to the exercise of public authority in France, (ii) those affecting public order, public health, or public safety, (iii) activities related to the production or trade of arms, munitions, and war materiel, and (iv) operations designed to circumvent the application of French laws and regulations (see also Chapter 13).

From the outset, public order was thus positioned at the core of the national interest concept. It emerged as the most legitimate basis for suspending or rejecting a

30. France, Decree No. 67-78 of January 27, 1967, implementing Law No. 66-1008 of December 28, 1966, on financial relations with foreign countries, Official Journal of the French Republic, No. 0025, January 29, 1967, p. 1073
31. France, Decree No. 89-938 of December 29, 1989, regulating financial relations with foreign countries, Official Journal of the French Republic, No. 0303, December 30, 1989, p. 16411, NOR: ECOX8910405D
32. France, Law No. 66-1008 of December 28, 1966, on financial relations with foreign countries, Official Journal of the French Republic, No. 0299, December 29, 1966, p. 11621
33. France, Decree No. 90-58 of January 15, 1990, amending and supplementing Decree No. 89-938 of December 29, 1989, regulating financial relations with foreign countries, Official Journal of the French Republic, No. 0013, January 16, 1990, p. 650, NOR: ECOX9010021D

foreign investment. However, this remains a flexible and evolving notion, which ultimately reflects prevailing conceptions of what constitutes a "peaceful and orderly society [34]."

In 1996, legislative value was conferred on the sectoral list defined by the 1990 Decree. The Law [35] of February 14, 1996, on financial relations with foreign countries, formally incorporated into statute the list of sectors relevant to the protection of national interests, without modifying the substance of the list set forth in the 1990 Decree. A first sign [36] of conceptual evolution nevertheless appeared with regard to how activities involving the production or trade of arms, munitions, and war materiel were to be interpreted. These were now to be understood as referring to equipment likely to affect "the technological capabilities of national defense."

The entire regime would later be codified by the Ordinance [37] of December 14, 2000, which established the legislative portion of the Monetary and Financial Code. From that point forward, Article L. 151-3 of the Monetary and Financial Codebecame the core statutory provision governing FDI screening in France.

However, it was an emblematic transaction, the takeover of Gemplus, that would challenge assumptions about the effectiveness of the French framework. The question of whether the French screening regime was operationally robust resurfaced in public debate [38] in 2002, following the acquisition of Gemplus by the private equity firm Texas Pacific Group (TPG). The appointment of Alex Mandl, a former board member of In-Q-Tel, a venture capital firm created by the CIA, as CEO of Gemplus intensified [39] fears of strategic entanglement between U.S. interests and the role of certain investment funds. This episode raised a fundamental question: Was the decree, as codified in the newly restructured Monetary and Financial Code, actually capable of covering the sectors France intended to protect under the banner of national interest?

The incident even led to the publication of a report [40] submitted to the Prime Minister in June 2003, titled, Economic intelligence, competitiveness and social cohesion (Intelligence économique, compétitivité et cohésion sociale), which stressed the

34. France, GUILLEMIN, Claire and LABAUDE, Hervé, "*La libéralisation des investissements directs étrangers en France*" Les Petites Affiches, April 12, 1996, No. 45, p. 12
35. France, Law No. 96-109 of February 14, 1996, on financial relations with foreign countries regarding foreign investments in France, Official Journal of the French Republic, No. 0039, February 15, 1996, p. 2385, NOR: ECOX9500155L
36. France, National Assembly, Report No. 2492 of January 18, 1996, MENUEL, Georges, Member of Parliament, submitted on behalf of the Committee on Finance, General Economy and Planning, on Bill No. 2347 supplementing Law No. 66-1008 of December 28, 1966, on financial relations with foreign countries regarding foreign investments
37. France, Ordinance No. 2000-1223 of December 14, 2000, on the legislative part of the Monetary and Financial Code, Official Journal of the French Republic, No. 0291, December 16, 2000, p. 20004, NOR: ECOX0000098R
38. France, Senate, Written Question without debate No. 0229S to the Minister of Foreign Trade, Official Journal of the Senate, April 2, 2003, p. 2385, AUTEXIER, Jean-Yves, Senator, CRC Group, Ministerial Reply, Official Journal of the Senate, May 7, 2003, p. 2862
39. France, National Assembly, Information Report No. 2202 of March 23, 2005, DEFLESSELLES, Bernard and MICHEL, Jean, Members of Parliament, submitted by the Committee on National Defense and the Armed Forces, on foreign capital participation in European defense industries, p. 25
40. France, Report to the Prime Minister, CARAYON, Bernard, "Economic Intelligence, Competitiveness and Social Cohesion," July 1, 2003, La Documentation française, 173 pages, available at https://www.vie-publique.fr/files/rapport/pdf/034000484.pdf (last accessed September 1, 2025)

urgent need for France to adapt its legal framework to the realities of global economic competition.

As a result, French authorities launched a new reform of the screening regime in 2003. From a legal procedural standpoint, the reform was somewhat unusual: the decree came before the law. This sequence is explained by the Government's initial assumption that it could extend FDI screening to cover the national defense sector without amending the legislative basis. This assumption proved incorrect, and following the amendment of the decree, the executive was ultimately compelled to revise the enabling legislation.

Thus, the French Government first issued the Decree [41] of March 7, 2003, regulating financial relations with foreign countries, which repealed the Decree [42] of December 29, 1989. This new decree required prior authorization for direct foreign investments only where they affected public order, public safety, or public health . However, both direct and indirect foreign investments became subject to screening if they concerned national defense.

In this updated regulatory text, which, notably, preceded the Law of August 1, 2003, by several months, the notion of public authority was removed, leaving only the concepts of public order and public safety. These were further defined, in part, by reference to activities prohibited under the French Penal Code.

These unlawful activities include:
—drug trafficking [43],
—fraudulent exploitation of a person's ignorance or state of vulnerability [44],
—pimping [45] and related organized networks,
—basic and aggravated money laundering [46],
—acts of terrorism [47],
—active bribery and trading in influence [48],
—participation in a criminal conspiracy [49],
—investments in the gambling sector, including casinos and gambling clubs,
—and in regulated private security activities [50].

Secondly, the decree targets foreign direct or indirect investments in France relating to national defense as well as arms and explosives, terms that replace the former reference to the "production or trade in arms, munitions, and war materiel." The prior wording, which only referred to "research, production or trade in arms," was deemed

41. France, Decree No. 2003-196 of March 7, 2003, regulating financial relations with foreign countries, Official Journal of the French Republic, No. 0058, March 9, 2003, pp. 4140–4142, NOR: ECOT0237030D
42. France, Decree No. 89-938 of December 29, 1989, regulating financial relations with foreign countries, Official Journal of the French Republic, No. 0303, December 30, 1989, p. 16411, NOR: ECOX8910405D
43. France, Criminal Code, Articles 222-34 to 222-39
44. France, Criminal Code, Article 223-15-2
45. France, Criminal Code, Articles 225-5, 225-6 and 225-10
46. France, Criminal Code, Article 324-1
47. France, Criminal Code, Articles 421-1 to 421-2-2
48. France, Criminal Code, Articles 431-1 to 433-2
49. France, Criminal Code, Articles 450-1 and 450-2-1
50. France, Internal Security Code, Article L. 611-1

too narrow by the French Government to encompass industrial activities involving dual-use goods, as defined in Council Regulation [51] (EC) No. 1334/2000 of 22 June 2000, or the production of components considered sensitive within the manufacturing chain of strategic equipment [52].

Finally, the decree also applies to Foreign Direct Investments (FDI) in France that are likely to pose "serious risks" to public health . This last criterion proved ineffective during the Sanofi–Aventis merger, particularly in light of Article 58 of the Treaty on the European Union. In that case, the French Government even invoked the fight against bioterrorism as a justification for applying the provisions of the Monetary and Financial Code. However, such an approach was ultimately found to be inconsistent with EU case law, especially the Scientology Church Association judgment [53], which interprets very narrowly the Member States' right to restrict the free movement of capital both within the Union and with third countries. In this ruling, the Court of Justice of the European Union reiterated that the EC Treaty "does not permit a system of prior authorization for foreign direct investments that merely defines, in general terms, the investments concerned as being likely to affect public order or public security, such that the parties concerned are not in a position to ascertain the specific circumstances in which prior authorization is required."

The 2003 decree thus required legislative validation, which was subsequently introduced during the emergency examination of the Financial Security Act before the French Senate. In a somewhat improvised move, a new article was added to complement the decree's list, empowering the Minister to oppose any foreign investment deemed liable to affect "national defense."

The first legislative amendment was introduced by Article 78 of the Financial Security Act [54] of 1 August 2003, which broadened the scope of sensitive activities to include national defense. The Government submitted an amendment to this effect during the Senate's urgent reading of the bill. The notion [55] of national defense is particularly broad in French law, encompassing military, civil, and economic defense. According to a ministerial circular [56] dated 14 February 2002, economic defense refers to the public authority's actions and initiatives to protect the economy and enterprises

51. European Union, Council Regulation (EC) No. 1334/2000 of June 22, 2000, setting up a Community regime for the control of exports of dual-use items and technology, Official Journal of the European Communities, L 159, June 30, 2000, p. 1

52. France, National Assembly, Information Report No. 1664 of June 9, 2004, CARAYON, Bernard, Member of Parliament, submitted by the Committee on Finance, General Economy and Planning, on the national economic security strategy

53. European Union, Court of Justice of the European Communities, March 14, 2000, "Association Église de Scientologie," Case C-54/99 European Court Reports 2000, p. I-01335, ECLI:EU:C:2000:124

54. France, Law No. 2003-706 of August 1, 2003, on financial security, Official Journal of the French Republic, No. 0177, August 2, 2003, p. 13220, NOR: ECOX0200186L

55. France, National Assembly, Report No. 807 of April 10, 2003, GOULARD, François, Member of Parliament, submitted on behalf of the Committee on Finance, General Economy and Planning, on the draft law, as adopted by the Senate, on financial security, Financial Security, p. 298, see new Article 56 ter (Article L. 151-3, Monetary and Financial Code): extension of the Minister's powers in controlling foreign investments

56. France, Ministry of the Economy, Finance and Industry, Circular of February 14, 2002, on economic defense, Official Journal of the French Republic, No. 0070, March 23, 2002, p. 5164, NOR: ECOZ0200005C

against various threats and to provide for the needs of national defense. This includes the production of military-use equipment not strictly classified as weapons or munitions.

Despite these clarifications, the 2003 reform was again deemed inoperative. A parliamentary report[57] on "national economic security strategy" highlighted the deficiencies of the mechanism established by the 7 March 2003 decree[58] and called for its overhaul. More importantly, the European Commission informed France that its regime was incompatible with EU law. Consequently, in 2004, a second legislative revision was carried out to bring France into compliance with its European commitments. The Monetary and Financial Code was amended again during the Senate's review of a bill on regulatory simplification. Article 30 of the Law[59] of 9 December 2004 introduced a new system that was, for the first time, explicitly compatible with EU obligations. As the French Government explained, it sought "to revise the legal framework in question in order to stabilize it and offer foreign investors greater legal certainty, allow for greater flexibility in negotiations with investors, and ensure compatibility with EU law." [60]

The 2004 law thus redefined the scope of foreign investments subject to prior authorization. Article 30 provided that "foreign investments in an activity conducted in France which, even occasionally, involves the exercise of public authority or falls within one of the following sectors shall be subject to prior authorization from the Minister of the Economy": on the one hand, "activities likely to affect public order, public security or the interests of national defense," and on the other hand, "activities relating to the research, production, or marketing of arms, munitions, powders and explosive substances."

This 2004 law formalized a more coherent list of sensitive sectors, no longer including public health. The new article also reaffirmed the relevance of the "exercise of public authority" as a core component of the screening regime, thereby reinforcing the original spirit of the 1966 framework, which centered on the protection of «National:interests." Accordingly, the law clarified the scope by reintroducing references to activities affecting public order and public security from the 1989 decree, integrating the expanded concept of national defense from the 2003 reform, and again covering the production and trade in arms and munitions, this time also explicitly including powders and explosive substances and incorporating research activities. Conversely, public health-related activities were no longer specifically targeted. Most importantly, the new system mandated the adoption of an implementing decree issued by the Conseil d'État to define the specific activities subject to prior authorization.

---

57. France, National Assembly, Information Report No. 1664 of June 9, 2004, CARAYON, Bernard, Member of Parliament, submitted by the Committee on Finance, General Economy and Planning, on the national economic security strategy
58. France, Decree No. 2003-196 of March 7, 2003, regulating financial relations with foreign countries, Official Journal of the French Republic, No. 0058, March 9, 2003, pp. 4140–4142, NOR: ECOT0237030D
59. France, Law No. 2004-1343 of December 9, 2004, on the simplification of the law, Official Journal of the French Republic, No. 0287, December 10, 2004, NOR: FPPX0400010L
60. France, Senate, Official Report of Debates, October 14, 2004, Sitting, Discussion on the draft law, adopted by the National Assembly after a declaration of urgency, on the simplification of the law, Amendment No. 91, available at https://www.senat.fr/seances/s200410/s20041014/s20041014001.html#SOM4 (last accessed September 1, 2025)

However, the 2004 legislation was perceived as introducing new restrictions on foreign investment. This dual legislative shift, within just eighteen months and adopted through legislative vehicles unrelated to investment control, along with the absence of meaningful parliamentary debate, contributed to the perception of a discreet return to economic protectionism[61] by the French Government . The Prime Minister[62], however, framed it differently, referring instead to "economic patriotism" and expressing the desire for "foreign investments, particularly those involving sensitive technologies linked to security and defense, including in their technological and health-related dimensions, to be more closely supervised."

The General Secretariat for National Defense (SGDN[63]) was entrusted with the task of updating the 2003 decree[64] to reflect the provisions of the 2004 legislation. At the request of the Ministry of the Economy, the SGDN initiated an interministerial process to clarify the scope of investments affecting national defense. A revision of the 7 March 2003 decree was thus planned in light of the new provisions introduced by Article 30 of the 2004 law.

In 2005, a new implementing decree[65] was prepared. It was formally announced by the Prime Minister on 27 July 2005 and was intended to establish in detail the nature and list[66] of sectors and activities subject to the authorization procedure under Article L. 151-3 of the Monetary and Financial Code. The draft decree explicitly referred to the protection of «National:interests."

The 2005 mechanism was ultimately formalized by the decree[67] of 14 May 2014, which expanded the list of investments subject to prior authorization. The main contribution of this decree was the introduction of the notion of "interests of the country", a term preferred over «National:interest", alongside the concept of "essential activities." These included activities involving goods, services, or technologies, including those ensuring the security and proper functioning of facilities and equipment, that are essential to safeguarding the interests of the country.

This historical overview illustrates the evolving nature of the concept of national interest in France's foreign investment screening regime and its successive legislative and regulatory expressions.

---

61. France, ATTALI, Bernard, "The End of Economic Nationalism", Le Figaro, 24 January 2005
62. France, Prime Minister VILLEPIN, Dominique, Press Conference, Paris, Hôtel de Matignon, 27 July 2005, last accessed September 1, 2025, available at https://www.vie-publique.fr/discours/148535-conference-de-presse-de-m-dominique-de-villepin-premier-ministre-sur
63. France, General Secretariat for National Defence (SGDN), official designation as of 2003
64. France, Decree No. 2003-196 of 7 March 2003 regulating financial relations with foreign countries, Official Journal of the French Republic, No. 0058, 9 March 2003, pp. 4140–4142, NOR: ECOT0237030D
65. France, Decree No. 2005-1739 of 30 December 2005 regulating financial relations with foreign countries and implementing Article L. 151-3 of the Monetary and Financial Code, Official Journal of the French Republic, No. 304, 31 December 2005, NOR: ECOX0508949D
66. France, Minister Delegate for Industry, LOOS, François, Statement, 29 August 2005, published in Les Échos, last accessed September 1, 2025, available at https://www.vie-publique.fr/discours/149652-declaration-de-m-francois-loos-ministre-delegue-lindustrie-dans-l
67. France, Decree No. 2014-479 of 14 May 2014 on foreign investments subject to prior authorization, Official Journal of the French Republic, No. 0112, 15 May 2014, NOR: ERNX1411012D

Essential Activities Connected to National Interests

The concept of essential activities was formally introduced by the Decree [68] of May 14, 2014, as previously referenced. This decree extended the scope of the Decree of December 30, 2005 to include activities that are essential to safeguarding the national interests of France in terms of public order, public security, or national defense. This terminology was subsequently reaffirmed in the Decree [69] of November 29, 2018, the Law [70] of May 22, 2019, and the Decree [71] of December 31, 2019. In doing so, the government significantly broadened the scope of strategic sectors falling under the prior authorization regime for foreign investors, using the concept of essential activities as a legal gateway.

Although the notion of "essential activities" has never been precisely defined, the decree aligns with the overarching logic of Article L. 151-2 of the French Monetary and Financial Code, which sets forth the powers of the Minister of the Economy, Industry, and Digital Affairs in matters related to the protection of national interests. It can be reasonably inferred that the notion of essential activities is conceptually close to the broader notion of the interests of the Nation.

The 2014 drafting was not coincidental. It was designed to ensure consistency with the requirements of European Union law, particularly with the standards established by the Court of Justice of the European Union (CJEU) [72]. The CJEU has consistently held that restrictions based on public order and public security are permissible only where a genuine and sufficiently serious threat exists to a fundamental interest of society. In this regard, it is understood that in the event of litigation, the interpretation of such concepts by the CJEU would take precedence, even in the context of national law.

Essential activities, therefore, encompass a broad array of business sectors and functions. The Decree [73] of May 14, 2014 specifies that the activities falling within its scope include those involving equipment, products, or the provision of services, including services that are related to the security and proper functioning of installations and facilities. The decree's wording was deliberately drafted in expansive terms, thereby granting the State considerable discretion in identifying which activities fall under the strategic domain.

As of 2014, these essential activities were delineated into six main sectoral categories:

---

68. Ibid
69. France, Decree No. 2018-1057 of 29 November 2018 on foreign investments subject to prior authorization, Official Journal of the French Republic, No. 0278, 1 December 2018, NOR: ECOT1816712D
70. France, Law No. 2019-486 of 22 May 2019 on Business Growth and Transformation, Official Journal of the French Republic, No. 0119, 23 May 2019, NOR: ECOT1810669L
71. France, Decree No. 2019-1590 of 31 December 2019 on foreign investments in France, Official Journal of the French Republic, No. 0001, 1 January 2020, NOR: ECOT1932857D
72. European Union, Court of Justice, 14 March 2000, "Association Église de Scientologie", Case C-54/99, European Court Reports 2000, p. I-01335, ECLI:EU:C:2000:124
73. France, Decree No. 2014-479 of 14 May 2014 on foreign investments subject to prior authorization, Official Journal of the French Republic, No. 0112, 15 May 2014, NOR: ERNX1411012D

—to the integrity, security, and continuity of supply in the fields of energy (including electricity, gas, hydrocarbons, or other energy sources) and water, in compliance with regulations enacted in the interest of public health;
—to the integrity, security, and continuous operation of networks and services in the transportation and electronic communications sectors;
—to the integrity, security, and continuous operation of any facility, installation, or infrastructure designated as being of vital importance (ouvrage d'importance vitale);
—to the protection of public health.

In 2018, the Minister of the Economy decided to expand the scope of essential activities set forth in the 2014 decree to include the digital and space sectors. To that end, he issued the Decree [74] of November 29, 2018, which added the following categories to the list of essential activities:
—Interception of communications, remote detection of conversations, or capture of computer data;
—Information systems security;
—Research and development activities relating to the items listed under Article L.2332-1 of the French Defense Code, concerning weapons, munitions, powders, and explosives for military use, as well as war materiel and equivalent items;
—Integrity, security, and continuity of space operations;
—Integrity, security, and continuous operation of specialized electronic and IT systems required for the missions of the National Police, the National Gendarmerie, civil security services, or for the exercise of public security missions by the Customs Administration;
—Activities involving cybersecurity, artificial intelligence, robotics,, additive manufacturing, and semiconductors [75];
—Dual-use goods and technologies listed in Annex I of the Council Regulation (EC) of May 5, 2009;
—Data hosting services, where compromise or disclosure of the data could impair the conduct of activities or harm interests related to any of the above two sectors.

Finally, with the adoption of the PACTE Act [76] (Loi PACTE) and the enactment of its implementing decree, the Government undertook a revision of the previous legislative and regulatory framework. The notion of national interests was formally enshrined in the statutory provisions of the law, while the Explanatory Memorandum [77] (notice) to the Decree [78] of December 31, 2019 referred to the broader concept

74. France, Decree No. 2018-1057 of 29 November 2018 on foreign investments subject to prior authorization, Official Journal of the French Republic, No. 0278, 1 December 2018, NOR: ECOT1816712D
75. Since 2020, 42 investment files involving companies operating in the electronics sector have been subject to foreign investment screening, including 24 specifically concerning firms active in the semiconductor industry. France, Ministry of the Economy and Finance, Annual Report on the Foreign Direct Investment Screening in France – 2023, p. 24, available at https://presse.economie.gouv.fr/publication-du-rapport-annuel-sur-le-controle-ief-en-2023 (last accessed 28 June 2025)
76. France, Law No. 2019-486 of 22 May 2019, on Business Growth and Transformation, Official Journal of the French Republic, No. 0119, 23 May 2019, NOR: ECOT1810669L
77. France, Decree No. 2019-1590 of December 31, 2019, on foreign investments in France, Official Journal of the French Republic, No. 0001, January 1, 2020, NOR: ECOT1932857D
78. France, Law No. 2019-486 of May 22, 2019, on Business Growth and Transformation, Official Journal of the French Republic, No. 0119, May 23, 2019, Articles 152 and 153, NOR: ECOT1810669L

of the interests of the country. This decree clarified the scope of covered activities, in particular by distinguishing between two categories:

—on the one hand, activities carried out in the listed sectors, understood in a broad sense and explicitly encompassing research and development (R&D);

—on the other hand, strict R&D activities relating to critical technologies and dual-use items. (See also Chapter 13 on sensitive activities.)

Given the absence of any statutory or regulatory cross-reference to a precise definition [79], and since no list can be considered exhaustive, the qualification of an activity as "essential" remains subject to the sovereign discretion of the French State.

The concept of national interest is closely aligned with that of the fundamental interests of the Nation.

While the defense of the national interest serves as the primary legal basis for derogating from the principle of free foreign investment in France, the 1966 legislation referred more broadly to the "interests of the Nation" (intérêts de la Nation) without providing a precise definition. It was only in subsequent legislative developments that the national interest was progressively characterized as encompassing public authority, national defense, public safety, and public order.

Over time, the term national interest has coexisted, and at times competed, with the notion of fundamental interests of the Nation (intérêts fondamentaux de la Nation). Unlike the former, the latter benefits from an explicit legal definition codified in the French Penal Code. Specifically, this concept is invoked in the legal treatment of crimes and offenses against the Nation, the State, and public peace . Article L. 410-1 of the Penal Code [80] defines fundamental interests of the Nation as including:

"its independence, the integrity of its territory, its security, the republican form of its institutions, its means of defense and diplomacy, the protection of its population in France and abroad, the balance of its natural environment and ecosystem, and the essential elements of its scientific, economic, and cultural heritage."

This definition clearly encompasses the criteria of public authority, national defense, public security, and public order, but does so in a broader and more systematic fashion. In a sense, the fundamental interests of the Nation form the conceptual backbone of national sovereignty, whether it relates to the structure of the State, its operational integrity, or its protection.

79. France, Decree No. 2019-1590 of December 31, 2019, on foreign investments in France – "*Notice: foreign investments must be subject to prior authorization when they concern activities essential to safeguarding the country's interests in terms of public authority, public order, public security, or national defense,*" Official Journal of the French Republic, No. 0001, January 1, 2020, NOR: ECOT1932857D, available at https://www.legifrance.gouv.fr/eli/decret/2019/12/31/ECOT1932857D/jo/texte (last accessed September 1, 2025)

80. Version in force since March 1, 1994. France, Article L. 410-1 of the Penal Code – "*The fundamental interests of the Nation include its independence, the integrity of its territory, its security, the republican form of its institutions, the means of its defense and diplomacy, the safeguarding of its population in France and abroad, the balance of its natural environment and living conditions, and the essential elements of its scientific and economic potential and cultural heritage*"

The Short-Lived Notion of Economic Sectors of National Interest

In parallel with the evolving notion of national interest, French public policy in the field of also sought to develop the idea of economic sectors of national strategic interest.

A landmark parliamentary report[81] in 2005 introduced the concept of "sensitive sectors" that ought to fall within the oversight of the Ministry of the Economy. At the time, the central figure of this policy was the High Official for (Haut Responsable chargé de l'Intelligence Économique, or HRIE), then attached to the Secretariat-General for National Defense (SGDN), an entity under the Office of the Prime Minister. One of the HRIE's key missions was to "reduce the vulnerability of strategic sectors to undesirable foreign takeovers." To this end, the HRIE coordinated the efforts of several key ministries: Defense, Economy, Finance and Industry, Interior, and Foreign Affairs.

In June 2004, the HRIE released a list of fifteen strategic sectors deemed particularly sensitive in light of national interest considerations.

The 2009 reform of France's economic intelligence framework invited a broader rethinking of the national strategy. As of 2007, the French government had initiated a review of the structure, with an emphasis, under the guidance of the General Secretary of the Élysée, on relocating strategic oversight back into the direct purview of the President of the Republic, following the model used for national security. One of the key challenges was to identify the economic sectors in which the State should concentrate its protection and support efforts.

As a result, the government created a new structure: the position of Interministerial Delegate for Economic Intelligence (Délégué interministériel à l'intelligence économique) was established by Decree[82] of September 16, 2009. This Delegate was tasked with identifying "economic sectors of national strategic interest." This marked the formal institutionalization of a new category of strategic sectors, focused exclusively on the economic dimension.

The Decree[83] of August 22, 2013, issued under Prime Minister Jean-Marc Ayrault, further reaffirmed this concept. Article 6 of the decree specified that:

"The Interministerial Delegate for Economic Intelligence identifies the economic sectors of national strategic interest."

This mission was of notable importance, as it required the Delegate's services to clarify and possibly define the scope of the concept. Moreover: "*He coordinates strategic monitoring to anticipate risks and threats likely to affect organizations and companies in these sectors and proposes all measures likely to prevent such risks and strengthen national capabilities in this domain.*"

---

81. France, National Assembly, Information Report No. 2202 of March 23, 2005, submitted by DEFLESSELLES, Bernard and MICHEL, Jacques, Members of Parliament, on behalf of the Committee on National Defense and Armed Forces, on the participation of foreign capital in European defense industries, p. 25
82. France, Decree No. 2009-1122 of September 17, 2009, on the Interministerial Delegate for Economic Intelligence, Official Journal of the French Republic, September 18, 2009, p. 15229, NOR: ECEX0921382D
83. France, Decree No. 2013-759 of August 22, 2013, on the Interministerial Delegate for Economic Intelligence, Official Journal of the French Republic, No. 0195, August 23, 2013, NOR: PRMX1321616D

Most significantly, this framework touched directly upon foreign investment screening policy. The Interministerial Delegate was henceforth involved in formulating "the Government's position on foreign investment matters." This overlap led to repeated calls for clarification [84], particularly with respect to the already applicable provisions of Article L. 151-3 of the Monetary and Financial Code.

The same decree emphasized that: "The Interministerial Delegate proposes measures to facilitate the financing of companies operating in economic sectors of national strategic interest. He coordinates the implementation of protection mechanisms for sensitive companiesHe also proposes, in coordination with the Secretariat-General for Defense and National Security, measures to reinforce the protection of national economic interests and of the State's and companies' scientific, technological, and economic assets."

Although this decree was repealed as of February 1, 2016, it nonetheless testified to a governmental desire to delineate the contours of national interest as it applies to economic sectors targeted by France's foreign investment screening mechanism.

* * *

The French foreign investment screening regime (Investissements Étrangers en France, or IEF) is structured around a fundamental principle and a single derogation.

The principle is that of free foreign investment in France, a core tenet of the country's open and attractive economic model. The derogation, however, is founded on the protection of national interests. While the notion of national interest remains circumstantial and evolving, it is important to recognize that since 1996 "*the net has continued to widen, while its mesh has continued to tighten.*"

This development reflects a long and deliberate process of institutional maturation. French authorities have gradually, yet consistently, moved toward a regime that is both more robust and more predictable for foreign investors. Despite the proliferation of legislative and regulatory instruments governing the system (see next chapter), the French approach to investment screening remains coherent, and its public policy objectives are well aligned, even amid the legal back-and-forth that has historically marked its evolution.

84. France, National Assembly, Written Question No. 38321, Official Journal of the National Assembly, September 24, 2013, p. 9859, submitted by MARLEIX, Olivier, Member of Parliament

Chapter 2

Legal Framework Governing the Foreign Direct Investment Screening in France

The French foreign investment screening mechanism, commonly referred to as contrôle IEF, has become a cornerstone of France's merger control framework, evolving since 1966 to address contemporary economic and national security challenges. This chapter outlines the core legal instruments and regulatory provisions that define and structure the French screening regime.

At the heart of the framework are Articles L. 151-1 et seq. of the French Monetary and Financial Code (French Monetary and Financial Code– CMF), which articulate the underlying principles, exceptions, and enforcement powers of the screening regime. Complementing them are Articles R. 151-1 et seq. of the CMF, which detail the procedural and operational aspects of the system (see Appendices A and B).

The Ministerial Order[85] of December 31, 2019 supplements these provisions by specifying both the documentation required for foreign investment filings and the list of critical technologies subject to control, thus emphasizing the technical and strategic considerations integral to the review process. In addition, recent Decrees of 2021, 2022, and 2023, which lowered control thresholds, will be analyzed to understand the most recent adaptations of the regulatory framework.

Moreover, Article 459 of the French Customs Code (Code des douanes) is considered, as it governs disputes involving cross-border financial relations and provides insight into the avenues available for litigation.

Finally, reference is made to the European Union Regulation of March 19, 2019, which establishes a cooperation mechanism among Member States for the screening of foreign direct investments (FDI), underscoring the importance of coordinated action across the European bloc.

85. France, Ministerial Order of December 31, 2019, on foreign investments in France, Official Journal of the French Republic, No. 0001, January 1, 2020, NOR: ECOT1937237A

Articles L. 151-1 et seq. CMF: Principles, Exceptions, and Enforcement Powers

The legal foundation for France's FDI screening regime originates in the 1966 Law on financial relations with foreign countries, now codified in Articles L. 151-1 et seq. of the CMF.

Article L. 151-1 sets forth the general principle of freedom of financial relations between France and foreign countries, stating that: "*Financial relations between France and foreign countries shall be free. This freedom shall be exercised in accordance with the provisions of this chapter and subject to France's international commitments.*" (See previous chapter)

Article L. 151-2 introduces the principal derogation to the freedom to invest, laying the legal basis for state intervention. Paragraph 1(c) of the article is of particular importance, as it allows foreign investments in France to be made subject to prior declaration, authorization, or control.

Article L. 151-3 defines the scope of the prior authorization regime, clarifying that restrictions apply only when specific conditions are met, most notably, the nature of the targeted activity. According to the article, the derogation is triggered where the activity:

- involves public authority,
- could adversely affect public order, public security, or national defense, or
- relates to the research, production, or marketing of arms, ammunition, powders, and explosive substances.

This definition directly echoes the concept of «National:interests" underlying the 1966 legislation. (See previous chapter and Chapter 13)

Article L. 151-3-1 establishes the enforcement powers of the Minister of the Economy, in cases where transactions are carried out without prior authorization or in breach of imposed conditions. Depending on the seriousness of the violation, the Minister[86] may:

- issue formal injunctions,
- impose daily penalties (astreintes),
- adopt protective measures (e.g., suspension of voting rights, appointment of a trustee, restriction on asset disposal or dividend payments), and
- impose financial penalties, as further provided in Article L. 151-3-2.

(See Chapters 21 and 22)

Article L. 151-4 stipulates that any transaction conducted in violation of the authorization regime is null and void. (See Chapter 21)

Article L. 151-5 requires all parties to respond to information requests by the public authorities, without being able to invoke trade secrecy. (See Chapter 20)

86. France, Ministry of the Economy, Finance, Industrial and Digital Sovereignty, Directorate General of the Treasury, "The police powers of the Minister of the Economy," Published on December 31, 2024, last accessed September 1, 2025, available at https://www.tresor.economie.gouv.fr/services-aux-entreprises/investissements-etrangers-en-france/les-pouvoirs-de-police-du-ministre-charge-de-l-economie

Article L. 151-6 mandates the publication of an annual report by the Government on foreign investment screening in France. This report must break down approved or rejected transactions by country of origin and by sector. It also provides a framework for parliamentary debate. (See also Chapters 5 and 20)

Article L. 151-7 introduces ex post parliamentary oversight of decisions taken by the Minister of the Economy in the context of foreign investment screening.

(See Chapter 5)

All Articles L. 151-3 to L. 151-7 are reproduced in Appendix A of this book.

Articles R. 151-1 et seq. CMF: Procedural Mechanisms and Administrative Structure

As laid out in the legislative portion[87] of the regime, the regulatory framework is detailed in a Council of State decree, which defines the nature of sensitive activities and investments subject to screening. It also sets out how authorization conditions may be reviewed or amended.

The Government, more precisely, the Minister of the Economy and Finance, is therefore responsible for specifying, via regulation, the entirety of the foreign direct investment screening mechanism in France. These rules are codified in Articles R. 151-1 to R. 151-12 of the CMF.

The first three articles define key terms:

- Article R. 151-1 defines the term foreign investor.
- Article R. 151-2 outlines what constitutes a covered transaction, including applicable thresholds.
- Article R. 151-3 lists the 22 sensitive sectors subject to screening.

Articles R. 151-4 to R. 151-11 govern the application process, including both the prior examination request and the authorization request.

Articles R. 151-12 to R. 151-15 concern enforcement and penalties.

Additional provisions govern matters common to both types of filings:

- Article R. 151-16 refers to the contents of the application file, with further detail delegated to a ministerial order (see next section).
- Article R. 151-17 authorizes the Minister to engage in international cooperation, particularly in coordination with EU mechanisms (see end of Chapter 6).

87. France, Monetary and Financial Code, Art. L. 151-3

The amended Ministerial Order of December 31, 2019: Filing Requirements and Critical Technologies

The amended Ministerial Order[88] of December 31, 2019 sets out the list of documents that must accompany a filing, whether for prior examination or authorization. (See Chapters 16 and 17)

In addition, the same Order gives effect to the Minister's regulatory authority under Article R. 151-3 III(1) to define the list of critical technologies subject to enhanced scrutiny. (See Chapter 13)

One advantage of using a ministerial order rather than a decree is its procedural flexibility: the list of critical technologies can be updated swiftly in response to emerging threats or industrial developments, without the formalities required for a full decree.

The 2023 Decree Lowers the Screening Threshold to 10% for Listed Companies

As a preliminary reminder, the PACTE Act[89] and its implementing decree had already reduced the threshold triggering foreign direct investment (FDI) screening in France (known as the IEF procedure) from 50% to 25%. During the COVID-19 pandemic, the French Minister of the Economy further lowered this threshold to 10% by decree[90], in an effort to prevent opportunistic market takeovers made possible by falling valuations resulting from the global economic slowdown. This measure was initially introduced as temporary. However, questions quickly arose as to whether it would be extended beyond 2020.

Several factors weighed in favor of maintaining the 10% threshold. From a political standpoint, Senator Bruno Retailleau, leader of the Les Républicains (LR) group in the Senate, publicly stated in June 2020 that he wished to see the lower threshold maintained, a call echoed by other members of parliament[91]. In addition, the French Economic, Social and Environmental Council (CESE), in its opinion[92] titled "For a Sustainable and Responsible Foreign Direct Investment Strategy in France", endorsed

88. France, Ministerial Order of December 31, 2019, on foreign investments in France, Official Journal of the French Republic, No. 0001, January 1, 2020, NOR: ECOT1937237A
89. France, Law No. 2019-486 of May 22, 2019, on Business Growth and Transformation, Official Journal of the French Republic, No. 0119, May 23, 2019, NOR: ECOT1810669L
90. France, Decree No. 2020-892 of July 22, 2020, on the temporary lowering of the threshold for the control of foreign investments in French companies whose shares are admitted to trading on a regulated market, Official Journal of the French Republic, No. 0179, July 23, 2020, NOR: ECOT2012085D
91. France, National Assembly, Written Question No. 32537 to the Minister of the Economy and Finance, Official Journal of the National Assembly, September 29, 2020, p. 6567, THIERIOT, Jean-Louis, Member of Parliament, Les Républicains (LR), Ministerial Reply, August 3, 2021, Official Journal of the National Assembly, p. 6208
92. France, Economic, Social and Environmental Council, COUVERT, Catherine and NIBOUREL, Christian, Opinion No. 2021-09, "For a sustainable and responsible foreign direct investment strategy in France," March 23, 2021, NOR: CESL1100009X, DILA, No. 41121-0009, ISSN 0767-4538, ISBN 978-2-11-155700-0

in its Recommendation No. 18 the extension of the 10% threshold until 2023, with a view to conducting an impact assessment at that time.

Most notably, the Minister of the Economy[93] himself justified the measure on substantive grounds: even a minority stake acquisition could pose a threat to France's national interests, particularly in the case of listed companies, where share ownership is by nature dispersed and control is difficult to assert. Consequently, a minority shareholder in such a company might still exert considerable influence over its strategic direction and sensitive operations. By contrast, in unlisted companies, where capital is typically concentrated in the hands of a few stakeholders, the ability of a minority investor to influence sensitive business decisions is significantly more limited.

Originally adopted as a temporary measure, the 10% threshold for acquisitions in French-incorporated companies listed on a regulated market was renewed twice, in 2021[94] and 2022[95]. It was then made permanent[96] in 2023, with effect from January 1, 2024.

On this matter, as well as on broader regulatory developments, the Foreign Direct Investment Screening Office (CIEF)

(Bureau du controle des investissements étrangers en France, or CIEF) holds advisory authority, pursuant to the provisions of its internal operating decree. The Council of State (Conseil d'État) may also intervene as necessary.

Article 459 of the French Customs Code Governs FDI-Related Offenses

Article 459 of the French Customs Code lays down the criminal penalties applicable to violations of French FDI regulations. It provides for a five-year prison sentence, confiscation of the assets constituting the offense, and fines ranging from the amount of the unlawful transaction up to twice that amount. (See Chapter 21.)

93. France, Senate, Written Question No. 16791 to the Minister of the Economy and Finance, Official Journal of the Senate, June 18, 2020, p. 2765, CONWAY-MOURET, Hélène, Senator, Socialist, Ecologist and Republican Group (SOCR), Ministerial Reply, June 10, 2021, Official Journal of the Senate, p. 3722
94. France, Decree No. 2021-1758 of December 22, 2021, extending the temporary lowering of the threshold for the control of foreign investments in French companies whose shares are admitted to trading on a regulated market, Official Journal of the French Republic, No. 0299, December 24, 2021, NOR: ECOT2133077D
95. France, Decree No. 2022-1622 of December 23, 2022, on the temporary lowering of the threshold for the control of foreign investments in French companies whose shares are admitted to trading on a regulated market, Official Journal of the French Republic, No. 0298, December 24, 2022, NOR: ECOT2233343D
96. France, Decree No. 2023-1293 of December 28, 2023, on foreign investments in France, definitively lowering the initial 25% threshold to 10%, Official Journal of the French Republic, No. 0301, December 29, 2023, NOR: ECOT2323089D

The European Regulation of March 19, 2019, Establishes a Common EU Framework for FDI Screening

In 2019, France, alongside Germany and Italy, supported the adoption of an EU-wide framework[97] for screening foreign direct investment originating from third countries. The shared objective of this initiative was to protect national security interests across the European Union through greater coordination and transparency.

Under this mechanism, France benefits from a dual-layered system: in addition to its own domestic screening regime (the IEF framework), it participates in a European-level alert and cooperation system coordinated by the European Commission. This mechanism facilitates information-sharing with other EU Member States, 23of which have adopted[98], or are in the process of adopting, national screening mechanisms, and with 4 others[99] that have not yet implemented such controls.

It is important to emphasize that the EU Regulation complements, rather than replaces, the French IEF regime . It applies exclusively to FDI originating from non-EU countries. While inspired by national security considerations akin to those underlying the U.S. CFIUS framework, the EU screening system is fundamentally distinct: the European Union is not a federal state, and matters of national security remain the sole prerogative of its Member States.

Accordingly, the EU mechanism is primarily intended to provide national authorities with enhanced information. The ultimate responsibility for safeguarding national interests continues to rest exclusively with the host Member State. A proper understanding of the Regulation is essential to grasp the implications of this reform, which entered into force in 2020. (See Chapter 6.)

* * *

The core legal framework for foreign investment screening in France is set out in the Monetary and Financial Code (Code monétaire et financier). The legislative provisions, particularly Articles L.151-1 et seq., define the overarching principles, the scope of derogations, and the enforcement powers of the State, while the regulatory provisions, Articles R.151-1 et seq., govern procedural modalities.

For reasons of flexibility, the French regime also relies on ministerial orders (arrêtés) to specify the list of supporting documents required in FDI filings, as well as to determine the list of critical technologies subject to review. This regulatory approach strikes a balance between legal predictability and adaptability, ensuring that the screening mechanism remains aligned with evolving threats to national interests.

---

97. European Union, Regulation (EU) 2019/452 of March 19, 2019, of the European Parliament and of the Council establishing a framework for the screening of foreign direct investments into the Union, Official Journal of the European Union, L 79I, March 21, 2019, pp. 1–14
98. Austria, Belgium, Czechia, Denmark, Estonia, Finland, Germany, Hungary, Ireland, Italy, Latvia, Lithuania, Luxembourg, Malta, the Netherlands, Poland, Portugal, Romania, Slovakia, Slovenia, Spain, Sweden
99. Bulgaria, Croatia, Cyprus, Greece

In addition to the Monetary and Financial Code, Article 459 of the Customs Code serves as the cornerstone of FDI-related enforcement and sanctions, while the 2019 EU Regulation provides a complementary supranational layer. Nevertheless, parties involved in foreign investment transactions are strongly encouraged to consult the official Guidelines issued by the French Treasury Department to better understand how the screening process is implemented in practice. (See next chapter.)

Chapter 3

The French FDI Screening Mechanism Is Framed by Guidelines

In addition to statutory and regulatory provisions, the French FDI screening mechanism is usefully framed by guidelines. Adopted in recent years, first in 2022 [100] and then in 2025 [101], as a follow-up to the PACTE Act, these guidelines are essential in assessing the predictability of the regime. They contribute to legal certainty by providing investors and their advisors with a clearer understanding of how the rules are applied. Issued by the Ministry of the Economy, the guidelines articulate the government's administrative doctrine in the review process.

In addition to the applicable legislative and regulatory instruments, the French foreign direct investment (FDI) screening mechanism, commonly referred to as the dispositif IEF, is further structured by a set of interpretive guidelines. Developed in recent years as a corollary to the PACTE Act [102], these guidelines play a critical role in enhancing the predictability of the screening process. They are issued by the Ministry of the Economy, which thereby articulates its enforcement doctrine and administrative practice.

Guidelines Are Essential to the Predictability of the Mechanism

While the existence of a clearly defined legal and regulatory framework, made available to stakeholders in advance, is a key element in ensuring procedural predictability, this alone does not suffice. It is equally important to establish an overarching interpretive and analytical framework that can shield foreign investments from arbitrary state intervention.

100. France, Ministry of Economy, Finance, Industrial and Digital Sovereignty, Directorate General of the Treasury, "Guidelines on the Foreign Direct Investment Screening in France," September 2022, published 8 September 2022, consulted 9 May 2024, available at https://www.tresor.economie.gouv.fr/services-aux-entreprises/investissements-etrangers-en-france
101. France, Ministry of Economy, Finance, Industrial and Digital Sovereignty, Directorate General of the Treasury, "Guidelines on the Foreign Direct Investment Screening in France," July 2025, published 30 July 2025, consulted 1 August 2025, available at https://www.tresor.economie.gouv.fr/services-aux-entreprises/investissements-etrangers-en-france
102. France, Law No. 2019-486 of May 22, 2019, on Business Growth and Transformation, Official Journal of the French Republic, No. 0119, May 23, 2019, NOR: ECOT1810669L

In this respect[103], the Organisation for Economic Co-operation and Development (OECD) has identified three key challenges that states must address:

The Organisation has identified three key challenges that states must address in the development and implementation of FDI screening frameworks:
(i) the need to establish a clear and structured framework in response to the broadening scope of foreign investment screening policies;
(ii) the imperative of strengthening international cooperation between screening authorities;
(iii) the assessment of the impact of such screening measures on the overall investment attractiveness of host countries.

On these matters, the OECD has maintained a consistent position[104] since 1986, aimed at fostering a favorable climate and fair procedures for investment screening.

This position aligns closely with contemporary approaches to economic security as well as with national narratives emphasizing economic patriotism. The OECD expressly acknowledges the legitimacy of restrictions on investment freedom when justified by national security concerns[105]. It has accordingly issued guidance[106] aimed at reconciling the protection of national security with the principle of investment openness.

In this context, the OECD Investment Committee reached consensus in 2008 on a set of Council Recommendations for investment policy, intended to preserve national security while upholding core commitments to liberal investment principles. These recommendations include:

These 2008 OECD Council Recommendations emphasize the following principles for investment policy in the context of national security:
—Non-discrimination. As a general rule, public authorities should adopt broadly applicable measures that ensure similar treatment for investors operating in comparable circumstances;
—Transparency and predictability. While it is in the interest of both investors and governments to preserve the confidentiality of sensitive information, regulatory objectives and enforcement practices must be as transparent as possible in order to enhance the predictability of outcomes;
—Codification and public availability. Laws and implementing regulations must be codified and made publicly accessible in an appropriate format (e.g., via a public

103. DUPEYRAT, op. cit., pp. 27–30
104. OECD, Recommendation of the Council concerning Member countries' measures relating to national treatment for reasons of public order and essential security interests, July 6, 1986, OECD/LEGAL/0226, accessed May 9, 2024, available at https://legalinstruments.oecd.org/en/instruments/OECD-LEGAL-0226
105. OECD, Directorate for Financial and Enterprise Affairs, Investment Committee, Report "Freedom of Investment, National Security and Strategic Industries: Sovereign Wealth Funds and Recipient Country Policies," April 4, 2008, DAF/INV(2008)5/REV1, last accessed September 1, 2025, available at https://one.oecd.org/document/DAF/INV(2008)5/REV1/en/pdf
106. OECD, Recommendation of the Council on guidelines for recipient country investment policies relating to national security, May 25, 2009, OECD/LEGAL/0372, last accessed September 1, 2025, available at https://legalinstruments.oecd.org/en/instruments/OECD-LEGAL-0372

register or online). In particular, the criteria used in investment reviews should be made publicly known;

—Prior notification. Governments should take appropriate steps to inform relevant stakeholders of any proposed changes in investment policies;

—Consultation. When contemplating reforms to their investment policy framework, public authorities should actively solicit feedback from interested stakeholders;

—Fair and predictable procedures. Foreign investment review procedures should be subject to strict deadlines. Commercially sensitive information submitted by the investor must be protected. Wherever feasible, legal provisions should enable the automatic approval of a transaction if no restrictive or conditional action is taken within a defined timeframe;

—Disclosure of investment policy actions. Governments should ensure that their actions under the investment policy regime are publicly communicated (e.g., through press releases, annual reports, or parliamentary briefings), while safeguarding sensitive and commercially strategic information;

—Proportionality of regulations. Any restrictions or conditions imposed on an investment must be no more stringent than necessary to address the relevant national security concerns, and should be avoided altogether if other available measures (e.g., licensing, competition policy, or financial regulation) are sufficient to mitigate the risk;

—National discretion over essential security interests. Each country has the sovereign right to determine what is necessary to protect its national security. This determination should be based on rigorous, context-sensitive risk assessments that reflect the institutional, economic, and geopolitical specificities of the state. There must be a clear link between the investment restriction and the identified national security risk;

—Targeted measures. Investment restrictions must directly address specific national security concerns rather than operate as blanket prohibitions;

—Adequate expertise. The design of security-based investment screening mechanisms must draw on appropriate national security expertise, as well as on the capacity to assess the broader policy implications of restricting versus permitting a transaction;

—Tailored responses. Where restrictions are applied, they must be proportionate to the specific risks posed by the investment in question. This includes the possibility of implementing mitigation agreements that address security concerns without entirely blocking the transaction;

—Measure of last resort. Investment restrictions should be considered only as a last resort, and only where alternative regulatory instruments (e.g., sectoral licensing, competition law, financial supervision) are inadequate to address the national security threat;

—Accountability. Effective accountability mechanisms should be established, including parliamentary oversight, judicial review, periodic impact assessments, and a requirement that decisions to block a transaction be taken at a sufficiently high level of government authority.

All of these OECD recommendations pursue a single objective: to provide foreign investors with the highest possible level of predictability during the screening and authorization process. As a member of the OECD, France has drawn upon these recommendations both in the drafting of its regulatory framework and in the elaboration of accompanying interpretive guidelines.

The Ministry of the Economy Issues Guidelines to Define Its Review Doctrine

Following the adoption of the PACTE Act [107] in 2019 and the enactment of its implementing decree on December 30, 2019, practitioners involved in France's foreign direct investment (FDI) screening regime widely recognized the need for further clarification on how the mechanism, commonly referred to as the dispositif IEF, should be understood and applied.

In this spirit, the publication of the first annual report [108] on FDI screening in France, along with several practical resources (including FAQs and templates [109] for filing an application under the screening regime), helped to identify areas of legal and procedural uncertainty.

In 2022, the Directorate General of the Treasury (Direction générale du Trésor, or DGT) continued this effort by issuing formal guidelines [110] intended to increase both transparency and predictability in the screening process. These guidelines followed a public consultation [111] held in March 2022 and were designed to provide stakeholders with a pedagogical and practical overview of (i) the scope of the applicable rules, (ii) the screening and authorization procedures, and (iii) the post-clearance monitoring obligations.

In 2025, the Directorate General of the Treasury (DGT) supplemented this work with the publication of an updated version. The 2025 edition of the FDI screening guidelines represents a significant deepening and consolidation compared to the 2022

---

107. France, Law No. 2019-486 of May 22, 2019, on Business Growth and Transformation, Official Journal of the French Republic, No. 0119, May 23, 2019, NOR: ECOT1810669L

108. France, Ministry of the Economy, Finance and Recovery, Directorate General of the Treasury, 2022 Annual Report, "Foreign Direct Investment Screening in France," published March 17, 2022, last accessed September 1, 2025, available at https://www.tresor.economie.gouv.fr/Articles/2022/03/17/publication-du-rapport-annuel-sur-le-controle-ief-en-2021

109. France, Ministry of the Economy, Finance and Recovery, Directorate General of the Treasury, Press Release, "FDI | Publication of standard application files for prior review or authorization requests under the French FDI screening mechanism," published February 22, 2022, last accessed September 1, 2025, available at https://www.tresor.economie.gouv.fr/Articles/2022/02/22/ief-publication-des-dossiers-types-pour-le-depot-des-demandes-d-examen-prealable-ou-d-autorisation-au-titre-de-la-reglementation-sur-le-controle-des-investissements-etrangers-en-france

110. See Point 1., in France, Ministry of the Economy, Finance, Industrial and Digital Sovereignty, Directorate General of the Treasury, "Guidelines on the Foreign Direct Investment Screening in France," September 2022, published September 8, 2022, accessed May 9, 2024, available at https://www.tresor.economie.gouv.fr/services-aux-entreprises/investissements-etrangers-en-france

111. France, Ministry of the Economy, Finance and Recovery, Directorate General of the Treasury, "Public consultation on the 2022 "Guidelines on the Foreign Direct Investment Screening in France," published March 24, 2022, accessed May 9, 2024, available at https://www.tresor.economie.gouv.fr/Articles/2022/03/24/consultation-publique-sur-les-lignes-directrices-2022-du-controle-des-investissements-etrangers-en-france

version. For the administration [112], this new edition, reflecting the most recent extensions of the scope of the regulation that entered into force on January 1, 2024, sets out the conditions under which screening applies to new types of investment transactions, including the crossing of the 10% voting rights threshold in a French-listed company by a non-European investor [113], and the acquisition of the French branch of a foreign company [114]. It also provides further clarification of the notion of critical raw materials .

The 2025 text thus harmonizes administrative doctrine with the practice accumulated since 2022 and introduces new sector-specific guidance, reflecting the State's determination to provide enhanced legal certainty for investors while at the same time broadening its ability to intervene in order to safeguard the national interest.

By clarifying the government's administrative doctrine, the publication of these guidelines offers stakeholders valuable insights into the practical operation of the regime. Crucially, the guidelines offer a high degree of legal certainty to all parties involved, since the DGT formally commits [115] to applying them consistently in all matters related to the screening of foreign investments in France.

According to Bruno Le Maire, Minister of the Economy, the issuance of these guidelines enhances France's investment attractiveness by increasing the predictability and legal certainty of the authorization process for foreign investors.

The DGT further explains that the guidelines were conceived as an educational and methodological tool, designed to support both the entities subject to the screening regime and their legal advisors in navigating the applicable rules and procedures.

These guidelines are therefore not binding in nature; rather, they serve to provide practical clarification and methodological guidance concerning the scope of the regime and the steps involved in the prior notification and authorization process.

Importantly, in the event of any divergence or interpretative difficulty between the guidelines and the applicable legislative or regulatory provisions, only the latter shall prevail. It is therefore the responsibility of the competent courts to resolve any potential conflicts of interpretation (see Chapter 22).

These guidelines may be updated or revised in the future to reflect legislative or regulatory changes, or to take into account evolving administrative doctrine or enforcement practice.

---

112. France, Ministry of the Economy, Finance and Industrial and Digital Sovereignty, Press Release No. 815, "Publication of the annual report on FDI screening in 2024," Paris, July 30, 2025, accessed August 22, 2025, available at https://www.tresor.economie.gouv.fr/Articles/2025/07/30/publication-du-rapport-annuel-sur-le-controle-ief-en-2024
113. France, Ministry of the Economy, Finance and Industrial and Digital Sovereignty, Directorate General of the Treasury, Guidelines on the Foreign Direct Investment Screening in France, July 2025, published July 30, 2025, accessed August 1, 2025, available at https://www.tresor.economie.gouv.fr/services-aux-entreprises/investissements-etrangers-en-france, Point 1.2.4.5: *"A downward crossing of the threshold, when the investor's shareholding falls below 10% of the voting rights, is not subject to any reporting requirement under the French FDI screening mechanism."*
114. Ibid., Point 1.4.2
115. France, Ministry of the Economy, Finance and Industrial and Digital Sovereignty, Directorate General of the Treasury, Press Release No. 108, "Guidelines on the Foreign Direct Investment Screening in France" published September 9, 2022, accessed September 1, 2025, available at https://presse.economie.gouv.fr/09-09-2022-controle-des-investissements-etrangers-en-france-publication-de-lignes-directrices

*
* *

The framing of the French FDI screening mechanism through regularly updated guidelines enhances the predictability of the review process, which is manifestly in the interest of the parties to a transaction.

These parties are thereby better positioned to anticipate the expectations of the administration in carrying out its mission of safeguarding the national interest. In any case, even though the Ministry of the Economy sets out its review doctrine through such guidelines, and even though its review policy is subject to parliamentary oversight (see Chapter 5), the Ministry of the Economy (see following chapter) nonetheless retains the sole authority to assess the mechanism as a whole.

Chapter 4

The Ministry of the Economy Is Responsible for Administering France's FDI Screening Regime

The question of which ministry is responsible for foreign direct investment (FDI) screening is a decisive one. It establishes the tone of interaction between the foreign investor and the host State. Like other market economies that have enshrined the principle of investment freedom, France has entrusted the screening of foreign investments (commonly referred to as contrôle IEF) to its Ministry of the Economy and Finance. Although this responsibility is operationally assigned to a dedicated review unit, referred to as the CIEF, the procedure is, in practice, interministerial and coordinated through the Interministerial Committee for Foreign Direct Investments Screenings in France (Comité interministériel des investissements étrangers en France –CIIEF).

The Ministry of the Economy Has Long Been the Lead Authority for FDI Screening

By designating the Minister of the Economy as the competent authority for investment screening, France has aligned itself with the practice observed in other liberal democracies. Notably, this responsibility was not assigned to the Ministry of the Armed Forces, despite the relevance of national defense interests, nor to the Ministry of the Interior, although it might have appeared logical given the references to public authority functions, public order, and national security.

Several reasons justify this institutional choice. First, the Ministry of the Economy is naturally inclined to promote investment liberalization and ensure the feasibility of transactions. This highlights the foundational principle that foreign investment is the rule, and restrictions are the exception. Second, foreign investors generally perceive the Ministry of the Economy as more attuned to the dynamics of globalized markets, thereby fostering trust.

As a result, the Minister of the Economy is ex officio the competent authority for foreign direct investment screening in France. This arrangement was reaffirmed on several occasions, including during the reform of France's economic security policy announced [116] in 2018 by then-Prime Minister Édouard Philippe. The legislative and

116. France, Prime Minister, PHILIPPE, Édouard, "Statement on the main lines of the Action Plan for Business Growth and Transformation (PACTE)," Lassigny, February 16, 2018, accessed May 9, 2024, available

regulatory amendments introduced by the PACTE Act and its implementing Decree [117] of November 29, 2018 [118], followed the same logic.

Within the Ministry of the Economy, the Directorate General of the Treasury (Direction générale du Trésor – DGT) has historically played a leading role in implementing the screening mechanism. This role was formalized by the Ministerial Order [119] of December 18, 2019, which structured the DGT into departments and sub-directorates. The Order states that the Sub-Directorate for Trade Policy, Investment, and the Fight Against Financial Crime is responsible for "implementing France's foreign investment screening regime."

The DGT emphasizes [120] that "FDI screening cannot be conducted in isolation from a deep understanding of the French business ecosystem and its financial needs," which is why this function naturally falls within its scope. The DGT has also made clear [121] that "the Directorate General of the Treasury, under the sole authority of the Minister of the Economy, is responsible for handling the screening process."

Other Administrative Bodies Contribute to the Screening System

Although the DGT is the lead authority, other directorates within the Ministry also contribute to the implementation of France's FDI regime. The General Directorate for Enterprises (Direction générale des entreprises – DGE) plays a particularly significant role with regard to economic security, notably through the Strategic Information and Economic Security Service (Service de l'information stratégique et de la sécurité économiques – SISSE).

Established [122] in January 2016, the SISSE is a nationally competent service [123] that coordinates the DGE's assessments of strategic sectors and acts as an early warning body for potentially sensitive foreign investments. Once an operation that may fall

---

at https://www.vie-publique.fr/discours/205026-declaration-de-m-edouard-philippe-premier-ministre-sur-les-grandes-li

117. France, Decree No. 2018-1057 of November 29, 2018, on foreign investments subject to prior authorization, Official Journal of the French Republic, No. 0278, December 1, 2018, NOR: ECOT1816712D
118. entered into force on January 1, 2019
119. France, Ministerial Order of December 18, 2019, on the organization of the Directorate General of the Treasury, Official Journal of the French Republic, No. 0300, December 27, 2019, NOR: ECOP1935021A
120. France, Ministry of the Economy, Finance and Recovery, Directorate General of the Treasury, Report, "Foreign investment control in France in 2021," March 2022, published March 17, 2022, accessed September 1, 2025, available at https://www.tresor.economie.gouv.fr/Articles/9aa76183-24a8-49ba-9466-179c5b29f99c/files/47b9b032-3d2b-4779-8327-15d3400045ab
121. See Point 2.1.3 in France, Ministry of the Economy, Finance and Industrial and Digital Sovereignty, Directorate General of the Treasury, "Guidelines on the Foreign Direct Investment Screening in France," July 2025, published July 30, 2025, accessed August 1, 2025, available at https://www.tresor.economie.gouv.fr/services-aux-entreprises/investissements-etrangers-en-france
122. France, Decree No. 2016-66 of January 29, 2016, establishing a Commissioner for Strategic Information and Economic Security and creating a national service with specific competence called "Strategic Information and Economic Security Service," Official Journal of the French Republic, No. 0025, January 30, 2016, NOR: EINX1531506D
123. France, Conseil d'État, 6th – 1st Combined Chambers, March 17, 2017, No. 398327, union "Finances centrales écoles" SPACEF CFDT
, ECLI:FR:CECHR:2017:398327.20170317I

under the FDI screening regime is detected, such as at the early stages of a planned acquisition, the SISSE or the competent ministry refers the matter to the DGT.

The CIEF: France's Dedicated Investment Screening Office

As previously mentioned, the control of foreign investments in France was significantly reformed in 2019 under the PACTE Act, with an associated increase in the resources dedicated to its enforcement.

One key institutional development was the creation, in January 2019, of a specialized review unit [124] within the DGT dedicated to foreign investment screening. This unit, initially referred to by its administrative code (MULTICOM4), was later renamed the CIEF [125] (Contrôle des investissements étrangers en France). Comprising six agents, the CIEF was established to handle the growing volume and complexity of screening cases resulting from regulatory reform [126].

The CIEF is responsible for implementing the legal and regulatory framework applicable to FDI screening, including the review of authorization and opinion requests submitted by foreign investors. Its functions are based on the provisions of the Ministerial Order [127] of December 18, 2019, which governs the organization of the Treasury Department. The Order provides that the relevant sub-directorate "implements the foreign investment screening regime. In cooperation with the Interministerial Committee for Foreign Direct Investments Screenings in France (CIIEF), for which it serves as the secretariat, it drafts and enforces the legal and regulatory framework, processes applications for authorization or opinion submitted by investors, and coordinates proposed decisions by the Minister of the Economy, including the exercise of police powers and sanctions established by law. It ensures transparency before Parliament and the public, in compliance with legally protected confidentiality rules. It participates in European and international fora concerning the control of foreign investments."

In response to a parliamentary inquiry [128], the government clarified that the Directorate General of the Treasury) relies on the CIIEF not only to review applications

124. France, Ministry of the Economy, Finance, Industrial and Digital Sovereignty, Directorate General of the Treasury, Department for Multilateral Affairs and Development – SAMD, Sub-directorate for Trade Policy, Investment and the Fight Against Financial Crime – MULTICOM, Office for the Foreign Direct Investment Screening in France – MULTICOM4
125. France, Directorate General of the Treasury, organizational chart referring to the "CIEF – Foreign investment control in France," September 2024, accessed September 1, 2025, available at https://www.tresor.economie.gouv.fr/Institutionnel/Niveau2/Pages/dec76c17-341b-4ca5-8a97-a8666a9ddaaa/files/d3cda4eb-5b68-4d72-aca7-7c75c86dd6ec
126. France, National Assembly, Written Question No. 35484 to the Minister of the Economy, Finance and Recovery, Official Journal of the National Assembly, January 12, 2021, p. 139, MARLEIX, Olivier, Member of Parliament, Les Républicains (LR), Ministerial Reply, Official Journal of the National Assembly, June 22, 2021, p. 5074
127. France, Ministerial Order of December 18, 2019, on the organization of the Directorate General of the Treasury, Official Journal of the French Republic, No. 0300, December 27, 2019, NOR: ECOP1935021A
128. France, National Assembly, Written Question No. 35484 to the Minister of the Economy, Finance and Recovery, Official Journal of the National Assembly, January 12, 2021, p. 139, MARLEIX, Olivier, Member of Parliament, Les Républicains (LR), Ministerial Reply, Official Journal of the National Assembly, June 22, 2021, p. 5074

under the FDI screening mechanism but also to monitor compliance with conditions attached to authorizations granted to foreign investors.

It is important to note, however, that the CIEF's role is strictly limited to reviewing transactions from the perspective of safeguarding national interests. The information collected during the screening process is not intended to be shared with other authorities, such as tax administrations, for unrelated purposes.

Finally, the CIEF represents France in EU and international discussions on investment screening. It acts as France's liaison at the Council of the European Union on FDI-related matters and serves as the national point of contact for the EU cooperation mechanism on investment screening, which has been in effect since October 11, 2020.

Screening Operates within an Interministerial Framework

The screening procedure operates within the framework of the Comité interministériel des investissements étrangers en France (CIIEF – Interministerial Committee on Foreign Investment in France). This committee brings together all ministries concerned by the foreign investment screening process, depending on the sector targeted by the applicable regulation.

Within this framework, the CIIEF's services ensure compliance with the commitments undertaken by foreign investors, notably through regular information disclosures that investors are required to provide to the administration (e.g., annual reports, meetings with designated points of contact), through information gathered by the administration's own means, and through on-site inspections whenever deemed necessary.

Monitoring compliance with the conditions attached to certain investment authorizations is performed jointly by the members of the CIIEF and the Service de l'information stratégique et de la sécurité économiques (SISSE – Strategic Information and Economic Security Service).

The committee is composed of approximately thirty civil servants from various ministries and state agencies, each contributing their specific expertise to assess the sensitivity of the French target's activities in terms of public security, public order, and national defense interests. Additional government entities may be consulted during the review process when specialized expertise is required. The CIIEF, thus composed, is tasked with implementing the legislative and regulatory framework governing foreign investment screening in France and with reviewing authorization requests and opinions submitted by investors.

In its capacity as the secretariat of the committee [129], the Office "Contrôle des investissements étrangers en France" (CIEF) – Foreign Direct Investment Screening Office (CIEF)) within the Directorate General of the Treasury (DGT) transmits each request to the ministries that are either directly affected by the proposed transaction or regularly involved in investment screening procedures.

129. DUPEYRAT, op. cit., p. 90

A broad range of government bodies may be consulted. In addition to the Ministry of the Armed Forces, these may include the Ministry of Health, the Ministry for the Ecological and Inclusive Transition, the Secrétariat général de la défense et de la sécurité nationale (SGDSN – General Secretariat for Defense and National Security), responsible for the protection of classified information, or the Agence nationale de la sécurité des systèmes d'information (ANSSI – National Cybersecurity Agency of France). The involvement of these entities depends on the specific business sector of the French target company.

This collaborative and often lengthy process is intended, first and foremost, to determine whether the investment in question falls within the scope of the screening mechanism, especially in light of the nature of the activities conducted by the French entity. If applicable, the review then seeks to identify the public interest objectives to be protected by the French State and the means by which such protection should be implemented, which may include attaching specific conditions to the authorization. Where such conditions are deemed necessary, the State prepares a draft letter of undertakings to be signed by the investor. This letter is then appended to the ministerial authorization, effectively transforming the authorization into a conditional one.

Although the committee meets several times a year, its operations are not governed by any specific statutory or regulatory instrument.In practice, each authorization request is referred by the CIEF to the competent government agencies for comment.

As highlighted by the mission [130] d'évaluation et de contrôle (MEC – Parliamentary Oversight Mission) of the French National Assembly in 2025, stakeholders interviewed during the fact-finding process emphasized that the opinions issued by the CIIEF are strictly advisory in nature and do not bind the Directorate General of the Treasury when issuing a final decision proposal.

Monitoring compliance with conditions imposed on foreign investors remains a core responsibility of the CIIEF, again in coordination with the SISSE. Any suspicion of a breach of an investor's undertakings is subject to a formal characterization process and may, where appropriate, lead to the initiation of sanction procedures.

This interministerial structure has been praised by the Parliamentary Committee of Inquiry on the French State's industrial policy decisions, which commended the IEF procedure for its interministerial character. The Commission [131] noted that "the screening mechanism owes its strength to its interministerial structure," adding that "the number of government departments involved in the Directorate General of the

130. France, National Assembly, Committee for the Assessment and Oversight of Public Policies, Fact-Finding Report No. 1453 by JOLIVET, François, and de LEPINAU, Hervé, Members of Parliament, on the evaluation of the Foreign Direct Investment Screening in France, Official Journal of the French Republic, May 27, 2025, text 45 of 69, published May 22, 2025, accessed Sept. 1st, 2025, available at https://www.assemblee-nationale.fr/dyn/17/rapports/cec/l17b1453_rapport-information

131. France, National Assembly, Report No. 897 rect., April 19, 2018, MARLEIX, Olivier (Chair), KASBARIAN, Guillaume (Rapporteur), Members of Parliament, submitted on behalf of the fact-finding committee tasked with reviewing the decisions of the State in matters of industrial policy, in light of recent corporate mergers, particularly Alstom, Alcatel, and STX, and the possible means to protect national industrial champions in a globalized trade context, Volume 1, consulted September 1, 2025, available at https://www.assemblee-nationale.fr/dyn/15/rapports/cepolind/l15b0897-ti_rapport-enquete

Treasury's) review process continues to grow. Ministerial offices are kept informed through the relevant administrations, and the entire chain of command is mobilized, up to the minister, when the sensitivity of the case so warrants."

It is also worth noting the particular role played by the Direction générale de l'armement (DGA – Defence Procurement Agency) in monitoring investor compliance with imposed conditions (see Chapter 20).

Finally, any suspicion of a breach of a legally binding undertaking triggers a formal characterization procedure and may result in sanctions being imposed.

*
* *

While the Ministry of the Economy has historically held primary responsibility for foreign investment screening, exercised through the CIEF within the Directorate General of the Treasury), the gradual reform and professionalization of the process have firmly embedded it within an interministerial framework. Parties to the transaction must be fully aware of this institutional reality. Moreover, as detailed in the following chapter, the screening mechanism itself is subject to parliamentary oversight, either through the procedure itself or within the broader framework of the legislature's general supervisory powers.

Chapter 5

Parliament Exercises Limited Oversight over the French FDI Screening Mechanism

The issue of parliamentary oversight over prior authorizations granted by the Minister of the Economy to foreign investors is a recurring theme in both French and international public debates. In many cases, legislative interventions [132], grounded in constitutional powers, have triggered major policy evolutions, most often in reaction to emblematic transactions.

In France, Parliament was for a long time absent from the foreign investment screening framework. It nevertheless entered the debate during the 2018 Parliamentary Committee of Inquiry on the State's decisions in matters of industrial policy. This development, together with the examination of the 2019 PACTE Law, led to the establishment of an official oversight mechanism under Article L. 151-7 of the Monetary and Financial Code. However, since that mechanism was designed to apply only after the conditions for the transaction's completion had expired, it has remained inoperative in practice. For this reason, Parliament decided in 2024 to enshrine in statute the possibility of holding a debate on the matter, and in 2025 the National Assembly launched an evaluation and oversight mission (Mission d'évaluation et de contrôle – MEC) on the screening regime. That said, sensitive transactions continue to be subject to recurrent political scrutiny, thereby paradoxically heightening the political risks affecting the completion of certain deals.

Parliament Had Long Been Absent from the FDI Screening Landscape

Historically, the supervision of foreign direct investment (FDI) in France has fallen under the exclusive responsibility of the executive branch and its administrative agencies. From the inception of a regulatory framework for FDI screening, control was

132. In the United States, the 2006 Dubai Ports World controversy prompted a major overhaul of the American foreign investment review framework, culminating in the adoption of the Foreign Investment and National Security Act (FINSA) in 2007. In France, a similar shift occurred following the work of the 2018 Parliamentary Committee of Inquiry tasked with reviewing the government's industrial policy decisions. This inquiry laid the groundwork for a revision of the French foreign direct investment (FDI) screening regime, leading to the adoption of the PACTE Act and the establishment of a parliamentary oversight mechanism. In the United Kingdom, the passage of the National Security and Investment Act in 2021 likewise introduced a form of parliamentary scrutiny, now exercised through the International Trade Committee of the House of Commons.

placed solely under government authority. The 1966 law entrusted the Government alone with the mission to "safeguard national interests," with no mention of Parliament. This arrangement reflected the Gaullist vision of a strong executive overseeing sovereign matters. Accordingly, the implementation of the screening regime was formalized by decree upon the recommendation of the Minister of the Economy.

Until recently, this "reserved domain" effectively excluded Parliament even from receiving information [133] about the process. In 2018, for instance, the Minister of the Economy responded to a parliamentary question by stating: "The Minister of the Economy and Finance is therefore not in a position to provide statistical information regarding decisions made under this procedure, given the security concerns the prior authorization process is designed to protect."

This posture ran counter to the constitutional reform [134] of 2008, which had aimed to expand Parliament's role in the oversight of public policy, including foreign direct investment screening . It is within this context that the National Assembly published a fact-finding report [135] on "non-EU investment and the protection of strategic European interests," and that the Minister of Industrial Recovery [136] was repeatedly questioned during the adoption of the May 14, 2014 decree [137] expanding the screening mechanism.

A Turning Point: The 2018 Parliamentary Inquiry Commission

The effective absence of parliamentary control came to an end in 2018 with the establishment of a parliamentary inquiry commission tasked with reviewing the FDI screening process and investigating landmark cases such as the sale of Alstom to General Electric, Alcatel to Nokia, and STX France to Fincantieri. This scrutiny, however, was exercised through the constitutional prerogatives of Parliament rather than through a dedicated legal mechanism under the Monetary and Financial Code.

Initiated by the opposition group "Les Républicains" under their annual right of initiative [138], the commission [139] was automatically placed on the legislative calendar.

133. France, National Assembly, Written Question No. 46 to the Minister of the Economy and Finance, Official Journal of the National Assembly, July 11, 2017, p. 3853, MARLEIX, Olivier, Member of Parliament, Les Républicains (LR), Ministerial Reply, Official Journal of the National Assembly, October 24, 2017, p. 5141

134. France, Constitutional Law No. 2008-724 of July 23, 2008, on the modernization of the institutions of the Fifth Republic, Official Journal of the French Republic, No. 0171, July 24, 2008, NOR: JUSX0807076L

135. France, National Assembly, Fact-Finding Report No. 1602, December 4, 2013, submitted by the Committee on European Affairs on extra-EU investments and the control of strategic European interests, by LAMBERT, Jean and MARTIN, Patrice Anato, Members of Parliament

136. France, National Assembly, Verbatim Record No. 76, May 20, 2014, sitting, Oral Questions to the Minister of the Economy, Industrial Recovery and the Digital Sector, Official Journal of the National Assembly, p. 3241 (ERHEL, Corinne, Member of Parliament, Socialist, Republican and Citizen Group – SRC) and p. 3242 (CHARTIER, Jérôme, Member of Parliament, Les Républicains – LR), ISSN 0242-6765

137. France, Decree No. 2014-479 of May 14, 2014, on foreign investments subject to prior authorization, Official Journal of the French Republic, No. 0112, May 15, 2014, NOR: ERNX1411012D

138. France, National Assembly, Resolution Proposal No. 271 of October 11, 2017, by JACOB, Christian, Member of Parliament, Les Républicains (LR), aiming to establish a commission of inquiry to examine State decisions on industrial policy, in light of recent corporate mergers, notably Alstom, Alcatel and STX, and possible means to protect national industrial flagships in a globalized trade context, accessed September 1st, 2025, available at https://www.assemblee-nationale.fr/dyn/15/textes/l15b0271_proposition-resolution

139. DUPEYRAT, op. cit., p. 230.

The National Assembly's Economic Affairs Committee, as the competent standing committee, designated Olivier Marleix (LR – Eure-et-Loir) as chair and Guillaume Kasbarian (LREM – Eure-et-Loir) as rapporteur. The resolution specifically sought to examine the French Government's decision-making process in authorizing the sale of Alstom to General Electric, especially after a parliamentary broadcast [140] revisited the controversial conditions of the deal.

Over a six-month period, the commission conducted numerous hearings, mapping the state of France's FDI screening mechanism and the protection of strategic sectors. Although opinions diverged on individual transactions, consensus emerged on the need to adapt the screening framework. The final report [141], adopted unanimously, emphasized the necessity of improving the control process for sensitive foreign investments and called for greater transparency in a regime that the commission nonetheless described as "relatively effective."

For Rapporteur Guillaume Kasbarian, the priorities were to better define what constitutes a "strategic" activity, enhance predictability for foreign investors, and improve parliamentary information rights. The report recommended extending the so-called "Montebourg Decree," strengthening the interministerial governance of the FDI screening process, and publishing detailed statistics to promote transparency.

The Government endorsed the conclusions of the inquiry commission and, during the parliamentary debates [142] on the PACTE Act [143] (Plan d'Action pour la Croissance et la Transformation des Entreprises), committed to providing Parliament with an annual report on foreign investments, mirroring the practice in the United States since 2007.

A major advancement came with the recommendation, put forward by the commission's rapporteur, to establish a parliamentary delegation [144] for economic security. The aim was to institutionalize a form of oversight more rigorous than mere committee hearings yet less confrontational than formal inquiry commissions. Ultimately, a compromise was reached: oversight would be exercised by a panel of qualified individuals, as enshrined in new Article L. 151-7 of the Monetary and Financial Code.

This marked a legal shift: for the first time since 1966, responsibility for foreign investment screening was no longer vested exclusively in the executive branch.

---

140. France, GENDREAU, David and LERAITRE, Alexandre, "Phantom War: The Sale of Alstom to General Electric," LCP, television documentary, 2017, ISAN No. 0000-0005-1974-0000-0-0000-0000-3
141. France, National Assembly, Report No. 897 rect., April 19, 2018, MARLEIX, Olivier (Chair), KASBARIAN, Guillaume (Rapporteur), Members of Parliament, submitted on behalf of the committee of inquiry tasked with examining State decisions in matters of industrial policy, in light of recent corporate mergers, notably in the cases of Alstom, Alcatel, and STX, and the possible means of protecting national industrial flagships in a globalized trade context, Volume 1, accessed May 9, 2024, available at https://www.assemblee-nationale.fr/dyn/15/rapports/cepolind/l15b0897-ti_rapport-enquete
142. France, National Assembly, Verbatim Record No. 20, September 14, 2018, Special Committee tasked with examining the bill on Business Growth and Transformation (No. 1088), Sitting of Friday, 9:30 a.m., accessed September 1, 2025, available at https://www.assemblee-nationale.fr/dyn/15/comptes-rendus/cspacte/l15cspacte1718020_compte-rendu
143. France, Law No. 2019-486 of May 22, 2019, on Business Growth and Transformation, Official Journal of the French Republic, No. 0119, May 23, 2019, NOR: ECOT1810669L
144. DUPEYRAT, op. cit., p. 238

In parallel, the Senate's Economic Affairs Committee pursued its own efforts to safeguard France's economic interests, organizing a series of hearings on foreign investments in companies deemed strategic.

Parliamentary Oversight Formally Established by the 2019 PACTE Act

Parliamentary oversight over the French foreign direct investment (FDI) screening regime was formally instituted in 2019 through the adoption of the PACTE Act (Law No. 2019-486 of May 22, 2019, on business growth and transformation). This legislation introduced Article L. 151-7 into the French Monetary and Financial Code, enshrining key recommendations issued by the 2018 Parliamentary Committee of Inquiry. Chief among these recommendations were the establishment of (i) an annual information mechanism on transactions reviewed by the Minister of the Economy, and (ii) an investigative power, both documentary and on-site, granted to designated members of Parliament.

In both instances, the oversight responsibilities are entrusted to the chairs of the parliamentary committees in charge of economic affairs and to the rapporteurs général of the finance committees in each chamber of Parliament. Given France's institutional and political equilibrium, the designated members are likely to belong to the majority group of each chamber. Each designated parliamentarian may delegate their oversight powers to another member of their respective committee.

This parliamentary oversight is primarily exercised through the executive branch's duty to inform the legislature. Accordingly, the Government is required to transmit to the designated members of Parliament an annual report detailing its actions "with respect to the protection and promotion of the Nation's economic, industrial, and scientific interests, as well as with respect to the screening of foreign investments under the procedure provided for in Article L. 151-3" of the Monetary and Financial Code.

This report includes a detailed analysis of the Government's strategy to protect and advance national economic, industrial, and scientific interests. It covers measures adopted in the field of economic security, efforts to safeguard strategic companies, related policy objectives, initiatives undertaken, and outcomes achieved.

The report also provides specific information on the prior authorization procedure applicable to foreign investments in activities carried out in France. This includes data on the number of authorization requests submitted to the Minister of the Economy, decisions to deny authorization, authorized transactions (both conditional and unconditional), the imposition of remedies under Paragraph II of Article L. 151-3, and the use of the Minister's sanctioning power pursuant to the same provision. However, the report explicitly excludes any information that could identify the individuals or legal entities subject to the authorization procedure.

In this framework, only the chairs of the economic affairs committees and the rapporteurs général of the finance committees are authorized to receive the annual report.

Beyond the reporting obligation, parliamentary oversight may also be exercised through powers traditionally associated with the broader constitutional missions of the French Parliament, namely, hearings, documentary and on-site investigations, and requests for information. Accordingly, the designated members (i.e., the committee chairs and finance rapporteurs général in both chambers) are jointly empowered to:

1° Hearings. The designated members of Parliament may hear testimony from the competent ministers, the Commissioner for Strategic Information and Economic Security (Commissaire à l'information stratégique et à la sécurité économiques), and the directors of the relevant central government departments, who may be accompanied by the advisors of their choice. These hearings, which are not open to the public, may include discussions of information identifying the natural or legal persons subject to the prior authorization procedure for foreign investments as provided under Article L. 151-3 of the Monetary and Financial Code;

2° Investigative powers. They may conduct any investigation, based on documentation or conducted on-site, relating to the Government's actions in the protection and promotion of France's economic, industrial, and scientific interests, as well as in the screening of foreign direct investment. These investigations [145], however, may not relate to foreign investments that are currently under review by the Minister of the Economy and that may give rise to a formal decision. All administrative information and documents requested in connection with such investigations must be provided to them, including any reports drawn up by agencies and departments in charge of administrative oversight, with the exception of information or documents protected by national defense secrecy.

Public Reporting, Limitations of Oversight, and the Emergence of Parliamentary Debate

The exercise of the oversight powers referred to in points (1) and (2) above must give rise to a public statement by each designated chair and rapporteur general before their respective committee. This may be accompanied by the publication of a report. In practice, members of Parliament regularly question [146] the Minister of the Economy in order to obtain statistical information on the implementation of the screening procedure.

However, in order to preserve both national security interests and trade secrecy, such communications, and any related reports, are strictly prohibited from disclosing information or assessments that would allow for the identification of natural or legal persons subject to the foreign investment screening procedure set forth in Article L. 151-3 of the Monetary and Financial Code.

---

145. Ibid., p. 135

146. France, Senate, Written Question No. 09362 to the Minister of the Economy and Finance, Official Journal of the Senate, March 14, 2019, p. 1364, CADIC, Olivier, Senator, Centrist Union Group (UC), Ministerial Reply, May 30, 2019, Official Journal of the Senate, p. 2862

Furthermore, in the course of their work, the designated chairs and rapporteurs général are authorized to submit joint recommendations and observations to the President of the Republic, the Prime Minister, and the relevant ministers. These are also transmitted to the Presidents of the National Assembly and the Senate.

The operational interface between the Government and Parliament for the purposes of transparency in the implementation of the screening mechanism is handled by the Foreign Direct Investment Screening Office (CIEF), the interministerial service responsible for processing prior authorization requests within the Ministry of the Economy, in coordination with other government departments.

Parliamentary Oversight Has Remained Practically Dormant

Four years after the introduction of the oversight mechanism under the PACTE Act, the former chair of the Parliamentary Committee of Inquiry formally questioned [147] the Minister of the Economy regarding the exercise of parliamentary oversight over France's foreign investment screening (known as IEF). He specifically requested statistical data on the number of hearings held and the number of investigations, documentary or on-site, carried out pursuant to Article L. 151-7 since its entry into force.

In response, the Minister of the Economy reiterated that Article L. 151-7 had established a framework for dialogue between the executive and legislative branches in matters of foreign investment screening. He was quick to clarify his interpretation that, although the provision allows designated parliamentary members to hear from relevant ministers or their representatives (including the Strategic Information and Economic Security Commissioner and the directors of the relevant central administrations), such hearings must be conducted behind closed doors.

Moreover, while confirming that parliamentarians may indeed conduct investigations on documents and on-site, the Minister emphasized that such investigations may not involve investments that are currently pending a decision by the Minister of the Economy. In other words, only completed transactions, those for which the authorization process has concluded, would be subject to potential oversight. This restrictive interpretation, which contradicts the original parliamentary intent behind the PACTE Act, renders the oversight procedure largely ineffective, stripping it of its core purpose: enabling real-time scrutiny of situations potentially detrimental to France's essential interests.

The Minister further confirmed that no hearings had been conducted pursuant to Article L. 151-7 since the enactment of the PACTE Act [148] on May 22, 2019. Although representatives of relevant authorities have appeared before Parliament in the context

147. France, National Assembly, Written Question No. 6278 to the Minister of the Economy, Finance, Industrial and Digital Sovereignty, Official Journal of the National Assembly, March 14, 2023, p. 2307, MARLEIX, Olivier, Member of Parliament, Les Républicains (LR), Ministerial Reply, Official Journal of the National Assembly, May 16, 2023, p. 4442

148. France, Law No. 2019-486 of May 22, 2019, on Business Growth and Transformation, Official Journal of the French Republic, No. 0119, May 23, 2019, NOR: ECOT1810669L

of broader inquiries into government action, particularly on topics such as competitiveness, economic intelligence, and national sovereignty, these discussions only tangentially addressed the functioning of the foreign investment screening mechanism.

With respect to the investigative powers granted under Article L. 151-7, the Minister acknowledged that his departments had not received any requests from the designated committee chairs or rapporteurs général for either document-based or on-site investigations.

Regarding the executive's reporting duty, the Minister affirmed that he had submitted annual reports to the designated members of Parliament, each summarizing the Government's actions in the area of foreign investment screening and presenting key statistical data.

Legislative Reform in 2024: Toward an Annual Parliamentary Debate

While the formal oversight procedure provided under Article L. 151-7 has remained largely dormant since its creation in 2019, parliamentary interest in France's foreign investment screening regime has not abated. On the contrary, emblematic transactions have prompted repeated parliamentary interventions.

More significantly, the issue of foreign direct investment screening re-emerged prominently in 2023 during the work [149] of the Senate's Economic Affairs Committee's fact-finding mission on the organization of economic intelligence in France. The mission examined strategic tools and frameworks to protect and reclaim national sovereignty.

Among the 23 recommendations unanimously adopted by the Committee was the proposal to "establish an annual parliamentary debate on economic intelligence that would take into account the publication of the annual report on foreign investment screening in France (IEF) and assess compliance with investors' commitments."

This recommendation took the form of a parliamentary initiative [150] within a broader effort to enhance national sovereignty. In 2024, it was formally introduced as an amendment during deliberations on draft legislation addressing foreign interference. The amendment was adopted by the Senate, despite opposition from the Government, and resulted in a significant legislative development: the formal inclusion of an annual parliamentary debate on the IEF mechanism. This provision is now codified under Article L. 151-6 of the Monetary and Financial Code.

In addition, the amendment specifies that the annual report submitted to the designated members of Parliament under Article L. 151-7 must henceforth include long-term monitoring of compliance by foreign investors with their commitments.

149. France, Senate, Fact-Finding Report No. 872, July 12, 2023, submitted on behalf of the Committee on Economic Affairs on economic intelligence, by LIENEMANN, Marie-Noëlle, Senator, and LEMOYNE, Jean-Baptiste, Senator, accessed September 1st, 2025, available at https://www.senat.fr/rap/r22-872/r22-8721.pdf

150. France, Senate, Bill No. 928 of September 21, 2023, aimed at making economic intelligence a tool for reclaiming national sovereignty, by LIENEMANN, Marie-Noëlle, LEMOYNE, Jean-Baptiste, BABARY, Serge, and MONTAUGÉ, Franck, Senators, accessed August 12, 2024, available at https://www.senat.fr/leg/ppl22-928.pdf

Even before the law was promulgated, and in light of persistent parliamentary interest in the FDI screening process, the Senate convened its first debate on the subject in 2024. Initiated by former Minister of Foreign Trade Jean-Baptiste Lemoyne, the debate approached the IEF mechanism through the lens of economic intelligence. Although held without a vote, the debate marked a milestone: for the first time, France's FDI screening regime was placed at the center of public and parliamentary discussion. Several high-profile transactions were addressed during the session (see next section).

A Parliamentary Debate on Foreign Investment Control Is Now Mandated by Law

Although the specific parliamentary oversight procedure introduced by Article L. 151-7 of the French Monetary and Financial Code in 2019 has remained largely dormant in practice, the French Parliament has not abandoned its interest in foreign direct investment (FDI) screening. Numerous interventions in both chambers over the years, often in connection with emblematic transactions, reflect the legislature's continued attention to the matter (see next section).

In particular, parliamentary focus on the national investment screening framework resurfaced in 2023 during the work of the Senate's Economic Affairs Committee, which conducted a fact-finding mission on France's economic intelligence architecture. The committee's objective was to explore new strategies to safeguard and reclaim the country's economic sovereignty.

Among the 23 unanimously adopted recommendations issued by the Committee was a proposal to "institute an annual parliamentary debate on economic intelligence, incorporating the publication of the annual report on the Foreign Direct Investment Screening in France and the monitoring of investor commitments."

This recommendation was carried forward as part of a broader parliamentary initiative focused on strengthening France's sovereignty. In 2024, the proposal was submitted as an amendment [151] to the bill on foreign interference and was adopted by the Senate, despite the Government's opposition. The amendment introduced a provision allowing for an annual parliamentary debate on the FDI screening mechanism, which is now codified in Article L. 151-6 of the Monetary and Financial Code.

The amendment also revised the reporting obligations under Article L. 151-7 by requiring that the annual report submitted to the presidents and general rapporteurs of the Economic and Finance Committees in each chamber include a longitudinal analysis of foreign investors' compliance with their commitments.

Even prior to the enactment of the legislation, and reflecting the broader political momentum surrounding the issue, the French Senate held its first debate [152] on the

151. France, Senate, Amendments Nos. 596, 595 and 593 of May 22, 2024, to the Bill on Foreign Interference in France (first reading), submitted by LEMOYNE, Jean-Baptiste, Senator, and others, accessed August 12, 2024, available at https://www.senat.fr/amendements/2023-2024/596/Amdt_25.html
152. France, Law No. 2024-850 of July 25, 2024, aimed at preventing foreign interference in France, Official Journal of the French Republic, No. 0177, July 26, 2024, NOR: IOMX2408435L

FDI screening regime in 2024. Spearheaded by former Minister of Foreign Trade Jean-Baptiste Lemoyne, the debate addressed the regime through the lens of economic intelligence[153]. Although it was a non-binding discussion, it marked a watershed moment by placing the screening mechanism squarely on the agenda of public and parliamentary scrutiny. During the session, a number of high-profile transactions were discussed (see next section).

The National Assembly Conducted an Evaluation of the Screening Mechanism in 2025

In 2024, the National Assembly included a formal evaluation of the "Foreign Direct Investment Screening in France" in the work program of its Committee for the Evaluation and Oversight of Public Policies (Comité d'évaluation et de contrôle des politiques publiques, CEC), following an initiative by the Rassemblement National political group. The CEC appointed two rapporteurs for this review: François Jolivet of the Horizons & Independents group and Hervé de Lépinau of the Rassemblement National group.

It is important to note that this evaluation did not fall within the scope of the dedicated parliamentary oversight procedure under Article L. 151-7 of the Monetary and Financial Code. Rather, it was undertaken pursuant to Parliament's broader constitutional mandate to evaluate public policies[154], carried out through the CEC, a cross-functional committee of the National Assembly. The CEC is chaired by the President of the Assembly and comprises thirty-six members appointed to reflect the proportional representation of political groups and the balance of standing committees.

To assess the French FDI screening regime, the mission employed a qualitative analytical methodology, including a review of academic and administrative literature, a series of stakeholder interviews, and the distribution of detailed questionnaires. The evaluation criteria focused on four key dimensions: (1) the effectiveness of the control mechanism; (2) the efficiency of its implementation; (3) the relevance of the mandatory prior authorization requirement and the list of strategic sectors; and (4) the coherence of the screening regime with other instruments of economic security.

The final report, released in 2025, offers an in-depth analysis of the system's operational performance and identifies several structural and procedural shortcomings. It puts forward approximately twenty recommendations aimed at strengthening the overall effectiveness of the screening framework.

Paradoxically, the absence of an enforceable mechanism for ongoing parliamentary control has led elected officials to resort to more traditional forms of political scrutiny over government decision-making. As a result, sensitive transactions that would otherwise remain confidential are frequently thrust into the public domain while still

153. France, Senate, Debates, Verbatim Record, May 29, 2024, "Foreign Direct Investment Screening in France as a tool of an economic intelligence strategy serving our sovereignty," LEMOYNE, Jean-Baptiste, Senator, RDPI Group, accessed July 9, 2024, available at https://www.senat.fr/cra/s20240529/s20240529.pdf

154. France, National Assembly, Rules of Procedure, Articles 98-1 and 146-2 to 146-7

under review. This politicization, often through parliamentary questions or media interventions, exposes deal participants to reputational risks and regulatory uncertainty, undermining transaction stability and investor confidence.

The National Assembly nonetheless conducted an evaluation of the screening mechanism in 2025

In 2024, at the initiative of the Rassemblement National group, the French National Assembly added to the agenda of the Committee for the Evaluation and Oversight of Public Policies (Comité d'évaluation et de contrôle des politiques publiques, CEC) an assessment of the "foreign direct investment screening mechanism in France." The Committee appointed two rapporteurs for the mission: François Jolivet, representing the Horizons & Indépendants (HI) group, and Hervé de Lépinau, representing the Rassemblement National (RN) group.

It is important to note that this assessment was not conducted under the specific parliamentary powers provided for in Article L. 151-7 of the Monetary and Financial Code (Code monétaire et financier), which governs parliamentary scrutiny of foreign direct investment screening. Rather, it falls within the broader constitutional mandate of Parliament to evaluate public policies. This mission was carried out by the CEC, a cross-cutting body within the National Assembly tasked with overseeing and assessing public policy implementation. The CEC is chaired by the President of the National Assembly and comprises thirty-six members, appointed in accordance with the principle of proportional representation of political groups and ensuring balanced representation from the standing committees.

To evaluate the French FDI screening regime, the mission employed a qualitative methodology based on a review of the academic and administrative literature, a series of interviews, and a set of questionnaires [155]. The assessment criteria focused on four key areas:

1. the effectiveness of the screening process,
2. the efficiency of the overall system,
3. the relevance of the prior authorization requirement and the list of strategic sectors subject to screening, and
4. the coherence of the FDI screening regime with other economic security instruments.

---

155. The rapporteurs structured their assessment of the mechanism around the following evaluative questions: Does the current list of sensitive activities subject to France's foreign investment screening (FDI screening) regime sufficiently capture the full range of national security-relevant sectors, and are the triggering thresholds for review appropriately calibrated ? Is the review process conducted by the French administration for foreign investment authorization requests efficient and of satisfactory quality ? Is there adequate oversight of the commitments made by foreign investors, and are such commitments subject to sufficiently frequent monitoring and effective sanctions in the event of non-compliance ? To what extent are decisions made under the French FDI screening regime coherently integrated into a broader economic security ecosystem (including domestic financing alternatives, security tools, risk analysis frameworks, intelligence monitoring, etc.) ? How does the effectiveness of France's foreign investment screening mechanism in strategic sectors compare to equivalent systems in place in the United States and other European Union Member States ?

The report [156], published in 2025, focuses on evaluating the efficiency of this regulatory mechanism, identifying its limitations, and proposing avenues for reform. It puts forward approximately twenty recommendations [157] aimed at improving the current framework.

---

156. France, National Assembly, Committee for the Assessment and Oversight of Public Policies, Fact-Finding Report No. 1453 by JOLIVET, François and de LEPINAU, Hervé, Members of Parliament, on the evaluation of the Foreign Direct Investment Screening in France, Official Journal of the French Republic, May 27, 2025, text 45 of 69, published May 22, 2025, accessed May 27, 2025, available at https://www.assemblee-nationale.fr/dyn/17/rapports/cec/l17b1453_rapport-information
157. Proposal No. 1: Adjust the legal framework governing foreign direct investment (FDI) screening in France to allow for a modular and graduated filtering mechanism, differentiating eligibility criteria, such as ownership thresholds and nationality-based requirements, based on the sensitivity level of the asset involved.
Proposal No. 2: Grant the French government the authority to intervene ex post in transactions completed in strategic sectors, where justified by national security considerations, following the model established under the UK National Security and Investment regime.
Proposal No. 3: Broaden the definition of qualifying investments to include operations beyond the acquisition of control under Article L. 233-3 of the Commercial Code, partial or full transfers of business branches, or threshold-crossings in voting rights, by expressly including greenfield investments.
Proposal No. 4: Expand the legal notion of "control" in an operational sense to reflect foreign influence, by amending Article R. 151-2 of the Monetary and Financial Code to include transactions conferring decisive influence, as well as certain non-controlling investments.
Proposal No. 5: Extend the list of strategic sectors referenced in Article R. 151-3 of the Monetary and Financial Code to include additional activities such as digital platforms and social networks, data center operations, banking and financial services, cultural sectors, certain real estate investments, emerging technologies, and artificial intelligence.
Proposal No. 6: Strengthen the staffing of the Foreign Direct Investment Screening Bureau (CIEF) within the Ministry of the Economy, in particular through the recruitment of legal experts specialized in corporate law to assist in identifying complex or sui generis corporate structures.
Proposal No. 7: Clarify and formalize the procedural steps involved in the review of authorization applications by the Interministerial Committee on Foreign Investments in France (CIIEF), through the issuance of an administrative circular.
Proposal No. 8: Enshrine in the Monetary and Financial Code the conditions that may be imposed on investors through commitment letters, including the explicit possibility of mandating proxy agreements in the defense sector, and requiring standardized evaluative indicators for all conditions imposed.
Proposal No. 9: Introduce a filing fee for foreign investment screening applications, calculated as a percentage of the transaction value, payable upon submission of the request.
Proposal No. 10: Establish a joint parliamentary delegation on economic security, composed equally of members from both chambers of Parliament, tasked with the ongoing oversight of the activities of the Foreign Direct Investment Screening Bureau (CIEF), investor compliance with imposed conditions, and the enforcement actions taken by the government.
Proposal No. 11: Amend the Monetary and Financial Code to remove existing barriers to parliamentary oversight of the FDI screening regime, by creating targeted mechanisms for information-sharing, effective procedures for ex post scrutiny of decisions made by the Minister of the Economy, and tools to assess investor compliance with imposed conditions.
Proposal No. 12: Require the Directorate General of the Treasury's annual report on FDI screening to include the nature and frequency of the main conditions imposed on investors, along with information on major acquisitions of strategic French companies by foreign investors.
Proposal No. 13: Clarify the application of the decree on the digital register of interest representatives, to ensure that lobbying activities conducted before the Directorate General of the Treasury on behalf of foreign investors are expressly recognized as falling under the scope of the French High Authority for Transparency in Public Life (HATVP) regulations.
Proposal No. 14: Develop a formal doctrine on economic intelligence through an interministerial directive, with a dedicated section on foreign investment screening, including anonymized decision summaries for use by government agencies, French businesses, and foreign investors.
Proposal No. 15: Increase awareness of the pre-filing procedure that complements FDI authorization requests, particularly among French businesses, and promote early engagement with the CIEF by foreign

Sensitive transactions are regularly subjected to political scrutiny

Paradoxically, the absence of effective parliamentary oversight over France's foreign direct investment (FDI) screening regime has led to the use of traditional political mechanisms to exert control over government decisions. As a result, transactions largely unknown to the general public are publicly exposed while still in progress, making it impossible to maintain confidentiality. Such premature disclosures introduce uncertainty and instability into investment processes and can severely compromise the success of transactions.

The Photonis Case

In 2019, during the acquisition of the French aerospace champion Latécoère by the American private equity fund Searchlight Capital Partners, another U.S. group, Teledyne Technologies, sought to acquire Photonis from the French fund Ardian. Photonis is a company specializing in optronic technologies, notably night vision devices used by the French armed forces, as well as components used in nuclear applications. The proposed acquisition aimed to create a "true war machine" [158] in the optronics field (infrared and light intensification) by merging Photonis with FLIR Systems. The resulting group would have emerged as a major global competitor to Lynred, the world's second-largest infrared imaging company, jointly owned by Safran and Thales.

---

investors to allow for anticipatory alignment of investment strategies with applicable screening requirements.

Proposal No. 16: Expand the scope of France's economic security policy by introducing an outbound investment screening mechanism to monitor and regulate foreign acquisitions initiated by French entities in strategic sectors abroad.

Proposal No. 17: Improve the circulation of strategic information among all services involved in economic security, in order to better anticipate threats and assess activity sensitivity; this includes the sharing of strategic benchmarks, updates on the evolving security environment, increased involvement of senior defense and security officials, and improved inter-agency intelligence sharing.

Proposal No. 18: Introduce a sovereign economic interest criterion as a mandatory consideration in the public procurement process for projects in the strategic sectors listed in Article R. 151-3 of the Monetary and Financial Code.

Proposal No. 19: Establish a specific interface between the Commercial Code and the Monetary and Financial Code to ensure the automatic triggering of sovereign control mechanisms whenever a foreign entity seeks to acquire a strategic French company undergoing judicial restructuring or liquidation.

Proposal No. 20: Promote coordination between the policy frameworks of the French Government Shareholding Agency (APE), the Caisse des Dépôts et Consignations, and Bpifrance, in order to facilitate the mobilization of public financial alternatives when a foreign investment in a strategic sector is rejected.

Proposal No. 21: Reinforce the intervention capacity of the French Government Shareholding Agency (APE) in highly strategic divestment cases by reallocating dividends from public enterprises to the Special Allocation Account for Government Shareholdings.

Proposal No. 22: Support the creation of investment funds accessible to the general public and specifically dedicated to financing various strategic industries, modeled on the recently launched Bpifrance Défense fund.

158. CABIROL, Michel, "Rachat de Photonis par Teledyne : la France a vraiment évité une catastrophe industrielle" La Tribune, published January 18, 2021, accessed May 9, 2024, available at https://www.latribune.fr/entreprises-finance/industrie/aeronautique-defense/rachat-de-photonis-par-teledyne-la-france-a-vraiment-evite-une-catastrophe-industrielle-872693.html

Against this backdrop [159], the French Prime Minister was formally approached by seventeen members of the National Assembly [160], all sitting on the Defense Committee. These parliamentarians raised serious concerns regarding the planned sale of the Bordeaux-based world leader in photodetection, particularly in the context of military aviation. Their alert focused on LIFI (Light Fidelity) photonic technology developed by Latécoère. They stressed that France's strategic autonomy depends on its ability to master key scientific, technological, and industrial capabilities. If the company came under U.S. control, they argued, any French defense equipment integrating LIFI could be subject to U.S. export restrictions under the International Traffic in Arms Regulations (ITAR), which prohibit the export of military goods containing American components. This parliamentary referral was all the more disruptive because the French government had initially approved the transaction, on the condition that an approved investor be granted a board seat and hold a 10% stake in Latécoère. In parallel with the National Assembly, the French Senate also voiced its opposition through multiple formal inquiries [161].

Following an assessment of several potential U.S. acquirers, Ardian selected Teledyne to enter into exclusive negotiations, based on a valuation of €500 million. At the same time, the French Defense Procurement Agency (DGA) attempted, unsuccessfully, to persuade Safran and Thales to acquire Photonis. The Director General for Armaments even declared [162] that Photonis was considered a strategic asset, and the DGA) had explicitly requested that both companies, as prime contractors in the optronics sector, examine the case.

As the proposed sale was undergoing review by the Directorate General of the Treasury) under the FDI screening regime, the French government ultimately rejected the deal. In a press release [163], it was the Minister for the Armed Forces, rather than the Minister of the Economy, who formally oversees the screening process, who announced that the State was actively working with French industrial and financial stakeholders to

---

159. DUPEYRAT, op. cit., p. 238
160. BAUER, Alain, DRIF, Alexandra and TREVIDIC, Marc, "*Défense : des députés sonnent l'alarme sur la vente d'actifs stratégiques à l'étranger*" Les Échos, November 27, 2019, accessed September 1st, 2025, available at https://www.lesechos.fr/industrie-services/air-defense/defense-des-deputes-sonnent-la-larme-sur-la-vente-dactifs-strategiques-a-letranger-1151287
161. France, Senate, Written Question No. 13500 to the Minister of the Economy and Finance, Official Journal of the Senate, December 19, 2019, p. 6204, LIENEMANN, Marie-Noëlle, Senator, CRCE-R Group, Ministerial Reply, February 27, 2020, Official Journal of the Senate, p. 1031
France, Senate, Written Question No. 13474 to the Minister of the Economy and Finance, Official Journal of the Senate, December 12, 2019, p. 6110, MICOULEAU, Brigitte, Senator, Les Républicains (LR), Ministerial Reply, February 27, 2020, Official Journal of the Senate, p. 1031
France, Senate, Written Question No. 14487 to the Minister of the Armed Forces, Official Journal of the Senate, February 27, 2020, p. 945, ALLIZARD, Pascal, Senator, Les Républicains (LR), Ministerial Reply, June 11, 2020, Official Journal of the Senate, p. 2685
162. France, Senate, Verbatim Record, October 2, 2019, Committee on Foreign Affairs, Defense and the Armed Forces, meeting of Wednesday, October 2, 2019, Finance Bill for 2020 – Hearing of Mr. Joël BARRE, Chief Executive for Armaments, accessed May 9, 2024, available at https://www.senat.fr/compte-rendu-commissions/20190930/etr.html
163. France, Ministry of the Armed Forces, Press Release, "Sovereignty of strategic companies:Company: Florence Parly announces that the State is working on an alternative solution for the takeover of Photonis," Paris, December 18, 2020, accessed May 9, 2024, available at http://www.oliviercadic.com/wp-content/uploads/2020/12/Communiqué-de-presse-Photonis-v-18-décembre-2020.pdf

craft a domestic takeover solution that would safeguard France's sovereignty. over Photonis. The company was described as essential to French military operations and a key contributor to industrial excellence and national defense capabilities.

The Minister further indicated that Teledyne's bid for Photonis had not been approved under the French FDI screening rules [164]. This decision, she explained, was taken in line with the State's commitment to protecting France's strategic interests and preserving the long-term future of a national technological champion. According to the Minister for the Armed Forces, the terms of Teledyne's acquisition offer failed to satisfy the government's requirements for preserving French sovereignty. in the defense sector.

Subsequently, the Ministry of the Armed Forces worked to identify a French-led alternative transaction involving industrial and financial stakeholders in the optronics field. This ultimately led to the acquisition of Photonis by the investment fund HLD, after which the company was renamed Exosens. At the time, the government made it clear that should Teledyne resubmit an application to acquire Photonis under the FDI screening regime, the proposal would be assessed in light of the conditions and objectives defined during the initial negotiations, namely, the reconciliation of national sovereignty. imperatives with the development needs of the French defense industry. In effect, this implied a likely rejection of any renewed attempt.

The Photonis case has since become emblematic of France's foreign investment screening regime. It exposed a structural disconnect between negotiations conducted with the Ministry of the Economy and the objections raised by the Ministry of the Armed Forces. For the sellers, this divergence had a chilling effect on the market and thwarted their valuation strategy. The difference between the price proposed by Teledyne and that ultimately accepted from the French seller resulted in a capital loss of €130 million. As such, the case stands as a clear example of how sectoral and political opposition can directly influence the valuation of a strategic transaction.

The Pont-à-Mousson SA Case

In 2019, the prospect of a potential sale by the French company Saint-Gobain of its subsidiary located in Pont-à-Mousson to its Chinese state-owned competitor, the Xinxing Group, prompted a formal question [165] in the Senate. On that occasion, a senator asked the Minister what measures were being implemented to ensure that the company's patents remained under French control, particularly within the framework of France's foreign direct investment (FDI) screening mechanism.

The Government responded by emphasizing that the specific nature of the pipelines manufactured in Pont-à-Mousson, used for water distribution, a basic utility [166],

164. within the meaning of prior authorization

165. France, Senate, Oral Question No. 0743G to the Minister of the Economy and Finance, Official Journal of the Senate, April 12, 2019, p. 5587, HUSSON, Jean-François, Senator, Les Républicains (LR), Ministerial Reply, April 11, 2019, Official Journal of the Senate, p. 5587

166. France, Monetary and Financial Code, Article R. 151-3: essential activities within the meaning of "II. – Activities liable to affect national defense interests, contributing to the exercise of public authority, or likely to affect public order and public security, when they concern infrastructures, goods or services essential to guarantee: ... 2° The integrity, security or continuity of water supply"

qualified the transaction for review under the French FDI screening framework. As the Government underlined, the pipelines produced in Pont-à-Mousson ensure access to a vital resource: water [167].

More broadly, given that current water networks in France experience an average loss rate of approximately 20%, the real strategic challenge for the future lies in preventing the loss of a raw material that is expected to become increasingly critical [168].

The Aubert & Duval Case

In 2020, the situation of the company Aubert & Duval, specialized in the production of materials [169] used in weapons systems, including submarines, aircraft, and armored vehicles [170], drew close attention from the French Ministry of the Armed Forces. As a key component of the French Defense Industrial and Technological Base (BITD – Base Industrielle et Technologique de Défense), the company was deemed strategically significant. On this occasion, the Minister of the Economy reiterated [171] that any potential foreign investment in the firm would fall under the scope [172] of the French foreign direct investment screening mechanism or IEF regime) and could only proceed with prior governmental authorization.

Subsequently, in order to safeguard the strategic interests associated with the company, the French State decided to go further by acquiring a stake in the firm and establishing a golden share [173] mechanism to secure its influence and veto rights over decisions affecting national security.

---

167. France, National Assembly, Oral Question No. 3146 to the Minister of the Economy and Finance, Official Journal of the National Assembly, June 25, 2020, p. 4638, POTIER, Dominique, Member of Parliament, Socialist Party (PS), Ministerial Reply, June 25, 2020, Official Journal of the National Assembly, p. 4638
168. France, National Assembly, Written Question No. 27339 to the Minister of the Economy and Finance, Official Journal of the National Assembly, March 10, 2020, p. 1811, POTIER, Dominique, Member of Parliament, Socialist Party (PS), Ministerial Reply, September 8, 2020, Official Journal of the National Assembly, p. 5988
169. A specialist in high-performance metallurgy, notably in the design, development, and manufacturing of forged and die-stamped parts, bars, and powders made from high-performance steels, superalloys, aluminum, or titanium.
170. Aubert & Duval manufactures the 155 mm gun barrel used on the CAESAR (truck-mounted artillery system).
171. France, Senate, Written Question No. 17089 to the Minister of the Armed Forces, Official Journal of the Senate, July 2, 2020, p. 3009, ALLIZARD, P, Senator, Les Républicains (LR), Ministerial Reply, November 5, 2020, Official Journal of the Senate, p. 5095
172. France, Decree No. 2019-1590 of December 31, 2019, on foreign investments in France, Official Journal of the French Republic, No. 0001, January 1, 2020, NOR: ECOT1932857D
173. France, Decree No. 2022-1182 of August 25, 2022, establishing a specific shareholding measure in the capital of the company Aubert & Duval SAS, Official Journal of the French Republic, No. 0198, August 27, 2022, NOR: ECOA2217072D

The Carrefour–Couche-Tard Case

In January 2021, the Canadian retailer "Alimentation Couche-Tard" considered launching a public takeover bid (OPA) for its French counterpart, the Carrefour Group. Barely had the project been discussed with the French Minister of the Economy, Bruno Le Maire, when Couche-Tard's founder, Alain Bouchard, withdrew from the €16 billion deal, drawing the consequences of the French government's outright opposition. The Minister justified his decision [174] before Parliament, stating that the State could not allow the acquisition of France's largest private-sector employer, responsible for 20% of the country's food distribution and a cornerstone of national food security, without firm resistance. The government, he argued, had a duty to safeguard the food security of the French people by ensuring secure supply chains.

The Minister further explained that his decision was, in his view, consistent both with the French Decree on Foreign Investments in France, which expressly subjects investments in the food distribution sector to prior review, and with the European regulation establishing food distribution as a matter of critical strategic importance. He also invoked the specific context in the aftermath of the COVID-19 pandemic, which had exposed the vulnerability of agricultural supply chains and the inability of certain products to circulate freely. For the government, protecting food security meant ensuring continuity across the entire value chain, from agricultural production to food processing and retail distribution.

This case is particularly revealing. While the Minister's analysis suggested that the contemplated acquisition could fall within the scope of the French Foreign Investment Screening (FIS) mechanism, particularly under the criterion of food security [175], it nonetheless raises procedural concerns. The investor was effectively informed of the final outcome, a refusal, without having submitted any formal request for either a prior examination or an authorization. This was clearly a political decision, rather than the result of a structured application of the FDI screening mechanism.

The case highlights the distinction between the predictability of the screening regime, i.e., the clarity of its procedural rules and review conditions, and the unpredictability associated with sovereign decision-making by the Minister of the Economy .

---

174. France, Senate, Oral Question No. 1606G to the Minister of the Economy and Finance, Official Journal of the Senate, January 21, 2021, p. 264, RAMBAUD, Didier, Senator, RDPI Group, Ministerial Reply, January 20, 2021, Official Journal of the Senate, p. 264

175. France, Monetary and Financial Code, Article R. 151-3: essential activity defined as "II. – Activities liable to affect national defense interests, contributing to the exercise of public authority, or likely to affect public order and public security, when they concern infrastructures, goods or services essential to guarantee: 9° The production, processing or distribution of agricultural products listed in Annex I to the Treaty on the Functioning of the European Union, where these contribute to the national food security objectives mentioned in points 1°, 17° and 18° of I of Article L. 1 of the Rural and Maritime Fishing Code"

The Eutelsat Case

In 2021, the hostile takeover bid launched by Altice for Eutelsat was the subject of a parliamentary question [176] in France. In his response, the Minister of the Economy recalled that, following the rejection of the acquisition proposal by Eutelsat's board of directors, on the grounds that the offer was too low, should Patrick Drahi, Chairman of Altice, raise his bid and the transaction eventually go through, such an acquisition could meet the conditions required to trigger the French foreign direct investment (FDI) screening mechanism. As such, it would require prior authorization pursuant to Article L. 151-3 of the Monetary and Financial Code (Code monétaire et financier). In other words, the State could invoke the FDI screening procedure to oppose the completion of the deal.

Ultimately, in June 2025, the Minister of the Economy and Finance, Éric Lombard, announced [177] that the French State would participate in the €1.35 billion capital increase launched by Eutelsat. Through the Agence des participations de l'État (APE, the French Government Shareholding Agency), the State subscribed to €717 million, representing approximately half of the total amount raised, thus increasing its equity stake to 29.99% following completion of the transaction.

The Yposkesi Case

In 2021, the South Korean conglomerate SK Holdings initiated the acquisition process of Yposkesi, a financially struggling French biotech company specializing in the contract manufacturing of viral vectors. Yposkesi was the first French pharmaceutical manufacturer fully dedicated to the production of gene and cell therapy drugs for the treatment of rare diseases. In April 2021, SK Group formally announced its acquisition of a 70% stake in the company from AFM-Téléthon and Bpifrance, with the stated aim of supporting Yposkesi's continued growth and development.

The transaction was brought to public attention during a Q&A session in the French Senate, where the Government acknowledged the strategic importance of the pharmaceutical industry, particularly in light of the COVID-19 crisis. The Minister of the Economy confirmed that the Yposkesi transaction was being reviewed under the framework governing foreign direct investment screening in France, specifically to determine the operation's eligibility for the regime and whether the State could exercise its right to block the acquisition [178].

---

176. France, Senate, Written Question No. 24818 to the Minister of the Economy and Finance, Official Journal of the Senate, October 14, 2021, p. 5863, LIENEMANN, Marie-Noëlle, Senator, CRCE-R Group, Ministerial Reply, April 28, 2022, Official Journal of the Senate, p. 2323

177. France, Ministry of the Economy, Finance, Industrial and Digital Sovereignty, Press Release No. 642, "Industrial and Digital Sovereignty: France strengthens its stake in Eutelsat's capital," Paris, June 19, 2025, accessed June 20, 2025, available at https://presse.economie.gouv.fr/souverainete-industrielle-et-numerique-la-france-renforce-sa-presence-au-capital-deutelsat/

178. France, Senate, Oral Question No. 1647G to the Minister of the Economy and Finance, Official Journal of the Senate, February 4, 2021, p. 720, HUGONET, Jean-Raymond, Senator, Les Républicains (LR), Ministerial Reply by the Minister for Industry, February 3, 2021, Official Journal of the Senate, p. 720

Ultimately, the investment by the South Korean group was granted the required prior authorization under France's foreign direct investment screening mechanism.

The Almaviva Santé Case

In 2021, during the ownership change of Almaviva Santé, France's fourth-largest private hospital group, 60% of the company was acquired by the Kuwaiti sovereign fund Wren House Infrastructure, while 16% was taken over by Bpifrance (the French public investment bank). On that occasion, the French Government reaffirmed [179] that companies operating in the healthcare sector are subject to heightened scrutiny, particularly in times of public health crises.

According to the Government, there was no ambiguity: foreign investments targeting French companies whose activities are essential to safeguarding public health are subject to France's foreign direct investment (FDI) screening mechanism and must receive prior authorization from the Minister of the Economy before completion.

Furthermore, the COVID-19 pandemic and the associated risk of opportunistic foreign takeovers, particularly in the healthcare sector, prompted France to strengthen its FDI screening regime . Notably, this led to the inclusion of biotechnology in the list of critical technologies covered by the screening mechanism.

The Lisa Aeronautics Case

In 2022, Lisa Aeronautics, a company based in the Savoie region of France and known for developing the Akoya seaplane, capable of taking off and landing on land, water, and snow, was placed under judicial proceedings and offered for sale. In early 2023, the Annecy Commercial Court approved the transfer of its assets for €90,000 to the Chinese company Zheilang Xingxle General Aviation Industry.

When questioned about the transaction, the French Minister of the Economy stated [180] that he could not comment on or intervene in ongoing judicial proceedings concerning individual cases. However, he did underscore that it would be up to the judge to consider all elements submitted as part of the case file, including those potentially relating to the applicability of the French foreign direct investment (FDI) screening mechanism.

It appears, however, that the possibility of the transaction falling within the scope of the FDI screening regime was not retained as a determining factor by the court [181].

---

179. France, Senate, Written Question No. 24387 to the Minister of the Economy and Finance, Official Journal of the Senate, September 16, 2021, p. 5338, DEMILLY, Stéphane, Senator, Centrist Union Group (UC), Ministerial Reply, April 28, 2022, Official Journal of the Senate, p. 2319

180. France, Senate, Written Question No. 06440 to the Minister of the Economy and Finance, Official Journal of the Senate, April 20, 2023, p. 2592, LIENEMANN, Marie-Noëlle, Senator, CRCE-R Group, Ministerial Reply, June 15, 2023, Official Journal of the Senate, p. 3800

181. France, Court of Appeal of Chambéry, 1st Chamber, Judgment of December 19, 2023, No. 23/00115, accessed September 1st, 2025, available at https://www.doctrine.fr/d/CA/Chambery/2023/CAP3D1982E3924B3708D0F6

The Exxelia Case

In 2022, the acquisition of the French company Exxeliaby the U.S.-based group Heico attracted parliamentary attention through a formal written question [182] submitted to the Government. According to media reports [183] at the time, the French authorities were ultimately unable to prevent the takeover of what was described as a "technological gem" by the American firm, due to the absence of a competing French offer capable of matching the attractiveness of Heico's bid. Nevertheless, in accordance with Article L. 151-3 of the French Monetary and Financial Code, the transaction was subject to prior authorization by the French Ministry of the Economy under the foreign investment screening mechanism. In this context, the French State negotiated a series of safeguards aimed at protecting national interests, including the issuance of a golden share [184] held by the French government.

The Saint-Gobain Case

In 2022, the French construction materials producer Saint-Gobain divested [185] its crystals and detectors division to a consortium led by SK Capital Partners, in partnership with Edgewater Capital Partners, two U.S. private equity firms specializing in advanced materials. This transaction provided the French Minister of the Economy with an opportunity, during a hearing before the Senate, to reaffirm [186] that the production of high-performance materials derived from crystalline structures, used across a broad spectrum of economic sectors, had not escaped the scrutiny of the foreign direct investment (FDI) screening authorities. Nevertheless, a prior authorization was ultimately granted, and the divestiture was allowed to proceed.

The Idemia Case

In 2022, the American private equity fund Advent International initiated the process of divesting Idemia, its French subsidiary specialized in digital security. Formed

182. France, National Assembly, Written Question No. 2307 to the Minister of the Economy, Finance, Industrial and Digital Sovereignty, Official Journal of the National Assembly, October 18, 2022, p. 4637, COLOMBIER, Caroline, Member of Parliament, Rassemblement National (RN), Ministerial Reply, December 20, 2022, Official Journal of the National Assembly, p. 6470
183. France, CABIROL, Michel, Press Article, Les Échos, "Défense : l'Américain Heico finalise le rachat sensible du français Exxelia," published January 18, 2024, accessed September 1st, 2025, available at https://www.lesechos.fr/industrie-services/air-defense/defense-lamericain-heico-finalise-le-rachat-sensible-du-francais-exxelia-1894840
184. France, Ministerial Order of March 24, 2023, deciding on the State's acquisition of a shareholding in the capital of Exxelia International SAS, Official Journal of the French Republic, No. 0075, March 29, 2023, text No. 9, NOR: ECOA2306736A
185. The Cristaux et Détecteurs division provides radiation detection solutions for medical imaging, security, nuclear safety, oil and gas exploration, and environmental monitoring, as well as sapphire-based products for the medical, industrial, electronics, and aerospace sectors.
186. France, Senate, Written Question No. 04516 to the Minister of the Economy and Finance, Official Journal of the Senate, December 22, 2022, p. 6573, LIENEMANN, Marie-Noëlle, Senator, CRCE-R Group, Ministerial Reply, May 18, 2023, Official Journal of the Senate, p. 3236

through the merger of Morpho Systèmes and Oberthur Technologies, Idemia, also partly owned by Bpifrance, supplies facial recognition systems and other biometric identification technologies, as well as identity verification tools for border control operations.

The company maintains close partnerships with governmental agencies, particularly in airport environments, to verify traveler identities and combat illegal immigration. It was also selected as a key contractor for France's national digital identity program.

In this context, the French Minister of the Economy publicly stated that the government was closely monitoring the proposed sale to ensure that Idemia's industrial and technological capabilities would remain sustainably located within French territory. He further indicated that the authorities would mobilize all available instruments to safeguard national interests. More specifically, the Minister confirmed [187] that any contemplated acquisition of Idemia by a foreign investor could fall within the scope of France's foreign direct investment (FDI) screening mechanism.

The Segault Case

In 2023, the proposed sale of Segault, a French SME with 80 employees owned by the Canadian industrial valve manufacturer Velan, raised national security concerns under France's foreign direct investment (FDI) screening regime. Segault is a key supplier to Naval Group, France's state-backed naval defense contractor, providing critical boiler valve components, including bonneted globe valves, angle bellows-sealed valves, pressurizer safety valves, non-return valves, instrumentation manifolds, and isolatable dynamic check valves, used in the construction and maintenance of France's nuclear submarines.

The transaction quickly evolved into a matter of public debate and climbed the ranks of governmental scrutiny [188]. What began as a series of parliamentary questions [189], addressed to the Minister of the Economy culminated in a direct inquiry [190]

---

187. France, National Assembly, Written Question No. 1390 to the Minister of the Economy and Finance, Official Journal of the National Assembly, September 20, 2022, LATOMBE, Philippe, Member of Parliament, MoDem Group, Ministerial Reply, November 22, 2022, Official Journal of the National Assembly, p. 5582

188. France, National Assembly, Written Question No. 6956 to the Minister of the Economy and Finance, Official Journal of the National Assembly, April 4, 2023, p. 3003, COLOMBIER, Caroline, Member of Parliament, Rassemblement National (RN)

189. France, National Assembly, Oral Question No. 763 to the Minister for Small and Medium-sized Enterprises, Trade, Crafts and Tourism, Official Journal of the National Assembly, April 12, 2023, GONZALEZ, José, Member of Parliament, Rassemblement National (RN) Group, Ministerial Reply, Official Journal of the National Assembly, April 12, 2023, p. 3739: "*Segault is a strategic company, and as you mentioned, the United States has a very aggressive regulatory framework, which could threaten the confidentiality of the technologies developed by Segault. Of course, this transaction will be subject to the foreign investment screening procedure.*"

190. France, National Assembly, Oral Question No. 712 to the Prime Minister, Official Journal of the National Assembly, March 29, 2023, p. 3169, MARLEIX, Olivier, Member of Parliament, Les Républicains (LR) Group, Ministerial Reply, Official Journal of the National Assembly, March 29, 2023

to the Prime Minister during a Government Question Time session and ultimately in a public announcement [191] by the Minister for the Armed Forces, Sébastien Lecornu, that the transaction would be vetoed. This announcement was made during parliamentary debates on the Military Planning Act [192] (Loi de programmation militaire).

It is important to highlight that, following the precedent set in the Photonis case, this marked only the second time that the Minister for the Armed Forces, who, as the competent line minister, plays a key role in the inter-ministerial review process, formally announced a rejection. However, the final authority to grant or withhold authorization under the FDI screening mechanism lies with the Minister of the Economy.

The Opella Case

In 2024, French pharmaceutical giant Sanofi entered into exclusive negotiations with U.S. private equity firm Clayton Dubilier & Rice (CD&R) for the sale of a 50% stake in its French subsidiary, Opella. Headquartered in France, Opella employs 11,000 people, operates in over 100 countries, and manages 13 high-end and strategically located production sites, along with four research and innovation centers. The company owns several flagship brands, including Allegra, Doliprane, and Dulcolax, and ranks as the world's third-largest player in the over-the-counter (OTC) medicines, vitamins, minerals, and dietary supplements market. Opella's products serve more than half a billion consumers globally.

From the outset, the transaction sparked significant public controversy in France, culminating in numerous questions [193] raised before the Government, debates which

191. France, National Assembly, Record of Proceedings, May 23, 2023, Second sitting of Tuesday, Minister Sébastien LECORNU's reply: "In substance, mechanisms already exist to block certain foreign investments. You mentioned Exxelia and Segault: I hereby publicly announce that, under this screening mechanism, the Ministry of the Armed Forces will veto the loss of operational control of Segault. This proves that the system works: let us be humble enough to acknowledge that others before us have addressed these issues in law." Accessed September 1st, 2025, available at https://www.assemblee-nationale.fr/dyn/16/comptes-rendus/seance/session-ordinaire-de-2022-2023/deuxieme-seance-du-mardi-23-mai-2023

192. France, Law No. 2023-703 of August 1, 2023, on military programming for the years 2024 to 2030 and including various provisions concerning defense, Official Journal of the French Republic, No. 0177, August 2, 2023, NOR: ARMD2305491L, accessed September 1st, 2025, available at https://www.assemblee-nationale.fr/dyn/16/dossiers/programmation_militaire_2024_2030

193. France, National Assembly, Oral Question No. 42 to the Minister of the Economy, Finance and Industry, "Sale of Opella by Sanofi," sitting of October 15, 2024, Official Journal of the National Assembly, No. 74, October 16, 2024, p. 5401, CHENU, Sébastien, Member of Parliament, Rassemblement National (RN), Minister's reply, October 15, 2024, Official Journal of the National Assembly, No. 74, October 16, 2024, p. 5401
France, National Assembly, Oral Question No. 43 to the Minister of the Economy, Finance and Industry, "Sale of Opella by Sanofi," sitting of October 15, 2024, Official Journal of the National Assembly, No. 74, October 16, 2024, p. 5402, RODWELL, Christopher, Member of Parliament, Ensemble pour la République (EPR), Minister's reply, October 15, 2024, Official Journal of the National Assembly, No. 74, October 16, 2024, p. 5402
France, National Assembly, Oral Question No. 50 to the Minister of the Economy, Finance and Industry, "Sale of Opella by Sanofi," sitting of October 15, 2024, Official Journal of the National Assembly, No. 74, October 16, 2024, p. 5407, CLOUET, Hadrien, Member of Parliament, La France insoumise (LFI), Minister's reply, October 15, 2024, Official Journal of the National Assembly, No. 74, October 16, 2024, p. 5407

extended into 2025 during parliamentary discussions[194] on "the loss of industrial sovereignty. and threats to strategic industries." In response to these concerns, the French State announced its decision to acquire a minority stake, between 1% and 2%, for a reported €100 to €150 million, through its public investment bank, Bpifrance. This equity stake came with voting rights and a board seat.

According to the Government, this capital investment was designed to provide the State with full access to strategic and operational information concerning Opella's activities, thereby ensuring early warning of any developments deemed inconsistent with prior commitments. More broadly, it was intended to enable the State to influence the company's long-term strategic trajectory in a manner aligned with France's economic sovereignty. objectives.

Asked why this capital investment was deemed necessary on top of the legally binding undertakings imposed under France's foreign investment screening regime (FDI Screening), the Government clarified that the transaction had been subject to an irrevocable unilateral agreement signed on October 20, 2024, between the State, the foreign investor, and the seller. The agreement imposed several obligations on the investor, including commitments to industrial development, job retention, local supply chains, and environmental protection. From the Government's perspective[195], the State's equity participation bolstered the enforceability of these commitments and enhanced the State's oversight capabilities.

It was further emphasized that this unilateral agreement, contractual in nature and not derived from any exercise of public authority, pursued objectives that were distinct from the foreign direct investment screening procedure. It did not preclude the Minister of the Economy, Finance, and Industrial and Digital Sovereignty. from exercising his statutory powers under the special police regime applicable to foreign investment screening in France. Those powers are aimed at safeguarding public order and public security, including the protection of public health.

France, National Assembly, Oral Question No. 55 to the Minister of the Economy, Finance and Industry, "Sale of Opella by Sanofi," sitting of October 15, 2024, Official Journal of the National Assembly, No. 74, October 16, 2024, p. 5411, PATRIER-LEITUS, Julie, Member of Parliament, La France insoumise (LFI), Minister's reply, October 15, 2024, Official Journal of the National Assembly, No. 74, October 16, 2024, p. 5411

France, National Assembly, Oral Question No. 84 to the Minister of the Economy, Finance and Industry, "Industrial, Food and Health Sovereignty," sitting of October 22, 2024, Official Journal of the National Assembly, No. 77, October 23, 2024, p. 5509, RUFFIN, François, Member of Parliament, Écologiste et Social (ES), Minister's reply, October 22, 2024, Official Journal of the National Assembly, No. 77, October 23, 2024, p. 5509

France, National Assembly, Oral Question No. 91 to the Minister of the Economy, Finance and Industry, "Sanofi," sitting of October 23, 2024, Official Journal of the National Assembly, No. 78, October 24, 2024, p. 5580, BENARD, Emmanuel, Member of Parliament, Gauche Démocrate et Républicaine (GDR), Minister's reply, October 23, 2024, Official Journal of the National Assembly, No. 78, October 24, 2024, p. 5580

194. France, National Assembly, Oral Question No. 478 to the Minister of the Economy, Finance and Industry, "Takeover of the Sanofi plant in Amilly," debate on the theme: "Loss of industrial sovereignty and damage to strategic industries," sitting of March 12, 2025, Official Journal of the National Assembly, No. 30, March 13, 2025, p. 2111, MÉNAGE, Thomas, Member of Parliament, Rassemblement National (RN), Minister's reply, March 12, 2025, Official Journal of the National Assembly, No. 30, March 13, 2025, p. 2111

195. France, National Assembly, Written Question No. 3493 to the Minister of the Economy, Finance, Industrial and Digital Sovereignty, "Tripartite Agreement between the State, Sanofi and CD&R," Official Journal of the National Assembly, No. 4 (Q), January 28, 2025, p. 2307, MARLEIX, Olivier, Member of Parliament, Les Républicains (LR), Minister's reply, Official Journal of the National Assembly, May 20, 2025, p. 3667

*
* *

Although the French Parliament exercises only limited oversight over the FDI screening regime, it is increasingly involved in high-profile or politically sensitive transactions. Some of these deals have been p. ublicly challenged or ultimately abandoned once they became politically untenable. For many lawmakers, it has become increasingly difficult to justify why the "representatives of the Nation" are not formally consulted on a mechanism ostensibly designed to "defend the Nation's interests."

This concern is particularly pronounced since the implementation of the EU framework for the screening of foreign direct investment (see next chapter). French parliamentarians have expressed surprise that other Member States are systematically notified of sensitive transactions occurring in France, whereas France's own Parliament lacks any genuine right of scrutiny.

Against this backdrop, the question of whether genuine parliamentary oversight should be established remains unresolved. In practice, this means that in addition to navigating the formal administrative process led by the Ministry of the Economy, foreign investors must also anticipate and manage the political dimensions that may emerge during or after the completion of a transaction. Political blowback may stem from local elected officials voicing concerns to Members of Parliament, or from competitors organizing counter-lobbying campaigns aimed at galvanizing parliamentary resistance.

The institutional risk is increasingly unpredictable and must be treated as a strategic factor in deal planning. A single topical parliamentary question can rapidly escalate into a full-scale hearing. Consequently, investors must factor in these political variables from the outset and prepare for fast-moving developments that may challenge the legal finality of an authorized transaction.

Chapter 6

The French FDI Screening Mechanism and Its Complementarity with the EU Screening Framework

To understand the economic sovereignty. challenges associated with the screening of foreign direct investments originating from third countries outside the European Union, it is essential to recall that the EU is, first and foremost, a market composed of sovereign States. At the heart of the issue lies the tension between, on one hand, the free movement of capital, and on the other, the national security prerogatives associated with the screening of foreign direct investment.

The EU Regulation on FDI screening, adopted in 2019, usefully complements [196] the French FDI screening mechanism ("dispositif IEF"), as it targets only transactions involving third countries and provides a broader assessment framework to national systems. While the French mechanism retains sole responsibility for protecting France's national interests, the EU framework offers valuable tools for intergovernmental cooperation by establishing formal "gateways" and "reference points" around the French system. The Regulation facilitates cooperation between France and other Member States with screening regimes analogous to the IEF, as well as those Member States without any FDI screening mechanism in place.

It should also be noted that the exchange of information under the Regulation is subject to strict safeguards, and the data requested must be limited to what is necessary for the purpose pursued. The only exception lies with the European Commission: if a transaction is deemed to present a risk to the interests of the Union as a whole, France must allow the Commission to conduct its own assessment independently.

An Enduring Vulnerability of the French FDI Screening System Within the European Union

Despite its robustness, the French FDI screening regime historically suffered from structural weaknesses within the context of the European Union, until the establishment of the EU-wide mechanism. These shortcomings stemmed from the difficulty of

196. DUPEYRAT, op. cit., p. 175 et seq.

reconciling national screening prerogatives with the principles of EU law, most notably, the free movement of capital enshrined in the EU's internal market.

As European integration progressed and the single market was completed, it became increasingly apparent that vulnerabilities affecting national security were, paradoxically, arising from within the internal market itself, vulnerabilities that France was institutionally incapable of addressing. In particular, it was possible for foreign investors to conceal their third-country origin by channeling acquisitions through European shell companies, thereby circumventing French screening rules altogether, even while acting under the influence or control of a third-country entity.

In practical terms, for many years, simply being a European company was enough to slip through the mesh of the French FDI screening net. As a result, the protection of France's economic interests was strictly limited to its own national territory, as the IEF mechanism had no extraterritorial application. Moreover, certain entities fell outside the scope of the screening mechanism solely on the grounds that they were subject to the control of a Member State of the European Union.

This situation revealed a broader structural issue: EU Member States lacked comprehensive visibility into the vulnerabilities [197] of their fellow Member States' screening frameworks, when such frameworks even existed, which was not always the case.

After decades spent constructing a zone of free trade and unrestricted capital flows, the European institutions changed course in 2019, just one year before the COVID-19 pandemic, by finally recognizing the legitimate aspirations of several Member States to safeguard strategic sectors, not only at the national level, but increasingly at the European level as well.

France's Role in the Genesis of the EU FDI Screening Framework

While the European Treaties acknowledge the possibility of restricting the free movement of capital and foreign investment within the European Union on grounds of public order and public security, they do not explicitly recognize national security as a general derogation, let alone as a legitimate ground for protectionism.

It was on this legal and political foundation that, in February 2017, three founding Member States of the European Community, Germany, France, and Italy, formally requested that the European Commission restrict foreign direct investments (FDI) in companies holding key technologies by introducing reciprocity requirements. This joint request marked a turning point [198] in the European Union's traditionally liberal approach

197. France, Economic, Social and Environmental Council (CESE), LION, Claude and MUGNIER, Olivier, Opinion No. 2022-013 of September 27, 2022, "Ambitions and levers for strategic autonomy of the European Union in the economic field, on a proposal by the Committee on European and International Affairs," NOR: CESL1100013X, DILA, No. 41122-0008, ISSN 0767-4538, ISBN 978-2-11-155718-5. "*The economic rules that have prevailed until now seem outdated: the rules of a level playing field are now distorted by the absence of reciprocity. In reaction, a more strategic culture is gradually emerging and common tools are being implemented (screening of foreign direct investments, revision of trade policy, industrial strategy...). Yet, a shared vision of economic autonomy within the EU has not yet gained consensus.*"

198. France, Ministry of the Economy, Finance and Recovery, Press Release, September 13, 2017, France, Germany, Italy, following President JUNCKER's State of the Union address, "The Commission's proposal for a regulation on the screening of strategic investments is a major step to ensure fair and equitable

to capital flows, prompting all EU institutions (the Parliament[199], the Council, and the Commission) to collaborate on designing a Union-wide FDI screening framework.

The new framework for reviewing foreign direct investment within the EU was built around two core principles: first, each Member State retains exclusive responsibility for assessing the impact of foreign investments on national security and public order within its territory; second, Member States must cooperate among themselves and with the European Commission to address risks posed by FDI originating from third countries.

In other words, France retained full sovereignty. in defining the national interests to be safeguarded in the context of a foreign direct investment, which did not, however, preclude the establishment of a European-level mechanism complementing the French FDI screening regime, aimed at assessing risks commonly faced by the Union's Member States from investments originating in third countries.

This reflection culminated in the adoption of Regulation[200] (EU) 2019/452 establishing a framework for the screening of foreign direct investments into the Union, which entered into force on April 10, 2019. Its application was phased in over eighteen months, becoming fully operational on October 11, 2020.

Article 1 of the Regulation[201] makes clear that its purpose is to set up a framework for the screening of FDI into the Union on grounds of security or public order, carried out by the Member States. In that regard, the Regulation aligns with the EU's expectations regarding lawful derogations to the free movement of capital and fits seamlessly with France's national FDI screening mechanism (the IEF regime). Moreover, the Regulation establishes a cooperation mechanism between Member States and between the Member States and the Commission, aimed at addressing FDI that may affect security or public order. Within this framework, the Commission is empowered to issue opinions on specific transactions, thereby creating a soft governance tool that is both advisory and persuasive in nature, albeit non-binding.

Importantly, both the recitals[202] and the operative provisions[203] of the Regulation underscore that it does not supersede the primary and exclusive responsibility of

---

competition in Europe and better protection in acquisition operations," available at https://www.economie.gouv.fr/communique-conjoint-france-allemagne-italie-suite-discours-État-union (last accessed September, 1st, 2025)

199. European Union, European Parliament, Legislative Resolution of February 14, 2019, on the proposal for a regulation of the European Parliament and of the Council establishing a framework for the screening of foreign direct investments into the European Union (COM(2017)0487 – C8-0309/2017 – 2017/0224(COD)), Official Journal of the European Union, C 449/673, December 23, 2020

200. European Union, Regulation (EU) 2019/452 of March 19, 2019, of the European Parliament and of the Council establishing a framework for the screening of foreign direct investments into the Union, Official Journal of the European Union, L 79I, March 21, 2019, pp. 1–14

201. European Union, Regulation (EU) 2019/452 of March 19, 2019, Article 1 "Subject matter and scope"

202. European Union, Regulation (EU) 2019/452 of March 19, 2019, Recital 7, "Foreign direct investment is an important source of growth, jobs and innovation. It enhances the competitiveness of European companies by contributing to their financing, creating new jobs, and promoting technology transfer. The Union is committed to maintaining an open investment environment, while also preserving its essential interests."

203. European Union, Regulation (EU) 2019/452 of March 19, 2019, Article 1(2), final sentence "This Regulation is without prejudice to the exclusive responsibility of each Member State for the protection of its national security, as provided for in Article 4(2) of the Treaty on European Union, and to the

Member States to protect their national security, as recognized under the Treaty [204] on the Functioning of the European Union (TFEU), including the protection of their essential security interests. Member States remain fully sovereign in this domain, especially in matters as vital as national security. That said, the exercise of this sovereign right must remain consistent with EU competition rules [205] and must never be used as a pretext for protectionist policies.

The Regulation underscores this respect for sovereignty. to such a degree that it even affirms the right [206] of a Member State not to establish any screening mechanism at all. Thus, the framework consists of non-binding, non-coercive, and flexible recommendations. It aims to fulfill two objectives: ensuring legal certainty and transparency on the one hand, and fostering greater harmonization and shared accountability on the other. As such, it does not supersede the French FDI screening mechanism. However, in the wake of the COVID-19 pandemic and the Commission's subsequent communication [207], Member States without an existing FDI screening framework were strongly encouraged to implement one.

Above all, the Regulation seeks to ensure legal certainty for foreign investors in the EU. In line with the Union's legal tradition, it explicitly aims to eliminate any form of discrimination against third countries. This objective mirrors that of the French regime, which likewise prioritizes predictability in FDI review procedures.

Furthermore, as part of its commitment to legal certainty, the Regulation [208] promotes transparency. Under its provisions, Member States are required to submit

---

right of each Member State to protect its essential security interests in accordance with Article 346 of the Treaty on the Functioning of the European Union."

204. European Union, Treaty on the Functioning of the European Union, Article 4(2) 2. Shared competences between the Union and the Member States apply in the following principal areas:
(a) internal market; (b) social policy, for the aspects defined in this Treaty; (c) economic, social and territorial cohesion; (d) agriculture and fisheries, excluding the conservation of marine biological resources; (e) environment; (f) consumer protection; (g) transport; (h) trans-European networks; (i) energy; (k) common safety concerns in public health matters, for the aspects defined in this Treaty.

205. Article 346 of the Treaty on the Functioning of the European Union (ex-Article 296 TEC)
1.The provisions of the Treaties shall not preclude the following rules:
(a) no Member State shall be obliged to supply information the disclosure of which it considers contrary to the essential interests of its security;
(b) any Member State may take such measures as it considers necessary for the protection of the essential interests of its security which are connected with the production of or trade in arms, munitions and war material; such measures shall not adversely affect the conditions of competition in the internal market regarding products which are not intended for specifically military purposes.
2. The Council may, acting unanimously on a proposal from the Commission, make changes to the list of products to which the provisions of paragraph 1(b) apply. That list was drawn up by the Council on 15 April 1958.

206. Regulation (EU) 2019/452 of the European Parliament and of the Council of 19 March 2019 establishing a framework for the screening of foreign direct investments into the Union, Article 1(3): "*No provision of this Regulation shall limit the right of each Member State to decide whether or not to screen a particular foreign direct investment within the framework of this Regulation.*"

207. European Union, European Commission, Communication, "Guidelines for Member States concerning foreign direct investment and the free movement of capital from third countries and the protection of Europe's strategic assets, ahead of the application of Regulation (EU) 2019/452 (FDI Screening Regulation)," (2020/C 99 I/01), Official Journal of the European Union, CI 99/1, March 26, 2020

208. Regulation (EU) 2019/452 of the European Parliament and of the Council of 19 March 2019 establishing a framework for the screening of foreign direct investments into the Union, Recital 32: "Nothing in this Regulation should limit the right of each Member State to protect its essential security interests.

annual reports [209] on the implementation of their respective screening mechanisms. Based on these reports, the Commission prepares and publishes an annual report on the implementation of the Regulation, which is submitted to the European Parliament and the Council, while preserving the confidentiality of sensitive information.

The Regulation also aims to enhance harmonization and accountability among stakeholders by reducing disparities and unnecessary complexity in administrative procedures, timelines, and eligibility criteria across Member States. Such inconsistencies can disadvantage foreign investors and may be exploited to circumvent national screening regimes through legal or financial structuring. To counter such risks, the Regulation requires Member States that have established screening mechanisms to adopt appropriate measures [210] to prevent circumvention and to comply with Union law. In addition, the Regulation outlines key elements [211] to guide the establishment of national screening mechanisms, thereby promoting clarity, legitimacy, and convergence among Member States. The French IEF regime fully embodies these objectives.

The European screening framework coordinates the French IEF mechanism and its counterparts across the European Union.

The European screening framework allows France's FDI screening mechanism (the IEF regime) to be effectively articulated with other national screening mechanisms within the European Union. From this perspective, the cooperation mechanism established between the Member States and the European Commission constitutes a significant and novel advancement.

It is important to reiterate that this mechanism does not aim to establish any form of Commission oversight over Member States, which retain full sovereignty. in assessing potential threats posed by foreign direct investment (FDI) to their national security and public order. Rather, the Commission's role operates as a facilitator, enabling Member

---

This Regulation should not affect the sole responsibility of the Member States for safeguarding their national security. In particular, measures taken for the protection of national security in connection with foreign direct investments should remain the sole responsibility of the Member States."

209. European Union, European Commission, "Report from the Commission to the European Parliament and the Council, Second Annual Report on the Screening of Foreign Direct Investments into the Union," {SWD(2022) 219 final}, Brussels, September 1, 2022, COM(2022) 433 final, available at https://eur-lex.europa.eu/legal-content/EN/TXT/HTML/?uri=CELEX:52022DC0433 (September 1st, 2025)

210. Regulation (EU) 2019/452 of the European Parliament and of the Council of 19 March 2019 establishing a framework for the screening of foreign direct investments into the Union, Recital 10 : "Foreign direct investment contributes to the Union's growth by enhancing its competitiveness, creating jobs, and bringing in capital, technologies, innovation, and expertise. The Union remains open to foreign direct investment. That openness is embedded in the Union's legal framework and is in line with its international commitments. At the same time, that openness is not unconditional. It must be balanced by appropriate mechanisms that allow the Union and the Member States to safeguard their essential interests."

211. Regulation (EU) 2019/452 of the European Parliament and of the Council of 19 March 2019 establishing a framework for the screening of foreign direct investments into the Union, Recital 15: "Member States and the Commission should cooperate with each other in relation to foreign direct investments to safeguard the Union's security, public order and strategic interests, with due regard to the competences of the Union and of Member States. In doing so, due account should be taken of the principles and values set out in Article 2 of the Treaty on European Union."

States to cooperate and assist each other whenever an FDI transaction in one Member State may adversely affect the security or public order of other Member States.

Each Member State thus preserves its full prerogative to screen and control FDI within its own jurisdiction. The Commission[212] has accordingly designed the cooperation[213] mechanism to respect the national specificities and sovereign will of each Member State.

The mechanism expressly distinguishes between Member States that have implemented a national screening mechanism and those that have not. The Commission[214] actively encourages Member States to submit annual reports detailing the implementation of their screening regimes. These reports should cover all decisions relating to the authorization, prohibition, or conditional approval of foreign direct investments, including mitigation measures, as well as decisions concerning investments that could adversely affect projects or programs of interest to the European Union.

The cooperation mechanism also includes a provision allowing third countries, whose inbound investments are subject to the Regulation, to engage in dialogue and cooperation[215] with the Commission. Both the Commission and the Member States are encouraged to liaise with competent authorities in third countries that share similar concerns regarding foreign direct investment screening, particularly in cases where such investments may pose risks to security or public order. This provision explicitly targets strategic cooperation with like-minded partners such as the United States, Canada, and Japan.

Administrative cooperation is expected to enhance the overall efficiency of Member States' screening frameworks and improve coordination both among Member States

---

212. European Union, Regulation (EU) 2019/452 of the European Parliament and of the Council of March 19, 2019, establishing a framework for the screening of foreign direct investments into the Union, Recital No. 16: "Member States should be able to provide comments to the Member State where the investment is planned or has been completed, irrespective of whether or not the latter has a screening mechanism in place or whether or not the investment is undergoing screening."
213. European Union, Regulation (EU) 2019/452 of the European Parliament and of the Council of March 19, 2019, establishing a framework for the screening of foreign direct investments into the Union, Recital No. 16: "It is appropriate to establish a mechanism enabling Member States to cooperate and assist each other where a foreign direct investment in one Member State is likely to affect the security or public order of other Member States."
214. European Union, Regulation (EU) 2019/452 of the European Parliament and of the Council of March 19, 2019, establishing a framework for the screening of foreign direct investments into the Union, Recital No. 22: "In order to allow Member States and the Commission to assess the likely impact of foreign direct investments, Member States should provide information relating to the ownership structure of the foreign investor and the target undertaking, the value and funding of the investment, its products, services and business operations, including, where relevant, information on the Member States in which they conduct relevant business operations, as well as the funding of the investment and its source."
215. European Union, Regulation (EU) 2019/452 of the European Parliament and of the Council of March 19, 2019, establishing a framework for the screening of foreign direct investments into the Union, Recital No. 29: "In order to ensure the effective and consistent implementation of this Regulation, the Commission should be able to issue opinions addressed to the Member State where the foreign direct investment is planned or has been completed, when that investment is likely to affect security or public order in more than one Member State, or when the investment is likely to affect a project or programme of Union interest. The Member State where the investment is planned or has been completed should give due consideration to the Commission's opinion and provide an explanation to the Commission in case its opinion is not followed."

and between Member States and the Commission. The Commission should also be in a position to monitor developments in FDI screening mechanisms implemented by third countries.

Ultimately, the European screening mechanism serves as an unprecedented instrument, acting as a shield against predatory behaviors and the strategic appetite of certain third countries.

The EU Regulation Applies Exclusively to Transactions Originating from Third Countries

The European regulation on foreign direct investment (FDI) screening operates as an additional control tower complementing the French IEF mechanism. Its primary objective is to target transactions initiated by foreign powers located outside the European Union. Accordingly, the regulation applies solely to investments originating from third countries, that is, countries that are not members of the European Economic Area, such as Canada, Russia, Japan, the United States, or China.

The regulation covers only those investment transactions carried out by non-European investors in one or more Member States of the European Union. Any transaction involving an entity that is a national of a third country to the European Union, and which forms part of the investor's control chain, must be notified to the European cooperation network pursuant to this regulation.

To that end, the regulation [216] provides clear definitions of both foreign investments and foreign investors, in order to facilitate its implementation. Under these definitions, a foreign direct investment is defined as any investment made by a foreign investor aimed at establishing or maintaining lasting and direct relationships with the enterprise or entrepreneur receiving the funds, with a view to conducting an economic activity in a Member State. This definition also includes investments that grant the investor the ability to effectively participate in the management or control of a company conducting economic activities.

The term "undertaking of a third country" refers to any undertaking constituted or otherwise organized under the laws of a third country. The regulatory framework [217] is designed to cover a wide spectrum of investment transactions, including those that establish or preserve direct and lasting links between third-country investors, including public entities, and undertakings engaged in economic activity within the Member States.

216. European Union, Regulation (EU) 2019/452 of the European Parliament and of the Council of March 19, 2019, establishing a framework for the screening of foreign direct investments into the Union, Article 2, "Definitions"

217. European Union, Regulation (EU) 2019/452 of the European Parliament and of the Council of March 19, 2019, establishing a framework for the screening of foreign direct investments into the Union, Recital 9

The EU Screening Mechanism as a Complementary Framework to the French FDI Control Regime

The European Union has established a screening and cooperation mechanism aimed at detecting predatory maneuvers by third countries targeting Europe's strategic assets. Rather than replacing national screening regimes, this mechanism is intended to provide additional input to Member States' economic security systems. Accordingly, when Member States, such as France, evaluate whether a foreign direct investment (FDI) originating from a third country may pose a threat to their security or public order, they may do so in collaboration with the European Commission and other Member States, taking into account all relevant factors.

The Regulation [218] provides that such relevant factors may include the potential impact of the investment on critical infrastructure, technologies (including key enabling technologies), and essential inputs for security or public order, where disruption, failure, loss, or destruction of such assets would have significant consequences in a Member State or across the Union.

It is also necessary to assess the specific context and circumstances surrounding the investment. For instance, whether the foreign investor is directly or indirectly controlled by a government of a third country, or whether the investor is involved in public investment programs or projects abroad. Although not codified in the Regulation's articles, the Commission [219] has recommended that Member States and the Commission itself may take into account any relevant information provided by economic operators, civil society organizations, or social partners such as trade unions concerning an FDI that may affect security or public order. This information advantage can prove valuable, as information often translates into power.

In addition, the Regulation permits the assessment of a broad range of potential impacts [220], from a foreign investment, such as on critical technologies, dual-use

---

218. European Union, Regulation (EU) 2019/452 of the European Parliament and of the Council of 19 March 2019 establishing a framework for the screening of foreign direct investments into the Union, Recital No. 13 "The cooperation provided for in this Regulation between Member States and the Commission should allow the Commission and the Member States to express their views on foreign direct investments likely to affect security or public order. It should not affect the power of Member States to maintain, amend or adopt mechanisms to screen foreign direct investments on grounds of security or public order, taking into account the need to preserve the balance between the aim of protection and the Union's attractiveness for foreign direct investment."
219. European Union, Regulation (EU) 2019/452 of the European Parliament and of the Council of 19 March 2019 establishing a framework for the screening of foreign direct investments into the Union, Recital No. 14 "This Regulation does not affect the right of Member States to prohibit or restrict foreign direct investments on grounds of security or public order. It is without prejudice to the application of stricter national rules in that respect, in compliance with Union law."
220. European Union, Regulation (EU) 2019/452 of the European Parliament and of the Council of 19 March 2019 establishing a framework for the screening of foreign direct investments into the Union, Article 4 – Factors that may be taken into consideration by Member States or the Commission
    In determining whether a foreign direct investment is likely to affect security or public order, Member States and the Commission may consider its potential effects on, inter alia: (a) critical infrastructure, whether physical or virtual, including energy, transport, water, health, communications, media, data processing or storage, aerospace, defence, electoral or financial infrastructure, and sensitive facilities, as well as land and real estate crucial for the use of such infrastructure; (b) critical technologies and dual-use items as defined in point 1 of Article 2 of Council Regulation (EC) No 428/2009, including

items [221], the supply of essential inputs [222] access to sensitive data, or on media freedom and pluralism. The breadth of this list reflects the need to account for existing regulatory frameworks and the varied policy sensitivities of the Member States.

This list has had a concrete influence on the French screening mechanism, which was amended [223] in 2020 to include both food security and media as sensitive sectors subject to national FDI screening. In determining whether a foreign investment may adversely affect national security or public order, Member States and the Commission may further consider whether the investor is state-controlled, has previously engaged in activities detrimental to security or public order, or is suspected of criminal or unlawful conduct.

These relevant factors serve not only as guidelines for France in terms of information-sharing but also as a basis for gathering intelligence relevant to the screening process. As such, the EU framework for FDI screening undeniably influences the national regime (known as the IEF – Investissements Étrangers en France – screening mechanism).

Procedural Timelines Are Designed to Align with the French IEF Regime

Under the Regulation, Member States retain discretion over their internal FDI screening timelines. However, these timeframes must be set in a manner that enables the timely consideration of comments from other Member States and of any opinion issued by the European Commission. The Regulation also underscores the importance of responding within reasonable time limits to requests for information, both initial and supplementary, in order to avoid undue delays.

---

artificial intelligence, robotics, semiconductors, cybersecurity, aerospace, defence, energy storage, quantum and nuclear technologies as well as nanotechnologies and biotechnologies; (c) supply of critical inputs, including energy or raw materials, as well as food security; (d) access to sensitive information, including personal data, or the ability to control such information; or (e) the freedom and pluralism of the media.

In assessing the impact of a foreign direct investment on security or public order, Member States and the Commission may also take into account, in particular: (a) whether the foreign investor is directly or indirectly controlled by the government, including state bodies or armed forces, of a third country, including through ownership structure or significant funding; (b) whether the foreign investor has already been involved in activities affecting security or public order in a Member State; or (c) whether there is a serious risk that the foreign investor engages in illegal or criminal activities.

221. European Union, Council Regulation (EC) No 428/2009 of 5 May 2009 setting up a Community regime for the control of exports, transfer, brokering and transit of dual-use items, Official Journal of the European Union, L 134/1, 29 May 2009, Article 2, point 1 – For the purposes of this Regulation, the following definitions shall apply: (1) 'dual-use items' shall mean items, including software and technology, which can be used for both civil and military purposes, and shall include all goods which can be used for the design, development, production or use of nuclear, chemical or biological weapons or of their means of delivery, including all items listed in Annex I.

222. In economic terms, "inputs" refer to the components used in the production process, as opposed to "outputs," which are the goods or services resulting from that process. Inputs may include raw materials, labor, and other production factors. In the agricultural sector, the term "inputs" typically refers to substances such as fertilizers and pesticides.

223. France, Decree No. 2019-1590 of December 31, 2019, on foreign investments in France, Official Journal of the French Republic [Journal Officiel de la République française], No. 0001, January 1, 2020, NOR: ECOT1932857D

As regards the French FDI screening framework (IEF), the implementation of the EU's cooperation mechanism does not result in any extension of the national screening timeline. The applicable timeframe [224] for processing an authorization request remains a maximum of 75 days: 30 working days for a standard review and up to 45 additional days if an in-depth investigation is launched.

Within this national deadline, time must also be allocated to accommodate the European cooperation mechanism. Specifically, upon France notifying the Commission and the other Member States of a transaction falling under the IEF screening mechanism involving an entity from a third country, the European process begins with a 15-day preliminary review period [225].

At the end of this 15-day period, three outcomes are possible:

1. if no response is issued, meaning that neither the Commission nor the Member States identify any risk associated with the notified transaction, the European cooperation procedure is concluded, and France may resume its national review process;
2. if the Commission or the Member States issue a comment or opinion providing relevant information to France, the European cooperation procedure is likewise concluded. France proceeds with its national screening, taking into account the comments and opinions received;
3. if the Commission or the Member States submit questions, particularly by requesting additional information from France,

If France endeavors to respond to the questions it has received, the time limits are suspended until such responses are provided. By the end of the sixteenth day at the latest, France must submit its replies to the Commission or the other Member States.

This initiates a second phase, lasting up to twenty days, during which the Commission and the Member States examine the responses submitted and conduct a more in-depth review of the transaction. At the end of this twenty-day period, they have two options:

1. either remain silent (as in Phase 1), in which case the EU cooperation procedure is deemed to be completed, and France may continue its national screening process;
2. or issue comments or an opinion containing any relevant information for the attention of France. In this case as well, the EU cooperation procedure is concluded. France then continues its review under the domestic FDI screening mechanism, taking into account the comments and opinions received;

In practice, requests for information may suspend the screening timeline in the reviewing Member State until a response is provided. Similarly, the procedure for

224. France, Ministry of the Economy, Finance and Recovery, Directorate General of the Treasury, "FAQ: Foreign Investment Screening in France" [« FAQ Le contrôle des investissements étrangers en France »], October 2023, p. 8, available at https://www.tresor.economie.gouv.fr/services-aux-entreprises/investissements-etrangers-en-france (last accessed September 1st, 2025)

225. France, Ministry of the Economy, Finance and Industrial and Digital Sovereignty, Directorate General of the Treasury, Annual Report 2025, "Foreign Direct Investment Screening in France ", published July 30, 2025, available at https://www.tresor.economie.gouv.fr/Articles/2025/07/30/publication-du-rapport-annuel-sur-le-controle-ief-en-2024 (last accessed July 31, 2025)

supplying additional information may, to some extent, extend the timeframes available to the Commission and the other Member States. However, such mechanisms may result in a degree of unpredictability for companies when compared to the current procedural framework. Furthermore, the possibility of ex post scrutiny of completed transactions raises important legal certainty concerns.

On this point, the French authorities [226] have emphasized that the timeframes linked to the EU-level notification procedure have no impact on the statutory deadlines of the French FDI screening mechanism (Investissements Étrangers en France – IEF).

In exceptional circumstances, where the screening Member State considers that its security or public order require immediate action, it must inform the other Member States and the Commission and may adopt a screening decision within a shorter timeframe than the one normally provided for in the second phase. In such cases, it must duly justify the need for urgent measures. The other Member States and the Commission will then endeavor to issue comments or deliver an opinion as promptly as possible.

Cooperation between the Member States and the Commission is facilitated through designated contact points established for this purpose.

See the "Diagram of the European Screening Mechanism" at the end of the chapter.

Finally, it is important to recall that, while the screening Member State must take due account of the comments made by other Member States and the opinion of the Commission, the final decision on whether to authorize or prohibit the investment rests solely with that Member State. In other words, France remains free to disregard alerts raised by another Member State or by the Commission. Overall, these procedures for issuing opinions and notifications are intended to enhance the economic security of the Member States.

The French FDI Screening Mechanism Retains Sole Responsibility for Protecting National Interests

Although the EU Regulation does not carry binding legal force, due notably to the nature of its drafting, it nonetheless provides directive guidance through its recommendations. It outlines a set of obligations and prerogatives that Member States should follow in order to comply with the expected standards and best practices underpinning the screening framework. These elements naturally influence the way France administers foreign direct investment screening under its national FDI regime (referred to as le dispositif IEF). However, they do not absolve France of its primary responsibility to safeguard its national interests.

The FDI screening framework clearly affirms that Member States remain solely responsible, and therefore solely competent, for determining how to protect their

226. See Point 2.2.3.1.3, France, Ministry of the Economy, Finance and Industrial and Digital Sovereignty, Directorate General of the Treasury, Guidelines on the Foreign Direct Investment Screening in France /, July 2025, published July 30, 2025, consulted August 1, 2025, available at https://www.tresor.economie.gouv.fr/services-aux-entreprises/investissements-etrangers-en-france,

essential security interests. Article 1 of Regulation (EU) 2019/452 confirms that national security falls under the exclusive responsibility of each Member State, in accordance with the Treaty [227] on the Functioning of the European Union (TFEU and, more specifically, Article 346 of the TFEU [228], which recognizes each Member State's right to protect its essential security interests.

Accordingly, it is up to each Member State, including France, to establish investment screening mechanisms that are appropriately tailored to its national security objectives. The Regulation [229] explicitly acknowledges that "Member States may maintain, amend, or adopt mechanisms to screen foreign direct investments on the grounds of security or public order." It also confirms that each Member State retains the absolute discretion [230] not to implement any screening mechanism at all.

Furthermore, the final decision regarding any foreign direct investment subject to screening, or any measure relating to an FDI that is not screened, rests exclusively with the Member State in which the investment is planned or has been completed. In other words, the European Commission does not hold decision-making authority over an FDI transaction that is subject to a Member State's screening procedure.

---

227. European Union, Treaty on the Functioning of the European Union, Article 4(2): Shared competence between the Union and the Member States applies in the following principal areas:
(a) internal market; (b) social policy, for the aspects defined in this Treaty; (c) economic, social and territorial cohesion; (d) agriculture and fisheries, excluding the conservation of marine biological resources; (e) environment; (f) consumer protection; (g) transport; (h) trans-European networks; (i) energy; (j) area of freedom, security and justice; (k) common safety concerns in public health matters, for the aspects defined in this Treaty.
228. European Union, Treaty on the Functioning of the European Union, Article 346 (ex Article 296 of the Treaty establishing the European Community (TEC)):
1. The provisions of the Treaties shall not preclude the application of the following rules:
(a) no Member State shall be obliged to supply information the disclosure of which it considers contrary to the essential interests of its security;
(b) any Member State may take such measures as it considers necessary for the protection of the essential interests of its security which are connected with the production of or trade in arms, munitions and war material; such measures shall not adversely affect the conditions of competition in the internal market regarding products which are not intended for specifically military purposes.
2. The Council may, acting unanimously on a proposal from the Commission, make changes to the list of products to which the provisions of paragraph 1(b) apply, as drawn up on April 15, 1958.
229. European Union, Regulation (EU) 2019/452 of the European Parliament and of the Council of 19 March 2019 establishing a framework for the screening of foreign direct investments into the Union, Article 3 – National screening mechanisms: 1. Member States may maintain, amend or adopt mechanisms to screen foreign direct investments on the grounds of security or public order, under the conditions and in accordance with the provisions of this Regulation. 2. Member States shall notify the Commission of their existing screening mechanisms by 10 April 2019. Member States shall notify the Commission of any newly adopted screening mechanism or any amendment to an existing screening mechanism within 30 days of its adoption. 3. Member States shall ensure that the screening mechanisms referred to in paragraph 1 comply with the following requirements: (a) transparency and non-discrimination between third countries; (b) the timeframes set by Member States shall allow for comments by other Member States and the Commission as referred to in Articles 6 and 7; (c) confidentiality of information exchanged in the screening process is protected; (d) foreign investors and the undertakings concerned have the possibility to seek recourse against screening decisions of the national authorities; (e) Member States shall establish contact points for the implementation of this Regulation and notify them to the Commission and other Member States.
230. European Union, Regulation (EU) 2019/452 of the European Parliament and of the Council of 19 March 2019 establishing a framework for the screening of foreign direct investments into the Union, Article 1(3):

That said, this national responsibility must be exercised in accordance with the rules and procedures that allow for the fulfillment of the European Union's broader objectives and prerogatives, particularly those concerning the freedom and protection of foreign investment within the internal market. Lastly, the Member State conducting the review must take into account the comments and opinions received through the cooperation mechanism.

European FDI Screening Framework Establishes Guiding Principles for National Regimes

Although the EU regulation on the screening of foreign direct investments does not carry binding legal force, it remains highly prescriptive in its recommendations and outlines several guiding principles, referred to as "guardrails", that Member States are strongly encouraged to follow.

These guardrails primarily include the adoption of transparent and non-discriminatory rules and procedures for national screening mechanisms applied to third-country investors. Each Member State retains the responsibility for defining the triggering conditions for review, the grounds on which screening decisions may be based, and the procedural rules applicable to each case. The regulation also encourages Member States to establish reasonable timelines for screening procedures and to implement anti-circumvention [231] measures designed to uphold the integrity of screening decisions. Particular attention should also be paid to national security and public order [232] risks arising from material changes in ownership structures or other essential characteristics of a foreign investor.

Furthermore, the framework [233] encourages Member States to take into account comments from other Member States and opinions issued by the European Commission. Where appropriate, such considerations should be reflected either through the

---

Nothing in this Regulation shall limit the right of each Member State to decide whether or not to screen a particular foreign direct investment within the framework of this Regulation.

231. European Union, Regulation (EU) 2019/452 of the European Parliament and of the Council of March 19, 2019, establishing a framework for the screening of foreign direct investments into the Union, Recital No. 6 : Foreign direct investments contribute to the Union's growth by enhancing its competitiveness, creating jobs and economies of scale, bringing in capital, technologies, innovation, expertise and access to markets.

232. European Union, Regulation (EU) 2019/452 of the European Parliament and of the Council of March 19, 2019, establishing a framework for the screening of foreign direct investments into the Union, Recital No. 11: It is essential to ensure the protection of sensitive information in the context of the cooperation mechanism between Member States and the Commission. This includes confidential information, commercially-sensitive information, information covered by national rules on confidentiality, and information the disclosure of which would be contrary to the essential interests of Member States' security.

233. European Union, Regulation (EU) 2019/452 of the European Parliament and of the Council of March 19, 2019, establishing a framework for the screening of foreign direct investments into the Union, Recital No. 17 : The framework for the screening of foreign direct investments should provide Member States and the Commission with the means to cooperate with each other in order to address risks related to foreign direct investment that could affect security or public order. In that context, Member States should be able to provide comments to the Member State where the foreign direct investment is planned or has been completed. The Commission should also be able to issue an opinion when a foreign direct investment is likely to affect security or public order in more than one Member State, or when it has relevant information in relation to that investment.

application of national measures or the development of broader policy responses, in accordance with the principle of sincere cooperation set forth in the Treaty on the Functioning of the European Union (TFEU[234]).

The regulation also calls for a thorough assessment of how best[235] to achieve the objectives of investment screening. This includes, inter alia, evaluating whether companies are required to collect or refrain from collecting certain information, as well as ensuring that other impacted Member States are duly notified of any such collection activities.

In joining the EU cooperation framework, Member States are subject to two main obligations:

1. General information-sharing duty: Member States conducting foreign investment screening must inform the Commission and the other Member States of such screening, even if the investment is not expected to produce cross-border effects.
2. General alert mechanism: Even in the absence of a formal screening procedure, Member States must notify the Commission and/or another Member State of any planned or completed foreign investment in another Member State that may affect security or public order. This obligation to alert remains valid for up to fifteen months following the completion of the transaction.

Finally, Member States are required to notify the Commission of any newly adopted screening mechanism, or any amendment to an existing mechanism, within thirty days of its entry into force. Through this approach, the European Union aims to foster greater coherence and harmonization among national screening regimes across the EU. Nonetheless, the effectiveness of a non-binding framework remains to be fully assessed in practice.

The IEF Mechanism Collects Information to Be Shared with Other Member States

France's foreign direct investment (FDI) screening mechanism[236], the IEF regime, includes a structured cooperation process with other EU Member States that also

234. European Union, Treaty on the Functioning of the European Union (TFEU), Article 4(3): "In the areas of research, technological development and space, the Union shall have competence to carry out activities, in particular to define and implement programmes; however, the exercise of that competence shall not result in Member States being prevented from exercising theirs."
235. European Union, Regulation (EU) 2019/452 of the European Parliament and of the Council of March 19, 2019, establishing a framework for the screening of foreign direct investments into the Union, Recital No. 24 : In order to ensure the effective implementation of this Regulation, the Union and the Member States should cooperate with the competent authorities of third countries in relation to issues of investment screening. Such cooperation may include sharing experience, best practices and information regarding investment trends.
236. European Union, Regulation (EU) 2019/452 of the European Parliament and of the Council of March 19, 2019, establishing a framework for the screening of foreign direct investments into the Union, Article 6, Official Journal of the European Union, L 79I, March 21, 2019, pp. 1–14, Article 6 – Annual reporting : Member States shall annually report to the Commission on foreign direct investments that took place within their territory. That report shall include information on the sectors, origin, and value of the investments, as well as on whether the investments were subject to screening or not, and the screening decisions taken, if any. The Commission shall present an annual report to the European Parliament and to the Council on the implementation of this Regulation, which shall be made public.

maintain FDI screening frameworks. The right to initiate this cooperation lies either with France in its capacity as a Member State or with the European Commission.

If France activates the cooperation mechanism, it must notify the European Commission and the other Member States, regardless of whether they themselves maintain a screening mechanism, of the foreign direct investment originating from a third country that is subject to review under the French regime. This notification must be accompanied, without undue delay, by a set of information [237] as outlined in Chapter 17 and Annex F.

The notification may also include a list of Member States whose public order or security may be affected by the transaction in question. Finally, and only if deemed necessary, the Member State conducting the screening, here, France, must indicate whether it considers the foreign direct investment at stake to potentially fall within the scope of the EU Merger Regulation [238].

Cooperation Between France and Member States Without National Screening Mechanisms

The European Regulation adopted in 2019 was also intended to facilitate the exchange of information among EU Member States that have chosen not to implement a national foreign direct investment (FDI) screening mechanism, while fully respecting their sovereign right not to do so. This initiative seeks to mitigate the risk that the absence of national screening in one Member State might undermine the economic security of others. Accordingly, the Regulation established a cooperation framework tailored to such situations.

This framework includes an alert or notification mechanism that allows a Member State, such as France, to submit comments to another Member State lacking a screening mechanism, if a foreign direct investment (FDI) in that State is likely to affect France's national security or public order. These comments are simultaneously shared with the European Commission, which in turn notifies the other Member States.

---

237. European Union, Regulation (EU) 2019/452 of the European Parliament and of the Council of March 19, 2019, establishing a framework for the screening of foreign direct investments into the Union, Article 9(2), Official Journal of the European Union, L 79I, March 21, 2019, pp. 1–14, Article 9(2) – Requests for information by the Commission, The request for information by the Commission shall be duly justified. It shall be limited to information necessary to assess the effects of the foreign direct investment on security or public order. The request shall set out the time limit within which the information is to be provided. The information requested may include in particular:
(a) the ownership structure of the foreign investor and of the target undertaking;
(b) the value of the investment;
(c) the products, services, and business operations of the foreign investor and of the target undertaking;
(d) the Member States in which the foreign investor and the target undertaking conduct relevant business operations;
(e) the funding of the investment and its source, including, when available, whether it involves funding from State bodies, including through concessional finance or subsidies;
(f) the date when the investment is planned or has been completed.

238. European Union, Council Regulation (EC) No. 139/2004 of January 20, 2004, on the control of concentrations between undertakings ("the EC Merger Regulation") (Text with EEA relevance), Official Journal of the European Union, L 24, January 29, 2004, pp. 1–22

In addition, the European Commission may issue an opinion addressed to a Member State if the investment in question appears likely to affect the security or public order of more than one Member State, or if it holds relevant information regarding the transaction. The Commission may issue such an opinion even where comments have already been submitted by other Member States. Furthermore, if at least one-third of the Member States express concern that an FDI poses a threat to their security or public order, the Commission is required to issue an opinion. The fact that such an opinion has been issued must be communicated to all other Member States.

The Regulation also provides for an evaluation right, exercisable in two distinct ways. First, a Member State may formally request the Commission to issue an opinion or invite other Member States to submit comments if it has reasonable grounds to believe that an FDI on its territory could jeopardize its security or public order. Any such comments or opinions must be duly substantiated. Second, a Member State or the Commission may request that the host Member State, where the FDI is planned or has taken place, provide all relevant information [239], even if the investment is not subject to national screening, when there is reason to believe that it may affect security or public order.

All information requests must be substantiated, proportionate, and strictly limited to what is necessary to issue an informed comment or opinion. The request must not impose an excessive burden on the Member State concerned, particularly in light of its choice not to adopt a screening mechanism. All requests for and responses to such information must be transmitted to the Commission concurrently.

The Regulation imposes clear procedural deadlines. Comments and opinions must be issued within 35 calendar days following receipt of the requested information. If the Commission needs to formulate an opinion in response to comments submitted by other Member States, an additional 15 calendar days are granted.

The Member State in which the FDI is taking place must take into account the comments submitted by other Member States and the Commission's opinion. Comments and opinions may be issued no later than 15 months after the completion of the FDI transaction. Cooperation occurs via designated national contact points.

These provisions do not apply to FDIs completed before April 10, 2019.

Proportionality and Purpose Limitation of Information Requests

The Commission [240] has emphasized that the cooperation mechanism should serve only to safeguard security and public order. It must not be diverted from this purpose.

239. European Union, Regulation (EU) 2019/452 of the European Parliament and of the Council of March 19, 2019, establishing a framework for the screening of foreign direct investments into the Union, Article 9: "Information required", Official Journal of the European Union, L 79I, March 21, 2019, pp. 1–14
240. European Union, Regulation (EU) 2019/452 of the European Parliament and of the Council of March 19, 2019, establishing a framework for the screening of foreign direct investments into the Union, Recital 18, Official Journal of the European Union, L 79I, March 21, 2019, pp. 1–14

Therefore, Member States must provide adequate justification for any request for information or comments related to a foreign investment in another Member State. The same justification requirement applies to the Commission when issuing an opinion or requesting information.

These safeguards are particularly important in situations where third-country investors are in competition with EU-based investors to acquire assets or pursue investments in a Member State. Screening practices must remain consistent with EU rules, including those relating to competition law. Member States must comply with EU law and with national legislation that conforms to EU requirements when transmitting requested information.

Pursuant to the Regulation [241], Member States must ensure that relevant information is shared promptly, without undue delay, with other Member States or the Commission when requested. Required information typically includes: the ownership structure of the foreign investor and target company; the approximate value of the investment; the products, services, and markets concerned; the Member States where the investor and target operate commercially; the financing and source of funds; and the anticipated or actual closing date of the transaction.

Where possible, Member States are encouraged to provide supplementary information. If a Member State is unable to provide the requested information despite its best efforts, it must inform the Commission and the other concerned Member States, explaining the reasons and detailing the steps taken to gather the information.

If no information is provided, any comments or opinions issued by other Member States or the Commission will be based solely on the information available to them. The Commission remains mindful of the risks associated with unjustified requests and stresses that screening cooperation must strike a balance between protecting national and Union interests and ensuring fair treatment of third-country investors.

Safeguards for Confidential Information Shared by France

The Regulation [242] mandates that confidential information, including commercially sensitive data, shared between Member States for screening purposes, be subject to strict confidentiality safeguards. This naturally applies to France, which remains bound by obligations to preserve the integrity of such data. Both the Commission and Member States must implement [243] all necessary measures to ensure confidentiality

241. European Union, Regulation (EU) 2019/452 of the European Parliament and of the Council of March 19, 2019, establishing a framework for the screening of foreign direct investments into the Union, Article 9: "Information required", Official Journal of the European Union [Journal officiel de l'Union européenne], L 79I, March 21, 2019, pp. 1–14
242. European Union, Regulation (EU) 2019/452 of the European Parliament and of the Council of March 19, 2019, establishing a framework for the screening of foreign direct investments into the Union, Recital 4, Official Journal of the European Union [Journal officiel de l'Union européenne], L 79I, March 21, 2019, pp. 1–14
243. European Union, Regulation (EU) 2019/452 of the European Parliament and of the Council of March 19, 2019, establishing a framework for the screening of foreign direct investments into the Union, Recital 30, Official Journal of the European Union [Journal officiel de l'Union européenne], L 79I, March 21, 2019, pp. 1–14

in accordance with Commission Decision[244] (EU, Euratom) 2015/443, Commission Decision[245] (EU, Euratom) 2015/444, and the agreement[246] adopted by the Council on the protection of classified information exchanged in the interest of the Union. National authorities must not declassify information without the prior written consent of the originator. Sensitive but non-classified information, or information provided in confidence, must be treated as such by the relevant authorities.

In addition to the obligation to safeguard confidential information, all processing of personal data must comply with applicable data protection legislation. National contact points and other entities involved in cooperation must comply with Regulation[247] (EU) 2016/679 of the European Parliament and of the Council (GDPR), while the Commission must adhere to Regulation[248] (EU) 2018/1725.

Article 3 of the Regulation[249] confirms that Member States are responsible for protecting confidential information, including commercially sensitive data, made available to the screening Member State. Despite the use of secure communication channels, foreign investors and target companies may express concerns regarding the reputational impact of screening mechanisms and the treatment of sensitive information in a context of increased cross-border data exchanges. Encrypted channels for information exchange are thus recommended.

Moreover, Member States may need to disclose substantial sensitive data concerning a particular investment project and the parties involved. This could potentially trigger parallel inquiries in other jurisdictions.

Lastly, it is essential that foreign investors and target companies retain the ability to challenge national screening decisions. The Regulation[250] therefore requires that Member States provide access to appropriate judicial remedies.

---

244. European Union, Commission, Decision (EU, Euratom) 2015/443 of March 13, 2015, on Security in the Commission, Official Journal of the European Union [Journal officiel de l'Union européenne], L 72/41, March 17, 2015, Document 32015D0443, ELI: http://data.europa.eu/eli/dec/2015/443/oj
245. European Union, Commission, Decision (EU, Euratom) 2015/444 of March 13, 2015, on the security rules for protecting EU classified information, Official Journal of the European Union [Journal officiel de l'Union européenne], L 72/41, March 17, 2015, p. 53, Document 32015D0444, ELI: http://data.europa.eu/eli/dec/2015/444/oj
246. European Union, Agreement between the Member States of the European Union, meeting within the Council, on the protection of classified information exchanged in the interest of the European Union, Official Journal of the European Union [Journal officiel de l'Union européenne], C 202/13, July 8, 2011
247. European Union, Regulation (EU) 2016/679 of the European Parliament and of the Council of April 27, 2016, on the protection of natural persons with regard to the processing of personal data and on the free movement of such data, and repealing Directive 95/46/EC (General Data Protection Regulation), Official Journal of the European Union [Journal officiel de l'Union européenne], L 119/1, May 4, 2016
248. European Union, Regulation (EU) 2018/1725 of the European Parliament and of the Council of October 23, 2018, on the protection of natural persons with regard to the processing of personal data by the Union institutions, bodies, offices and agencies and on the free movement of such data, and repealing Regulation (EC) No 45/2001 and Decision No 1247/2002/EC, Official Journal of the European Union [Journal officiel de l'Union européenne], L 295/39, November 21, 2018
249. European Union, Regulation (EU) 2019/452 of the European Parliament and of the Council of March 19, 2019, establishing a framework for the screening of foreign direct investments into the Union, Article 3(4), Official Journal of the European Union [Journal officiel de l'Union européenne], L 79I, March 21, 2019, pp. 1-14
250. European Union, Regulation (EU) 2019/452 of the European Parliament and of the Council of March 19, 2019, establishing a framework for the screening of foreign direct investments into the Union, Article

As the French Minister of the Economy has emphasized [251], France, like all Member States, is not obliged to disclose any information that it considers contrary to its essential national security interests.

France's Obligation to Engage with the European Commission in Cases of Union Interest

The European Commission plays a significant role in inter-State procedures when a foreign investment involves a project or program of Union interest. This is particularly relevant in transactions subject to screening by Member States, as the application for prior authorization must disclose any participation in Union-related projects or programs, or any financial support derived from EU funds. These programs are listed [252] in Article 8 of Regulation (EU) 2019/452 and encompass initiatives deemed substantial in terms of EU financing or governed by Union law concerning critical infrastructure, technologies, or inputs essential to public security and public order.

The list of covered programs [253] includes the European Global Navigation Satellite Systems (GNSS), the European Geostationary Navigation Overlay Service (EGNOS), and

---

3(5), Official Journal of the European Union [Journal officiel de l'Union européenne], L 79I, March 21, 2019, pp. 1–14

251. France, National Assembly, Written Question No. 35024 to the Minister of the Economy, Finance and Recovery, Official Journal of the National Assembly [Journal Officiel de l'Assemblée nationale], December 15, 2020, p. 9103, MARLEIX, Olivier, Deputy, Les Républicains (LR), ministerial reply, Official Journal of the National Assembly [Journal Officiel de l'Assemblée nationale], September 28, 2021, p. 7175

252. European Union, Regulation (EU) 2019/452 of the European Parliament and of the Council of March 19, 2019, establishing a framework for the screening of foreign direct investments into the Union, Recital No. 3
"*Certain foreign direct investments may pose a risk to security or public order in the Member States or in the Union. It is thus necessary to provide a framework for the screening of foreign direct investments into the Union on grounds of security or public order. The framework for the screening of foreign direct investments should allow Member States and the Commission to take into account all relevant factors when screening such investments, including the effects on critical infrastructure, critical technologies, including key enabling technologies, supply of critical inputs, such as energy or raw materials, access to sensitive information or the ability to control such information, or the freedom and pluralism of the media.*"

253. European Union, Regulation (EU) 2019/452 of the European Parliament and of the Council of March 19, 2019, establishing a framework for the screening of foreign direct investments into the Union, Annex, "List of projects or programmes of Union interest":
1 - European GNSS programmes (Galileo and EGNOS), Regulation (EU) No. 1285/2013 of the European Parliament and of the Council of December 11, 2013, on the implementation and exploitation of European satellite navigation systems and repealing Council Regulation (EC) No. 876/2002 and Regulation (EC) No. 683/2008 of the European Parliament and of the Council, Official Journal of the European Union, L 347/1, December 20, 2013
2 - Copernicus, Regulation (EU) No. 377/2014 of the European Parliament and of the Council of April 3, 2014, establishing the Copernicus Programme and repealing Regulation (EU) No. 911/2010, Official Journal of the European Union, L 122/44, April 24, 2014
3 - Horizon 2020, Regulation (EU) No. 1291/2013 of the European Parliament and of the Council of December 11, 2013, establishing Horizon 2020, the Framework Programme for Research and Innovation (2014–2020) and repealing Decision No. 1982/2006/EC, Official Journal of the European Union, L 347/104, December 20, 2013
4 - Trans-European Transport Networks (TEN-T)), Regulation (EU) No. 1315/2013 of the European Parliament and of the Council of December 11, 2013, on Union guidelines for the development of the trans-European transport network and repealing Decision No. 661/2010/EU, Official Journal of the European Union, L 348/1, December 20, 2013

the Galileo satellite navigation and radionavigation program. It also covers Copernicus (the EU's Earth observation program), Horizon 2020 (the European R&D Framework Program for 2014–2020), and the European Defence Industrial Development Programme (EDIDP). Additionally, it includes the Trans-European Transport Network (TEN-T), which aims to establish a seamless transportation system for goods and passengers across Member States, with an objective of 90,000 km of high-quality roads and highways by 2020. The list further includes the Trans-European Energy Networks (TEN-E) and Trans-European Telecommunications Networks, as well as the Permanent Structured Cooperation (PESCO), a provision of the Lisbon Treaty enabling deeper defense integration among a group of EU Member States.

The annual reports of the European Commission provide useful insight into France's active role within the Union screening mechanism.

- First Annual Report (2021) [254]

This first report covered the period from the entry into force of the Regulation (October 11, 2020) through June 30, 2021. It thus represents the initial implementation phase of the EU cooperation mechanism.

As regards France, out of a total of 265 notifications submitted to the Commission by 11 Member States, more than 90% originated from five countries: France, Germany, Italy, Spain, and Austria. From the very first year of application, France established itself as one of the principal contributors, thereby confirming its leading role in deploying the cooperation mechanism. It was also among the 12 Member States that amended their domestic screening regimes to adapt them to the new European and economic constraints.

In terms of covered activities, as elsewhere in the EU, the most affected sectors were manufacturing and information and communication technologies (ICT).

---

5 - Trans-European Energy Networks (TEN-E), Regulation (EU) No. 347/2013 of the European Parliament and of the Council of April 17, 2013, on guidelines for trans-European energy infrastructure and repealing Decision No. 1364/2006/EC and amending Regulations (EC) No. 713/2009, (EC) No. 714/2009 and (EC) No. 715/2009, Official Journal of the European Union, L 115/39, April 25, 2013

6 - Trans-European Telecommunications Networks, Regulation (EU) No. 283/2014 of the European Parliament and of the Council of March 11, 2014, on guidelines for trans-European networks in the area of telecommunications infrastructure and repealing Decision No. 1336/97/EC, Official Journal of the European Union, L 86/14, March 21, 2014

7 - European Defence Industrial Development Programme (EDIDP), Regulation (EU) 2018/1092 of the European Parliament and of the Council of July 18, 2018, establishing the European Defence Industrial Development Programme aiming at supporting the competitiveness and innovation capacity of the Union's defence industry, Official Journal of the European Union, L 200/30, August 7, 2018

8 - Permanent Structured Cooperation (PESCO), Council Decision (CFSP) 2018/340 of March 6, 2018, establishing the list of projects to be developed under PESCO, Official Journal of the European Union, L 65/24, March 8, 2018

254. European Union, European Commission, "Report from the Commission to the European Parliament and the Council, First Annual Report on the Screening of Foreign Direct Investments into the Union," {SWD(2021) 334 final}, Brussels, November 23, 2021, COM(2021) 714 final, available at https://eur-lex.europa.eu/legal-content/FR/TXT/HTML/?uri=CELEX:52021DC0714 (last accessed September 1, 2025)

As for the types of notified transactions, most concerned mid-sized operations (€10–100 million), although several ICT transactions reached values in the billions.

With respect to the screening procedure, Phase 1 absorbed the vast majority of notifications; only a limited number of French transactions moved to Phase 2, primarily in manufacturing and ICT.

- Second Annual Report (2022) [255]

The second report covered the year 2021, the first full year following entry into force of the Regulation, marking a stage of consolidation of the EU cooperation mechanism.

Out of 414 notifications submitted by 13 Member States, more than 85% came from five countries: France, Germany, Italy, Spain, and Austria. France thereby confirmed its status as a major contributor, after already being one of the five States responsible for more than 90% of transmissions in the first report.

As elsewhere in the EU, the French notifications focused on ICT, manufacturing, financial services, wholesale and retail trade, and construction.

At the Union level, the majority of notified transactions were valued below €500 million, though a significant proportion (34%) exceeded that threshold, ranging from €1 to approximately €30 billion. In France, as in the EU overall, investment centered on mid-sized operations (€10–100 million), but several large transactions in ICT and healthcare were also notified.

As regards procedure, 86% of French notifications (in line with other Member States) were rapidly closed in Phase 1. By contrast, 11% were escalated to Phase 2 for in-depth review, notably in manufacturing (defense, aerospace, semiconductors, energy) and ICT.

Finally, the report noted improved processing times, as the average response period for Phase 2 requests from the Commission decreased from 31 days (Report 2021) to 22 days in 2021.

- Third Annual Report (2023) [256]

The third report covered the year 2022, the second full year of application of the Regulation. It marked a phase of intensified activity of the EU cooperation mechanism, with an increased volume of notifications and improved interstate coordination.

---

255. European Union, European Commission, "Report from the Commission to the European Parliament and the Council, Second Annual Report on the Screening of Foreign Direct Investments into the Union," {SWD(2022) 219 final}, Brussels, September 1, 2022, COM(2022) 433 final, available at https://eur-lex.europa.eu/legal-content/FR/TXT/HTML/?uri=CELEX:52022DC0433 (last accessed September 1, 2025)
256. European Union, European Commission, "Report from the Commission to the European Parliament and the Council, Third Annual Report on the Screening of Foreign Direct Investments into the Union{SWD(2023) 329 final}, Brussels, October 19, 2023, COM(2023) 590 final, available at https://eur-lex.europa.eu/legal-content/FR/TXT/HTML/?uri=CELEX:52023DC0590 (last accessed September 1, 2025)

In 2022, 15 Member States transmitted notifications to the Commission, totaling 423 cases. As in prior years, more than 85% came from five countries, including France alongside Germany, Italy, Spain, and Austria. France thus remained among the foremost contributors, confirming the trend observed since 2020 and 2021.

Sectorally, French notifications concentrated, as across the EU, on ICT, manufacturing (including defense, aerospace, and semiconductors), energy, healthcare, and biotechnology.

In terms of transaction size, most French cases involved mid-sized operations (€10–500 million), but several transactions exceeding €1 billion were examined, notably in ICT and energy. The United States remained the primary source of notified investors, followed by the United Kingdom and China, reflecting the broader patterns highlighted by the Commission.

As regards procedure, approximately 87% of French cases were processed swiftly in Phase 1, with roughly 9% requiring in-depth Phase 2 review, mainly in ICT, energy, and sensitive manufacturing.

Finally, France was also among the Member States most active in issuing comments on cases notified by other Member States, underscoring its leading role in European cooperation.

- Fourth Annual Report (2024) [257]

The fourth report covered the year 2023, the third full year of application of the Regulation. This occurred in a context of declining global FDI flows (–15%) but reinforced European screening mechanisms. By 2023, 24 Member States, including France, had adopted screening regimes, and 17 submitted notifications to the Commission.

France again ranked among the principal contributors, together with Germany, Italy, Spain, and Austria, accounting for the majority of nearly 620 total notifications. It thus remained a driving force of the European framework, both in terms of volume and active participation in interstate exchanges.

Sectorally, French notifications focused on ICT, manufacturing (defense, aerospace, space, semiconductors), energy, healthcare, and biotechnology. A notable novelty in 2023 was the notification of significant transactions related to critical raw materials .

As for transaction size, French notifications concerned mainly mid-sized deals (€10–500 million), though several very large transactions exceeding €1 billion were also recorded. The principal origins of investors were the United States, the United Kingdom, and China, a trend also confirmed by the Commission at EU level.

With respect to procedure, approximately 85% of French cases were handled in Phase 1, while about 12% required in-depth Phase 2 review, primarily in energy, ICT,

257. European Union, European Commission, "Report from the Commission to the European Parliament and the Council, Fourth Annual Report on the Screening of Foreign Direct Investments into the Union," {SWD(2024) 234 final}, Brussels, October 17, 2024, COM(2024) 464 final, available at https://eur-lex.europa.eu/legal-content/FR/TXT/HTML/?uri=CELEX:52024DC0464 (last accessed September 1, 2025)

and critical raw materials . France also made extensive use of its prerogatives to comment on cases notified by other Member States, actively contributing to pan-European cooperation. In the same spirit, upon publication [258] of its 2025 Annual Report, the Directorate General of the Treasury) reiterated that France continued to participate actively in the EU cooperation mechanism and in the ongoing revision process.

Reform of Regulation 2019/452: Strengthening the French FDI Screening Mechanism

Despite the added value of the cooperation mechanism, it remains subject to several limitations. As highlighted in a report [259] by the French National Assembly's fact-finding and evaluation mission, these include increased regulatory complexity for transaction parties, as well as persistent fragmentation among national screening regimes. Synchronizing Member State frameworks remains a significant challenge, particularly regarding scope, timelines, covered sectors, decision-making procedures, and risk-assessment criteria.

During hearings, the European Commission [260] emphasized that "this fragmentation [...] may seriously impair the effectiveness and efficiency of the cooperation mechanism, create barriers within the internal market, and reduce the EU's attractiveness to foreign investors." Similarly, the European Court of Auditors [261] noted in its special report, three years after the entry into force of the EU framework, that "important limitations remain at the EU-27 level that hinder the framework's effectiveness and efficiency in addressing risks to security and public order." The Court specifically pointed to a lack of coordination in applying the Regulation, uncertainty around the definition of critical sectors, and divergent interpretations of key concepts among Member States, an issue that directly affects the initial filtering of transactions, as foreign investor status and involvement in sensitive activities are frequently both present.

---

258. France, Ministry of the Economy, Finance and Industrial and Digital Sovereignty, Directorate General of the Treasury, Annual Report 2025, "Foreign Direct Investment Screening in France," published July 30, 2025, available at https://www.tresor.economie.gouv.fr/Articles/2025/07/30/publication-du-rapport-annuel-sur-le-controle-ief-en-2024 (last accessed July 31, 2025)
259. France, National Assembly, Committee for the Evaluation and Oversight of Public Policies, Information Report, No. 1453, by Members of Parliament JOLIVET, François and de LEPINAU, Hervé, on the evaluation of foreign direct investment screening in France, Official Journal of the French Republic, May 27, 2025, text 45 of 69, published May 22, 2025, available at https://www.assemblee-nationale.fr/dyn/17/rapports/cec/l17b1453_rapport-information (last accessed May 27, 2025)
260. France, National Assembly, Committee for the Evaluation and Oversight of Public Policies, Hearing of April 23, 2025, as part of the evaluation of foreign direct investment screening in France, Denis Redonnet, Deputy Director-General of the Directorate-General for Trade (DG Trade) of the European Commission, Chief Trade Enforcement Officer, responsible for Directorates F and G, accompanied by Mr. Damien Levie, Head of Unit Trade.F.4 ("Technology and Security, FDI Screening"), and Mr. Florent Herlitz, Senior Administrator in charge of the foreign direct investment screening file
261. European Union, European Court of Auditors, Special Report No. 27/2023, "Screening of foreign direct investment in the EU – The framework is in place, but significant limitations hinder effective management of security and public order risks", September 26, 2023

Notably, the EU institutions, having once regarded investment screening as a form of economic protectionism, have now aligned in recognizing the importance of such mechanisms to safeguard strategic European interests.

In response to these criticisms, the Commission introduced five initiatives [262] in 2024 aimed at enhancing the EU's economic security, including a legislative proposal to revise Regulation 2019/452. While acknowledging that the 2019 framework had met its initial objectives, namely, establishing a formal channel for Member States and the Commission to exchange information on FDIs, the proposed reform includes:

- A mandatory requirement for all Member States to implement a national FDI screening mechanism for reasons of public security and public order;
- An extension of the cooperation mechanism to include intra-EU investments by EU-based investors that are directly or indirectly controlled by entities from non-EU countries, whereas the original Regulation applied only to investors expressly originating from third countries;
- The inclusion of greenfield investments made by foreign-controlled entities in the scope of screening;
- A defined list of strategic assets and critical technologies subject to enhanced oversight.

In 2025, following interinstitutional negotiations, the European Parliament and the Council [263] reached a political agreement on a revised Regulation strengthening the EU framework for screening foreign direct investments. The new text will require all Member States to operate FDI screening mechanisms based on harmonised core rules and to assess foreign investments in a common set of sensitive and strategic sectors, including areas such as media, critical raw materials and transport infrastructure, as well as certain intra-EU transactions where the ultimate investor is established in a third country. The Regulation awaits formal adoption by the Parliament and the Council and is expected to enter into force in the first half of 2026, with application starting 18 months after its entry into force.

France's Recourse to Other Forms of International Cooperation

Beyond the European screening mechanism, French law [264] provides for additional avenues of international cooperation. Under Article R.151-17 of the French Monetary and Financial Code, the competent administrative authorities, namely, the Foreign Direct Investment Screening Office (CIEF), may engage in international cooperation to verify information provided by foreign investors, including the origin of funds.

262. European Union, European Commission, Communication from the Commission to the European Parliament and the Council – Advancing European Economic Security: Presentation of Five New Initiatives, Brussels, January 24, 2024, COM(2024) 22 final, available at https://eur-lex.europa.eu/legal-content/FR/TXT/PDF/?uri=CELEX:52024DC0022 (last accessed June 17, 2025)

263. European Union, European Commission, *Commission welcomes political agreement on strengthened EU framework for screening of foreign direct investments*, Press Release IP/25/3007, 11 December 2025, available at https://ec.europa.eu/commission/presscorner/detail/en/ip_25_3007 (last accessed 11 December 2025).

264. France, Decree No. 2019-1590 of December 31, 2019, on foreign investments in France, Official Journal of the French Republic, No. 0001, January 1, 2020, NOR: ECOT1932857D

The Minister of the Economy has emphasized[265] that his office maintains regular administrative dialogue with third countries to exchange views on FDI screening frameworks and share best practices. These exchanges, however, do not involve sharing case-specific information, which remains protected by trade secret and national security obligations, both under French law and under the domestic laws of the third countries involved.

The Minister also reiterated[266] that the Directorate General of the Treasury) (DG Trésor) represents France in all European and international forums dedicated to foreign investment screening. It participates in the European Commission's expert groups on FDI matters, as well as in the working groups of the EU Council. The CIEF serves as France's designated point of contact with the European Commission and other Member States under the EU cooperation mechanism, which became operational on October 11, 2020.

*
* *

In a context marked by growing awareness across Europe of the potential national security and strategic risks associated with foreign investments, France's domestic FDI screening regime (the "IEF mechanism") is now complemented by the EU's broader framework. The exchange of information with other Member States enables France to better detect and evaluate potentially hostile foreign investment strategies on European soil. Moreover, international cooperation, both within and outside the EU, further enhances the robustness of this risk-based assessment approach.

---

265. France, National Assembly, Written Question No. 35024 to the Minister of the Economy, Finance and Recovery, Official Journal of the National Assembly, December 15, 2020, p. 9103, by Member of Parliament MARLEIX, Olivier (Les Républicains group), ministerial reply published in the Official Journal of the National Assembly, September 28, 2021, p. 7175, reported on February 16, 2021
266. France, Ministry of the Economy, Finance and Industrial and Digital Sovereignty, Directorate General of the Treasury, Annual Report 2024, "Foreign Direct Investment Screening in France," published July 30, 2025, available at https://www.tresor.economie.gouv.fr/Articles/2025/07/30/publication-du-rapport-annuel-sur-le-controle-ief-en-2024 (last accessed July 31, 2025)

Diagram of the European screening mechanism [267]

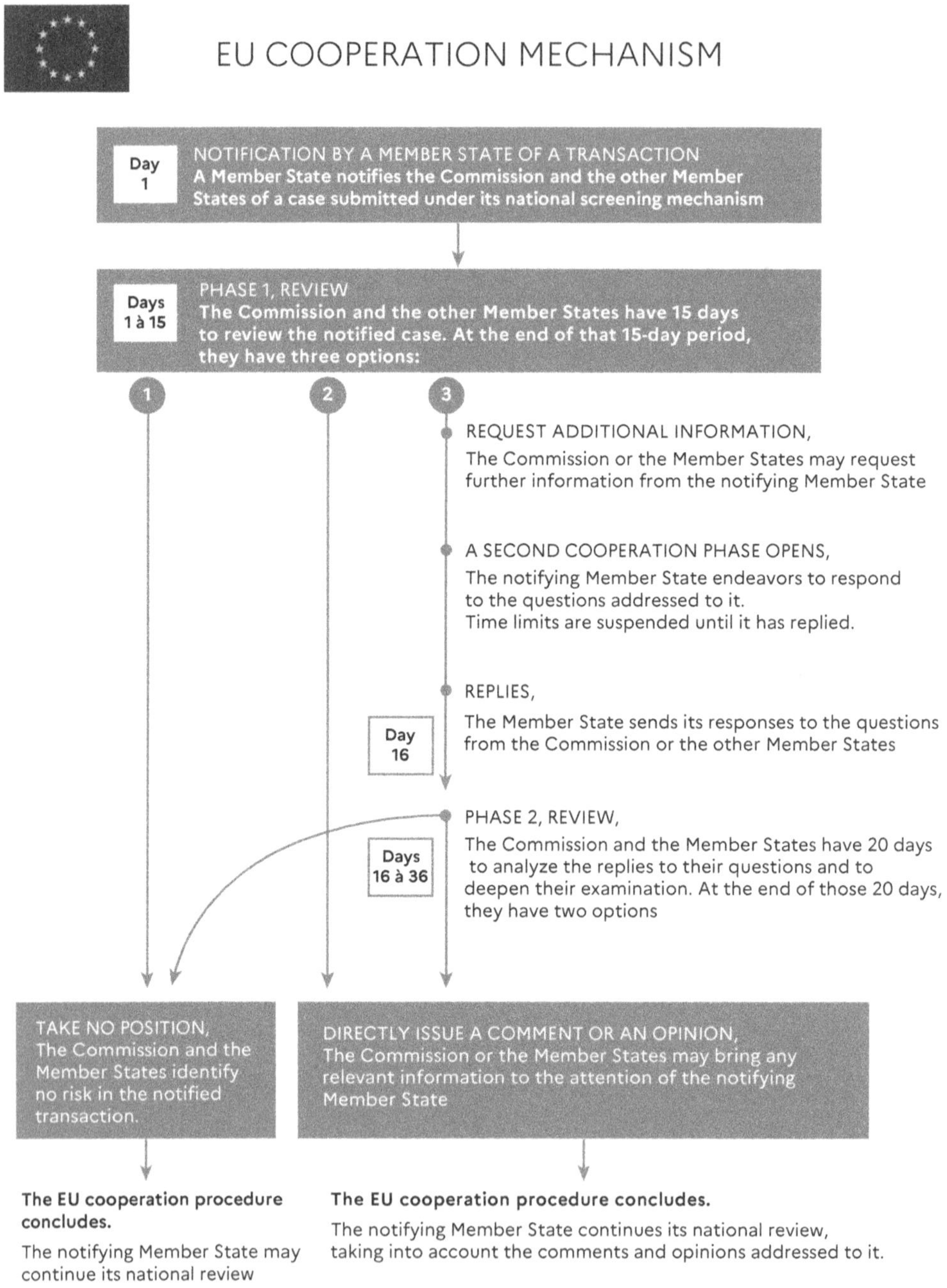

267. Diagram prepared in accordance with Articles L. 321-1 et seq. of the Code of Relations between the Public and the Administration (CRPA) – source: France, Ministry of the Economy, Finance and Industrial and Digital Sovereignty, Directorate General of the Treasury, Annual Report 2024, "Foreign Direct Investment Screening in France," published July 30, 2025, available at https://www.tresor.economie.gouv.fr/Articles/2025/07/30/publication-du-rapport-annuel-sur-le-controle-ief-en-2024 (last accessed July 31, 2025)

Chapter 7

The IEF Screening Mechanism Operates Alongside Other National Interest Protection Frameworks

The French foreign investment screening mechanism (IEF) is not the only legal tool available to the French State to safeguard national interests. As emphasized [268] by the Conseil d'État (France's highest administrative court), certain investments in specific companies, regardless of whether the investor is foreign or domestic, may threaten fundamental interests of the Nation. In such cases, the core objective of public intervention is the protection of the national interest through appropriate regulatory measures.

These national interests, often referred to as "superior," "sensitive," or "strategic", may be protected through the exercise of public authority, including via the enactment of laws and regulations that establish exceptional rights in favor of the State. These derogatory provisions grant the government legal prerogatives designed to ensure the preservation of the most critical national assets and capabilities.

This overarching approach is reflected in three other key legislative regimes in addition to the IEF mechanism:

- The regime of "specific action" (action spécifique), which is part of the government's policy as a shareholder and provides the State with enhanced rights in certain strategic companies;
- The legal framework governing sensitive exports, which regulates the transfer of dual-use or military-related technologies and goods;
- The legal regime for the protection of the Nation's scientific and technical potential (PPST), which aims to shield sensitive knowledge and research from undesirable foreign influence or exfiltration.

The purpose of this chapter is therefore to demonstrate that the IEF mechanism is only one instrument among several available to the French State in its mission to protect the national interest. In practice, these instruments are often used in a complementary manner and may be jointly mobilized when a proposed transaction raises issues of national concern. As such, all parties to a transaction that may trigger national interest considerations must anticipate and account for this broader legal and institutional context.

268. France, Council of State, Guide to Economic Policy Tools, Fact Sheet No. 20, "Protection of strategic interests in companies, 2022–2023 edition," accessed September 1st, 2025, available at https://www.conseil-etat.fr/publications-colloques/etudes/guide-des-outils-d-action-economique

State Shareholding as a Tool for Safeguarding National Interests

In addition to its authority to screen foreign direct investments, the French State also acts as a shareholder in strategic companies to safeguard the Nation's economic security. Unlike nationalizations, which confer direct control over companies through full or majority ownership, public shareholding in sensitive sectors does not seek to manage the company's operations. Rather, its purpose is to ensure that the entity does not engage in conduct contrary to France's national interest.

Through public equity stakes, France has developed sovereign investment instruments designed to protect its economic sovereignty. In this way, public finances, the so-called "main publique" or "public hand", are deployed in pursuit of the same overarching goal: the protection of the Nation's essential interests. Public investment is thus intended to play a pivotal role in the structuring of equity transactions, particularly mergers and acquisitions involving companies operating in strategic sectors.

In such contexts, the State may position itself at the negotiating table, not in its capacity as a regulator through foreign investment screening, but rather as a shareholder alongside the existing owners or the prospective purchaser of the target company. To do so, it may rely on a range of tools, including public investment vehicles and certain sovereign prerogatives that go beyond ordinary corporate law.

The Role of Bpifrance: Supporting Innovative and Strategic Enterprises

Established by Law [269] of December 31, 2012, Bpifrance is a cornerstone of France's public support policy for innovative businesses. In addition to its mission of fostering entrepreneurship and innovation, Bpifrance is regularly mobilized to support or secure companies deemed strategic by the French State acting as a shareholder. Given the overlap between its areas of intervention and those covered by France's foreign investment screening mechanism (IEF), Bpifrance is often called upon in parallel, as was the case in 2024 during the sale of Opella to the private equity fund Clayton, Dubilier & Rice (CD&R).

Bpifrance operates pursuant to an investment doctrine [270] first published in 2014, which outlines the guiding principles of its financing and equity operations, and clarifies its position as a public policy tool in service of business development, innovation, regional revitalization, and the structuring of strategic sectors and industrial value chains.

Bpifrance's action is built around four core objectives:

(i) Supporting SMEs and mid-sized firms with growth potential: Bpifrance primarily targets very small businesses (TPEs), small and medium-sized enterprises (SMEs),

269. France, Law No. 2012-1559 of January 1, 2013, on the creation of the Public Investment Bank, Official Journal of the French Republic, No. 0001, January 1, 2013, NOR: EFIX1235147L

270. France, Bpifrance, Instruction No. 2014/0042 of April 14, 2014, Bpifrance's Intervention Doctrine, available at https://www.bpifrance.fr/content/download/3499/46658/version/2/file/DoctrineBpifranceavril2014.pdf (last accessed June 27, 2025)

and intermediate-sized companies (ETIs) that are considered future leaders in their industries or value chains.

(ii) Promoting innovation: Innovation is a central priority of Bpifrance's mandate. Its support spans the entire value chain, from early-stage R&D to growth capital for innovative companies, particularly in emerging and strategic sectors such as new technologies, the environment, health, and the green and energy transitions. Many of these sectors coincide with those identified as sensitive under the French FDI screening regime .

(iii) Revitalizing local economies: Through privileged partnerships with regional governments, Bpifrance anchors its efforts in local territories, where it contributes to the preservation of industrial ecosystems and job creation. The safeguarding of industrial capabilities and know-how is also a core dimension of France's economic security policy.

(iv) Structuring strategic sectors and industrial value chains: Bpifrance plays a role in consolidating and strengthening key sectors such as aerospace, agri-food, automotive, biotechnology, cleantech and green services, rail, nuclear energy, and robotics,. In certain cases, this is achieved through the creation and management of sector-specific funds. Once again, this sector-based approach aligns closely with the logic underpinning the regulation of foreign investments in sensitive areas.

While Bpifrance operates in pursuit of the collective interest, a concept distinct from national interest, its missions often converge with the goals of France's economic security doctrine. This convergence authorizes Bpifrance to intervene when strategic assets are at stake.

This is particularly true of its equity investments in the form of seed capital, venture capital, growth capital, and buyout capital. Bpifrance's priorities are set out in a five-year strategic plan developed through consultations with representatives of the State and the bank's National Steering Committee. This plan identifies priority areas for innovation-related activities, including:

- Industrial sectors, through the "Industry Plan," which targets health, nuclear energy, and defense;
- Advanced technologies, through the "Tech Plan," which covers AI, cybersecurity, and software;
- Creative and cultural industries, and
- Greentech.

Bpifrance manages a wide range of investment funds [271] aligned with these objectives. One notable example is the Lac d'Argent Fund (LAC1), launched in 2019 at the initiative of the Minister of the Economy, Bruno Le Maire, as a strategic response to the limitations of legal FDI screening in protecting sensitive French companies. Managed by Bpifrance Investissement, a portfolio management company licensed by the French Financial Markets Authority (AMF), LAC1 is a hybrid fund that combines public

271. France, National Assembly, Committee for the Evaluation and Oversight of Public Policies, Fact-Finding Report, No. 1453, by JOLIVET F. and de LEPINAU H., Members of Parliament, on the evaluation of foreign direct investment screening in France, Official Journal of the French Republic, May 27, 2025, text 45 of 69, published May 22, 2025, available at https://www.assemblee-nationale.fr/dyn/17/rapports/cec/l17b1453_rapport-information (last accessed May 27, 2025)

and private capital, with a target size of €10 billion. Its mission is to ensure capital stability for major publicly listed French companies by supporting them through financial, technological, and environmental transitions, while defending them against activist investors. The fund is governed by an independent investment committee that operates free from political influence, in strict compliance with regulatory reporting obligations.

To date, LAC1 has made strategic minority investments in several French industrial champions, including Arkema, EssilorLuxottica, and Veolia. Through these operations, the fund seeks to deliver long-term strategic value while contributing to sound corporate governance. Its hybrid and patriotic structure exemplifies the emergence of a new form of sovereign public finance deployed in the service of national economic independence and competitiveness.

Bpifrance also invests in funds dedicated to disruptive technologies. For example, it manages the Deep Tech 2030 Fund on behalf of the French State under the France 2030 investment plan, and the Innovation Défense Fund, launched in 2021 to finance early-stage and venture capital operations involving dual-use or civilian startups developing high-potential, defense-related technologies.

The targeted sectors include energy, quantum computing, artificial intelligence, data analytics, virtual and augmented reality, simulation, connectivity, advanced materials, semiconductors, sensors and emitters, autonomous vehicles, robotics, cybersecurity, and space technologies.

In 2025, Bpifrance participated in the second €100 million fundraising round for Alice & Bob, a French leader in quantum computing. Existing investors from the first round (Elaia Partners, Breega, Supernova Invest, and Bpifrance) renewed their support, alongside new entrants such as Future French Champions, AXA Venture Partners, and the European Innovation Council.

The Role of the Government Shareholding Agency (APE): Safeguarding Deep Sovereignty[272]

Established[273] in 2004, the French State Shareholding Agency (Agence des participations de l'État, APE) was initially tasked with defending and promoting the State's equity interests, separating this function from the oversight traditionally exercised by sectoral ministries such as Transport, Culture, Defense or Energy. Its creation marked a turning point in the reassertion of the State as a shareholder in the economy, following two decades of market-driven privatizations during the 1980s and 1990s.

Over time, the APE's mission evolved from a purely patrimonial function to a broader sovereign instrument. In 2010, a State Commissioner was appointed and placed under the direct authority of the Minister of the Economy, reinforcing the

272. DUPEYRAT, op. cit.,

273. France, Decree No. 2004-963 of September 9, 2004, establishing the national service "Agence des participations de l'État" (State Holdings Agency), Official Journal of the French Republic, No. 211, September 10, 2004, text No. 5, NOR: ECOZ0400043D

agency's strategic role. A ministerial order[274] in 2012 further clarified the agency's institutional positioning within the Ministry of the Economy and Finance (MINEFI).

As the embodiment of the French shareholder-State, the APE invests equity capital in companies considered strategic by the French government, with a view to stabilizing ownership structures or supporting long-term development and transformation. It exercises the full range of prerogatives attached to shareholding, including voting rights in general meetings and influence over the composition of corporate boards. These powers enable the State to exert meaningful control and pursue sovereign interests through corporate governance.

A major shift occurred in 2014, when the government issued new guidelines defining the strategic objectives[275] of State ownership. This coincided with the adoption of Ordinance[276] of August 20, 2014, which overhauled the legal framework governing the State's shareholding activities and aimed to give the State as shareholder a level of influence comparable to that of private investors. For the first time, France formalized an investment doctrine encompassing broader objectives than the mere protection of national industrial champions.

In the field of strategic interest protection, the role of the APE has since been reinforced by the May 14, 2014 Decree[277] on foreign investment screening in France (known as the Montebourg Decree), adopted in the wake of General Electric's proposed acquisition of Alstom in April 2014. That episode, retrospectively seen as a missed opportunity, highlighted the need for greater synergy between the foreign investment screening mechanism (IEF) and the State's equity tools.

A further strategic shift occurred in 2017, in a context of constrained public finances and growing challenges linked to ecological, industrial, and technological transitions. The government decided to streamline the State's equity portfolio and refine its intervention doctrine around three priority pillars:

- companies that contribute to national sovereignty. (notably in defense and nuclear energy);
- companies performing public service missions or providing services of general interest where market regulation alone is insufficient to safeguard the public interest;
- companies facing critical financial difficulties whose failure could pose systemic risks.

---

274. France, Ministerial Order of June 29, 2012, on the procedures for the exercise of the powers of the Minister of the Economy and Finance and the Minister of Industrial Recovery concerning the national service "Agence des participations de l'État" (State Holdings Agency), Official Journal of the French Republic, No. 0151, June 30, 2012, p. 10661
275. France, Council of Ministers Communication, January 15, 2014, "The Government Shareholding Strategy," accessed June 20, 2025, available at https://www.economie.gouv.fr/files/files/directions_services/agence-participations-etat/Documents/Communiques/2014-01-15-Conseil_des_ministres-CP-Strategie_de_l'Etat_actionnaire.pdf
276. France, Ordinance No. 2014-948 of August 20, 2014, on the governance and equity transactions of publicly owned companies, Official Journal of the French Republic, No. 0194, August 23, 2014, NOR: FCPT1414784R
277. France, Decree No. 2014-479 of May 14, 2014, on foreign investments subject to prior authorization, Official Journal of the French Republic, No. 0112, May 15, 2014, p. 8062

The COVID-19 pandemic (2020) and the war in Ukraine (2022) brought sovereignty. issues back to the forefront and led to a reassessment of the State's investment doctrine, with four main considerations:

- the continued need to support businesses impacted by crisis;
- economic sovereignty. and reindustrialization imperatives;
- environmental requirements that are accelerating business model transformation;
- digital and technological disruption requiring sovereign responses.

Several emblematic equity acquisitions illustrate the new direction taken by the APE:

In June 2024 [278], as part of a broader Franco-Belgian industrial cooperation framework, the French State acquired a 10% stake in John Cockerill Defense (JCD), alongside Belgium's sovereign wealth fund SFPIM, which also took a 10% interest. This followed JCD's acquisition of Arquus (formerly Renault Trucks Defense). Anchored in a bilateral memorandum of understanding signed by the French President and the Belgian Prime Minister, the deal aimed to establish a leading joint industrial hub in ground defense systems. A shareholders' agreement ensures both States maintain control over strategic decisions and safeguard national interests.

In October 2024 [279], the APE confirmed the French State's subscription of €300 million to the capital increase of Orano, a key player in the nuclear fuel cycle. Following the transaction, the State held a 90.33% majority stake. The recapitalization supported France's nuclear energy strategy, the transition to a decarbonized economy, and long-term fuel supply security, most notably through expansion of the Georges Besse II enrichment plant at Tricastin. Japan's JNFL and MHI retained minority stakes (4.83% each), preserving a long-standing strategic partnership.

In December 2024 [280], the State acquired an 80% stake in Alcatel Submarine Networks (ASN) from Nokia. This strategic transaction aimed to reinforce France's digital sovereignty. and secure control over critical subsea communication infrastructure, key assets given that 99% of global data traffic transits through undersea cables. The agreement allows for a future increase in the State's stake to 100%, while Nokia maintains a temporary minority interest to facilitate operational transition.

In June 2025 [281], the State submitted a firm offer to acquire Atos' Advanced Computing business, covering high-performance computing and supercomputer technologies vital to

278. France, Ministry of the Economy, Finance, Industrial and Digital Sovereignty, Press Release, Paris, June 27, 2024, "The French State acquires an equity stake in the Belgian company John Cockerill Defense," accessed June 20, 2025, available at https://www.economie.gouv.fr/files/files/directions_services/agence-participations-etat/Documents/Communiques/CP_JCockerill-APE.pdf

279. France, Ministry of the Economy, Finance and Industry, Press Release No. 068, Paris, October 24, 2024, "The Government Shareholding Agency (APE) confirms the State's €300 million subscription to Orano's capital increase," accessed June 20, 2025, available at https://presse.economie.gouv.fr/lagence-des-participations-de-letat-ape-confirme-la-souscription-de-letat-a-hauteur-de-300-meur-a-laugmentation-de-capital-dorano/

280. France, Ministry of the Economy, Press Release No. 97 of 5 November 2024, "The French State acquires 80% of Alcatel Submarine Networks (ASN) to ensure the strategic control of submarine connectivity infrastructures", Official website of the Ministry of the Economy

281. France, Ministry of the Economy, Finance, Industrial and Digital Sovereignty, Press Release No. 534 of June 2, 2025, "The French State takes a major step forward in its project to acquire part of Atos Group's

the French defense and industrial base. The carve-out excluded non-strategic Vision AI activities. Other sensitive assets of the Atos group had already been placed under State protection in November 2024 via preferred shares granting veto rights over strategic decisions.

Also in June 2025[282], the Minister of the Economy, Éric Lombard, announced a €717 million public subscription to a €1.35 billion capital increase by Eutelsat. This investment raised the State's stake to 29.99%. The goal was to support Eutelsat's strategic positioning in low Earth orbit (LEO)satellite constellations, an area central to Europe's digital sovereignty. Eutelsat remains the only European operator with assets in both geostationary (GEO) and LEO orbits and plays a key role in developing the IRIS sovereign constellation. This strategic equity investment is aimed at supporting Eutelsat's expansion in the fast-growing segment of low Earth orbit (LEO) satellite constellations, a sector deemed critical to European digital sovereignty. Eutelsat is currently the only European operator with a dual presence in both geostationary orbit (GEO) and low Earth orbit (LEO), positioning it as a key pillar in the development of IRIS^2, the EU's future sovereign satellite constellation. The transaction is backed by Eutelsat's major reference shareholders, including Bharti Space, CMA CGM, and the Fonds Stratégique de Participations[283] (Strategic Investment Fund). According to the French Government, this investment represents a pivotal step in shaping Europe's space future, reaffirming that the construction of a competitive, resilient, and sovereign space industry lies at the heart of both French and European strategies for secure connectivity.

Today, the APE is France's principal public shareholder, managing a portfolio worth over €80 billion. Despite this substantial figure, its size remains relatively modest given the sovereign ambitions pursued. The portfolio remains heterogeneous, notably in publicly listed[284] companies such as EDF (83.7%), ADP (50.6%), Airbus Group (11.1%), Engie (24.1%), Safran (13.2%), Thales (25.7%), Orange (13.45%), Renault (15%), Air France/KLM (14.3%), Dexia (5.7%) and CNP (1.1%) as of June 2018.

Although the APE does not directly participate in the IEF screening procedure, it plays an incidental yet active role in cases where the protection of essential interests requires equity-based interventions. In practice, the APE may be involved when screening results lead the government to consider acquiring preferred shares in a company, thus securing strategic influence while maintaining limited capital exposure.

'Advanced Computing' business," Paris, accessed June 20, 2025, available at https://presse.economie.gouv.fr/letat-francais-franchit-une-etape-decisive-dans-son-projet-dacquisition-dune-partie-de-lactivite-advanced-computing-du-groupe-atos/

282. France, Ministry of the Economy, Finance, Industrial and Digital Sovereignty, Press Release No. 642 of June 19, 2025, "Industrial and digital sovereignty: France increases its stake in Eutelsat," Paris, accessed June 20, 2025, available at https://presse.economie.gouv.fr/souverainete-industrielle-et-numerique-la-france-renforce-sa-presence-au-capital-deutelsat/

283. The Fonds Stratégique de Participations (FSP – Strategic Investment Fund) is a long-term investment vehicle whose shareholders and board members are drawn from seven major French insurance companies: BNP Paribas Cardif, BPCE Assurances, CNP Assurances, Crédit Agricole Assurances, Groupama, Société Générale Assurances, and Suravenir.

284. France, State Shareholder Report 2024, Agence des participations de l'État, annex to the Finance Bill, October 2023, PDF, available at https://www2.assemblee-nationale.fr/static/16/pdf/Annexes_PLF/Rapport_%C3%89tat_actionnaire.pdf, last accessed June 27, 2025

Legal Framework Governing Special Rights in Strategic Sectors

When the French State becomes a shareholder, it may rely on a range of legal tools to help protect strategic assets. Most of these instruments derive from general corporate law rather than special statutory provisions. They include shareholder agreements, bespoke contractual arrangements, and preference shares.

The "Golden Share" Mechanism Under EU Law

Among the legal instruments available to the French State to safeguard strategic assets is the so-called action spécifique, or "golden share", which grants the State special rights to preserve national interests and sovereign prerogatives. This mechanism was revised in 2015 and again in 2019 to reinforce [285] the legal framework governing corporate governance and equity transactions involving companies with public capital participation.

The golden share is historically [286] rooted in the liberalization and privatization wave initiated in France during the 1980s. Beginning in 1986, the French State launched a broad privatization program, yet retained a degree of control over certain companies returned to the private sector. As Jérémie Houet [287] notes, this type of shareholding arrangement "*can be described as a security representing a portion of a company's capital that carries special rights. These rights grant the holder powers of such scope that, under normal circumstances, only a majority stake would entitle them to exert similar influence over both the shareholding structure and the management of the company.*"

The legal basis for the golden share was first established in France by Law [288] of August 6, 1986 on privatization procedures. Article 10 of that law authorized the French State to convert an ordinary share into a "specific share" (action spécifique) carrying exceptional rights. Specifically, the Minister of the Economy was empowered

285. DUPEYRAT, op. cit., pp. 158–170
286. ibid.
287. HOUET, Jean, "Golden Shares under European Union Law", Studies, Larcier Publishing, March 20, 2015, 450 p., EAN/ISSN 9782804476878
288. France, Law No. 86-912 of August 6, 1986, on the implementation procedures for the privatizations decided by Law No. 86-793 of July 2, 1986, authorizing the government to take various economic and social measures, Official Journal of the French Republic, August 7, 1986, p. 9695, Article 10: "*...A decree shall determine, for each of the concerned companies, whether the protection of national interests requires that an ordinary share held by the State be converted into a specific share endowed with all or part of the rights defined below. If so, said decree shall also pronounce this conversion. The rights that may be attached to a specific share are as follows: 1° Prior approval by the Minister of the Economy when a person, acting alone or in concert, crosses one or more thresholds set in the decree mentioned in the first paragraph above, calculated as a percentage of the share capital or voting rights; 2° The appointment to the board of directors or supervisory board, as the case may be, of one or two State representatives designated by decree, without voting rights; 3° The power to oppose, under conditions set by a decree adopted by the Conseil d'État, decisions to dispose of assets or certain types of assets of the company or its subsidiaries, or to pledge them as collateral, that may harm national interests. The institution of this share takes effect by operation of law. Except in cases involving national independence, the specific share may be definitively converted into an ordinary share by decree at any time.*"

to issue a decree requiring prior approval for any acquisition exceeding 10% of the company's share capital, if deemed necessary to protect «National:interests." Law [289] of July 19, 1993 further expanded the State's powers by allowing the appointment, by decree, of one or two non-voting State representatives to the company's board of directors or supervisory board, as applicable. It also introduced a veto right, exercisable under a Council of State decree, over asset transfers or the use of assets as collateral when such transactions might undermine national interests [290].

The European Commission has long scrutinized golden share regimes. In the EU internal market, freedom of establishment and the free movement of capital are considered fundamental principles. In a 1997 communication [291], the Commission warned Member States that "restrictions on intra-Community investment and discriminatory measures are incompatible with the Treaty provisions on capital movements and the right of establishment, unless they fall within one of the exceptions provided for in the Treaty. By contrast, non-discriminatory measures are permissible if they are based on objective, stable, and publicly known criteria and if they are justified by overriding reasons of general interest. In all cases, the principle of proportionality must be respected."

The Commission also encourages Member States to proactively notify any potential restrictions on capital flows or establishment rights. Nevertheless, it reaffirms that the decision to privatize a public undertaking lies within the exclusive economic policy competence of each Member State.

The Court of Justice of the European Union (CJEU) has consistently invalidated golden share regimes that are deemed discriminatory. Its case law [292] distinguishes between discriminatory measures, those restricting foreign investors' access to capital or to managerial control, and non-discriminatory measures. The Court closely examines whether national rules impose foreign ownership thresholds or require prior governmental approval for share acquisitions, or whether both mechanisms are used in combination. Such measures are generally held to constitute serious infringements of fundamental Treaty freedoms and are therefore prohibited.

289. France, Law No. 93-923 of July 19, 1993, on privatization, Official Journal of the French Republic, No. 166, July 21, 1993, p. 10255, NOR: ECOX9300080L

290. France, National Assembly, Report, No. 2498, January 19, 2015, FERRAND, Richard, General Rapporteur, Member of Parliament, on behalf of the special committee responsible for examining, following the initiation of the accelerated procedure, Bill No. 2447 on growth and economic activity

291. European Union, European Commission, Communication of July 19, 1997, on certain legal aspects concerning intra-Community investment, Official Journal of the European Communities, No. C 220/15, July 19, 1997, pp. 15–18, Document 31997Y0719(03)

292. European Union, Court of Justice of the European Communities, Commission v Portuguese Republic, Case C-367/98, Judgment of June 4, 2002, para. 37, ECLI:EU:C:2002:326
European Union, Court of Justice of the European Communities, Commission v French Republic, Case C-483/99, Judgment of June 4, 2002, para. 36, ECLI:EU:C:2002:327
European Union, Court of Justice of the European Communities, Commission v Kingdom of Belgium, Case C-503/99, Judgment of June 4, 2002, para. 37, ECLI:EU:C:2002:328
European Union, Court of Justice of the European Communities, Commission v Kingdom of Spain, Case C-463/00, Judgment of May 13, 2003, para. 52, ECLI:EU:C:2003:272
European Union, Court of Justice of the European Communities, Commission v United Kingdom, Case C-98/01, Judgment of May 13, 2003, para. 39, ECLI:EU:C:2003:273
European Union, Court of Justice of the European Communities, Trummer and Mayer, Case C-222/97, Judgment of May 16, 1999, paras. 20–21, ECLI:EU:C:1999:143

France was found in breach of EU law in this respect. In its judgment[293] of June 4, 2002 in Commission of the European Communities v. French Republic (Case C-483/99), the Court held that the special rights held by the French Minister of the Economy in the former public oil company Elf-Aquitaine, including prior approval for shareholding threshold crossings and veto rights over the transfer or pledge of company shares, were not justified on public security grounds. Although the Court acknowledged that concerns relating to public policy or security may, in certain circumstances, warrant a Member State's influence over formerly public undertakings operating in strategic sectors, it held that such influence may not be justified by reference to Article 295 of the EC Treaty (now Article 345 TFEU) relating to ownership regimes. In short, property regimes cannot serve as a basis for derogating from fundamental Treaty freedoms such as the free movement of capital.

However, this strict stance is not absolute. Both the Commission and the Court recognize that derogations may be permitted under Articles 56 and 63 of the Treaty on the Functioning of the European Union (TFEU), provided they are based on legitimate public order or public security grounds and satisfy the principle of proportionality. On that basis, the Court upheld the Belgian golden share regime, emphasizing that it was non-discriminatory, justified by an overriding reason of general interest, clearly defined by law, and proportionate to the stated objective.

The 2015 Reform Aligns French Law with European Union Requirements

It is in light of these considerations that France undertook its first reform of the "golden share" mechanism (action spécifique) in 2015. Aware of the need to bring its domestic legislation into compliance with European Union law, France revised the rules governing special rights in the context of the enactment of Law[294] No. 2015-990 of August 6, 2015, on Growth, Economic Activity, and Equal Opportunity. The impact assessment[295] accompanying the draft legislation recalled that preferential rights granted by Member States to retain a degree of control over privatized companies operating in major or sensitive strategic sectors may constitute restrictions on the fundamental freedoms enshrined in the Treaties, insofar as such rights are liable to hinder or reduce the attractiveness of direct investments from operators based in other Member States. However, such mechanisms are not inherently unlawful under EU law.

The 2015 legislation introduced a graded approach to the rights attached to the golden share, depending on the nature of the interests at stake. The most stringent regime is now restricted to the defense sector. Under this framework, the executive

293. European Union, Court of Justice of the European Communities, Commission v French Republic, Case C-483/99, Judgment of June 4, 2002, ECLI:EU:C:2002:327

294. France, Law No. 2015-990 of August 6, 2015, on growth, economic activity and equal opportunities, Official Journal of the French Republic, No. 0181, August 7, 2015, p. 13537, NOR: EINX1426821L

295. France, National Assembly, Bill No. 2447 of December 10, 2014, on growth and economic activity, Impact Assessment, Volume 2, NOR: EINX1426821L / Bleue-1

may, on a case-by-case basis, determine by decree which of the prerogatives enumerated by statute shall apply to a specific golden share.

The new legal framework for golden shares, as established by the 2015 law [296], is consistent with EU requirements. Notably, the reform removed the previous reference to the "protection of national interests," replacing it with language aligned with EU law: "the protection of the essential interests of the country in matters of public order, public health, public security, or national defense." This new wording is better tailored to the legal standards of the European Union.

Furthermore, to ensure consistency with EU case law, the amended Article 31-1 of the French Privatization Act now stipulates that "the rights attached to a special share shall in each case be defined in such a way as to be necessary, appropriate, and proportionate to the objectives pursued."

Under the 2015 framework, the golden share may confer three types of rights on the State. These rights include:

The 2015 law provides that a golden share may confer on the State the following three types of rights:

1° Prior approval by the Minister of the Economy for threshold crossings
The prior authorization of the Minister in charge of the Economy may be required where a person, acting alone or in concert, crosses one or more of the thresholds set forth in Article L. 233-7, I of the French Commercial Code. The specific thresholds subject to approval are determined by the decree establishing the golden share. A distinct threshold may be set for acquisitions made by foreign persons or entities under foreign control, within the meaning of Article L. 233-3 of the same Code, acting alone or in concert. Such authorization may only be withheld if the proposed transaction is likely to harm the essential interests of the country for which the golden share was instituted.

2° Appointment of a non-voting government representative
The golden share may confer the right to appoint a representative of the French State, without voting rights, to the board of directors, the supervisory board, or the equivalent deliberative body of the company, as applicable. The appointment is made in accordance with the procedures laid down in the decree establishing the golden share.

3° Veto power over certain asset transfers
The State may be granted the power to oppose, under regulatory conditions, any decision involving the transfer or pledging of company assets, or certain categories of such assets, by the company or its subsidiaries, where such transactions are likely to affect the essential interests of the country.

296. France, Law No. 2015-990 of August 6, 2015, on growth, economic activity and equal opportunities, Article 186, Official Journal of the French Republic, No. 0181, August 7, 2015, p. 13537, NOR: EINX1426821L

The Golden Share Regime Is Strengthened for Companies Linked to National Security

The legal framework applicable to golden shares is reinforced when it comes to companies operating in sectors connected to national security. The new Article 186 of the 2015 law introduces a specific provision targeting undertakings whose activities fall within the scope of Articles 55, 56, and 223 of the Treaty establishing the European Community, namely, activities involving the exercise of public authority, public security, public health, or national defense. In the case of such companies, any shareholding exceeding 5% acquired by foreign natural or legal persons, or by entities under foreign control, as defined in Article L. 233-3 of the French Commercial Code, acting alone or in concert, is subject to prior approval by the Minister in charge of the Economy.

A similar provision was initially included in the draft legislation submitted to the Conseil d'État (Council of State), which ultimately recommended its removal in favor of the general prior approval procedure laid down in paragraph 4 of the same article, applicable to various thresholds, including the 5% threshold.

The State may therefore choose between the general authorization regime and this sector-specific mechanism. The 2015 law [297] reiterates that "the institution of a golden share takes effect by operation of law. Except in cases involving national independence, the golden share may at any time be definitively converted into an ordinary share by decree." Accordingly, no amendment to the company's articles of association is required for the golden share to be legally effective.

However, this ministerial discretion is curtailed where national independence is at stake, a phrase that is both particularly forceful and relatively vague. It constitutes a constitutional reference, as Article 5 of the French Constitution designates the President of the Republic as the guarantor of "national independence, territorial integrity, and compliance with treaties."

Speculatively, one may wonder whether this wording implies that the President of the Republic could invoke this constitutional responsibility to direct the Minister of the Economy to block the conversion of a golden share into an ordinary share.

The 2019 Reform Reinforces the Protection of National Interests

During the parliamentary review of the PACTE Act, it became apparent that the scope of application for the French State's golden shares was overly narrow. The Government observed that, although golden shares allow the State to maintain a degree of control over strategic companies, they had in practice been used in only a limited number of cases. It therefore concluded that protecting strategic enterprises required a broader approach, one that could no longer rely solely on majority ownership stakes.

297. France, Law No. 2015-990 of August 6, 2015, on growth, economic activity and equal opportunities, Official Journal of the French Republic, No. 0181, August 7, 2015, p. 13537, NOR: EINX1426821L

Accordingly, the French Government undertook a second reform of the golden share regime in 2019. Article 154 of the PACTE Act[298] amended Article 31-1 of Ordinance[299] of August 20, 2014, on the governance and capital transactions of State-owned companies, which had been introduced by Article 186 of Law[300] of August 6, 2015.

In the explanatory memorandum[301] to the 2019 legislation, the Government reiterated that golden shares allow the State to retain control over sensitive assets held by companies operating in strategically important sectors, particularly in cases of State divestiture. This mechanism was not new. The Government further acknowledged that such preferential rights constitute a derogation from the EU principles of free movement of capital and freedom of establishment, and can only be justified under the exceptions provided by the Treaty on the Functioning of the European Union (TFEU), which allows Member States to restrict these freedoms for certain public interest reasons. Under EU law, a golden share may only be justified where it serves "the protection of the essential interests of the country in matters of public order, public health, public security, or national defense."

In this regard, the case law of the Court of Justice of the European Union (CJEU) requires that any such measures, as well as the procedures for their adoption, must be non-discriminatory, justified by an objective of general interest, and proportionate to the aim pursued. The principles of necessity and proportionality are thus central. It was with a view to strict compliance with EU law and CJEU jurisprudence that the Government proposed to revise the golden share regime.

Additionally, the Government emphasized that this measure is fully consistent with the broader policy communicated to investors: foreign investment is welcome, and France believes in the economic benefits of open markets. However, foreign investors must understand that their operations must comply with French rules and sovereign interests, just as they must in other countries, even those most favorable to free trade. Market openness only makes sense when it is governed by clear rules that define both its benefits and its potential limits. The golden share is therefore presented as a targeted instrument, used only when strictly necessary, and with rights that are proportionate to the public interest objective pursued. It represents a pact of trust between the State and economic actors, intended to strengthen the protection of strategic assets in the interest of both the Nation and the companies concerned.

First, the PACTE Act[302] extended the possibility of instituting a golden share even outside the context of a State divestment, as had previously been required by the first

298. France, Law No. 2019-486 of May 22, 2019, on Business Growth and Transformation, Official Journal of the French Republic, No. 0119, May 23, 2019, NOR: ECOT1810669L

299. France, Ordinance No. 2014-948 of August 20, 2014, on the governance and capital transactions of publicly owned companies, Official Journal of the French Republic, No. 0194, August 23, 2014, NOR: FCPT1414784R

300. France, Law No. 2015-990 of August 6, 2015, on growth, economic activity and equal opportunities, Official Journal of the French Republic, No. 0181, August 7, 2015, p. 13537, NOR: EINX1426821L

301. France, National Assembly, Bill No. 1088 of 18 June 2018 on the Growth and Transformation of Companies (PACTE Act), Explanatory Memorandum, 19 June 2018, consulted on 9 May 2024, available at https://www.assemblee-nationale.fr/dyn/15/textes/l15b1088_projet-loi#D_non_amendable_1

302. France, Law No. 2019-486 of May 22, 2019, on Business Growth and Transformation, Official Journal of the French Republic, No. 0119, May 23, 2019, NOR: ECOT1810669L

paragraph of Article 31-1 of the aforementioned Ordinance. This amendment enables enhanced protection of strategic companies in which the State or Bpifrance holds a minority interest, provided that such a measure is justified by "the protection of the essential interests of the country in matters of public order, public health, public security, or national defense" and that it remains strictly proportionate to that objective. The law expressly targets companies engaged in activities covered by Article L. 151-3, I of the French Monetary and Financial Code.

From the Government's perspective, the earlier version of the law unduly limited the State's ability to safeguard its strategic assets by conditioning the creation of a golden share on a downward crossing of a shareholding threshold (one-third, one-half, or two-thirds of the capital). Legally, however, neither constitutional law nor EU law requires such a trigger event: the only relevant legal standards for instituting a golden share are the necessity and proportionality of the rights attached to it. From a policy standpoint as well, the prior threshold requirement constrained the use of golden shares to cases in which the State already held a substantial stake, thereby preventing the protection of certain strategic firms in which the State's participation was more limited.

The PACTE Act[303] introduced a new form of golden share (action spécifique[304]) that may be established under the following conditions:

(i) in the capital structure of any company listed in the annex to the decree establishing the French State Shareholding Agency (Agence des participations de l'État, or APE), as it stood on January 1, 2018, irrespective of the level of State ownership;

(ii) in any publicly traded company in which Bpifrance or one of its subsidiaries held at least 5% of the share capital as of January 1, 2018. Where such companies do not have their registered office in France, a golden share may be established instead in their French-incorporated subsidiaries. This provision addresses the need to strengthen the protection of assets essential to French sovereignty., even as international industrial cooperation remains necessary in many strategic sectors.

Secondly, the PACTE Act clarified the rights attached to golden shares. While the three existing prerogatives introduced by the 2015 reform were retained, two clarifications were made:

(i) The definition of "transfer" (cession) was refined to explicitly encompass all transactions that may affect strategic assets protected under a golden share arrangement, including intragroup restructurings. This ensures that implementing decrees for golden shares can address any reorganization that may, deliberately or otherwise, circumvent State prerogatives or exclude protected assets from the scope of protection. Both the former and revised legal language cover tangible and intangible assets, a key point to ensure the inclusion of intellectual property rights within the scope of protection.

(ii) The law also specified the conditions under which the Minister of the Economy may access the information necessary to exercise rights associated with the golden share. In particular, this enables the Minister to assess the broader economic and

303. France, Law No. 2019-486 of May 22, 2019, on Business Growth and Transformation, Official Journal of the French Republic, No. 0119, May 23, 2019, NOR: ECOT1810669L

304. DUPEYRAT, op. cit., pp. 168–173

social environment surrounding the protected assets, including their territorial connection to France and their structural integrity. Importantly, the categories of information subject to disclosure are not exhaustive.

Finally, the rules governing the modification of a golden share over time were clarified to provide predictability to investors and stakeholders. Henceforth:

(i) Golden shares may be amended during their lifespan, regardless of the entity in which they were initially established. As justifications for the protection of strategic assets evolve over time, due to technological innovation and changes in the geopolitical or economic environment, the rights associated with a golden share may be increased or reduced, provided such changes meet the legal standards of necessity and proportionality in light of the public interest objectives pursued.

(ii) Each golden share is subject to periodic review by the French administration with respect to the companies involved. Beyond the strict conditions required for its initial establishment, the State undertakes to re-evaluate at least every five years the necessity and relevance of the decree establishing the golden share. This five-year review ensures that protection measures remain both adequate and proportionate to the underlying public interest. For instance, if a company involved in national defense sees certain technologies become commoditized while others emerge as critical to national sovereignty, the French authorities will reduce the protection for the former and strengthen safeguards for the latter. The quinquennial review serves as a formal mechanism to ensure such adjustments are implemented.

The Options Available to the French State as Shareholder: Special Shares, Preferred Shares, Shareholders' Agreements and Strategic Safeguard Conventions

The scope of the French State's equity holdings may be identified through the list of 84 entities[305] managed by the French Government Shareholding Agency (Agence

305. 1. Air and Airport Transport : Aéroport de Bordeaux-Mérignac, Aéroport de La Réunion-Roland Garros, Aéroport de Marseille-Provence, Aéroport de Montpellier-Méditerranée, Aéroport de Strasbourg-Entzheim, Aéroport de Toulouse-Blagnac, Aéroport Martinique-Aimé Césaire, Aéroports de Paris (ADP), Société aéroportuaire de Guadeloupe Pôle Caraïbes.
2. Rail and Urban Transport : Société nationale SNCF, Société des chemins de fer luxembourgeois, RATP.
3. Road Transport and Infrastructure Concessions : Caisse nationale des autoroutes, Société concessionnaire française pour la construction et l'exploitation du tunnel routier sous le Mont-Blanc (ATMB), Société des autoroutes Rhône-Alpes (AREA), Société française du tunnel routier du Fréjus (SFTRF).
4. Maritime, Inland Waterway, and Port Infrastructure Transport : Compagnie générale maritime et financière (CGMF), Grand port maritime de Bordeaux, Grand port maritime de Dunkerque, Grand port maritime de la Guadeloupe, Grand port maritime de la Guyane, Grand port maritime de la Martinique, Grand port maritime de La Réunion, Grand port maritime de La Rochelle, Grand port maritime de Marseille, Grand port maritime de Nantes Saint-Nazaire, Grand port fluvio-maritime de l'Axe – Seine, Société internationale de la Moselle.
5. Defense, Security and Sovereignty : Airbus Group SE, Dassault Aviation, Défense conseil international (DCI), GIAT Industries SAS, KNDS NV, Naval Group, Odas, Sofema, SNPE SAS, Société technique pour l'énergie atomique, Thales, TSA SAS.
6. Energy and Strategic Resources : Areva, Électricité de France (EDF), ENGIE, Eramet, Eurenco Holding SAS, Orano.

des participations de l'État, APE), in particular as updated by the Decree [306] of 3 November 2023, which amended the annex to the Decree of 9 September 2004, as well as through the APE's annual report [307].

Within this list, the State exercises different types of shareholder prerogatives depending on the specific national interest it seeks to protect. These include the holding of special shares (actions spécifiques) or preferred shares (actions de préférence), as well as the implementation of shareholders' agreements and conventions for the protection of national strategic interests entered into between the State and the relevant entities.

The French State currently holds a special share in six companies:

—Thales Group [308]: A global leader in high-technology solutions for the defense and security sectors. Some of its technologies are deemed essential to national sovereignty and are therefore subject to specific safeguards. The special share entitles the State to require prior approval from the Minister of the Economy for any direct or indirect crossing of thresholds representing one-tenth or a multiple of one-tenth of the company's capital or voting rights. To date, all such threshold crossings have been approved, including Dassault Aviation's increased stake in Thales in 2009. The State also has the right to appoint a non-voting representative to the board of directors and to veto the disposal or pledge of strategic assets defined by decree. Notably, no such veto has been exercised since the establishment of this special share.

—Herakles [309] (now Safran Ceramics): A subsidiary of the Safran Group, acting as its R&D center for high-temperature composite materials with critical applications in

7. Finance, Public Investment and Restructuring : Bpifrance EPIC, Caisse nationale des autoroutes, Consortium de réalisation (CDR), Dexia, FSI Equation SAS, SOGEPA, Société de prise de participation de l'État (SPPE).
8. Audiovisual, Culture and Media : Arte France, France Médias Monde, France Télévisions, Radio France.
9. Technologies, Telecommunications and Digital : IN Groupe, Orange.
10. Industry and Shipbuilding : Chantiers de l'Atlantique.
11. Automotive and Civil Aeronautics : Renault, Safran.
12. Public Services, Logistics and Postal Sector : La Poste, Semmaris.
13. Health and Biotechnology : Laboratoire français du fractionnement et des biotechnologies (LFB).
14. Gaming and Leisure : La Française des jeux, Casino d'Aix-les-Bains.
15. Housing and Planning : Société pour le logement intermédiaire SAS.
16. Currency and Secure Printing : La Monnaie de Paris, IN Groupe.
17. Technical and Diplomatic Cooperation : Civipol, Odas.
18. Intermodal Transport / Territorial Policy : Fonds pour le développement d'une politique intermodale des transports dans le massif alpin (FDPITMA).

306. France, Decree No. 2023-1017 of November 3, 2023, amending Decree No. 2004-963 of September 9, 2004, establishing the national service with specific competence "Agence des participations de l'État", Official Journal of the French Republic, No. 0257, November 5, 2023, NOR: ECOA2325244D

307. France, Government Shareholding Agency (APE), Report on the State as Shareholder 2024, Annex to the Draft Finance Bill for 2024, October 17, 2023, accessed May 9, 2024, available at https://www.budget.gouv.fr/documentation/jaunes-budgetaires-2024/rapport-relatif-letat-actionnaire

308. France, Decree No. 97-190 of March 4, 1997, establishing a specific share held by the State in the capital of Thomson CSF, Official Journal of the French Republic, No. 54, March 5, 1997, p. 3484, NOR: ECOT9751571D

309. France, Decree No. 2011-268 of March 14, 2011, establishing a specific share held by the State in the capital of SNPE Matériaux Énergétiques, Official Journal of the French Republic, No. 0062, March 15, 2011, p. 4674, NOR: EFIT1105845D

solid propulsion. These technologies are considered essential to France's sovereignty. and nuclear deterrent capabilities.

—Engie[310]: In this energy group, the State holds a right to oppose any decision to sell or pledge strategic assets located within French territory, such as natural gas transmission pipelines, gas distribution infrastructure, underground gas storage facilities, and liquefied natural gas terminals. These infrastructures are considered vital for the continuity and security of France's gas supply.

—KNDS[311] (formerly Nexter Systems SA): A manufacturer of medium- and large-caliber weapon systems and munitions. The special share is used to ensure the security of supply and the preservation of innovation capacity in this strategic sector.

—Eramet SA[312]: A major mining and metallurgical company and one of the world's leading producers of alloy metals such as nickel and manganese, which are used to enhance steel properties, along with high-performance alloys and specialty steels used in industries such as aerospace, energy, and tooling.

—Aubert & Duval SAS[313]: A global leader in high-performance steels, superalloys, titanium, and aluminum, and a strategic supplier to the aerospace sector.

The French State[314] also holds preferred shares[315] in the following companies:

—ADIT (Agence pour la Diffusion de l'Information Technologique), the European leader in strategic intelligence, risk prevention and management, regional economic intelligence, and business diplomacy;

—Aubert & Duval SAS, a French metallurgical company supplying high-performance alloys and long products used in the aerospace, defense, energy, tooling, motorsport, and medical sectors;

—ArianeGroup SAS, a joint venture that designs and manufactures ballistic missiles and Ariane launchers, ensuring sovereign access to space for France and Europe;

---

310. France, Decree No. 2007-1790 of December 20, 2007, establishing a specific share held by the State in the capital of Gaz de France SA, Official Journal of the French Republic, No. 0296, December 21, 2007, p. 20659, NOR: ECET0773708D

311. France, Decree No. 2015-1586 of December 4, 2015, establishing a specific share held by the State in the capital of Nexter Systems SA, Official Journal of the French Republic, No. 0283, December 6, 2015, p. 22496, NOR: FCPA1528253D

312. France, Decree No. 2022-206 of February 18, 2022, establishing a specific share in the capital of Eramet SA, Official Journal of the French Republic, No. 0043, February 20, 2022, NOR: ECOA2130115D. The ordinary share held by the State in the capital of Eramet SA was converted into a specific share in order to protect France's essential interests in the field of materials critical to national defense needs in the aeronautics, naval, land and nuclear sectors, notably with respect to the preservation of innovation, design and production capacities, as well as the security of supply of such materials.

313. France, Decree No. 2022-1182 of August 25, 2022, establishing a specific share in the capital of Aubert & Duval SAS, Official Journal of the French Republic, No. 0198, August 27, 2022, NOR: ECOA2217072D

314. France, Ministry of the Economy, Finance, Industrial and Digital Sovereignty, Agence des participations de l'État, "2022–2023 Activity Report," October 17, 2023, accessed September 1st, 2025, available at https://www.economie.gouv.fr/files/2024-02/REA23_RA_vf.pdf?v=1715076968

315. France, Commercial Code, Article L. 228-11: "*At the time of the company's formation or during its existence, preferred shares may be issued, with or without voting rights, and carrying special rights of any kind, whether temporary or permanent." The preference may be financial (e.g., special dividend rights) or political (e.g., enhanced voting or information rights). It may be positive (granting an additional right) or negative (restricting or eliminating a right), with no requirement for a balance between advantages and disadvantages. Preferred shares may be issued by all types of joint-stock companies, whether listed or not.*"

—Bpifrance SA, France's public investment bank, whose mission is to finance and support the development of French enterprises;
—Compagnie industrielle des lasers [316] (CILAS), a subsidiary of MBDA and Safran Electronics & Defense, specialized in the development and production of high-tech military laser-optics systems;
—Exxelia International SAS [317], a designer and manufacturer of high-reliability passive components and subsystems for critical functions and markets. On August 3, 2023, the Ministry of the Economy announced [318] that the French State had converted its ordinary share into a preferred share, thereby finalizing the process to secure its strategic interests following the acquisition of Exxelia by the U.S.-based group Heico;
—France Donges-Metz [319], a company operating petroleum pipelines;
—GEAST [320], formerly a joint venture between General Electric and Alstom in the field of civilian nuclear power. On October 2, 2018, Alstom's stake was sold to General Electric. The State retained a preferred share granting it veto rights over strategic decisions likely to affect French national interests;
—Safran Ceramics, a subsidiary of Safran and part of the former Herakles group, active in the French aerospace industry;
—Société nationale maritime Corse Méditerranée (SNCM), formerly Compagnie générale transméditerranéenne (CGTM), a French maritime company operating ferry and mixed cargo-passenger services between mainland France and Corsica, Sardinia, Algeria, and Tunisia;
—Société de financement local (SFIL), a public development bank established on February 1, 2013, to ensure stable financing for local public entities in France;
—Société Le Nickel [321] (SLN), a New Caledonia-based company and subsidiary of Eramet, the world's leading producer of ferronickel;
—Solinter Holding [322], a real estate investment company.

---

316. France, Ministerial Order of February 15, 2022, authorizing the acquisition by the State of an equity stake in Compagnie industrielle des lasers (CILAS), Official Journal of the French Republic, No. 0061, March 13, 2022, text No. 16, NOR: ECOA2205013A
317. France, Ministerial Order of March 24, 2023, authorizing the acquisition by the State of an equity stake in Exxelia International SAS, Official Journal of the French Republic, No. 0075, March 29, 2023, text No. 9, NOR: ECOA2306736A
318. France, Ministry of the Economy, Finance, Industrial and Digital Sovereignty, Press Release No. 1099, "The State converts the share it holds in the capital of Exxelia International into a preferred share," Paris, August 29, 2023, accessed May 9, 2024, available at https://presse.economie.gouv.fr/29082023-letat-transforme-laction-quil-detient-au-capital-de-la-societe-exxelia-international-en-action-de-preference/
319. France, Ministerial Order of January 5, 2022, authorizing the acquisition by the State of an equity stake in Société Française Donges-Metz, Official Journal of the French Republic, No. 0015, January 19, 2022, text No. 11, NOR: ECOA2138625A
320. France, Ministerial Order of October 1, 2015, authorizing the acquisition of a share in the company GEAST, Official Journal of the French Republic, No. 0233, October 8, 2015, text No. 16, NOR: FCPA1522494A
321. France, Ministerial Order of July 6, 2016, authorizing the acquisition of a share in the company Le Nickel-SLN, Official Journal of the French Republic, No. 0161, July 12, 2016, text No. 16, NOR: FCPA1618468A
322. France, Ministerial Order of April 18, 2016, authorizing the acquisition of a share in the company Solinter Holding, Official Journal of the French Republic, No. 0095, April 22, 2016, text No. 18, NOR: FCPA1608221A

The State may also enter into shareholder agreements to safeguard national interests.

To protect strategic sectors, the French government may rely on contractual or corporate rights, including rights granted under a company's bylaws or via shareholder agreements [323] with the company or its partners. As noted by former Minister Michel Sapin [324], "these agreements, often confidential, are far more decisive than the mere level of ownership." A shareholder holding only one-third of a company's capital may obtain a veto over strategic decisions, such as employment, technology transfers, or relocations, while a majority shareholder may voluntarily forgo certain prerogatives.

Typically, shareholder agreements entered into by the State include three types of clauses [325]:

—Governance-related clauses, which may require company executives to notify the State in advance of specific decisions or to obtain its prior approval for actions exceeding defined thresholds;

—Transfer and capital-related clauses, which may impose restrictions or obligations concerning the transfer of shares. These include:

- approval clauses (requiring the consent of other shareholders before selling shares),
- preemption rights (granting priority in acquiring shares being sold),
- tag-along rights (allowing minority shareholders to join in the sale under the same terms),
- and liquidity clauses (defining exit strategies, including the option for investors to mandate a financial advisor if the company is not sold or listed within a set timeframe);

—Clauses relating to shareholder-executives, which may impose obligations or grant specific rights to shareholders holding key operational positions. For instance, "bad leaver" clauses impose penalties if a manager leaves the company under certain conditions.

Examples of known shareholder agreements include the following strategic companies:

—Thales: agreement [326] dated December 28, 2006 between TSA and Alcatel-Lucent, with Dassault joining via a subsequent agreement effective May 19, 2009, replicating key

323. DUPEYRAT, op. cit., pp. 170–173

324. France, National Assembly, Committee Report No. 39, March 22, 2018, Fact-Finding Committee on State Decisions in Industrial Policy in Light of Recent Mergers, Particularly in the Cases of Alstom, Alcatel, and STX, and on Means to Protect Strategic French Industrial Assets in a Globalized Economy, Hearing of Mr. Michel Sapin, accessed September 1st, available at https://www.assemblee-nationale.fr/dyn/15/comptes-rendus/cepolind/l15cepolind1718039_compte-rendu

325. France, National Assembly, Report No. 897 rect., April 19, 2018, MARLEIX, Olivier (Chair), KASBARIAN, Guillaume (Rapporteur), Members of Parliament, submitted on behalf of the fact-finding committee on State decisions in industrial policy in light of recent mergers, particularly in the cases of Alstom, Alcatel and STX, and on means to protect national industrial flagships in a globalized economy, Volume 1, accessed September 1st, 2025, available at https://www.assemblee-nationale.fr/dyn/15/rapports/cepolind/l15b0897-ti_rapport-enquete

326. France, Ministry of the Economy, Finance and Industry, Commission for Equity Interests and Transfers, Opinion No. 2006-A.C.-6 of December 28, 2006, on a capital increase of Thales reserved for Alcatel-Lucent, Official Journal of the French Republic, No. 3, January 4, 2007, text No. 104, NOR: ECOT0651088V

provisions of the original November 18, 1999 shareholder pact between Alcatel, Thales, and Groupe Industriel Marcel Dassault (GIMD);
—Airbus Group: shareholder agreement between GZBV (Germany), SEPI (Spain), and Sogepa (France);
—Dassault Aviation: shareholder agreement [327] concluded on June 21, 2013 between the State, Airbus, and EADS;
—Dassault Aviation: separate bilateral convention [328] between the French State and GIMD, signed in 2014;
—PSA Group (now Stellantis): shareholder agreement effective April 29, 2014.

The State may also enter into strategic interest protection agreements, including:
—Thales: Strategic Interest Protection Agreement;
—Safran: Agreement on the Protection of Strategic and Defense Assets, signed December 21, 2004 with Sagem and SNECMA; amended on March 31, 2011;
—Airbus Group: National Security Agreement with the French State;
—Airbus Group: Contract concerning ballistic missile programs;
—MBDA: Agreement concluded between Airbus, MBDA, and the French State;
—KNDS (formerly Nexter): Convention [329] between the French State and Honosthor (involving Nexter and KMW).

In conclusion, equity stakes enable the French State to intervene proportionately to protect national interests. This shareholder "toolbox" complements the FDI screening mechanism (dispositif IEF), which serves the same objective of safeguarding national interests but applies exclusively to foreign investment transactions.

Parties to a transaction not subject to FDI screening should nonetheless be aware that the State may still enter the company's capital via the special share mechanism.

Regulation of sensitive exports

• The Regulation of Sensitive Export Controls

Unlike the French FDI Screening Mechanism (dispositif IEF), which can be broadly characterized as seeking to determine whether the State has legitimate grounds to refuse a foreign investor access to a domestic company based on national interest considerations, the regulatory regime governing the export of sensitive goods is, by its very nature, prohibitive. It operates on the inverse logic: the default is prohibition, and the core question becomes whether the State has legitimate grounds to authorize the export of strategic or sensitive materials to non-EU countries.

---

327. France, Ministry of Defense and Ministry of the Economy, Finance, Industrial and Digital Sovereignty, Press Release No. 106/216, "The State announces the signing of an agreement with Groupe Industriel Marcel Dassault, majority shareholder of Dassault Aviation," Paris, November 28, 2014, accessed September 1st, 2025, available at https://www.economie.gouv.fr/files/files/directions_services/agence-participations-etat/L'Etat_annonce_la_signature_d'une_convention_avec_le_Groupe_Industriel_Marcel_Dassault%2C_actionnaire_majoritaire_de_Dassault_Aviation.pdf

328. Ibid.

329. France, Ministry of Finance and Public Accounts, Commission for Equity Interests and Transfers, Opinion No. 2015–A.C.–4 of November 25, 2015, on the transfer of Nexter Systems to the private sector, Official Journal of the French Republic, No. 0279, December 2, 2015, text No. 110, NOR: FCPA1529209V

That said, the analytical prism in both regimes is essentially the same: the protection of the national interest. Any company targeted for acquisition that operates within the scope of such regulations must assume its business activities are of a sensitive nature, and that such sensitivity will prompt careful scrutiny by public authorities.

• Export Controls Within the EU Framework

As a matter of principle, exports from France to third countries are generally unrestricted, pursuant in particular to Regulation [330] (EU) No. 2015/479 of 11 March 2015 on the common rules for exports.

Nevertheless, the French Conseil d'État has clarified [331] that certain restrictions are permissible, notably under Article 36 of the Treaty on the Functioning of the European Union (TFEU), which allows Member States to maintain export restrictions on grounds such as public morality, public order, public security, the protection of health and life of humans and animals, the preservation of plants, the protection of national treasures possessing artistic, historical or archaeological value, or the protection of industrial and commercial property.

Further, Article 346(1)(b) TFEU provides that "any Member State may take such measures as it considers necessary for the protection of the essential interests of its security which are connected with the production of or trade in arms, munitions and war material." However, such measures "must not adversely affect the conditions of competition in the internal market regarding products which are not intended for specifically military purposes."

As regards defense-related products, Directive [332] 2009/43/EC of 6 May 2009 (as amended) establishes a harmonized system of intra-EU transfer licenses for defense suppliers. However, Article 1(2) of the Directive expressly states that it "shall not affect the discretion of Member States with regard to policy on the export of defense-related products" outside the European Union.

Accordingly, in cases where a contemplated transaction fails to meet all three eligibility criteria for review under the French FDI Screening Mechanism, the State may still intervene on the basis of export control regulations due to the sensitive nature of the company's activities.

• National Control of Military Equipment

At the national level, the principal regime applicable to the export of war materials is set out in Articles L. 2335-2 et seq. of the French Defense Code (Code de la défense).

---

330. European Union, Regulation (EU) 2015/479 of March 11, 2015, of the European Parliament and of the Council, on the common rules for exports (codified text), Official Journal of the European Union, L 83/34, March 27, 2015
331. France, Conseil d'État, Guide to Economic Action Tools, Sheet No. 20, "*Protection des intérêts stratégiques dans les entreprises*, version 2022-2023," accessed September 1st, 2025, available at https://www.conseil-etat.fr/publications-colloques/etudes/guide-des-outils-d-action-economique
332. European Union, Directive 2009/43/EC of May 6, 2009, of the European Parliament and of the Council, simplifying the conditions of transfers of defence-related products within the Community (Text with EEA relevance), Official Journal of the European Union, L 146/1, June 10, 2009

This regime is grounded in a principle of prohibition, mitigated by a system of prior authorizations and ongoing interministerial coordination.

Many of the activities and goods covered by this regime overlap with those subject to the FDI screening regime [333]. Notably, Article L. 2335-4 provides that "the competent administrative authority may at any time, under conditions set forth by a decree issued by the Conseil d'État, suspend, modify, revoke or withdraw export licenses it has issued, on grounds of compliance with France's international commitments, protection of essential security interests, public order or public security, or due to failure to comply with the conditions specified in the license."

By specifically referencing "essential security interests, public order or public security," this export screening regime for war materials follows the same rationale of national interest protection as the French FDI Screening Mechanism.

Here again, there is significant overlap between the types of activities falling within both regulatory frameworks, particularly research, production, and commercialization of ammunition, powders, and explosive substances.

- **The Control of Dual-Use Goods**

As French authorities have emphasized [334], the export of dual-use goods is governed, like other goods, by the general rules of the World Trade Organization. Nevertheless, WTO rules recognize that exceptions are permissible for national security reasons.

Although such goods are part of global trade flows, their sensitive nature places them under strict governmental control. Export authorizations may be required, and export bans are possible. Exporters of dual-use goods must therefore submit formal applications for export authorization. A lack of administrative response within five months constitutes a de facto refusal.

At the European level, dual-use items are defined in Regulation [335] (EU) 2021/821 as "items, including software and technology, which can be used for both civil and military purposes, and shall include all goods which can be used for the design, development, production or use of nuclear, chemical or biological weapons or their means of delivery, including all goods which can be used both for non-explosive uses and for any assistance in the manufacture of nuclear weapons or other nuclear explosive devices."

The overlap with the list of sensitive activities referenced in the FDI Screening Mechanism is again significant. Any party to a transaction involving such items must

333. France, Monetary and Financial Code, Articles L. 151-3 and R. 151-3

334. France, Ministry of the Economy, Finance, Industrial and Digital Sovereignty, Directorate General for Enterprises, "Report to Parliament on the Export of Dual-Use Goods from France, July 2023," published August 30, 2023, accessed September 1st, 2025, available at https://www.entreprises.gouv.fr/files/files/Publications/2023/Rapports/rap-2023-sbdu.pdf

335. European Union, Regulation (EU) 2021/821 of May 20, 2021, of the European Parliament and of the Council, establishing the Union regime for the control of exports, brokering, technical assistance, transit and transfer of dual-use items (recast), Official Journal of the European Union, L 206/1, June 11, 2021

assess whether the operation could fall within the scope of either (or both) regulatory regimes.

In practical terms, activities involving dual-use goods are highly likely to attract heightened scrutiny from French authorities when the acquirer is a foreign investor. Indeed, Article R. 151-3 of the French Monetary and Financial Code (Code monétaire et financier) explicitly includes such goods within the scope [336] of the FDI Screening Mechanism.

French authorities provide numerous examples [337] of dual-use items that illustrate the complexity of this regulatory landscape, such as:

- Glass-lined steel tanks used either in the food industry or for the manufacture of chemical weapons;
- Carbon fiber fabrics used for golf clubs, helicopter blades, or weapons of mass destruction delivery systems;
- Seals and valves used in industrial processing or nuclear reactors;
- Inertial navigation systems for commercial aircraft or missiles;
- Spark gaps used in lithography or to trigger explosives;
- Viral strains used for medical research or biological weapons;
- 3D simulation games or guidance systems for missile targeting;
- Machine tools for either civil or military machining;
- Remote-controlled model aircraft or tactical delivery systems capable of destruction.

These examples underscore the inherent duality of such goods and the critical importance of export control and FDI screening frameworks in safeguarding France's essential security interests.

The Regulatory Framework for the Protection of France's Scientific and Technological Potential (PPST)

Among the activities protected by the French State, the "scientific and technological potential of the Nation" (Protection du Potentiel Scientifique et Technique de la Nation, or PPST) holds a special place. This concept [338] is closely tied to the notion of "fundamental interests of the Nation" expressly referenced in Article 410-1 of the French Penal Code [339] (Code pénal), which forms the legal foundation for measures

336. European Union, Activities related to dual-use goods and technologies listed in Annex IV of Regulation (EC) No 428/2009 of May 5, 2009, of the Council, establishing a Community regime for the control of exports, transfer, brokering and transit of dual-use items, Official Journal of the European Union, L 134/1, May 29, 2009

337. France, Ministry of the Economy, Directorate General for Enterprise, "Monitoring issues related to dual-use goods and technologies," available at https://www.entreprises.gouv.fr/la-dge/nos-missions/suivre-les-questions-relatives-aux-biens-et-technologies-double-usage (last accessed September 1, 2025)

338. DUPEYRAT, op. cit., p. 46

339. France, French Penal Code, Article 410-1: *"For the purposes of this Title, the fundamental interests of the Nation shall mean its independence, the integrity of its territory, its security, the republican form of its institutions, the means of its defense and diplomacy, the protection of its population both in France and abroad, the balance of its natural environment and ecosystem, and the essential elements of its scientific and economic potential and its cultural heritage."*

taken to safeguard national sovereignty. According to the definition adopted by the French Secretariat-General for Defense and National Security (SGDSN), this potential comprises all tangible and intangible assets related to basic and applied scientific research and technological development.

To protect this national asset, France established in 2011 a dedicated framework [340] to prevent the misappropriation or diversion of strategic know-how. The 2013 White Paper [341] on Defense and National Security reaffirmed the PPST as a key national security objective. The system's purpose is to shield both public and private entities from undue access to their sensitive knowledge, know-how, and strategic technologies. It is designed to provide enhanced protection against the illicit appropriation of information.

The legal and administrative protection granted under this framework is anchored in the control of both physical and virtual access to sensitive information. This is implemented through the designation of zones à régime restrictif (ZRRs, or "restricted access areas"), which are specific locations within entities where strategic research or production activities take place, and which warrant protection due to their value for national competitiveness or technological sovereignty.

The list [342] of protected scientific and technical sectors is set forth by a decree [343] issued by the Prime Minister on July 3, 2012. Implementation guidance is provided

340. France, Decree No. 2011-1425 of November 2, 2011, implementing Article 413-7 of the Criminal Code and concerning the protection of the Nation's scientific and technical potential, Official Journal of the French Republic, No. 0256, November 4, 2011, p. 18562, NOR: PRMX1118649D

341. France, Presidency of the Republic, White Paper Commission on Defense and National Security, GUEHENNO, Jean-Marie, White Paper on Defense 2013, 2013, Paris, La Documentation française, Directorate of Legal and Administrative Information, p. 107, ISBN: 978-2-11-009358-5, available at https://www.vie-publique.fr/rapport/33131-livre-blanc-sur-la-defense-et-la-securite-nationale-2013 (last accessed May 9, 2024)

342. France, List of Protected Scientific and Technical Sectors:
Biology, Medicine and Health: 11. Molecular and cellular biology. 12. Biomolecules, pharmacology, therapeutics. 13. Physiology, biology of organisms, populations, and interactions. 14. Clinical research, technological innovation, public health.
Chemistry: 21. Materials chemistry. 22. Organic, inorganic, and industrial chemistry. 23. Theoretical, physical, and analytical chemistry. 24. Materials engineering.
Mathematics and Its Interactions: 31. Mathematics and its interactions.
Physics: 41. Elementary particles and theoretical physics. 42. High-temperature plasmas. 43. Dense media, materials, and components. 44. Dilute media and fundamental optics. 45. Nuclear physics.
Agricultural and Ecological Sciences: 51. Environmental biology, population biology, ecology. 52. Organism biology; animal, plant, and microbial biotechnologies. 53. Agri-food biotechnologies, food sciences.
Earth and Universe Sciences, Space: 61. Astronomy, astrophysics. 62. Solid earth and surface layers. 63. Earth and fluid envelopes.
Information and Communication Sciences and Technologies: 71. Automation, manufacturing systems. 72. Signal and image processing. 73. Electronics, microelectronics, nanoelectronics, and microwaves. 74. Micro-nanosystems and sensors. 75. Optical and photonic systems. 76. Computer science and applications.
Engineering Sciences: 81. Process engineering. 82. Cold plasmas. 83. Power electronics. 84. Electrical engineering. 85. Acoustics. 86. Biomechanics and bioengineering. 87. Energy systems, thermal engineering, combustion. 88. Fluid mechanics. 89. Civil engineering. 810. Mechanical engineering, manufacturing systems, transport. 811. Solid mechanics, materials, structures, and surfaces. 812. Missiles, weapons, defense sciences and technologies.

343. France, Ministerial Order of July 3, 2012, concerning the protection of the Nation's scientific and technical potential, Official Journal of the French Republic, No. 0155, July 5, 2012, p. 11051, NOR: PRMX1227979A

by an interministerial circular[344] dated November 7, 2012. Notably, many of the protected sectors under this framework overlap with those considered sensitive under France's Foreign Investment Screening mechanism (dispositif IEF).

The PPST framework forms part of a broader regulatory ecosystem designed to safeguard national security. It complements:
(i) the regime for the protection of national defense secrets;
(ii) the security framework for activities of vital importance, notably through the points d'importance vitale (PIV) system, which protects against physical threats;
and (iii) the government's economic security and intelligence policy.

This interministerial framework is coordinated[345] by the SGDSN and operationalized by various ministries, including those in charge of Agriculture, Defense, Economy, Energy, Environment, Research, Health, and Transportation. Each ministry implements the system through its own defense and security officials, adapting the procedures to their specific sectoral risks and needs.

Since 2012, the PPST framework has primarily relied on voluntary participation by research institutions and private-sector actors. Through dialogue with State authorities, any entity may request an assessment of the sensitivity of its activities and, where appropriate, opt into the PPST framework. This collaborative approach enables tailored protection measures based on each entity's exposure and available resources.

In practical terms, the PPST offers participating entities legal and administrative safeguards, including the ability to:
—control physical and logical access to restricted areas (ZRRs), subject to prior review by the relevant ministry;
—obtain legal protection against malicious acts threatening the integrity, competitiveness, or reputation of the entity (e.g., data theft, unauthorized disclosure, cyber-intrusions, anti-competitive behavior);
—receive support from government services to raise the entity's overall security posture;
—designate and train a responsible team aware of national security concerns;
—join a trusted community conducive to research and industrial partnerships.

In 2024, the PPST regime was strengthened[346] to simplify and clarify the procedures for granting access authorizations to ZRRs[347]. Effective as of January 1, 2025, the reform introduced a contraventional regime (i.e., administrative penalties) to sanction (i) violations of the obligations governing the protection and management of ZRRs and (ii) obstruction of the duties of personnel responsible for securing such

344. France, Interministerial Circular No. 3415/SGDSN/AIST/PST of November 7, 2012, on the implementation of the system for protecting the Nation's scientific and technical potential, NOR: PRMD1238889C
345. France, Prime Minister, Secretariat-General for National Defense and Security (SGDSN), Protecting the Nation's Scientific and Technical Potential, published November 22, 2022, available at https://www.sgdsn.gouv.fr/nos-missions/proteger/proteger-le-potentiel-scientifique-et-technique-de-la-nation (last accessed September 1st, 2025)
346. France, Decree No. 2024-430 of May 14, 2024, containing various provisions relating to the protection of the Nation's scientific and technical potential, Official Journal of the French Republic, No. 0111, May 15, 2024, NOR: PRMD2334561D
347. France, Criminal Code, Article R. 413-5-1

areas. These rules primarily target research organizations, laboratories, universities, engineering schools, and companies, including directors and managers of sites hosting restricted zones.

Advancing the Objectives of the 2025 French Strategic Review

In 2025, the French foreign direct investment screening regime (Investissements Étrangers en France, IEF) assumed a central role in fulfilling Strategic National Review [348] (RNS) Objective No. 3, which calls for preparing the economy for wartime conditions. Economic security has thereby become a pillar of national defense, particularly with respect to the preservation, protection, and development of the Defense Industrial and Technological Base (BITD) . By 2030, the French economy and industrial capabilities are expected to meet the operational needs of the armed forces and domestic security services in the event of a major extraterritorial conflict and its spillover effects on national territory.

Against the backdrop of an ongoing "fog of economic war," the interministerial economic security framework, overhauled in 2019, will be particularly mobilized to detect and address threats targeting companies contributing to the national defense effort. Within this framework, the regulation of foreign investments in companies forming part of the BITD will be subject to heightened vigilance.

The Strategic National Review thus introduces an additional layer of alert for those companies identified under Objective No. 3 as requiring protection, preservation, and promotion, which will consequently be subject to particularly close scrutiny in the context of IEF screening.

*
* *

As evidenced, the French foreign direct investment screening regime (Investissements Étrangers en France, IEF) operates in parallel with other regulatory frameworks and public policies designed to safeguard the national interest and national defense. These include, inter alia, the regulatory framework governing the Protection of the Nation's Scientific and Technical Potential (Protection du potentiel scientifique et technique de la Nation, PPST), the framework applicable to the control of sensitive exports, the regime pertaining to the Scientific and Technical Potential of the Nation (Potentiel scientifique et technique de la Nation, PPST), as well as the strategic objectives pursued through the Strategic National Review (Revue nationale stratégique, RNS). Collectively, these regulations and objectives form an ecosystem surrounding transactions that involve strategic concerns for the State, and more specifically, certain activities deemed sensitive.

---

348. France, Prime Minister, General Secretariat for Defence and National Security (SGDSN), National Strategic Review – 2025 Update, point 238, published on July 13, 2025, accessed on July 15, 2025, available at https://www.sgdsn.gouv.fr/files/files/Publications/20250713_NP_SGDSN_Actualisation_2025_RNS_FR.pdf

Beyond the question of eligibility under the FDI screening regime, it is in the best interest of the parties to any transaction involving a sensitive activity to assess whether one or more of these other regulatory frameworks may apply to their deal. Only a comprehensive approach to the contemplated transaction can provide the necessary legal certainty and ensure its smooth execution, in the mutual interest of all stakeholders involved.

Chapter 8

The French FDI Screening Procedure Is Free of Charge

From the perspective of the parties to a transaction, particularly the foreign investor, it is essential to note that submitting a request for authorization or a prior review under the French foreign direct investment (FDI) screening regime does not incur any filing fee. In other words, the procedure is free of charge.

However, parties should be aware that the process may generate indirect costs that must be anticipated and factored into the planning of the transaction.

No Filing Fees for FDI Screening or Prior Review Requests

Under French administrative law, regulatory authorizations may either be subject to a fee or be free of charge, depending on factors such as the nature of the authorization, the sector involved, and the regulatory objective.

In the case of foreign direct investment screening, France has adopted a principle of default gratuity. This means that no fees are charged for submitting a request for authorization (filed by the foreign investor) or a request for prior review (filed by the target company).

This approach contrasts with the practice in other jurisdictions, most notably the United States, which introduced a filing fee system as part of the FIRRMA reform [349] of 2018. Under U.S. law, the amount of the filing fee is proportionate to the value of the transaction and is determined based on several factors, including the fair market value of the target company. The payment methods are regulated by statute, and while there are limited exemptions and few instances of refunds, the withdrawal of a voluntary notice does not trigger additional fees. Importantly, timely payment is a precondition for the notice to be deemed formally submitted and reviewable.

349. United States, Public Law No. 115-232, John S. McCain National Defense Authorization Act for Fiscal Year 2019, including the Foreign Investment Risk Review Modernization Act of 2018 (FIRRMA), Section 1723 ("Funding"), August 13, 2018, 132 Stat. 1636, H.R. 5515, 538, published by the U.S. Government Publishing Office (GPO), available at https://www.govinfo.gov/app/details/PLAW-115publ232 (last accessed September 1st, 2025).

Indirect Costs of the French Screening Procedure

Although the French screening procedure does not entail direct fees, it does involve indirect costs, primarily related to transaction advisory services.

Among these are:

- The gathering of information required to compile a complete and compliant request for authorization or prior review;
- Legal and regulatory counsel, often involving external law firms or internal legal departments;
- The administrative burden associated with preparing the file, which can take several weeks to complete.

This process is typically conducted by the transaction parties themselves and should ideally be anticipated as early as possible, either when the investment project is first agreed upon or once informal discussions with the French authorities begin.

The burden tends to be higher for third-country investors, who may be required to complete an English-language information form (see Chapter 17 and Annex E), which may overlap with but also go beyond the information typically required under domestic French procedures.

In this regard, both the acquiring party and the target company should designate within their respective organizations a point person specifically responsible for overseeing the information-gathering process. Ideally, this person should hold a senior position to ensure that sensitive questions receive timely and meaningful responses from top management.

Depending on the size and complexity of the transaction, it may be necessary to allocate a near full-time resource to this task. This can be challenging, given that the person in question must be sufficiently senior to access the entirety of the company's decision-making organs.

Once collected, the information must be consolidated, typically by the advisors responsible for preparing and submitting the authorization or prior review request to the French Treasury's FDI review unit (CIEF) . It is strongly recommended to provide advisors with full access to the relevant documentation upfront, rather than reactively supplying missing pieces during the course of the review.

Upon completion of the information-gathering process (see Chapter 17), the parties may then proceed to file their request for authorization or prior review (see Chapter 16).

These indirect costs must be factored into the transaction timeline and budget, even if the filing itself is free of charge.

* * *

While no filing fee is required to submit a request under the French FDI screening mechanism, the transaction parties must anticipate that the procedure entails significant indirect costs. Still, these pale in comparison to the potential loss in valuation or deal failure that could result from a poorly prepared submission leading to a denial or conditional clearance by the French State.

Chapter 9

The FDI Screening Mechanism Operates in Compliance with Public Transparency Standards

Foreign investment screening is, by its very nature, a political process. It involves discretionary assessments grounded in considerations of public order, public security, and more broadly, national security. This process unfolds against a geopolitical backdrop marked by the reality of foreign interference.

In practice, although the examination of a prior authorization request is formally centralized through a single window, the CIEF office, a given transaction may nonetheless require interactions with other institutional bodies involved in one capacity or another. In all cases, the objective remains the same: initiating communication with a public decision-maker with the aim of influencing a public decision, in this instance the granting of prior investment authorization.

The critical issue, therefore, is determining at what point such communication falls within the normal scope of the administrative review procedure, or conversely, constitutes an act of influence that must be declared as such to the High Authority for Transparency in Public Life (Haute Autorité pour la transparence de la vie publique, HATVP).

For the parties to the transaction, the stakes go beyond the applicable sanctions regime; their reputation is at risk in a market where the preservation of the national interest is paramount. For public decision-makers, the concern lies in guarding against any influence strategy that lacks transparency.

The Issue of Influence in the Context of FDI Screening Procedures

Ensuring transparency and credibility in national economic security mechanisms requires a clear determination of whether communications with public authorities concerning foreign direct investment (FDI) in France fall within the scope of disclosure obligations to the High Authority for Transparency in Public Life (Haute Autorité pour la transparence de la vie publique – HATVP). Given the stakes of national security and the protection of France's essential interests, it is critical that public officials involved in the FDI screening process be capable of identifying any form of influence or interference to which they are subject and that all relevant parties be held accountable, especially during the review of their stated intentions.

This issue was notably raised [350] during the 2018 parliamentary inquiry conducted by the National Assembly's Commission of Inquiry on the State's industrial policy choices. That investigation highlighted a widespread disregard for public transparency obligations among investors, advisors, and government officials alike. Transactions with direct implications for national interests were too often conducted behind closed doors, within insular networks favoring privileged relationships [351].

As Commission Chair Olivier Marleix noted at the time, "In practice, it seems that in our country the prevailing habit is to first seek a green light from the highest level of the State, with the formal authorization procedure then carried out by the administration." The criticism was not aimed at influence activities per se, but at the inversion of the authorization process: decisions on whether to approve foreign investments were sometimes made by senior government officials, ministers, the Prime Minister, or even the President, before the competent authorities had completed their legal and technical review. This dynamic raises additional economic security concerns, as influence activities, even when legitimate, can also be deployed by foreign powers seeking to undermine, delay, or manipulate the autonomy of the screening process.

From the lawmakers' perspective, the entire FDI procedure should be subject to minimum transparency standards governing interest representation, whether the actors involved are official or informal. As Commission Rapporteur Guillaume Kasbarian concluded, "Transparency in influence activities relating to the authorization of foreign investments is also a key issue in protecting our national interests."

The Commission directly challenged the stance taken by investment bankers [352], who argued that they were not "lobbyists" within the meaning of the law because "actions taken to obtain an individual decision from the administration are not considered lobbying activities." This position allowed them to avoid registering with the

350. DUPEYRAT, op. cit., pp. 236–240

351. France, National Assembly, Report No. 897 rect., April 19, 2018, MARLEIX O., Chair, KASBARIAN G., Rapporteur, Members of Parliament, produced on behalf of the fact-finding committee tasked with reviewing the State's decisions on industrial policy in light of recent corporate mergers, particularly in the cases of Alstom, Alcatel, and STX, as well as potential measures to protect France's national industrial champions in a globalized market economy, Volume 1, foreword: "*If this fact-finding committee has caused discomfort, it is because it has disrupted political, administrative and business practices rooted in a culture of insider dealings. This exposure has unsettled those actors who are not accustomed to being held accountable for the rights and prerogatives conferred on them by law, or for the flexibility they allow themselves in complying with public transparency rules*," accessed May 9, 2024, available at https://www.assemblee-nationale.fr/dyn/15/rapports/cepolind/l15b0897-ti_rapport-enquete

352. France, National Assembly, Verbatim Report No. 41, fact-finding committee on the State's decisions in industrial policy in light of recent corporate mergers, particularly the cases of Alstom, Alcatel and STX, and on potential means of protecting France's national industrial champions in a globalized economy, chaired by Mr. Olivier MARLEIX, open hearing of Mr. David de ROTHSCHILD, Chairman of Rothschild & Co, Mr. Grégoire CHERTOK and Mr. Nicolas BONNAULT, Managing Partners, and Ms. Caroline NICO, Director of Communications, Thursday, March 22, 2018, session at 2:30 p.m., BONNAULT N., Managing Partner, Rothschild & Co: "*As far as we are concerned, we can only operate within the framework of the applicable decree and the guidelines issued by the High Authority for Transparency in Public Life (HATVP). For transactions that require an individual decision, such as foreign investments in France, the current interpretation is that actions by those seeking an authorization do not constitute lobbying*," accessed May 9, 2024, available at https://www.assemblee-nationale.fr/dyn/15/comptes-rendus/cepolind/l15cepolind1718041_compte-rendu

HATVP and to sidestep related obligations. However, the Commission found this argument to be especially problematic, noting that "the remuneration of investment banks depends on the successful completion of transactions. They therefore have a strong incentive to persuade the State to grant its authorization." The Commission's conclusion was unequivocal: "This practice must change."

This debate arises [353] because many actors involved in FDI screening procedures seek to exploit the legal framework governing public transparency to avoid its application. A frequent reference is made to the Decree [354] of 9 May 2017, which in Article 1 states: "*The act of requesting, pursuant to legislative or regulatory provisions, the granting of an authorization or the benefit of an advantage to which one is legally entitled, as well as submitting an administrative appeal or undertaking a procedural step required by law for obtaining such authorization or benefit, shall not be considered a communication within the meaning of the previous paragraph.*"

Under this interpretation, all parties involved in the FDI screening process, including their legal and financial advisors, are bound by law to seek prior authorization . As part of that obligation, they must communicate with the Strategic Investment Screening Unit (CIEF) and/or other public authorities to comply with regulatory requirements. As such, they argue they are exempt from interest representation obligations, including the need to disclose the purpose of their action, the officials contacted, or any budget allocated to influence efforts.

This was the core argument invoked by investment banks [355] during the parliamentary inquiry to justify their refusal to comply with transparency requirements. However, the Commission rejected this interpretation, stressing that "*it overlooks the fact that the administration does not operate under a rule of automatic entitlement [compétence liée], but exercises discretionary authority and must therefore remain free from undue influence.*" Lawmakers emphasized that transparency obligations apply to all actors and that the legislature had made clear its intention to subject investment banks to those requirements. As former Minister of the Economy Michel Sapin stated [356] in reference to the 2017 Decree he signed: "*Such a decree could not have exempted entire categories of potential interest representatives, because only the law has the authority to do so.*"

353. DUPEYRAT, op. cit., pp. 240–246
354. France, Decree No. 2017-867 of May 9, 2017, on the digital register of interest representatives, Official Journal of the French Republic, No. 0109, May 10, 2017, NOR: ECFM1706418D
355. France, National Assembly, Verbatim Report No. 41, fact-finding committee on the State's decisions in industrial policy in light of recent corporate mergers, particularly the cases of Alstom, Alcatel and STX, and on potential means of protecting France's national industrial champions in a globalized economy, chaired by Mr. Olivier MARLEIX, open hearing of Mr. David de ROTHSCHILD, Chairman of Rothschild & Co, Mr. Grégoire CHERTOK and Mr. Nicolas BONNAULT, Managing Partners, and Ms. Caroline NICO, Director of Communications, Thursday, March 22, 2018, session at 2:30 p.m., accessed September 1st, 2025, available at https://www.assemblee-nationale.fr/dyn/15/comptes-rendus/cepolind/l15cepolind1718041_compte-rendu
356. France, National Assembly, Verbatim Report No. 39, fact-finding committee on the State's decisions in industrial policy in light of recent corporate mergers, particularly the cases of Alstom, Alcatel and STX, and on potential means of protecting France's national industrial champions in a globalized economy, chaired by Mr. Olivier MARLEIX, open hearing of Mr. Michel SAPIN, former Minister, Thursday, March 22, 2018, session at 9:30 a.m., accessed May 9, 2024, available at https://www.assemblee-nationale.fr/dyn/15/comptes-rendus/cepolind/l15cepolind1718039_compte-rendu

This legal and policy analysis was reaffirmed in 2025 in the final report of the National Assembly's fact-finding and oversight mission on foreign direct investment screening . The report[357] confirmed the persistence of influence activities operating outside the purview of HATVP oversight. It identified, on one hand, the existence of grey areas in terms of transparency, particularly in the case of foreign state-sponsored economic influence strategies, and, on the other, structural limitations that hinder the ethical oversight of law firms and financial advisors representing foreign investors before the Directorate General of the Treasury) (DG Trésor). The mission ultimately recommended[358] "strengthening the ethical oversight of interest representatives."

The HATVP Considers Certain IEF Advisors as Interest Representatives

To determine whether a party or advisor involved in the French foreign investment screening procedure (procédure IEF) qualifies as engaging in influence activities, reference must first be made to Law[359] No. 2016-1691 of December 9, 2016, on transparency, anti-corruption, and the modernization of economic life. This law defines the legal framework applicable to interest representation in France, commonly understood as lobbying.

In essence, the law defines lobbying as (i) communication (ii) initiated by a legal entity (iii) with a public official (iv) for the purpose of influencing public decision-making. The law establishes a registration requirement for such activities in a centralized public register of interest representatives. Entities subject to this requirement include private legal persons, public establishments or groupings engaged in industrial or commercial activities, and organizations listed under Title I, Book VII of the French Commercial Code and under Title II of the French Artisans' Code. This applies regardless of whether the contact is made by a company executive, employee, or member.

The law also provides that "natural persons who are not employed by a legal entity" but "who engage in a professional activity meeting the statutory criteria" are likewise considered interest representatives. Conversely, the law exempts certain categories[360] from the registration obligation, based on the nature of their activities or roles.

357. France, National Assembly, Committee for the Evaluation and Oversight of Public Policies, Fact-Finding Report No. 1453, by JOLIVET F. and de LEPINAU H., Members of Parliament, on the evaluation of foreign direct investment screening in France, Official Journal of the French Republic, May 27, 2025, text 45 of 69, published May 22, 2025, accessed May 27, 2025, available at https://www.assemblee-nationale.fr/dyn/17/rapports/cec/l17b1453_rapport-information

358. Proposal No. 13: Clarify the application of the decree on the digital register of interest representatives so that representation activities carried out with the Directorate General of the Treasury on behalf of a foreign investor are included in the list of advocacy actions subject to the rules of the High Authority for Transparency in Public Life.

359. France, Law No. 2016-1691 of December 9, 2016, on transparency, anti-corruption, and the modernization of economic life, Official Journal of the French Republic, No. 0287, December 10, 2016, Text No. 2, NOR: ECFM1605542L

360. France, Law No. 2013-907 of October 11, 2013, on the transparency of public life, Official Journal of the French Republic, No. 0238, October 12, 2013, Text No. 1, Article 18-2: "The following shall not be considered as interest representatives (...) (a) Elected officials, when acting in the course of their mandate; (b) Political parties and groups, in the exercise of their mission as defined in Article 4 of the

During parliamentary debates [361] on the adoption of the law, the scope of entities required to register gave rise to significant controversy. The question was raised whether investment banks, private equity firms, or financial advisory firms should be considered legal persons engaging in lobbying and therefore be subject to registration with the Haute Autorité pour la Transparence de la Vie Publique (HATVP).

The legislature ultimately clarified that such entities do fall within the scope of the law. In fact, one of the examples discussed during the debates explicitly concerned investment banks advising on foreign investment transactions. The conclusion of the debates was unequivocal: investment banks, financial advisory firms, and similar advisors are subject to the same registration obligations as traditional public affairs or lobbying firms.

The position of the HATVP on this issue is particularly illuminating. The HATVP made its position known in two stages.

When consulted [362] specifically about the application of the lobbying rules to the foreign investment review procedure, the authority issued a number of clarifying responses [363]. These were subsequently incorporated into updated guidance [364] issued in 2023.

In practice, for matters relating to the French FDI screening mechanism, the HATVP conducts a dual analysis based on the legal form of the organization (the organic criterion) and the nature of its activities (the material criterion).

On the organic criterion (the legal nature of the organizations concerned), the HATVP considers whether an entity falls within one of the two categories contemplated by law: legal persons and natural persons.

For legal persons, the HATVP has clearly stated that investment banks and law firms are indeed legal entities falling within the scope of the law, on equal footing with public affairs, lobbying, communications, or strategy firms. According to the HATVP, if the legislature had intended to exclude these categories, it would have expressly

---

Constitution; (c) Civil servant unions and, within the scope of the negotiation provided for in Article L.1 of the Labor Code, employee trade unions and employer professional organizations; (d) Religious associations, in their dealings with the Minister and ministerial departments responsible for religious affairs; (e) Associations representing elected officials, when performing the missions set out in their statutes."

361. France, National Assembly, Verbatim Report, June 8, 2016, First sitting of Wednesday, 14th legislature, Ordinary session 2015–2016, discussion of Amendment No. 484, accessed September 1st, 2025, available at https://www.assemblee-nationale.fr/14/cri/2015-2016/20160207.asp

362. France, National Assembly, "Letter from the Chairman of the Parliamentary Committee of Inquiry on State Decisions in Industrial Policy, Olivier Marleix, to Mr. Jean-Louis Nadal, President of the High Authority for Transparency in Public Life," dated April 19, 2018, available from MARLEIX, Olivier, Member of Parliament

363. France, High Authority for Transparency in Public Life, "Letter from Mr. Jean-Louis Nadal, President, to Mr. Olivier Marleix, Member of Parliament," dated September 21, 2018, available from MARLEIX, Olivier, Member of Parliament

364. France, High Authority for Transparency in Public Life, Publication, October 1, 2023, "Register of Interest Representatives, Guidelines: New Version," accessed June 5, 2025, available at https://www.hatvp.fr/wordpress/wp-content/uploads/2023/09/Lignes-directrices_nouvelles-version_entree-en-vigueur-au-01102023_VF.pdf

done so in the exemption provisions. Since this is not the case, such entities are presumed subject to the framework.

That said, even where the organic criterion is met, the HATVP reserves the right to examine on a case-by-case basis whether the material criterion is satisfied. In this context, the authority may conduct desk reviews or onsite inspections to verify compliance, including disclosure of the client's name, the type of public officials contacted, and the budget allocated to the influence campaign.

As to natural persons, the HATVP recalls that individuals engaged in professional lobbying activities, regardless of their business structure (e.g., liberal profession, sole proprietorship, micro-enterprise, EIRL, umbrella company arrangement), are deemed interest representatives if they meet the criteria. This includes informal groups or associations formed to work on foreign direct investment screening matters, provided the material threshold is met. Even an association focused on FDI screening may be subject to registration if its activity qualifies as lobbying.

The material criterion (the activity concerned) requires two cumulative conditions to be met:

1. The entity or individual must engage in lobbying activities; and
2. Lobbying must be the main or regular activity of at least one individual within the organization.

The HATVP defines lobbying activity by reference to Article 18-2 of the Law[365] of October 11, 2013, which describes it as "seeking to influence public decision-making, notably the content of a law or regulation, by initiating communication with a designated public official."

According to Article 1 of the implementing decree[366] of May 9, 2017, such communication must be initiated by the interest representative and excludes certain types of contact.

In practice, five cumulative conditions must be met for a communication to qualify as lobbying:

1. There must be a communication between the interest representative and a public official;
2. The official must fall within the categories listed in Article 18-2 of the 2013 law;
3. The communication must be initiated by the interest representative;
4. It must relate to an existing or future public decision;
5. Its objective must be to influence that decision.

For this purpose, the HATVP defines "communication" broadly. It includes:

- Any in-person meeting, regardless of context (e.g., dedicated meeting, professional lunch, trade fair, club meeting);
- Any phone or video call or electronic message exchange;

365. France, Law No. 2013-907 of October 11, 2013, on the transparency of public life, Official Journal of the French Republic, No. 0238, October 12, 2013

366. France, Decree No. 2017-867 of May 9, 2017, on the digital register of interest representatives, Official Journal of the French Republic, No. 0109, May 10, 2017, NOR: ECFM1706418D

- Any letter, email, or private message sent electronically;
- Any direct and named interaction with a public official via social media.

If multiple contacts are made within a short period with the same official and concern the same matter, they count as a single communication. However, if a single message (e.g., email) is addressed to multiple public officials, each instance is counted separately for reporting purposes.

The organization of an event involving public officials may also constitute a lobbying action if certain elements are present, such as the officials' attendance and participation, the opportunity for direct exchanges, or discussions relating to specific public decisions or legal frameworks.

Accordingly, in light of the clarifications provided by the HATVP, any gathering, whether an association, conference, club, forum, or similar professional venue, addressing the issue of foreign direct investment screening must be regarded as a lobbying entity carrying out an interest representation activity. It is likewise essential to ensure that any potential funding of such gatherings by foreign entities (companies, law firms, embassies) cannot be construed as interference. It is therefore strongly recommended that parties to a transaction, and in particular their counsel, anticipate this dimension in preparation for possible HATVP oversight.

The HATVP Distinguishes Cases Involving the Issuance of Individual Decisions

The issue of interpreting and classifying communicationsin light of the organizational and material criteria arises with particular acuity in the context of communications relating to individual decisions . This is precisely the situation encountered in connection with an authorization request under the IEF procedure.

As a general principle, to determine whether a communication seeking an individual decision constitutes an interest representation activity, the High Authority for Transparency in Public Life (HATVP) draws the following distinction: any communication, other than a mere procedural or administrative step, intended to influence a public decision-maker before the formal review process has begun is considered an act of interest representation.

This logic specific to the IEF regulatory framework must not, however, mislead the parties to a transaction regarding their disclosure obligations on transparency in public life before the HATVP. They must therefore consider that any interaction not falling stricto sensu within the procedures expressly set forth in the provisions of the foreign direct investment screening regime under the Monetary and Financial Code falls within the scope of the HATVP disclosure requirements. Such an approach offers the most effective means of ensuring both legal certainty and the protection of the parties' reputation in the transaction.

Conversely, where a communication with a public official is undertaken for the purpose of processing a request under the conditions laid down by a legislative or regulatory text, the HATVP takes the position that such communication does not constitute an act of interest representation. Accordingly, it is clear that communications carried out within the framework and in accordance with the conditions of an authorization request under Articles R.151-5 et seq., as well as those relating to a prior request for review of an activity under Article R.151-4, fall within this category and therefore do not need to be declared.

All other forms of contact, however legitimate or well-intentioned, must be viewed as influence activities and may trigger the corresponding reporting obligations. It is up to each interest representative to evaluate whether a given communication falls within or outside the scope of these rules based on its true intent and substance.

Specifically, the following scenarios are excluded from the definition of interest representation:

- Before filing a request: communications limited to announcing the intent to file, clarifying the nature and scope of the transaction, or scheduling procedural steps;
- During the review process: all communications between the applicant and the competent administrative authority handling the request;
- Following a denial: communications related to a gracious, hierarchical, or judicial appeal;
- Following an approval: communications limited to the implementation and monitoring of the individual decision.

All other communications, however well-intentioned, must be regarded as interest representation activities. It is therefore incumbent upon each interest representative to assess these criteria in light of the actual purpose of his or her communication with a public official.

The HATVP also provides guidance on individual decisions involving the exercise of a legal right. Under Article 1 of Decree [367] No. 2017-867 of 9 May 2017, communications seeking a benefit that constitutes a legal entitlement for eligible individuals or entities do not qualify as interest representation. However, this exception does not apply to FDI authorization requests. The issuance of an investment authorization is a discretionary act, not a right.

This was confirmed [368] by the 2018 parliamentary inquiry into France's industrial policy, which underscored that "the administration is not bound by law [compétence liée] and must remain protected from undue influence."

Therefore, within the IEF regulatory framework, the HATVP is likely to exempt only those communications with the Investment Screening Unit (CIEF), which is designated by regulation as the central point of contact for applicants. Foreign investors, and,

367. France, Decree No. 2017-867 of May 9, 2017, on the digital register of interest representatives, Official Journal of the French Republic, No. 0109, May 10, 2017, NOR: ECFM1706418D

368. France, National Assembly, Report No. 897 rect., April 19, 2018, MARLEIX, Olivier, Chair, KASBARIAN, Guillaume, Rapporteur, Members of Parliament, submitted on behalf of the Commission of Inquiry on State decisions in industrial policy in light of recent corporate mergers, including the cases of Alstom, Alcatel and STX, and on the means to protect national industrial champions in a globalized trade environment, Volume 1, accessed September, 1st, 2025, available at https://www.assemblee-nationale.fr/dyn/15/rapports/cepolind/l15b0897-ti_rapport-enquete

where applicable, target companies, are required by law to engage with CIEF in order to comply with the screening procedure. Moreover, the CIEF coordinates the interagency process by gathering the views of other relevant ministries and authorities, making it the mandatory and exclusive interlocutor for applicants.

By contrast, any communication initiated with authorities outside of the CIEF, such as the Directorate General of the Treasury) (DG Trésor), the Minister's Office, the Minister of the Economy, or other institutional actors involved in the process (e.g., the Directorate General for Enterprises (DGE), the Interministerial Department for Economic Security (SISSE), the Defence Procurement Agency (DGA), the General Secretariat for Defense and National Security (SGDSN), the National Cybersecurity Agency (ANSSI), high-level defense officials, or even the Prime Minister or the Office of the President), is likely to be regarded as an attempt to influence a public decision. In the context of IEF, that decision is the granting of prior authorization to invest.

The question of disclosure also arises with respect to public officials themselves. French lobbying laws do not currently require public decision-makers to verify whether their interlocutors are properly registered as interest representatives, nor do they require them to report such communications. Yet this legal gap may expose officials to criticism, especially in high-stakes FDI screening cases and in the context of parliamentary oversight. Public officials may be accused of negligence if they appear insufficiently vigilant regarding influence operations conducted by transaction parties, including those with ties to foreign powers.

To mitigate such risks, public officials are encouraged to request formal mandates from their interlocutors confirming their status as interest representatives. These mandates, aligned with HATVP guidance (see Appendix H), help clarify the scope of each party's obligations and demonstrate the official's awareness of the economic security implications at stake.

• The HATVP Also Monitors Foreign Influence

The transparency of practices employed by actors seeking favorable decisions from the French State is increasingly viewed as an issue of economic security, and even of national sovereignty. It lies at the heart of efforts to combat foreign influence.

According[369] to the High Authority for Transparency in Public Life (HATVP), "the proliferation of direct and indirect influence operations conducted by foreign states, combined with their lack of traceability and inherent complexity, poses significant risks to national democratic processes. Hostile actions contrary to national interests can be carried out without public awareness, even though public decisions must be made in the general interest and in service of the national interest. Regulating the influence of foreign interests on public decision-making is therefore necessary to preserve the integrity and transparency of the decision-making process."

369. France, High Authority for Transparency in Public Life, News & Analysis, July 16, 2024, "The French Framework for Regulating Foreign Influence," accessed June 5, 2025, available at https://www.hatvp.fr/lobbying/actualites/le-dispositif-francais-dencadrement-de-linfluence-etrangere/2

This objective is aligned with the fundamental purpose of the French foreign investment screening regime (FDI screening, or procédure IEF), which is itself designed to safeguard against foreign interference [370].

The relationship between the FDI screening regime and foreign interference was examined in detail during the 2023 parliamentary inquiry [371] dedicated to this topic. During the hearings, the head of the Strategic Information and Economic Security Service (SISSE) confirmed that the classification of a foreign investment in France as foreign interference is conducted "on a case-by-case basis." The analysis combines a well-defined doctrinal framework, based on national lists of strategic actors requiring protection, with a flexible risk-based approach tailored to the profile of the foreign investor. SISSE evaluates "who is behind the investment fund, what capital is involved, who the ultimate beneficial owner is, and whether there are links to foreign states," in order to develop "a risk map of the investor." Importantly, an investor located within the European Union is not automatically treated as benign, since "EU-based structures may be used as investment vehicles by third-party interests, including for legal or tax reasons."

Following the inquiry, a legislative proposal aimed at preventing foreign interference in France was introduced. The bill's rapporteur [372] in the National Assembly recommended, among other measures, permanently maintaining the 10% ownership threshold that triggers the FDI screening procedure for non-EU investments, and extending its application to all companies, including privately held firms.

The issue of how to address non-listed companies is indeed raised. Although these companies may fall outside the formal scope of the IEF procedure, the report emphasized that SISSE, in collaboration with the Directorate of Defense Intelligence and Security (DRSD) and the General Directorate for External Security (DGSE), is actively monitoring them. SISSE's analysis in such cases covers the full supply chain, including first- and second-tier subcontractors. In connection with Chapter 7 of this volume, it is essential to note that a transaction's ineligibility under the IEF criteria does not exempt it from scrutiny by the State, or from the reach of other public policies related to economic sovereignty.

The Organisation for Economic Co-operation and Development (OECD) also raised concerns about foreign influence, observing [373] that for a long time, "the French

370. France, OECD (2024), Strengthening Transparency and Integrity in Foreign Influence Activities in France: A Tool to Address the Risks of Foreign Interference, OECD Public Governance Reviews, OECD Publishing, Paris, p. 19, accessed May 28, 2025, available at https://doi.org/10.1787/d6e6e8e9-fr

371. France, National Assembly, Report No. 1311, June 1, 2023, TANGUY, Jean-Philippe, Chair, LE GRIP, Constance, Rapporteur, Members of Parliament, on behalf of the Commission of Inquiry into Political, Economic and Financial Interference by Foreign Powers, States, Organizations, Companies, Interest Groups, Private Individuals, Aimed at Influencing or Corrupting Opinion Leaders, Decision-Makers or French Political Parties, Volume 1, accessed June 10, 2025, available at https://www.assemblee-nationale.fr/dyn/16/rapports/cion_lois/l16b2343_rapport-fond

372. France, National Assembly, Report No. 2343, March 13, 2024, HOULIÉ, Sacha, Member of Parliament, Rapporteur, submitted on behalf of the Law, Legislation and General Administration Committee of the Republic, on Bill No. 2150 aimed at preventing foreign interference in France, accessed June 10, 2025, available at https://www.assemblee-nationale.fr/dyn/16/rapports/cion_lois/l16b2343_rapport-fond

373. France, OECD (2024), Strengthening Transparency and Integrity in Foreign Influence Activities in France: A Tool to Address the Risks of Foreign Interference, OECD Public Governance Reviews, OECD Publishing, Paris, p. 37, accessed May 28, 2025, available at https://doi.org/10.1787/d6e6e8e9-fr

registry of interest representatives covered only a limited subset of actors engaged in influence activities on behalf of foreign governments and state-linked organizations." In practice, lobbying activities carried out on behalf of non-EU foreign states were often not registered with the HATVP.

In response to such gaps, and in light of the growing prevalence of influence operations falling outside its regular oversight mechanisms, the HATVP has begun targeting foreign state-backed influence strategies directly.

First, in October 2023, the HATVP issued [374] a new version of its guidelines, explicitly stating that consulting and law firms acting on behalf of foreign public authorities are required to register with the Authority whenever they engage in interest representation directed at French public officials, as defined by the law.

Second, and more significantly, in 2024, this position was reinforced by the enactment of Law [375] No. 2024-850 of 25 July 2024 on the prevention of foreign interference in France. Among other provisions, the law created a separate digital registry of foreign influence activities, maintained by the HATVP. Distinct from the lobbying registry, this new register logs activities declared by any person acting on behalf of a foreign principal, meaning a non-EU foreign power, foreign public entity, or political party or group established outside the European Union. These activities must aim to influence public decision-making, including the legislative process, public policy formulation, or France's European or foreign policy.

These activities must be declared to the HATVP under the conditions set forth in the Decree of July 31, 2025, which defines the registration and reporting requirements applicable to activities falling within the scope of foreign interference, establishing the framework for an accessible and transparent digital registry. As of October 1, 2025, any natural or legal person acting on behalf of a foreign principal will be required to register with the HATVP registry. Such registration must occur within 15 business days once the statutory conditions giving rise to the obligation are met. The registry is designed to centralize all information relating to foreign interference, thereby ensuring comprehensive monitoring.

This aspect of the fight against foreign interference was described as critical by the rapporteurs of the 2025 fact-finding and oversight mission on foreign direct investment screening . In their report [376], they underscored that "since relationships between foreign investors and French public authorities involve intermediaries,

374. France, High Authority for Transparency in Public Life, Register of Interest Representatives, "Guidelines: New Version, Effective as of October 1, 2023," p. 17, accessed May 28, 2025, available at https://www.hatvp.fr/wordpress/wp-content/uploads/2023/09/Lignes-directrices_nouvelles-version_entree-en-vigueur-au-01102023_VF.pdf

375. France, Law No. 2024-850 of July 25, 2024, aimed at preventing foreign interference in France, Official Journal of the French Republic, No. 0177, July 26, 2024, NOR: IOMX2408435L

376. France, National Assembly, Committee for the Evaluation and Oversight of Public Policies, Information Report No. 1453, JOLIVET, François, and de LEPINAU, Hervé, Members of Parliament, on the evaluation of foreign direct investment screening in France, Official Journal of the French Republic, May 27, 2025, text 45 of 69, published May 22, 2025, see "Strengthening Ethical Oversight of Interest Representatives," p. 104, accessed May 27, 2025, available at https://www.assemblee-nationale.fr/dyn/17/rapports/cec/l17b1453_rapport-information

including consulting firms, investment banks, and law firms, the FDI screening procedure is particularly vulnerable to economic influence threats." The rapporteurs added: "The involvement of foreign investors' legal and financial advisors in the conduct of the IEF procedure currently lacks a clear legal framework with respect to transparency. Yet, according to the rapporteurs, such a framework is essential to ensuring sustainable oversight and to effectively protecting France's economic sovereignty." .

* * *

The French FDI screening regime operates within a broader legal and institutional framework aimed at ensuring public transparency, and even foreign interference. Within that context, the issue of influence over public decision-makers, especially when it arises during the official screening process, must be addressed with the utmost rigor. While the HATVP draws clear distinctions between types of influence and procedural interactions, it remains in the best interest of the transaction and its parties to ensure that no doubt can be cast on the foreign investor's willingness to respect the decision-making autonomy of French public authorities. Influence must not be used to circumvent the procedure or, worse, to compromise the national interest.

Part Two

The Rationale Underlying France's Foreign Investment Screening Mechanism

As a general principle, the French foreign investment screening mechanism (the IEF regime) is grounded in the imperative to safeguard the national interest. As expressly stated in French law, it is because the Government is entrusted with the responsibility of protecting national interests [377] that it is permitted to depart from the principle of free foreign investment and subject the establishment, modification, or liquidation of foreign investments in France to a system of declaration, prior authorization, or regulatory control.

To determine whether a foreign investment falls within the scope of this national interest exception, it is essential to adopt a legally operable method. This requires reliance on a legal definition that clearly delineates the perimeter of the screening mechanism.

In practice, the screening mechanism applies only when three cumulative criteria are met (see Chapter 10). These conditions are set forth in Articles R.151-1, R.151-2, and R.151-3 of the French Monetary and Financial Code (Code monétaire et financier). First, the investment must involve a foreign investor (see Chapter 11). Second, the investment must take a form that qualifies under the relevant legal provisions when targeting a French legal entity (see Chapter 12). Third, the transaction must involve a business activity deemed sensitive by the French State (see Chapter 13).

377. France, Monetary and Financial Code, Article L. 151-2

Chapter 10

The filing of an application is required where three cumulative criteria are met

Determining whether, and under what conditions, a given investment transaction falls within the scope of France's foreign investment screening mechanism (IEF) is a fundamental issue. This assessment shapes both the legal obligations incumbent upon the parties and, more broadly, the overall credibility of the regime in light of its mission to safeguard the national interest.

Foreign investors and their legal counsel must be aware that the screening mechanism only applies when three cumulative conditions are satisfied. These pertain respectively to: (i) the investor's status, (ii) the nature of the transaction, and (iii) the type of business activity targeted. These three criteria are codified in Articles R.151-1, R.151-2, and R.151-3 of the French Monetary and Financial Code (Code monétaire et financier).

The cumulative nature of these criteria has several consequences. Most notably, it renders the filing of a prior authorization request mandatory, unless a specific derogation applies, for instance, where the investor has already lawfully acquired prior control over the same entity. However, there are two exceptions to that derogation which always prevail: (i) when the investor is unable to comply with previously imposed conditions, or (ii) when the contemplated transaction involves the full or partial transfer of a business line.

Moreover, the cumulative assessment must take into account the timing of the transaction, meaning that the three criteria must be evaluated in light of the specific circumstances at the relevant moment of the operation.

The three cumulative criteria are set forth in Articles R. 151-1, R. 151-2, and R. 151-3 of the French Monetary and Financial Code.

As reiterated by the French authorities [378], an investment transaction must be subject to prior review and approval by the Minister of the Economy whenever the following three cumulative conditions are met:

378. France, Ministry of the Economy, Finance and Industrial and Digital Sovereignty, Directorate General of the Treasury, "Guidelines on the Foreign Direct Investment Screening in France" / July 2025, published July 30, 2025, see Point 1, accessed August 1, 2025, available at https://www.tresor.economie.gouv.fr/services-aux-entreprises/investissements-etrangers-en-france

Foreign investment screening in France is only triggered if three cumulative conditions are met, as defined under the French Monetary and Financial Code:

1. the presence of a foreign investor within the meaning of Article R. 151-1 of the Monetary and Financial Code;
2. the execution of a foreign investment transaction targeting a French-law entity within the meaning of Article R. 151-2 of the same Code;
3. the performance by the target entity of one or more activities deemed to participate, even occasionally, in the exercise of public authority, or which are likely to affect public order, public security, or national defense interests, as defined in Article R. 151-3 of the Code.

These provisions [379] apply throughout Metropolitan France as well as in overseas départements and collectivities, including New Caledonia, French Polynesia, and the Wallis and Futuna Islands.

The Combined Presence of All Three Criteria Makes the Filing of an Authorization Request Mandatory

Two key consequences arise from the cumulative nature of these eligibility criteria regarding the requirement to submit an authorization request.

The first is that if all three criteria are met, the foreign investor is legally required to submit a prior authorization request, subject only to a narrow exemption, itself limited by two exceptions. In other words, when the three criteria are jointly satisfied, the investor has no legal alternative but to file, failing which they expose themselves to enforcement measures and penalties.

The second consequence is that, conversely, if even one of the three criteria is not met, the investor is not under any legal obligation to file a request. This opens a space for strategic discretion, and, in some cases, intentional silence, particularly where the investor or the target company may have a vested interest in avoiding notification. As a result, circumvention strategies may emerge, particularly focusing on the two most malleable criteria: (i) the characterization of the investor as "foreign" under French law, and (ii) the determination of whether the transaction qualifies as a foreign investment, including questions of control, the crossing of the 10% voting rights threshold [380], or the acquisition of all or part of a business line.

The procedures for submitting the application file forming part of the authorization request are set out in Chapter 17.

379. France, Monetary and Financial Code, Articles L. 732-5, L. 733-5 and L. 734-5
380. France, Decree No. 2023-1293 of December 28, 2023, on foreign investments in France, lowering the initial threshold from 25% to 10% on a permanent basis, Official Journal of the French Republic, No. 0301, December 29, 2023, NOR: ECOT2323089D

A Derogation from the Authorization Requirement Exists When Control Has Already Been Acquired

Article R. 151-7 of the French Monetary and Financial Code establishes an exception to the requirement to file a prior authorization request. (see detailed discussion in Chapter 12)

Specifically, a foreign investor is exempt from this obligation when the ultimate controlling entity within the ownership chain, understood in accordance with Article [381] R. 151-1, II, had already acquired control over the target entity before the contemplated investment, as defined under Article L. 233-3 of the French Commercial Code.

If, despite this exception, a request for authorization is nevertheless submitted, the acknowledgment of receipt issued by the French authorities will explicitly state that the application is without object.

It should be noted that prior to the amendment [382] that entered into force on January 1, 2024, Article R. 151-7 contained not one but three distinct categories [383] of exceptions.

Two Situations Require the Filing of an Authorization Request Regardless

While an exemption may apply where the investor has previously acquired control, French regulations [384] still require the State to review certain categories of investment operations. This safeguard is designed to prevent abuse of the procedure, particularly where an earlier authorization might be circumvented to the detriment of the Nation's interests.

---

381. France, Monetary and Financial Code, Article R. 151-1, II: "*For the purposes of this Chapter, a control chain refers to the group composed of an investor referred to in points 3° or 4° of I and the persons or entities that control it. All persons and entities belonging to a control chain shall be deemed investors within the meaning of this Chapter.*"
382. France, Decree No. 2023-1293 of December 28, 2023, on foreign investments in France, Official Journal of the French Republic, No. 0301, December 29, 2023, NOR: ECOT2323089D
383. France, for reference: "1° where the investment was made between entities belonging to the same group, that is, entities directly or indirectly owned more than 50% in capital or voting rights by the same shareholder; 2° where the investor crossed, directly or indirectly, alone or in concert, the threshold of 25% of the voting rights in the capital of an entity over which it had previously acquired control pursuant to an authorization granted under point 1° of Article R. 151-2; 3° where the investor acquired control, within the meaning of Article L. 233-3 of the Commercial Code, of an entity in which it had previously crossed the 25% voting rights threshold, directly or indirectly, alone or in concert, pursuant to an authorization granted under point 3° of Article R. 151-2, provided that such acquisition had been subject to prior notification to the Minister of the Economy. Unless objected to by the Minister, this new authorization was deemed granted after a period of thirty days following notification, under conditions specified by ministerial order."
384. France, Ministry of the Economy, Finance and Industrial and Digital Sovereignty, Directorate General of the Treasury, Guidelines on the Foreign Direct Investment Screening in France /, July 2025, published July 30, 2025, consulted August 1, 2025, available at https://www.tresor.economie.gouv.fr/services-aux-entreprises/investissements-etrangers-en-france, see Point 1.4.2

Accordingly, even where the exemption formally applies, a prior authorization request must be filed in the following two scenarios :

1° where the investment undermines conditions imposed under a previous authorization

An authorization is required where the investment would prevent the investor from complying with conditions previously imposed under a prior authorization, as set forth in Article R. 151-8, II of the French Monetary and Financial Code.

This applies to investments involving one or more French entities previously acquired under a conditional authorization, where the relevant conditions remain in force. The investment must have the effect of obstructing compliance with those conditions, this could include a variety of situations, such as:
—the dissolution or disappearance of the foreign entity originally responsible for compliance with the conditions;
—the division of the French entity's activities among multiple entities;
—the integration of the French entity into a different part of the investor's corporate group, subjecting it to foreign legislation that could jeopardize the continuity or security of its activities; or
—the integration of the French entity into a part of the investor's group that falls within the scope of Article R. 151-10 of the Monetary and Financial Code.

2° where the investment involves transferring all or part of a strategic business line abroad

An authorization is required when the investment involves the transfer abroad of all or part of a business line falling within the strategic sectors listed in Article R. 151-3 of the French Monetary and Financial Code.

In such cases, the exemption from the prior authorization requirement does not apply. The rule targets operations involving the outbound transfer of strategic activities, regardless of whether the French entity has previously been subject to screening under the FDI regime. Examples include:
—the direct acquisition by a foreign entity of all or part of a business line belonging to a French company;
—the acquisition by a foreign entity of a branch of a French company;
—however, intra-group transactions between French subsidiaries of the same foreign investor remain exempt from the authorization requirement. With respect to this latter point, the 2025 Guidelines issued by the French administration expressly clarified that a branch is covered by the foreign investment screening regime when it constitutes the operational vehicle of a foreign company in France.

Accordingly, the investor must submit a formal prior authorization request in both such cases.

Conversely, acquisitions of all or part of a business line carried out between French entities belonging to the same corporate group as the investor remain exempt from any prior authorization requirement.

The obligation to file a notification or a new request in the event of crossing the 10% threshold

The administration recalls[385] that it is mandatory to file a prior notification in the case of an investment transaction consisting of crossing the threshold of 10% of the voting rights in a French law company whose shares are admitted to trading on a regulated market and whose activities fall within the scope of Article R. 151-3 of the Monetary and Financial Code.

This type of transaction may give rise to two possible filings:
—either a prior notification under the last paragraph of Article R. 151-5 of the Monetary and Financial Code, following which a waiver of the authorization requirement arises after a period of ten business days, unless opposed by the Minister;
—or a formal prior authorization request under the same conditions as a "classic" prior authorization request.

According to the administration, filing a prior notification is intended to be preferred over submitting a prior authorization request.

Failure to file either a notification or an authorization request may give rise to administrative enforcement or sanctions in cases of investments carried out without authorization, or where authorization has been obtained fraudulently, as set out under the applicable enforcement and sanction measures.

The filing of a prior notification is carried out according to the same procedures as those applicable to a prior authorization request (see Chapter 17).

The FDI Screening Regime Also Takes Into Account the Timing of the Investment Operation

As clarified by the French administration[386], Article R. 151-2 of the Monetary and Financial Code is intended to apply to investments that are to be carried out at a specific, identifiable date, not to future operations subject to uncertainty. This principle governs the assessment of whether the three cumulative criteria for FDI screening are met.

Accordingly, the decision as to whether a transaction is subject to screening is made on the basis of the legal and factual circumstances existing at the date the investment is completed.

However, certain investment structures involve mechanisms whereby a foreign investor acquires the right to invest at a future, and potentially uncertain, date. This may occur through convertible instruments (e.g., convertible bonds, share warrants,

385. France, Ministry of the Economy, Finance and Industrial and Digital Sovereignty, Directorate General of the Treasury, "Guidelines on the Foreign Direct Investment Screening in France," / July 2025, published July 30, 2025, see Point 2.3.1, accessed August 1, 2025, available at https://www.tresor.economie.gouv.fr/services-aux-entreprises/investissements-etrangers-en-france
386. ibid., Point 1.2.5.

call options) or contractual arrangements (e.g., shareholder agreements or security arrangements that trigger upon certain events). In such cases, the investment only becomes subject to the screening mechanism once the transaction becomes certain and enforceable.

The French authorities have confirmed [387], for example, that the conversion of bonds with share warrants into equity qualifies as a notifiable foreign investment under the FDI screening regime, where such conversion results in the crossing of the 25% voting rights threshold.

*
* *

The FDI screening mechanism is a key consideration in any M&A transaction involving a foreign investor, as it applies whenever three cumulative criteria are met (see following chapters). However, transaction parties may find themselves unsettled by a legal framework that grants them discretion to assess whether those criteria are met, while effectively requiring them, if not as a matter of law, then in practice under certain conditions, to submit either a formal authorization request or, at the very least, a prior examination request.

In 2024 [388], a total of 392 filings related to foreign investments were submitted to the Directorate General of the Treasury) (Direction Générale du Trésor – DGT), compared to to 309 in 2023 and 325 in 2022. This figure includes authorization requests submitted by foreign investors, prior examination requests concerning the activities of a French company, filed either by the foreign investor or the French target entity, as well as notifications of the crossing of the 10% voting rights threshold in a listed company by a non-EU investor.

---

387. France, National Assembly, Committee for the Evaluation and Oversight of Public Policies, Information Report No. 1453, by JOLIVET, François, and de LEPINAU, Hervé, Members of Parliament, on the evaluation of foreign direct investment screening in France, Official Journal of the French Republic, May 27, 2025, text 45 of 69, published on May 22, 2025, last accessed May 27, 2025, available at https://www.assemblee-nationale.fr/dyn/17/rapports/cec/l17b1453_rapport-information

388. France, Ministry of the Economy, Finance and Industrial and Digital Sovereignty, Directorate General of the Treasury, Annual Report 2024, "Foreign Direct Investment Screening in France," published July 30, 2025, accessed July 31, 2025, available at https://www.tresor.economie.gouv.fr/Articles/2025/07/30/publication-du-rapport-annuel-sur-le-controle-ief-en-2024

Chapter 11

FDI Screening Requires the Involvement of a Foreign Investor

The first of the three cumulative conditions triggering the screening of a foreign investment is the involvement of a foreign investor.

The key challenge lies in defining the notion of a foreign investor in a manner that is consistent, on the one hand, with the overarching objective of protecting national interests, and on the other hand, with applicable legal standards.

As recalled [389] by the Ministry of the Economy, the regime applies to any natural person of foreign nationality, or to any French national who is not a tax resident in France. It also applies to any legal entity governed by foreign law, or to any French entity controlled either by a foreign-law entity or by a natural person of foreign nationality.

Moreover, any person or entity forming part of the control chain of the investor, whether of the direct investor or of the ultimate controlling entity, is deemed to be an investor for the purposes of the French FDI screening framework.

By Definition, the Foreign Investor Is Not French

The designation of an investor as "foreign" is central to determining whether the contemplated transaction may pose a threat to national interests.

Accordingly, one of the core elements of the French FDI screening framework lies in drawing a clear distinction between, on the one hand, "France" and, on the other hand, "foreign countries," which here refers to all jurisdictions other than France.

In this regard, after three decades of globalization and economic internationalization (1990–2020), crossing a national border no longer suffices to determine whether an investor qualifies as foreign. The government must therefore rely on a broader set

389. France, Ministry of the Economy, Finance and Industrial and Digital Sovereignty, Directorate General of the Treasury, "Conditions for a Transaction Subject to Prior Authorization," published December 30, 2024, accessed September 1, 2025, available at https://www.tresor.economie.gouv.fr/services-aux-entreprises/investissements-etrangers-en-france/les-conditions-d-une-operation-soumise-a-autorisation-prealable

of criteria in order to develop a legally and economically workable definition of a foreign investor.

A purely geographical [390] approach would prove inadequate for the purposes of the FDI screening regime, even if it may remain relevant in terms of statistical classification by country or sector. For example, under the methodology [391] adopted in the 6th edition of the IMF Balance of Payments Manual, geographical classifications are based solely on the immediate source of capital flows. If a U.S. company invests in France through a subsidiary established in another country, such as the Netherlands, the reported stock of foreign direct investment will attribute the transaction to the Netherlands, not to the United States, which is the ultimate beneficiary of the investment.

Sectoral classification is similarly limited: it is based on the economic activity assigned to each resident company in the French commercial register maintained by INSEE. No adjustments are made to reclassify holding companies, for example, according to the core activity of their corporate group.

Likewise, the concept of "residency" is not retained [392], although it is essential in determining whether a transaction falls within the balance of payments framework. Residency is defined as the center of predominant economic interest of a natural or legal person. Residents include individuals or entities whose primary economic activities are located in France, while non-residents include individuals who usually live abroad and foreign entities in respect of their foreign establishments. This definition of residency depends not on nationality but on the location of economic activity.

As a result, none of these approaches, geographic origin, sectoral affiliation, or residency, forms the basis of the legal definition of a foreign investor under the French screening regime.

Lawmakers could have considered using the notion of the "international nature" of an investment as a basis. Legally speaking [393], this notion is assessed in relation to the purpose and scope of the governing instrument [394]. In the context of free movement, an investment is considered international when it involves a cross-border capital flow, as reflected in the balance of payments, an OECD- or EU-type definition. However, this approach is statistical and accounting-based, relying heavily on the residency criterion, and fails to account for the national security or geopolitical implications at stake.

In the same vein, tax residency could have been adopted as a relevant criterion, but this was also rejected (see further below).

---

390. DUPEYRAT, op. cit., pp. 92–96
391. International Monetary Fund, Balance of Payments and International Investment Position Manual, Sixth Edition (BPM6), 2013, ISBN 978-1-46238-087-9 (PDF), accessed May 9, 2024, available at https://doi.org/10.5089/9781589068155.069
392. France, Banque de France, "Balance of Payments and International Investment Position – Annual Report 2022," Banque de France, published online July 20, 2023, accessed September 1st, 2025, available at https://www.banque-france.fr/fr/publications-et-statistiques/publications/la-balance-des-paiements-et-la-position-exterieure-de-la-france-2022
393. DUPEYRAT, op. cit.,
394. France, CARREAU, Dominique, and JUILLARD, Patrick, Droit international économique, 2nd edition, Paris, Dalloz, Précis collection, 2005, pp. 1129 et seq., EAN 9782247060252

Ultimately, when the objective is the protection and safeguarding of national interests (see Chapter 1), which forms the legal basis for derogating from the general freedom to invest, the nationality of the investor becomes a more relevant and decisive factor than residency. The real question is: what is the nationality of the investor who, once the investment is completed, will be able to exercise control or influence over the direction of the target entity?

The French FDI screening regime defines four criteria to determine whether an investor qualifies as "foreign"

From an operational standpoint, the notion[395] of "foreign investor" has been formally delineated by the Decree[396] of December 31, 2019, which codified Article R. 151-1 of the French Monetary and Financial Code. Under this provision, the term "foreign investor" refers to:

1° any natural person of foreign nationality;

2° any French national who is not domiciled in France within the meaning of Article 4 B of the French General Tax Code[397];

3° any entity governed by foreign law;

4° any French-law entity[398] controlled by one or more of the persons or entities referred to in items 1°, 2°, or 3° above.

---

395. It was the Decree of January 27, 1967, implementing the 1966 law on the control of foreign investments, that first introduced in France a legal definition of the "foreign" nature of an investment. At the time, "France" encompassed "continental France, Corsica, the overseas departments, and, except for the French Somaliland Coast, the overseas territories. The Principality of Monaco was assimilated to France." As for "Abroad," it was literally defined as "countries other than France" as previously specified.
Later, the Decree of March 7, 2003, regulating financial relations with foreign countries, established the nationality criterion of the investor in the following terms: it referred to a "foreign-law company or a non-resident natural person" (that is, a person whose primary center of interest is located abroad).
See DUPEYRAT, op. cit., p. 94.

396. France, Decree No. 2019-1590 of December 31, 2019, on foreign investments in France, Official Journal of the French Republic, No. 0001, January 1, 2020, NOR: ECOT1932857D

397. France, Tax Code (CGI), Article 4 B:
1. The following are considered to have their tax domicile in France:
a. Individuals whose household or principal place of residence is located in France;
b. Those who pursue a professional activity in France, whether salaried or not, unless they can demonstrate that such activity is carried out in France on an ancillary basis. Executives of companies whose registered office is located in France and whose annual turnover exceeds €250 million are deemed to carry out their main professional activity in France, unless proven otherwise. For companies that control other entities under the conditions set out in Article L. 233-16 of the Commercial Code, the turnover is understood as the sum of their own turnover and that of the entities they control. The term "executives" in the second paragraph of this subsection b includes the chairman of the board of directors when he or she also serves as chief executive officer, the chief executive officer, deputy chief executive officers, the president and members of the management board, managing partners, and any other officers with equivalent duties;
c. Those who have the center of their economic interests in France.
2. The following are also considered to have their tax domicile in France: civil servants of the State, local authorities, and public hospital services who perform their duties or are assigned abroad and who are not subject in that foreign country to personal income tax on all of their income.

398. The Decree of May 7, 2012 introduced the category of French-law companies controlled by foreign entities. It provided that French companies controlled by foreign investors (whether from third countries or EU Member States) would be subject to the regime applicable to EU investors. The key interest of the measure was to subject French companies controlled by foreign nationals to the French FDI screening

In practical terms, all foreign investors, regardless of their nationality, fall within the scope of the French foreign investment screening framework.

As regards criterion 1°, the French administration [399] interprets "foreign national" as any individual holding a nationality other than French. Such individuals are therefore classified as foreign investors.

For criterion 2°, determining whether a French national is not domiciled in France requires reference to Article 4 B of the General Tax Code. Notably, the French tax residency of a foreign national does not disqualify them from being considered a foreign investor. Conversely, a French national is considered a foreign investor when they are fiscally domiciled abroad.

Under Article 4 B [400], an individual is deemed fiscally domiciled in France if they meet any of the following conditions:

—they maintain their primary residence or habitual abode in France;

—they carry out a professional activity in France, whether salaried or not, unless they can demonstrate that such activity is incidental;

—they have the center of their economic interests in France;

—they are government agents performing duties or assigned to missions in a country where they are not subject to personal taxation on their worldwide income.

In cases of dual or multiple nationality, the presence of French nationality exempts the individual from the foreign investor classification, provided they are fiscally domiciled in France. However, dual or multiple nationals nationals domiciled abroad are treated as foreign investors. In such cases, their "foreignness" fulfills one of the three cumulative conditions required to trigger the FDI screening process.

With respect to Monegasque investors, the administration specified [401] in its 2022 guidelines that a natural person of Monegasque nationality qualifies as a foreign investor. However, if such a person also holds French nationality, they are then considered French. In the same vein, pursuant to the provisions of Article R. 152-11, paragraph 1, of the Monetary and Financial Code, a natural person of French nationality who is fiscally domiciled in Monaco is not regarded, for the purposes of the FDI screening regulations, as a foreign investor.

---

mechanism. Ultimately, investment transactions carried out by a French-law company controlled by (i) a natural person who was a national of a country other than France, (ii) a company whose registered office was located outside France, or (iii) a French national residing outside France, were also made subject to prior authorization. See DUPEYRAT, op. cit., p. 94.

399. See Point 1.1.1 in France, Ministry of the Economy, Finance and Industrial and Digital Sovereignty, Directorate General of the Treasury, "Guidelines on the Foreign Direct Investment Screening in France," July 2025, published July 30, 2025, accessed August 1, 2025, available at https://www.tresor.economie.gouv.fr/services-aux-entreprises/investissements-etrangers-en-france

400. France, Ministry of the Economy and Finance, Bulletin Officiel des Finances Publiques – Impôts (BOFiP), "IR – Champ d'application et territorialité – Personnes imposables et domicile fiscal," accessed September 1st, 2025, available at https://bofip.impots.gouv.fr/bofip/1910-PGP.html/identifiant%3DBOI-IR-CHAMP-20120912

401. See Point 1.1.1 in France, Ministry of the Economy, Finance and Industrial and Digital Sovereignty, Directorate General of the Treasury, "Guidelines on the Foreign Direct Investment Screening in France," September 2022, published September 8, 2022, accessed September 1, 2025, available at https://www.tresor.economie.gouv.fr/services-aux-entreprises/investissements-etrangers-en-france

The criterion of tax residence is assessed at the time of the transaction, based on the individual's habitual residence. A post-closing change of tax residency does not retroactively trigger a screening obligation, unless it is determined that the change was intended to circumvent French regulations.

With respect to legal entities, the French administration[402] considers that any entity governed by foreign law qualifies as a foreign investor. Accordingly, any entity, regardless of its legal form, that is subject to the law of a foreign State, including Monaco, whether that State is a member of the European Union (EU) or a third country outside the EU, is deemed a foreign investor.

It should be recalled that Article R. 151-1 of the Monetary and Financial Code, as revised by the Decree[403] of December 30, 2019, eliminated[404] the former distinction between, on the one hand, entities established in a Member State of the European Union or a party to the Agreement on the European Economic Area, and, on the other hand, entities established in third countries outside the European Union.

However, this broad classification raises interpretive challenges. While Article R. 151-2 refers to "entities," French domestic law does not provide a precise definition of this term.

The French administration faces a genuine legal challenge insofar as domestic law does not provide a clear statutory definition of the concept, even though the applicable regulation explicitly refers to it. In practice, the administration relies on the notion of "entity" as defined under European Union law[405], namely "an organized grouping of persons and assets enabling the pursuit of an economic activity with its own purpose." The Court of Justice of the European Union (CJEU) has consistently applied[406] this concept of entity to encompass any structure or organization that conducts an economic activity, regardless of its legal form or status[407].

---

402. France, Ministry of the Economy, Finance and Industrial and Digital Sovereignty, Directorate General of the Treasury, "Guidelines on the Foreign Direct Investment Screening in France" July 2025, published July 30, 2025, see Point 1.1.2, accessed August 1, 2025, available at https://www.tresor.economie.gouv.fr/services-aux-entreprises/investissements-etrangers-en-france
403. France, Decree No. 2019-1590 of December 31, 2019, on foreign investments in France, Official Journal of the French Republic, No. 0001, January 1, 2020, NOR: ECOT1932857D
404. Prior to this reform, a distinction had to be made with the category of "third countries," which encompassed all jurisdictions outside the European Economic Area (EEA) and Liechtenstein, the latter being excluded due to the absence of an administrative assistance convention. In other words, the member states of the European Economic Area (EEA) and Liechtenstein were not subject to the same regime as third countries such as the United States or China. This tripartite differentiation between "France," "European states," and "third countries" in practice facilitated circumvention strategies. That distinction has now been abolished.
405. European Union, Court of Justice of the European Communities, Judgment of March 11, 1997, Case C-13/95, Ayse Süzen v. Zehnacker Gebäudereinigung GmbH Krankenhausservice, ECLI:EU:C:1997:141, I-1259, Document 61995CJ0013, European Court Reports 1997 I-01259, paragraph 13
406. European Union, Court of Justice of the European Communities, Judgment of April 23, 1991, Case C-41/90, Klaus Höfner and Fritz Elser v. Macrotron GmbH, ECLI:EU:C:1991:161, I-1979, Document 61990CJ0041, Reports of Cases 1991 I-01979, paragraph 21: "the concept of an undertaking encompasses every entity engaged in an economic activity, regardless of the legal status of the entity and the way in which it is financed."
407. ibid

In a 1999 judgment[408], the Court of Justice of the European Communities defined the notion of "economic entity" as "an organized grouping of persons and assets enabling the pursuit of an economic activity with its own purpose." By way of interpretation, the French administration therefore considers that the notion of entity extends both to organized groupings vested with legal personality[409] and to those without it.

The scope of the concept is thus potentially very broad. To overcome this ambiguity, the French administration mainly refers to the interpretative guidance of the Court of Justice of the European Union(CJEU) . Accordingly, the administration takes the view that a foreign entity is to be understood as "*an organized grouping, whether or not vested with legal personality, without prejudice to the laws applicable in each State, enabling the pursuit of an activity and governed, as to its incorporation and operation, by non-French law.*"

Consequently, for the purposes of the French FDI screening regime (Investissements Étrangers en France – IEF), a foreign entity covers a wide range of private bodies (companies, branches, associations, trusts, investment vehicles, foundations, business groupings) as well as public bodies (States, local governments, and other public or semi-public entities) governed by non-French law. The administration had already clarified[410] in its first set of guidelines issued in 2022 that SPACs (Special Purpose Acquisition Companies), as listed investment vehicles incorporated under foreign law, may therefore qualify as foreign investors.

The fourth criterion captures any French-law entity (regardless of its legal form, commercial company, civil society, association, foundation, GIE, etc.) that is under the control of one or more foreign investors as defined above:
—a foreign natural person;
—a French national domiciled for tax purposes outside France and Monaco;
—a foreign-law entity.

A European Company (SE), governed by the Council Regulation[411] of October 8, 2001, and having its registered office in France, is deemed to be a French-law entity,

---

408. European Union, Court of Justice of the European Communities, Judgment of December 2, 1999, Case C-234/98, G. C. Allen et al. v. Amalgamated Construction Co. Ltd, ECLI:EU:C:1999:594, Document 61998CJ0234, Reports of Cases 1999 I-08643: "The concept of an economic entity refers to an organized grouping of persons and of assets enabling the exercise of an economic activity which pursues a specific objective."

409. In 2024, 44% of ultimate investors were financial investors (compared to 43% in 2023), 28% were natural persons (compared to 24% in 2023), and 27% were industrial investors (compared to 33% in 2023). Legal entities are classified either as industrial or financial investors. Source: France, Ministry of the Economy, Finance and Industrial and Digital Sovereignty, Directorate General of the Treasury, Annual Report 2024, "Foreign Direct Investment Screening in France," published on July 30, 2025, last accessed July 31, 2025, available at https://www.tresor.economie.gouv.fr/Articles/2025/07/30/publication-du-rapport-annuel-sur-le-controle-ief-en-2024

410. This clarification is significant, as when investing in a SPAC, the investor does not know precisely how the funds raised by the company will ultimately be allocated. The investor only knows that the company intends to invest in a certain type of businesses or sectors. The decision therefore rests on a matter of trust in the managers.

411. European Communities, Council Regulation (EC) No. 2157/2001 of October 8, 2001, on the Statute for a European company (SE), Official Journal of the European Communities, L 294/1, November 10, 2001, ELI: http://data.europa.eu/eli/reg/2001/2157/oj

subject to French law pursuant to Articles L. 229-1 and L. 210-3 of the French Commercial Code. Accordingly, it is not treated as a foreign investor, unless it is itself controlled by a foreign investor. In 2025, the administration clarified that a European company whose registered office is located outside French territory qualifies as a foreign investor, even if its operational headquarters is located in France.

In general, it would be more accurate, within the meaning of Article R. 151-1, to refer to the "foreign status of the investor" rather than to the "foreign investor" per se.

Finally, Article R. 151-10 of the Monetary and Financial Code [412], introduced by the same 2019 Decree [413], requires that investors disclose any connections with foreign states or public bodies when submitting a prior authorization request. Such affiliations may be grounds for denial of authorization [414].

Similarly, the origin-of-funds investigation, undertaken under international cooperation mechanisms referenced in Article R. 151-17, is not in itself a criterion for distinguishing between foreign and French investors. A payment initiated from a French bank account does not preclude the investor from being qualified as a foreign person or entity under the FDI screening framework.

The Administration Also Assesses Whether the Investor Is Under Foreign Control

Beyond the regulatory definition of a "foreign" investor set forth in points 1°, 2°, and 3° of Article R. 151-1 of the French Monetary and Financial Code, the French Treasury administration also scrutinizes the actual nationality of the investor. This inevitably raises the question of the control chain and ultimate control. This issue is addressed in point 4° of the same article, which covers any French-law [415] entity controlled by one or more individuals or entities of foreign nationality or established under foreign law.

Identifying the control chain is key to safeguarding the Nation's interests. The French government must be able to assess whether various investment vehicles might be used as proxies to facilitate indirect takeovers by foreign investors, some potentially acting on behalf of foreign states. Consequently, the investor's status cannot be

412. DUPEYRAT, op. cit.,

413. France, Decree No. 2019-1590 of December 31, 2019, on foreign investments in France, Official Journal of the French Republic, No. 0001, January 1, 2020, NOR: ECOT1932857D

414. France, Monetary and Financial Code, Article R. 151-10: "...The minister may take into account the fact that the investor has ties with a foreign government or public body."

415. As a reminder, the Decree of May 7, 2012 introduced the category of French-law entities controlled by foreign persons. It provided that French companies under foreign control, whether by third-country or EU investors, would be subject to the regime applicable to EU investors. The key purpose was to bring under the French FDI screening framework those French companies that are effectively controlled by foreign interests. Accordingly, investments carried out by (i) a French-law entity controlled by a natural person who is a national of a country other than France, (ii) a company with its registered office located outside of France, or (iii) a French national residing abroad were also subject to prior authorization procedures.
DUPEYRAT, op. cit.,

determined solely by reference to the law of the country in which it is incorporated; the full control chain must be analyzed to assess any actual risk.

To that end, paragraph II of Article R. 151-1 defines the "control chain" as encompassing any investor composed of: (i) any foreign-law entity, or (ii) any French-law entity controlled by one or more individuals or entities that are either foreign nationals, French nationals not domiciled[416] in France for tax purposes, or foreign-law entities.

In short, all persons and entities forming part of the control chain qualify as "investors" for purposes of French FDI rules.

This approach entails two main consequences[417]:

—First, any member of the control chain may submit the authorization application on behalf of all investors within the chain, pursuant to Article R. 151-5 of the Monetary and Financial Code;

—Second, each member of the control chain is deemed an investor. Therefore, if just one member qualifies as a foreign investor under French FDI rules, the entire investment is considered to originate from a foreign investor. For example, a control chain composed of French entities or individuals, but including one foreign national, non-resident French national, or foreign-law entity (including an investment vehicle), qualifies as foreign, even if the ultimate controlling investor is French[418].

Legally, control is assessed[419] primarily by reference to Article[420] L. 233-3 of the Commercial Code. If control cannot be established under that standard, a subsidiary

---

416. France, Tax Code, Article 4 B

417. France, Ministry of the Economy, Finance and Industrial and Digital Sovereignty, Directorate General of the Treasury, "Guidelines on the Foreign Direct Investment Screening in France," July 2025, published July 30, 2025, see Point 1.1.3, accessed August 1, 2025, available at https://www.tresor.economie.gouv.fr/services-aux-entreprises/investissements-etrangers-en-france

418. "The classification as a non-European investor takes into account both the direct investor and all entities or natural persons forming its chain of control (Art. R. 151-1 of the Monetary and Financial Code). In cases where there are multiple investors (as in co-control situations), the presence of at least one non-European investor results in the classification as a non-European investor, regardless of the origin of the other ultimate investors." Source: France, Ministry of the Economy, Finance and Industrial and Digital Sovereignty, Directorate General of the Treasury, Annual Report 2024, "Foreign Direct Investment Screening in France," published July 30, 2025, accessed July 31, 2025, available at https://www.tresor.economie.gouv.fr/Articles/2025/07/30/publication-du-rapport-annuel-sur-le-controle-ief-en-2024

419. The Monetary and Financial Code incorporates the definition of foreign investment established by the Commercial Code, in particular Article L. 233-3, since Decree No. 2005-1739 of December 30, 2005. This extension allows for the inclusion of situations in which a minority investor, such as an investment fund, holds veto rights over certain key decisions through statutory or contractual provisions. As a result, foreign investments are not limited to majority acquisitions but also encompass cases of joint control or negative control, where influence over the target entity may be exercised without holding a majority of voting rights.

420. France, Commercial Code, Article L. 233-3, version in force since December 5, 2015

I. - For the purposes of Sections 2 and 4 of this Chapter, a natural or legal person shall be deemed to control another entity where:

1° They directly or indirectly hold a portion of the capital conferring a majority of the voting rights in the general meetings of that company;

2° They alone hold a majority of the voting rights in that company pursuant to an agreement entered into with other partners or shareholders, provided such agreement is not contrary to the company's interests;

test based on paragraph III of Article L. 430-1 of the same code[421] applies. In performing this analysis, the administration refers to the interpretation provided by the French Competition Authority's 2020 merger control guidelines[422], subject to any updates.

During its review, the Foreign Investment Screening Bureau (Bureau du CIEF) evaluates the investor's nationality at all levels of the ownership structure. The foreign character of the investment is determined by assessing the entire ownership chain of the direct acquirer. If any link in that chain qualifies as foreign, the investment is considered foreign. Investors are also required to notify the Directorate General of the Treasury (DGT) of any changes to the control chain, even after authorization or completion of the transaction.

Investment vehicles, regardless of their legal form or jurisdiction of incorporation, are considered investors under Article R. 151-1. They may be foreign investors in their own right, regardless of the nationality or domicile of their asset manager.

For instance, if a French holding company is controlled by a Luxembourg investment fund managed by a French asset management company, that Luxembourg fund qualifies as a foreign investor under the applicable regulation.

By contrast, the creation of a French investment vehicle by a group of foreign investors, none of whom exercises control within the meaning of Article L. 233-3 or Section III of Article L. 430-1 of the French Commercial Code, does not in itself constitute a transaction subject to foreign investment screening in France. The transactions carried out by such a vehicle are not deemed to be investment operations, since the vehicle, in this case, does not qualify as a foreign investor[423].

However, the administration does not adopt a categorical position on such situations. It takes into account the diversity of forms and legal structures of investment

3° They in fact determine, by the voting rights at their disposal, the decisions made at the general meetings of that company;
4° They are a partner or shareholder of that company and have the power to appoint or remove the majority of the members of the administrative, executive, or supervisory bodies of that company.
II. – Control is presumed when a person directly or indirectly holds more than 40% of the voting rights and no other partner or shareholder directly or indirectly holds a larger share than theirs.
III. – For the same purposes, two or more persons acting in concert shall be deemed to jointly control another entity where they in fact determine the decisions taken at general meetings.

421. France, Commercial Code, Article L. 430-1, paragraph III
III. – For the purposes of this Title, control results from rights, contracts, or other means which, either separately or jointly and having regard to the relevant factual or legal circumstances, enable a decisive influence to be exercised over the activity of an undertaking, and in particular:
—rights of ownership or use over all or part of the assets of an undertaking;
—rights or contracts that confer a decisive influence over the composition, deliberations or decisions of the undertaking's corporate bodies.

422. France, Competition Authority, "Guidelines on merger control – 2020," July 23, 2020, last accessed September 1st, 2025, available at https://www.autoritedelaconcurrence.fr/sites/default/files/Lignes_directrices_concentrations_2020.pdf

423. France, Ministry of the Economy, Finance, Industrial and Digital Sovereignty, Directorate General of the Treasury, "Guidelines on the Foreign Direct Investment Screening in France July 2025, Point 1.2, published July 30, 2025, accessed August 1, 2025, available at https://www.tresor.economie.gouv.fr/services-aux-entreprises/investissements-etrangers-en-france

funds, whether established within the European Union or in third countries, and conducts a case-by-case analysis of the control chain of such funds in light of Articles L. 233-3 and L. 430-1(III) of the French Commercial Code. The administration then examines the specific features of each structure, including the rights and obligations of the investors on the one hand and, where applicable, of the management company on the other. Particular attention is paid to the fund's mode of management (internal or external) as well as, where relevant, to the provisions of the fund's governing rules.

This tailored analysis directly impacts the content of the authorization application. Under Article 1 of the amended Ministerial Order [424] of December 31, 2019 on foreign investments in France, where the control chain includes one or more investment funds, documentation must be submitted identifying the fund manager (s) and the individuals or entities controlling them.

In a 2020 decision [425], the French Conseil d'État ruled that the applicant is required to disclose the identity of the fund's manager, and, if the manager is a legal entity, the natural persons or public bodies controlling it. However, there is no obligation to identify every investor in the fund.

In that case, the transaction involved an investment fund and the identity of the fund manager was properly disclosed. The petitioners argued that the administration should have gone further and traced control to the ultimate beneficial owners, as is the case for regular corporate entities. The government countered that, unlike majority shareholders in corporations, fund investors do not control the fund; that function lies with the fund manager. The Conseil d'État agreed, finding that disclosure of the manager's identity is sufficient to establish control for purposes of the IEF regime .

The government's representative even imagined [426] a scenario in which a fund is merely a façade for hidden investors who dictate decisions that should lawfully be made by the manager. But only in such cases of suspected abuse would the administration conduct a deeper investigation into the fund's substance. Such inquiries would not occur during the initial application process, which does not require disclosure of all unit holders, since they do not exercise operational control over the target.

As summarized by the French Treasury [427]: "*If one link in the control chain qualifies as foreign under the regulation, the investor is deemed foreign.*"

---

424. France, Ministerial Order of December 31, 2019, on foreign investments in France, Official Journal of the French Republic, No. 0001, January 1, 2020, NOR: ECOT1937237A

425. France, Council of State (6th–5th Combined Chambers), Decision No. 422580 of 3 April 2020, M. and Mme B... v. FII Co and Warwick Capital Partners, ECLI:FR:CECHR:2020:422580.20200403, listed in the tables of the Recueil Lebon, holding that "for a transaction carried out by an investment fund, it is for the applicant to indicate the identity of the fund manager and, where that manager is itself a legal person, the identity of the natural persons or public entities controlling it; and by finding that no provision requires the identification of all investors participating in that fund, the court did not err in law."

426. France, Council of State, HOYNCK, Stéphane, Public Rapporteur, Conclusions, Session of March 4, 2020, Decision No. 422580 of April 3, 2020, M. and Mme. B... and Warwick Capital Partners, judgment delivered on April 3, 2020, last accessed September 1st, 2025, available at https://www.conseil-etat.fr/fr/arianeweb/CRP/conclusion/2020-04-03/422580?download_pdf

427. France, Ministry of the Economy, Finance and Recovery, Directorate General of the Treasury, "FAQ on Foreign Investments in France," January 2025, p. 3, accessed September 1, 2025, available at https://www.tresor.economie.gouv.fr/Institutionnel/Niveau2/Pages/f149e66d-6df2-4726-a594-3d95409d7a46/files/7d5e95fd-ca16-496d-815a-4242973300f4

For a more practical perspective, the 2025 annual report[428] specifies that in 2024, most screened investments, 65 percent, were carried out by ultimate controlling investors from outside the European Union (compared to 67.4 percent the previous year). The principal countries of origin for these ultimate investors were the United States, the United Kingdom, and Switzerland.

Investors controlled from within the European Union and the European Economic Area accounted for 35 percent of the authorization requests submitted. The leading countries of origin for these investors were Luxembourg, Germany, and the Netherlands, which remained unchanged compared to 2023.

The Administration Also Investigates Foreign Influence

The potential existence of foreign influence within the control chain is equally critical. Article R. 151-1 allows the French authorities not only to examine ultimate control but also to consider any form of foreign control or influence.

If control within the meaning of Article L. 233-3 of the Commercial Code cannot be established, the administration may nonetheless assess whether the investor is subject to decisive operational, economic, or political influence from third parties, even those with no equity ties. If such influence is found, and if it enables or could enable actions contrary to France's essential national interests, the investment may be lawfully restricted[429].

The administration therefore considers both **control by** and **influence over** the investor. This includes cases in which a French ultimate investor acts through foreign-law intermediaries, rendering the transaction notifiable under the IEF regime due solely to the presence of a foreign-controlled intermediary.

Investigating such influence can be particularly complex when the investor is a listed company or when shareholders are based outside the EU. In these cases, authorities must trace the highest level of governance and decision-making. Investors are strongly encouraged to proactively share full and transparent information with the Treasury. Failure to do so can slow down the review process and raise concerns about the transaction's true nature.

Once authorization is granted, this question of control and influence remains relevant for monitoring compliance with imposed conditions. The regime has been

428. France, Ministry of the Economy, Finance and Industrial and Digital Sovereignty, Directorate General of the Treasury, Annual Report 2024, "Foreign Direct Investment Screening in France," published July 30, 2025, accessed July 31, 2025, available at https://www.tresor.economie.gouv.fr/Articles/2025/07/30/publication-du-rapport-annuel-sur-le-controle-ief-en-2024

429. The OECD also addresses the issue of the ultimate nationality of the investor. This is a common challenge faced by all member countries: how to determine the investor's true nationality, in other words, to identify who ultimately controls the investing entity. Among OECD members, there is no consensus on the effectiveness of nationality as the most appropriate criterion, particularly when the State is dealing with financial investors such as investment funds or hedge funds. The issue becomes even more pronounced in cases where investments are structured through offshore financial centers or tax havens. Nevertheless, ultimate control remains a relevant and meaningful concept in this context.

adapted to ensure the administration can identify those individuals or entities within the control chain responsible[430] for fulfilling undertakings and can hold them accountable in case of breach. Any change, however minor, in the control chain post-authorization must also be reported to the authorities.

At the same time, while the investor must disclose the entire control chain, particularly in cases involving multiple shareholders, this does not entitle the investor to share the authorization or its conditions with co-investors. This is due to the government's desire to prevent sensitive information from being disclosed to a foreign shareholder who, though present in the control chain, is not deemed a threat. This is a matter not only of trade secrecy but of national security, as key details in the authorization and the related undertakings must be kept confidential.

As the French administration recalls[431], the Minister may also take into account any links existing between the investor and a foreign government or public entity.

These links may take multiple forms: equity-related (direct or indirect ownership interests in the investor, including through state-owned enterprises or public bodies, or any decisive public influence), financial (subsidies, loans, grants, or tax exemptions), political or decisive influence (power to appoint directors, to determine strategic decisions, or to shape the operational framework of the business), or submission to a specific regulatory regime imposing extraordinary obligations toward a State (such as mandatory disclosure of information or prior authorization requirements for strategic decisions).

Accordingly, while the French foreign investment screening mechanism is applied without discrimination based on the investor's nationality, the existence of links with a foreign government or public entity is considered as a factor in the risk assessment. Special attention is given to opaque or complex investment structures and arrangements.

Lastly, foreign influence is assessed through multiple lenses, and certain countries receive heightened scrutiny, even though France officially maintains a non-discriminatory approach. China is one such example. A Senate information report[432] recently highlighted the Chinese government's refocusing of its influence tools toward the economic sphere. In this context, French intelligence services closely monitor[433] entities

430. France, Monetary and Financial Code, Article R. 151-8, "II. – Where the investment authorization is subject to conditions, it shall designate, among the investors within the meaning of Article R. 151-1 II, on whose behalf the authorization was requested, the investor or investors responsible for complying with those conditions."

431. France, Ministry of the Economy, Finance and Industrial and Digital Sovereignty, Directorate General of the Treasury, "Guidelines on the Foreign Direct Investment Screening in France," July 2025, published July 30, 2025, see Point 2.2.3.3, accessed August 1, 2025, available at https://www.tresor.economie.gouv.fr/services-aux-entreprises/investissements-etrangers-en-france

432. France, Senate, Information Report No. 873, September 29, 2021, submitted on behalf of the fact-finding mission on extra-European state influences in French higher education and academia and their consequences, GATTOLIN A., Senator, accessed September 1st, 2025, available at https://www.senat.fr/rap/r20-873/r20-873.html

433. France, Senate, Written Question No. 02204 to the Minister of the Interior, Official Journal of the Senate, August 4, 2022, p. 4108, KAROUTCHI R., Senator, Les Républicains (LR) group, ministerial reply, March 30, 2023, Official Journal of the Senate, p. 2217

active in strategic sectors, operators of vital importance (OIVs and PIVs), and institutions hosting sensitive facilities (ZRRs), especially within the framework of the national Scientific and Technical Potential Protection (PPST) regime. The General Directorate for Internal Security (DGSI) monitors various threats, including legal and financial takeovers, cyberattacks, intrusions, destabilization, data theft, and reputational harm.

The Administration Also Assesses the Investor's Integrity

As part of its review of whether a transaction involves a foreign investor, the French administration also conducts a due-diligence process to assess the investor's personal and professional integrity. This assessment is not directly tied to the investor's nationality but rather focuses on their conduct and reputation in the marketplace.

This integrity review is critical, as it may serve as grounds for the Minister of the Economy to deny authorization. The Minister may determine that the investor does not qualify as a "foreign investor" under the applicable regime solely [434] because there are "serious doubts regarding the investor's integrity." An investor's integrity may be called into question if, for instance, they have been convicted of financial fraud or other white-collar crimes, sentenced to a term of imprisonment, or maintain connections with a foreign state deemed to pose a threat to France's essential national interests.

Such assessments are typically conducted by the Strategic Information and Economic Security Service (Service de l'information stratégique et de la sécurité économiques – SISSE) or by French intelligence services, on behalf of the Interministerial Committee for Foreign Direct Investments Screening (Comité interministériel du contrôle des investissements étrangers en France – CIEF) .

The French Government has clarified the consequences of a negative integrity assessment in the context of a transaction reviewed by Parliament. It emphasized [435] that if an investor's integrity is in doubt, the proposed investment may be denied authorization, and the transaction may not proceed (see Chapter 22).

This possibility is also confirmed by French administrative case law. In particular, the Council of State (Conseil d'État) upheld the Government's decision in a case involving a challenge brought by "Pathé France Holding" against the deferral of a foreign direct investment transaction. In its ruling [436], the Court affirmed that the Minister of the Economy is entitled, when assessing potential risks to public order or national

434. France, Ministry of the Economy, Finance, Industrial and Digital Sovereignty, Directorate General of the Treasury, "Conditions for a Transaction Requiring Prior Authorization," published on May 23, 2023, available at https://www.tresor.economie.gouv.fr/services-aux-entreprises/investissements-etrangers-en-france/les-conditions-d-une-operation-soumise-a-autorisation-prealable (last accessed May 9, 2024)
435. France, National Assembly, Written Question No. 9625 to the Minister of the Economy, Finance and Industrial and Digital Sovereignty, Official Journal of the National Assembly, July 4, 2023, TANGUY J.-Ph., Member of Parliament, Rassemblement National (RN) group, ministerial reply, August 29, 2023, Official Journal of the National Assembly, p. 7761
436. France, Council of State, 6th / 2nd Sub-Sections, Decision No. 160550 of April 15, 1996, published in the Recueil Lebon

security, to consider both the conduct of the individual or entity benefiting from the investment and the origin of the funds used to finance the transaction.

In that case, the record showed that the acquirer's behavior raised serious concerns about their integrity (including criminal convictions, even if later pardoned or amnestied), as well as suspicions surrounding the origin of the funds. Accordingly, the Minister was justified in concluding that the proposed acquisition posed a threat to public order and in deciding to defer the transaction.

*
* *

While the presence of a "foreign investor" is the first of the three cumulative criteria that trigger the screening procedure, it is not always straightforward. Although the legal framework sets out four alternative tests for determining whether an investor qualifies as "foreign," this classification alone is insufficient to settle the matter.

For this reason, the administration further examines whether the investor is ultimately under foreign control and, beyond integrity, whether they are subject to foreign influence. Paradoxically, while the French foreign investment screening mechanism operates within the broader EU framework on FDI filtering, the French approach remains resolutely national in scope. It thereby excludes any possibility of reclassification that could arise solely from an investor's establishment within another Member State of the European Union.

Chapter 12

FDI screening also requires that the investment target a specific French-law entity

An investment made by a foreign investor must be submitted for prior review by the Minister of the Economy if it qualifies as an investment operation in a French-law entity. The investment operation in a French target company therefore constitutes the second cumulative condition, in addition to the foreign nature of the investor, discussed in the previous chapter. A summary table for this chapter is provided at the end.

The specific nature of the investment is assessed based on the control or influence it confers

The Minister will examine the nature of the transaction to determine whether it qualifies as an investment and must therefore be authorized. For a transaction to be considered an investment, reference must be made to Article R. 151-2 of the French Monetary and Financial Code [437], which provides that an investment, for the purposes [438] of Article L. 151-3 (public authority, public order, public security, national defense), includes the following operations by a foreign investor as defined in paragraph I of Article R. 151-1:

1° acquiring control, within the meaning of Article L. 233-3 of the French Commercial Code, of a French-law entity or of an establishment registered with the French Trade and Companies Register;

2° acquiring all or part of a business line of a French-law entity;

3° crossing, directly or indirectly, alone or in concert, the threshold of 25% of voting rights in a French-law entity;

437. France, Decree No. 2019-1590 of December 31, 2019, on foreign investments in France, Official Journal of the French Republic, No. 0001, January 1, 2020, NOR: ECOT1932857D, Article 1

438. "...any activity which, in France and even on an occasional basis, either participates in the exercise of public authority, or is likely to impair public order, public security, or national defense interests, or, finally, is related to the research, production or marketing of weapons, munitions, powders, and explosive substances."

4° crossing, directly or indirectly, alone or in concert, the threshold[439] of 10% of voting rights in a French-law company whose shares are admitted to trading on a regulated market.

Important[440] clarification: items 3° and 4° apply only to third-country investors outside the European Union. They do not apply to individuals who are nationals of an EU Member State or of a State party to the European Economic Area Agreement that has concluded an administrative assistance convention with France to combat fraud and tax evasion, and who are domiciled in one of those States; nor do they apply to entities whose entire chain of control, within the meaning of paragraph II of Article R. 151-1, is governed by the laws of such States or whose members are nationals of and domiciled in one of those States.

The French administration assesses the specific nature of an investment beyond the strict scope of regulatory categories.

In practice, the administration examines any type of investment and does not consider itself bound by a rigid classification. Investment transactions and structures are inherently diverse and therefore are not exhaustively enumerated in the applicable regulations. The list is illustrative rather than limitative. By way of example, the administration[441] specifies that transactions falling within the scope of Article R. 151-2 of the Monetary and Financial Code may include acquisitions of shares or equity interests, mergers, contributions in kind, transfers, or exchanges of shares, whether effected for consideration (e.g., a sale) or gratuitously (e.g., gifts or donations).

Furthermore, the administration underscores that the concept of the target entity of the investment must be construed broadly, in a manner comparable to the assessment of a corporate investor. It encompasses a wide range of organizational forms such as corporations, foundations, trusts, and similar structures (see Chapter 11).

Foreign Direct Investment (FDI) screening in France covers any foreign investment targeting a French-law entity

Regardless of the nature of the investment, be it the acquisition of control (as provided under point 1°), the purchase of all or part of a branch of activity (point 2°), or the crossing, even indirectly, of a threshold in voting rights (points 3° and 4°), the operation must necessarily target an entity governed by French law in order to satisfy the second cumulative criterion (the nature of the transaction) that triggers the FDI

439. The initial 25% threshold was permanently lowered to 10% by Decree No. 2023-1293 of December 28, 2023, on foreign investments in France, Official Journal of the French Republic, No. 0301, December 29, 2023, NOR: ECOT2323089D

440. ibid

441. France, Ministry of the Economy, Finance and Industrial and Digital Sovereignty, Directorate General of the Treasury, Guidelines on the Foreign Direct Investment Screening in France, July 2025, Point 1.2, published July 30, 2025, accessed August 1, 2025, available at https://www.tresor.economie.gouv.fr/services-aux-entreprises/investissements-etrangers-en-france

screening regime . The first criterion relates to the foreign status of the investor (see Chapter 11).

As previously stated [442], the French authorities interpret the notion of "entity," in this context a French-law entity, in light of the case law of the Court of Justice of the European Union(CJEU) . According to the CJEU, an "entity" encompasses any structure or organization engaging in an economic activity, regardless of its legal status or form. In a 1999 judgment [443], the CJEU defined the concept of economic entity as "a combination of human and material resources enabling the pursuit of a specific economic objective." Based on this interpretation, the French administration considers the notion of entity to include both organized structures endowed with legal personality and those without it.

As a general rule, a French-law entity refers to any entity established under and governed by French national law. This includes private legal persons, such as commercial companies, civil companies, economic interest groupings (GIE), and associations. Certain private legal entities may also be entrusted with the management of public services. Additionally, it includes public legal persons such as the French State and its various administrative subdivisions, local authorities, and public institutions.

The administration [444] emphasizes that the concept of entity should be construed broadly, encompassing a wide range of organizational forms including corporations, foundations, trusts, and other comparable structures (see Chapter 11).

In 2023, the Minister of the Economy expanded [445] the scope of the FDI screening mechanism to include acquisitions of control over French branches of foreign-law entities engaged in sensitive activities relevant to public order, public security, or national defense interests. This reform aimed [446] to respond to the growing complexity of investment structures and to mitigate the risk of circumvention of the regulation by foreign investors. Whereas the scope of the screening mechanism initially covered only French-law companies, it was extended to include any establishment registered in the French Trade and Companies Register (Registre du commerce et des sociétés).

---

442. European Union, Court of Justice of the European Communities, Judgment of April 23, 1991, Case C-41/90, Klaus Hëfner and Fritz Elser v. Macrotron GmbH., ECLI:EU:C:1991:161, I-1981, Document 61990CJ0041, Reports of Cases 1991 I-01979, para. 21: "the concept of an undertaking encompasses every entity engaged in an economic activity, regardless of the legal status of the entity and the way in which it is financed."
443. European Union, Court of Justice of the European Communities, Judgment of December 2, 1999, Case C-234/98, G. C. Allen and Others v. Amalgamated Construction Co. Ltd, ECLI:EU:C:1999:594, Document 61998CJ0234, Reports of Cases 1999 I-08643: "The concept of an economic entity refers to an organized grouping of persons and assets enabling the exercise of an economic activity pursuing a specific objective."
444. France, Ministry of the Economy, Finance and Industrial and Digital Sovereignty, Directorate General of the Treasury, Guidelines on the Foreign Direct Investment Screening in France July 2025, Point 1.2, published July 30, 2025, accessed August 1, 2025, available at https://www.tresor.economie.gouv.fr/services-aux-entreprises/investissements-etrangers-en-france
445. France, Decree No. 2023-1293 of December 28, 2023, on foreign investments in France, Official Journal of the French Republic, No. 0301, December 29, 2023, NOR: ECOT2323089D
446. France, Ministry of the Economy, Finance, Industrial and Digital Sovereignty, Directorate General of the Treasury, Annual Report 2024, "Foreign Direct Investment Screening in France," published on June 4, 2024, accessed on June 6, 2024, available at https://www.tresor.economie.gouv.fr/Articles/c7ec36f3-6df0-4cf8-82aa-9c772917afeb/files/249123ae-5a3b-45dd-8f6f-5f84b2fc0c0a

As the administration recalls, this extension complements the existing coverage of branch transfers (point 2° of Article R. 151-2 of the French Monetary and Financial Code), which already allowed for the review of acquisitions of branches of French-law entities involved in sensitive activities.

The screening mechanism also applies to any establishment registered in the French Trade and Companies Register (registre du commerce et des sociétés – RCS).

The French administration has clarified [447] the situation of an acquisition involving the control of an establishment registered in the Trade and Companies Register (RCS) in France. This situation, expressly covered by Decree No. 2023-1293 of December 28, 2023 on foreign investments in France, which entered into force on January 1, 2024, introduced into Article R. 151-2, paragraph 1 of the Monetary and Financial Code this new category of investment.

The notion of an establishment registered in the Trade and Companies Register must be understood within the meaning of Articles L. 123-1 et seq. of the Commercial Code. Accordingly, under Article R. 151-2 of the Monetary and Financial Code, an investment includes the acquisition, by a foreign investor, of control over a foreign-law entity holding an establishment registered in the French Trade and Companies Register.

Likewise, the acquisition, by a foreign investor, of control over a French-law entity holding such an establishment is also considered to constitute the acquisition of control over a French-law entity.

By contrast, the acquisition of control over an establishment registered solely in the National Business Register (Registre National des Entreprises), within the meaning of Articles L. 123-36 et seq. of the Commercial Code, without registration in the Trade and Companies Register, does not fall within the scope defined by Article R. 151-2 of the Monetary and Financial Code.

FDI screening in France does not apply to the creation of a French legal entity (greenfield investment).

Only investment transactions carried out by a foreign investor in French-law entities that, at the date of the transaction, engage in sensitive activities within the meaning of Articles L. 151-3 and R. 151-3 of the Monetary and Financial Code require the prior authorization of the Minister.

447. France, Ministry of the Economy, Finance and Industrial and Digital Sovereignty, Directorate General of the Treasury, "Guidelines on the Foreign Direct Investment Screening in France," July 2025, Point 1.2.2, published July 30, 2025, accessed August 1, 2025, available at https://www.tresor.economie.gouv.fr/services-aux-entreprises/investissements-etrangers-en-france

Accordingly, the creation of entities in France[448] by a foreign investor to develop an activity in France, also referred to as "creation investments" or "greenfield investments", does not fall within the scope of the French FDI screening regime .

This does not, however, prejudice the application of the regime to any subsequent investment transaction carried out within the newly incorporated entity[449], whether in the form of an equity transaction or the acquisition of an establishment registered with the Trade and Companies Register (Registre du Commerce et des Sociétés, RCS) or of a business unit belonging to a French-law entity.

It should be noted that, although greenfield investments are not covered by the FDI screening regime under the eligibility criteria, conversely, in the case of a transaction involving a foreign investor originating from a third country outside the European Union, the investor must complete the "Request for Information from the Investor" form (see Annex E), which expressly provides for the reporting of this type of investment.

Furthermore, the administration emphasizes[450] that the lack of eligibility under the French FDI screening regime does not necessarily mean that the activities of the company concerned by the investment are not considered sensitive for the national interests protected by the regime. This does not exclude the potential application of other regulations aimed at safeguarding national interests (see Chapter 7).

Finally, parties to a transaction should bear in mind that this issue is at the core of ongoing parliamentary discussions, with the 2025 fact-finding and oversight mission[451] of the National Assembly recommending an extension[452] of the regime's scope to include this category of investment.

FDI screening does not apply to intra-group transactions

Under the French framework governing foreign direct investment (FDI), the question arises as to whether intra-group transactions are subject to the FDI screening

---

448. France, Business France, Press Release, February 29, 2024, "France strengthens its attractiveness in an unstable global context," published on February 29, 2024, accessed on May 27, 2025, available at https://media.businessfrance.fr/actualites/la-france-consolide-son-attractivite-dans-un-contexte-mondial-instable-61a5-0fea0.html

449. France, Ministry of the Economy, Finance, Industrial and Digital Sovereignty, Directorate General of the Treasury, "Guidelines on the Foreign Direct Investment Screening in France July 2025, published on July 30, 2025, accessed on August 1, 2025, available at https://www.tresor.economie.gouv.fr/services-aux-entreprises/investissements-etrangers-en-france

450. Ibid. Point 2.2.3.2.1

451. France, National Assembly, Committee for the Evaluation and Oversight of Public Policies, Information Report No. 1453 by JOLIVET, François and de LEPINAU, Hervé, Members of Parliament, on the evaluation of foreign direct investment screening in France, Official Journal of the French Republic, May 27, 2025, text 45 of 69, published on May 22, 2025, accessed on May 27, 2025, available at https://www.assemblee-nationale.fr/dyn/17/rapports/cec/l17b1453_rapport-information.

452. Proposal No. 3: Broaden the definition of eligible investments to include types of transactions other than the acquisition of control within the meaning of Article L. 233-3 of the Commercial Code, the acquisition of all or part of a branch of activity, or the crossing of a threshold of voting rights, by inserting the mention of creation investments ("greenfield investments").

mechanism. These operations may involve transactions between companies belonging to the same corporate group, or between a parent company and one or more of its subsidiaries, whether in the form of financing arrangements, the purchase of goods or services, the granting of a loan, or, most relevant here, the execution of an investment transaction, a sale, or an asset transfer.

From a regulatory standpoint, the Monetary and Financial Code establishes an exception to the obligation to file a prior authorization request in this specific case. Article R. 151-7(I) of the Monetary and Financial Code provides that "the investor is exempt from the authorization requirement ... where the ultimate investor in the control chain, within the meaning of Article R. 151-1(II), had, prior to the contemplated transaction, already acquired control, within the meaning of Article L. 233-3 of the Commercial Code, of the entity subject to the investment."

Accordingly, in the context of an intra-group transaction, namely, an investment transaction carried out between entities belonging to the same corporate group, that is, entities directly or indirectly held by more than 50 percent of the share capital or voting rights by the same shareholder, the administration clarifies [453] that the investor is exempt from the obligation to file a prior authorization request.

In such a case, the exemption applies because the ultimate investor in the control chain has already acquired control, within the meaning of Article L. 233-3 of the Commercial Code, of the entity that is the target of the investment. Therefore, if an application is nonetheless filed despite the benefit of this exemption, the investor will be informed that the request is moot.

This rule must be assessed ab initio, meaning that the entities concerned must already belong, prior to the contemplated transaction, to the same group under the control, within the meaning of Article L. 233-3 of the Commercial Code, of the ultimate investor in the control chain, and not as a result of the contemplated transaction. The exemption from prior authorization for an intra-group reorganization is evaluated solely by reference to Article L. 233-3 of the Commercial Code, and not, as may be the case for determining the status of a foreign investor, by reference to Article L. 430-1(III) of the Commercial Code.

The administration nonetheless emphasizes that, as this rule constitutes a derogation from a mandatory requirement, its scope of application is to be construed narrowly.

As such, the mere existence of a controlling shareholder across several entities is not sufficient to qualify for the exemption, unless this shareholder holds, directly or indirectly, more than 50% of the capital or voting rights in each of those entities.

Likewise, the mere fact that the shareholders of the investor are the same as those of the target entity does not suffice to qualify for the intra-group exemption provided

453. France, Ministry of the Economy, Finance, Industrial and Digital Sovereignty, Directorate General of the Treasury, "Guidelines on the Foreign Direct Investment Screening in France July 2025, Point 1.4, published on July 30, 2025, accessed on August 1, 2025, available at https://www.tresor.economie.gouv.fr/services-aux-entreprises/investissements-etrangers-en-france

for in Article R. 151-7 of the Monetary and Financial Code, insofar as such shareholders do not necessarily exercise control, within the meaning of Article L. 233-3 of the Commercial Code, over the target entity of the investment.

Likewise, where entities are held by multiple shareholders acting jointly, even if each holds over 50% collectively, this joint control does not bring the entities within the scope of the intra-group exemption.

The exemption also does not apply to the transfer of a stake in an entity from one investment fund to another, even when both funds are managed by the same asset management company, unless that management company itself holds more than 50% of the capital or voting rights in each of the funds concerned, which is rarely the case in practice.

Similarly, so-called continuation fund transactions, in which a newly created fund acquires the assets of a fund reaching the end of its life cycle, are not automatically exempted, even where the same management company is involved, unless the conditions for the intra-group exemption set out in Article R. 151-7 of the French Monetary and Financial Code are strictly met. That provision requires that the parties to the transaction must belong to the same group as defined by the regulatory threshold of ownership or voting rights.

On this point, the French Cour de Cassation [454] (Supreme Court for civil and commercial matters) has held that the exercise of voting rights by an asset management company on behalf of a venture capital mutual fund (Fonds Commun de Placement à Risque) does not confer control over the target company to the management company. Therefore, the management company is not deemed part of the same group as the fund or the underlying portfolio company for purposes of the intra-group exemption under corporate law.

Consequently, the eligibility of an intra-group transaction for exemption from the FDI screening procedure is subject to a case-by-case analysis, taking into consideration the legal structure of the entities involved, the nature of the fund, whether its management is internal or delegated, and the specific governance features of the investment vehicle.

What are the three categories of investment transactions subject to FDI screening ?

1°: Acquisition of control over the target entity

The first trigger for FDI screening is the acquisition of control over a French legal entity. When the foreign investor's transaction targets such an entity, the French

454. France, Court of Cassation, Social Chamber, Judgment of March 20, 2019, No. 17-19.595, ECLI:FR:CCASS:2019:SO00469, published in the Bulletin: "*Pursuant to Article L. 233-3, I, 1°, of the French Commercial Code, to which Article L. 2331-1 of the French Labor Code refers, a company is deemed to control another when it directly or indirectly holds a portion of the capital conferring the majority of voting rights at the general meetings of that company. A court of appeal which finds that it has not been established that a management company of a risk mutual fund directly or indirectly holds any portion of the capital of a holding company, rightly concludes that said management company cannot be considered, under the combined provisions of Articles L. 233-3, I, 1°, and L. 233-4 of the Commercial Code, as controlling the subsidiary of the holding company.*"

administration will determine whether the transaction constitutes a change of control. This assessment is made strictly[455] in reference to Article L. 233-3 of the French Commercial Code, which provides the sole legal basis for defining control in this context.

Control is assessed exclusively under Article L. 233-3 of the French Commercial Code

In assessing the first type of triggering event, namely, where a foreign investment in a French-law entity results in the acquisition of control over that entity, the relevant definition of "control" applied by the CIEF examining authorities is that set forth in Article L. 233-3 of the French Commercial Code.

Under this provision, any natural or legal person is deemed to control another entity in any of the following circumstances:

a) where it directly or indirectly holds a portion of the share capital conferring the majority of voting rights in the general meetings of the target company;
b) where it alone holds the majority of voting rights pursuant to an agreement entered into with other shareholders or partners, provided that such agreement is not contrary to the interests of the company;
c) where, by virtue of the voting rights it holds, it is in a position to effectively determine the decisions adopted at the company's general meetings;
d) where it is a shareholder or partner in the company and has the authority to appoint or remove the majority of the members of the company's management, administrative, or supervisory bodies.

In addition, control is presumed to exist where a person, acting alone, directly or indirectly holds more than 40% of the voting rights and no other shareholder or partner holds a greater share.

Lastly, two or more persons acting in concert are deemed to jointly control a company where they effectively determine the decisions adopted at its general meetings.

A key clarification must be emphasized here: only Article L. 233-3 of the French Commercial Code applies in determining control for the purposes of the first scenario referred to in Article R. 151-2 of the French Monetary and Financial Code. Put differently, in contrast to the definition of control used to qualify a foreign investor under Article R. 151-1 of the same Code, which does refer to Article L. 430-1 of the Commercial Code relating to merger control, the definition of control over a French-law entity (the investment target) is strictly and exclusively grounded in Article L. 233-3. This distinction is essential: it underscores that two separate legal definitions of "control" are used under the FDI screening regime, one for identifying a foreign investor, and another for characterizing the French entity subject to the investment.

455. and not, as may be the case for the determination of foreign investor status, by reference to Article L. 430-1(III) of the Commercial Code

Control over the Target Entity May Be Either Direct or Indirect

Another important point is that foreign investments involving the acquisition of control over a French-law entity are subject to the French FDI screening mechanism (IEF), regardless of whether such control is direct or indirect.

Direct control is assessed on the basis of voting rights held directly within the French target entity.

Indirect control is also recognized and is grounded in Article L. 233-3 of the French Commercial Code.

In practice, the administration[456] assesses indirect control by aggregating the voting rights held by a company in the target entity with those held, directly or indirectly, by any other entities that it controls.

The control of a French-law entity by a foreign investor may also be acquired through one or several intermediary entities. In such cases, Article L. 233-4 of the French Commercial Code applies, which provides that: "Any equity interest, even below 10 percent, held by a controlled company shall be deemed to be indirectly held by the company that controls such company."

Control over the Target Entity May Be Either Legal (de jure) or Factual (de facto)

The FDI screening mechanism also covers transactions resulting in the acquisition of either de jure or de facto control over a French-law entity[457].

The administration will determine the nature of the ultimate control exercised over the target entity.

De jure control is evaluated by the administration[458] based on the voting rights acquired in the target company (or companies) constituting the French-law entity. The most typical case of de jure control is that of an investor holding the majority of voting rights in general meetings. This corresponds to the scenario described in paragraph 1° of Article L. 233-3 of the Commercial Code.

Another scenario may arise where a foreign investor acquires, on its own, the majority of voting rights pursuant to an agreement concluded with other partners or shareholders, provided that such agreement is not contrary to the interests of the company (Article L. 233-3, I, 2° of the French Commercial Code).

---

456. See Point 1.2.1.1 in Min. Econ. Fin. Ind. Sov. Dig., DG Treasury, "Guidelines on the Foreign Direct Investment Screening in France" July 2025, published July 30, 2025, accessed August 1, 2025, available at https://www.tresor.economie.gouv.fr/services-aux-entreprises/investissements-etrangers-en-france

457. This distinction was first set out in the 2022 guidelines but was later abandoned in the 2025 guidelines, with the administration now referring instead to the "characterization" of control. The author has retained the original 2022 presentation.

458. See Point 1.2.1.2 in Ministry of the Economy, Finance, Industrial and Digital Sovereignty, Directorate General of the Treasury, "Guidelines on the Foreign Direct Investment Screening in France July 2025, published July 30, 2025, last accessed August 1, 2025, available at https://www.tresor.economie.gouv.fr/services-aux-entreprises/investissements-etrangers-en-france

In this context, the administration recalls that the entire Article L. 233-3 applies. Accordingly, an investor, whether a natural or legal person, is presumed to exercise control where it holds, directly or indirectly, more than 40% of the voting rights in the target entity, and no other shareholder or partner holds a larger share (see paragraph II of Article L. 233-3 of the Commercial Code).

De facto control refers to situations in which the investor does not hold a majority of voting rights but nonetheless enjoys effective power to determine the decisions adopted at the general meetings of the target entity. (see Article L. 233-3, I, 3° of the French Commercial Code).

By way of example, the acquisition by a shareholder of a minority fraction of voting rights may amount to a takeover where, at the time of such acquisition, special voting rights, such as double voting rights, are granted to the investor, or where the investor holds the power to appoint or remove the majority of the members of the company's management, administrative, or supervisory bodies (Article L. 233-3, I, 4° of the French Commercial Code). The same applies where the investor is vested with specific prerogatives set forth in a shareholders' agreement or in the bylaws, such as particular veto rights, or the authority to appoint the majority of the members of the company's governing bodies.

The existence of de facto control is established based on a case-by-case analysis of the specific legal and factual elements granted to the investor in the course of a given transaction. This includes a review of the shareholding structure of the target company, in particular the dispersion of share capital and attendance rates at general meetings, to determine whether the investor, despite holding a minority stake, effectively controls the general meetings and, by extension, the target entity.

Close attention is also given to the bylaws, shareholders' agreements, and any non-voting or multiple-voting shares or equity interests that may be issued in connection with an investment transaction, particularly with respect to non-voting or multiple-voting shares or contractual veto rights that may be provided. The administration recommends that these elements be described in detail as of the filing of the authorization request.

The control of the target entity may be either exclusive or joint

Under the French foreign investment screening mechanism (FDI screening), any acquisition of control over a French-law entity qualifies as a notifiable transaction, whether the control is exercised on an exclusive or joint basis.

Exclusive control refers to a situation in which a single investor, whether a natural or legal person, exercises control over the target entity.

Joint control, by contrast, refers to a situation in which two or more investors, natural or legal persons, jointly control the target entity. In this respect, paragraph III of Article L. 233-3 of the French Commercial Code provides that "two or more entities acting in concert shall be deemed to jointly control another when they in fact determine the decisions taken at shareholders' meetings. " However, the French administration specifies that the notion of "concerted action" referred to in paragraph III of

Article L. 233-3 must be interpreted autonomously from the notion provided under Article L. 233-10 of the same Code [459].

According to the administration's interpretation, the notion of joint control as defined in Article L. 233-3 III presupposes the existence of a concerted arrangement between the co-investors, typically embodied in a legally binding agreement, such as the articles of association or a shareholders' agreement, through which the parties agree to implement a common policy vis-à-vis the target company and determine, in fact, the decisions taken at the general meetings. Such arrangements often grant co-controllers veto rights over strategic decisions, thereby ensuring that they effectively influence shareholder resolutions.

The administration [460] distinguishes between standard minority protection rights, typically granted to safeguard the financial interests of a minority shareholder, and specific rights that confer influence over the operational activities of the target entity.

For instance, veto rights granted to a minority investor over the appointment or dismissal of executive officers, the execution of any investment or contract regardless of a monetary threshold, or the approval of the target company's budget or business plan may be deemed sufficient to confer joint control, provided another entity simultaneously holds similar controlling rights under Article L. 233-3 of the Commercial Code.

Similarly, the existence of governance clauses in the articles of association or a shareholders' agreement, such as conflict resolution mechanisms or temporary transfer restrictions, may also support a finding of joint control.

Importantly, joint control may exist even when one of the parties holds a sufficient fraction of the voting rights to unilaterally determine shareholders' resolutions in the absence of such an agreement, provided that a concerted action agreement exists [461].

---

459. French Commercial Code, Article L. 233-10

I. – Persons shall be deemed to be acting in concert where they have entered into an agreement to acquire, dispose of, or exercise voting rights, with a view to pursuing a common policy toward the company or to obtaining control of such company.

II. – Such an agreement shall be presumed to exist:

1° Between a company and the chairman of its board of directors and its chief executive officers or members of its management board or its managing directors;

2° Between a company and the companies it controls within the meaning of Article L. 233-3;

3° Between companies controlled by the same person or persons;

4° Between the shareholders of a simplified joint-stock company (SAS) with respect to the companies it controls;

5° Between the trustee and the beneficiary of a trust arrangement, where the beneficiary is also the settlor.

III. – Persons acting in concert shall be jointly and severally liable for compliance with the legal and regulatory obligations to which they are subject.

460. See Point 1.2.1.3 in Ministry of the Economy, Finance, Industrial and Digital Sovereignty, Directorate General of the Treasury, "Guidelines on the Foreign Direct Investment Screening in France," July 2025, published July 30, 2025, last accessed August 1, 2025, available at https://www.tresor.economie.gouv.fr/services-aux-entreprises/investissements-etrangers-en-france

461. France, Commercial Chamber of the Court of Cassation, Judgment No. 09-16.112 of June 29, 2010, published in the Bulletin, *"Joint control as defined in Article L. 233-3 III of the Commercial Code is not ruled out merely because one of the concert parties holds a majority that, absent the agreement between them, would enable it to unilaterally determine the outcome of shareholder meetings. Accordingly, a court of appeal was correct in finding that the mere fact that one company holds 80% of the voting rights in*

As regards transitions between forms of control, the administration considers [462] that a shift from joint control to exclusive control (or vice versa) does not qualify as a notifiable transaction under Article R. 151-2 of the French Monetary and Financial Code. Accordingly, a foreign investor who already holds joint control over a French entity is not required to file a prior authorization request should they acquire exclusive control. Likewise, a transition from exclusive to joint control is not considered a notifiable event. This means that variations in shareholding by a foreign investor who already exercises exclusive or joint control over a French entity do not in themselves trigger the requirement to file a prior authorization request.

The notion of control encompasses both EU and non-EU investors

Foreign acquisitions of control over French entities are subject to the French FDI screening mechanism (Dispositif IEF), regardless of whether the investor is established within or outside the European Union. Indeed [463], under Article R. 151-2, 1° of the French Monetary and Financial Code (Code monétaire et financier), operations involving the acquisition of control over a French-law entity fall within the scope of the regime when carried out by any foreign investor as defined under Article R. 151-1 of the same Code, irrespective of their geographical origin.

What matters for the purposes of the screening regime is the nature of the control acquired, not whether it originates from an EU or non-EU investor.

2° Eligibility of Investments Involving the Total or Partial Acquisition of a Business Line of the Target Entity

The screening mechanism also covers the total or partial acquisition of a business line (branche d'activité) of a French-law target entity.

First, according to the French authorities [464], transactions falling under point 2° of Article R. 151-2 of the French Monetary and Financial Code, i.e., the acquisition of a business line of a French-law target entity, are eligible for review and apply to all foreign investors as defined in Article R. 151-1 of the same Code, whether they are based within the European Union or outside it.

Second [465], the French FDI screening regulations do not provide an autonomous definition of the notion of a "business line," even though the concept is explicitly referenced. As a result, the French administration refers to definitions established by

---

shareholders' meetings while another holds 20% does not preclude the latter from exercising control over the former."

462. See Point 1.2.1.4 in Ministry of the Economy, Finance, Industrial and Digital Sovereignty, Directorate General of the Treasury, "Guidelines on the Foreign Direct Investment Screening in France," July 2025, published July 30, 2025, last accessed August 1, 2025, available at https://www.tresor.economie.gouv.fr/services-aux-entreprises/investissements-etrangers-en-france

463. Ibid, See Point 1.2.

464. Ibid, see Point 1.2.3

465. Ibid

national and EU case law. According to the French Court of Cassation[466], a business line can be defined as *"a set of elements enabling autonomous operation, i.e., a set capable of functioning independently under normal conditions."* The Court of Justice of the European Communities[467] (CJEC) similarly held that a branch may constitute a business line if it consists of "a collection of assets and personnel capable of contributing to the pursuit of a specific business activity."

Furthermore, Article R. 151-2, 2° of the Monetary and Financial Code expressly refers to the "total" or "partial" acquisition of a business line, meaning all or part of such a line. The mere acquisition of certain assets cannot be qualified as the acquisition of an entire business line, but it may nonetheless be considered a partial acquisition thereof within the meaning of Article R. 151-2.

By way of illustration, and subject to a case-by-case analysis, the administration considers that a partial business line acquisition may include the direct or indirect acquisition by a foreign investor of any of the following components:
—a portfolio of sensitive contracts;
—a significant number of intellectual property rights necessary for the operation of the relevant business line;
—the assignment of a patent or the grant of an exclusive or non-exclusive license to a patent;
—equipment, vehicles, furniture, and machinery used in the operation of the business line;
—any one of the above elements, provided that it is essential for the conduct of the sensitive activity concerned.

Lastly, other definitions of "business line" may be found in French administrative practice. According[468] to INSEE (the National Institute of Statistics and Economic Studies), a business line is defined as a grouping of homogeneous production units that manufacture goods or provide services classified under the same item of the relevant economic activity nomenclature. INSEE is also responsible for maintaining and supervising the nomenclature of business lines in France. There are approximately 700 business lines officially recognized in the French economy.

3° Eligible investments include those resulting in the crossing of a voting-rights threshold in the target entity

The screening mechanism also applies to investments that, directly or indirectly, whether individually or in concert with others, result in the crossing of a certain threshold of voting rights. That threshold is set at 25% when it concerns the holding

466. France, Court of Cassation, Commercial Chamber, February 6, 1990, Decision No. 88-16.827, unpublished: "...the notion of a branch of activity refers to all the elements that constitute an autonomous operation capable of functioning by its own means..."

467. European Union, Court of Justice of the European Communities, October 13, 1992, Case C-50/91, Commerz-Credit-Bank, ECLI:EU:C:1992:386: "A branch constitutes a branch of activity within the meaning of Article 7(1)(b) of Council Directive 69/335/EEC of July 17, 1969, concerning indirect taxes on the raising of capital, insofar as it constitutes a combination of assets and personnel capable of contributing to the performance of a specific activity."

468. INSEE, "Enterprise," statistical definition, last accessed August 1, 2025, available at https://www.insee.fr/fr/metadonnees/definition/c1560.

of voting rights in a French-law entity. It is lowered to 10% when it concerns the holding of voting rights in a French-law company whose shares are admitted to trading on a regulated market.

The threshold crossing initially refers to the exceeding of 25% of the voting rights.

Under Article R. 151-2, 3° of the French Monetary and Financial Code, foreign direct investment in a French legal entity is subject to prior authorization where it results in the investor, directly, indirectly, alone or acting in concert, crossing a 25% voting rights threshold.

This triggering event is construed strictly by the French Treasury Department[469]: the threshold is deemed crossed only when the foreign investor's total voting rights strictly exceed 25% of the voting rights in the target French entity.

The calculation must include all shares carrying enhanced voting rights (e.g., preferred shares) and must exclude those devoid of voting rights. It should be emphasized that only the crossing of the 25% threshold constitutes an eligible investment operation under this provision. The crossing of higher thresholds (e.g., 50%, 75%, or even 100%) is not covered by this screening criterion, absent a corresponding acquisition of contro

l.

It should be noted that only the crossing of the 25% voting rights threshold in the target entity qualifies as an investment. Consequently, the crossing of the 50%, 75%, or 100% thresholds of voting rights does not constitute an eligible voting rights threshold crossing within the meaning of Article R. 151-2 of the French Monetary and Financial Code.

In the same vein, it is the upward crossing of a threshold that triggers the applicability of the prior authorization regime, not a downward movement. The administration[470] has confirmed this position with respect to the lowering of the threshold to 10% of voting rights in the case of listed companies (see below).

---

469. See Point 1.2.4.1 in Ministry of the Economy, Finance and Industrial and Digital Sovereignty, Directorate General of the Treasury, "Guidelines on the Foreign Direct Investment Screening in France," July 2025, published July 30, 2025, accessed August 1, 2025, available at https://www.tresor.economie.gouv.fr/services-aux-entreprises/investissements-etrangers-en-france

470. See Point 1.2.4.5 in Ministry of the Economy, Finance and Industrial and Digital Sovereignty, Directorate General of the Treasury, "Guidelines on the Foreign Direct Investment Screening in France" July 2025, published July 30, 2025, accessed August 1, 2025, at https://www.tresor.economie.gouv.fr/services-aux-entreprises/investissements-etrangers-en-france: "The downward crossing of the threshold, when the investor's shareholding falls below the 10% threshold of voting rights, is not subject to any reporting obligation under the French FDI screening mechanism."

The crossing of the 10% threshold applies more strictly to the voting rights of listed companies.

Under the regulation (Article R. 151-2, 4° of the Monetary and Financial Code), the threshold is lowered to 10% when it concerns the holding of voting rights in a French-law company whose shares are admitted to trading on a regulated market. This is an autonomous triggering threshold.

In 2025, the administration clarified [471] that, for purposes of the French foreign direct investment screening regime (FDI Screening), thc notion of a "regulated market" is not defined autonomously but by reference to Articles L. 421-1 et seq. of the Monetary and Financial Code and Articles 511-1 et seq. of the General Regulation of the French Financial Markets Authority (Autorité des marchés financiers – AMF). This definition encompasses regulated markets located in France, in the European Union, and in the States parties to the Agreement on the European Economic Area (EEA) .)

Consequently, French companies listed on non-regulated markets, such as Euronext Growth, do not fall within the scope of this provision. Likewise, French companies listed on markets located outside the EU are not covered by this rule.

The operation must, moreover, be carried out by an investor from outside the European Union or from a State party to the European Economic Area Agreement that has entered into an administrative assistance convention with France for the purpose of combating fraud and tax evasion.

It was the Decree [472] of 28 December 2023 on foreign investments in France that made permanent the lowering of the threshold from 25% to 10%. This 10% threshold had originally been introduced [473] in the context of the COVID-19 pandemic [474] in order to shield French listed companies engaged in sensitive activities from opportunistic acquisitions. The question of temporary thresholds has therefore been definitively settled for companies listed on a regulated market.

The key point to retain is that the 10% voting-rights threshold in a French company whose shares are admitted to trading on a regulated market triggers screening only under the following conditions:

—it does not apply to individual investors who are nationals of a Member State of the European Union or of a State party to the Agreement on the European Economic Area that has concluded with France an administrative assistance convention for combating tax fraud and tax evasion, provided that such individuals are domiciled in one of those States;

471. Ibid.

472. France, Decree No. 2023-1293 of 28 December 2023 on foreign investments in France, Official Journal of the French Republic, No. 0301, 29 December 2023, NOR: ECOT2323089D

473. As a reminder, the original 25% threshold was temporarily lowered to 10% in 2020, 2021, and 2022.

474. France, Ministry of the Economy, Finance, Industrial and Digital Sovereignty, Press Release, No. 458, December 22, 2022, "Extension in 2023 of the temporary measure lowering the threshold triggering FDI screening in French listed companies on a regulated market," accessed September 1, 2025, available at https://presse.economie.gouv.fr/22122022-prorogation-en-2023-de-la-mesure-dabaissement-temporaire-du-seuil-declenchant-le-controle-ief-dans-les-societes-francaises-cotees-sur-un-marche-reglemente/

—it does not apply to an investor constituted by an entity in which all members of the control chain, within the meaning of Article R. 151-1 II of the Monetary and Financial Code, are subject to the law of one of those same States, or are nationals of and domiciled in one of those States;
—it applies only to investments made in companies listed on a regulated market;
—it is subject to an accelerated procedure: the foreign investor crossing the 10% voting-rights threshold must notify the Directorate General of the Treasury. According to the administration [475], this constitutes a legal obligation [476]. The investor may opt either for prior notification or for a prior authorization request (notification being the preferred route according to the administration), but in all cases a filing must be made. The notification dossier is lighter than the prior authorization application (see Chapter 10).

Failure to file either a notification or an authorization request may lead to enforcement measures or sanctions in the event of carrying out an investment without authorization, or in the event of obtaining authorization fraudulently (see Chapter 21).

The Minister of the Economy then has a period of ten business days to determine whether the contemplated transaction must be referred to a more in-depth review, based on the filing of a complete authorization request. Absent an objection by the Minister within this ten-day period following notification, the exemption from the requirement to file an authorization request arises implicitly.

Moreover, the notifying party remains free [477] to withdraw its notification request at any time.

Finally, it should be recalled that the downward crossing of the 10% voting rights threshold, i.e., where the investor's participation falls below 10%, does not give rise to any declaration requirement under the French FDI screening regime . Conversely, the upward crossing of the 25% threshold of voting rights in a French entity whose shares are admitted to trading on a regulated market, if it occurs after a prior crossing of the 10% threshold that has already been subject to FDI screening, triggers a new review under the FDI screening regime and requires the investor to file a new authorization request.

Indirect Threshold Crossings

To account for de facto control or influence over the target entity, indirect threshold crossings must also be assessed.

For the purposes of the administration [478], the calculation of an indirect threshold crossing is made by aggregating the total number of voting rights:

475. See Point 2.3 in Ministry of the Economy, Finance, Industrial and Digital Sovereignty, Directorate General of the Treasury, "Guidelines on the Foreign Direct Investment Screening in France," July 2025, published July 30, 2025, accessed August 1, 2025, at https://www.tresor.economie.gouv.fr/services-aux-entreprises/investissements-etrangers-en-france
476. Ibid, Point 2.3.1.
477. Ibid. Point 2.3.5.
478. Ibid. Point 1.2.4.3.

—held by an investor, whether a legal entity or a natural person, in the target company; or
—held by any other companies directly or indirectly controlled by that investor, regardless of the legal form or nationality of such companies, in the target company.

The computation method follows Article L. 233-4 of the French Commercial Code, which attributes to the controlling parent company all voting rights held by subsidiaries under its control.

This rule prevails over any other method, in particular the "product of shareholdings" approach. It entails two consequences:
—pursuant to this rule, a foreign investor acquiring control of a target entity that holds, directly or indirectly, more than 10% or 25% of the voting rights of a French subsidiary is deemed to have indirectly crossed the threshold in that French subsidiary; and
—furthermore, a foreign investor crossing the 10% or 25% voting rights threshold in a target entity is also deemed to have indirectly crossed the threshold in the French subsidiaries controlled by that entity.

Accordingly, the indirect crossing of the 10% or 25% voting rights threshold by an investor in a French-law entity is assessed solely on the basis of the shareholdings held by companies directly or indirectly controlled by that investor.

A foreign investor crossing the 25% voting rights threshold in a French-law target entity is deemed to have indirectly crossed the threshold in the French subsidiaries controlled by that entity.

Thus, in the case of a foreign investment in a French group, the scope of review triggered by a threshold crossing includes:
(i) the French parent company in which the threshold is directly crossed by the foreign investor, and
(ii) the French subsidiaries controlled by that parent company for which the threshold crossing is indirect.

If the threshold crossing occurs directly in a foreign-law company, the French subsidiaries controlled by that foreign parent company are included within the scope of review to the extent the threshold crossing is indirect. Conversely, French subsidiaries that are not directly or indirectly controlled by the parent company are excluded.

By contrast, if a French investment vehicle is created by a group of foreign investors, none of whom individually holds control within the meaning of Article L. 233-3 or Article L. 430-1(III) of the French Commercial Code, the threshold crossing in a French-law entity by such vehicle does not constitute an investment transaction within the meaning of Article R. 151-2 of the Monetary and Financial Code.

The rule derived from the French Commercial Code prevails over any other rule, such as, for example, the "product of shareholdings" method.

Threshold Crossing by Acting in Concert

For the purposes of the administration [479], the notion of "acting in concert" is interpreted, in the case of a threshold crossing, in accordance with Article L. 233-10 of the French Commercial Code. Entities are deemed to be acting in concert when they have entered into an agreement to acquire, transfer, or exercise voting rights with a view to pursuing a common policy toward the company or to obtaining control thereof.

Thus, concerted action requires an understanding among the parties to coordinate their conduct with respect to a given company, creating reciprocal obligations among them. The mere fact that two or more entities act in the same way toward a company is not sufficient to establish concerted action.

The agreement binding the concert parties need not be in writing; it may be express or implied. Accordingly, the interpretation of concerted action giving rise to a threshold crossing under the FDI screening regime is not limited to the mere existence of a shareholders' agreement. In the absence of such a written agreement, concerted action may be demonstrated by a body of serious, specific, and consistent indicia [480].

Without being exhaustive, the administration may consider as constituting joint control those clauses of an agreement that evidence cohesion and solidarity justified by the common interest of the parties, such as provisions concerning long-term non-transferability, coordinated restrictions on respective shareholdings, reciprocal approval for any acquisition or transfer, or tag-along rights.

To be characterized as concerted action, the agreement must therefore pursue the objective of establishing a common policy toward the company. The purpose of such a policy may consist in managing the parties' shareholdings with respect to the target entity, in managing the target entity itself, in acquiring or transferring voting rights, or in arranging for the joint exercise of control over the company. It may also pursue the objective of obtaining control of a French-law entity.

Finally, Article L. 233-10 of the French Commercial Code provides that an agreement constituting concerted action is presumed to exist:

—between a company, the chairman of its board of directors, and its chief executive officers or the members of its management board or its managers;

—between a company and the companies, it controls within the meaning of Article L. 233-3;

—between companies controlled by the same person(s);

—between the shareholders of a simplified joint-stock company (société par actions simplifiée, SAS) with respect to the companies it controls;

—between a trustee and the beneficiary of a trust agreement, if that beneficiary is also the settlor.

479. France, Ministry of the Economy, Finance and Industrial and Digital Sovereignty, Directorate General of the Treasury, "Guidelines on the Foreign Direct Investment Screening in France July 2025, published July 30, 2025, see Point 1.2.4.4, consulted August 1, 2025, available at https://www.tresor.economie.gouv.fr/services-aux-entreprises/investissements-etrangers-en-france

480. France, Court of Cassation, Commercial Chamber, May 15, 2012, No. 11-11.633, ECLI:FR:CCASS:2012:CO00545

The administration further clarified [481] in its 2025 guidelines that, in cases where a non-EU or non-EEA investor and an EU or EEA investor acting in concert each acquire a stake of less than 25% or 10% of the voting rights in a French-law company whose shares are admitted to trading on a regulated market, but where their combined holdings exceed one of those thresholds, only the acquisition of the stake by the non-EU or non-EEA investor is likely to constitute an investment transaction.

Personal and Territorial Scope: Focus on Non-European Investors

The crossing of voting rights thresholds applies exclusively to non-European investors

In the same manner as the administration determines the foreign nature of an investor (see Chapter 11), it also defines the category of investors subject to the 25% voting rights threshold and the 10% voting rights threshold in a French-law company whose shares are admitted to trading on a regulated market (see below).

According to the administration [482], the direct or indirect crossing, whether alone or in concert, of the 25% voting rights threshold referred to in Article R. 151-2(3) of the Monetary and Financial Code, as well as the 10% threshold applicable to French-law companies listed on a regulated market, referred to in Article R. 151-2(4) of the same Code, does not apply to investors from the European Union.

Nor does it apply to investors from a State party to the Agreement on the European Economic Area that has concluded an administrative assistance convention with France for the purpose of combating tax fraud and tax evasion. As a reminder, the EEA member states that are not members of the European Union but have concluded such a convention with France are, as of today: Iceland, Liechtenstein, and Norway.

The obligation to seek prior authorization does not apply to threshold crossings of 25 percent of the voting rights in a French-law entity, or 10 percent of the voting rights in a French-law company whose shares are admitted to trading on a regulated market, where such acquisition does not result in control within the meaning of Article L. 233-3 of the French Commercial Code, when the investment concerns a French-law company by:
—individuals who are nationals of a Member State of the European Union, Iceland, Liechtenstein, or Norway, and who are domiciled in one of these States;
—legal entities where the entire chain of control consists of entities that (i) are governed by the law of one of the EU Member States, Iceland, Liechtenstein, or Norway, or (ii) are nationals of and domiciled in one of these States.

Accordingly, threshold crossings of 25 percent (Article R. 151-2, 3° of the French Monetary and Financial Code) and 10 percent (Article R. 151-2, 4° of the same

481. France, Ministry of the Economy, Finance and Industrial and Digital Sovereignty, Directorate General of the Treasury, "Guidelines on the Foreign Direct Investment Screening in France July 2025, Section 1.2.4.4, published July 30, 2025, consulted August 1, 2025, available at https://www.tresor.economie.gouv.fr/services-aux-entreprises/investissements-etrangers-en-france
482. Ibid, see Point 1.2.4.2.

Code[483]) by an investor of British nationality or subject to the law of the United Kingdom have, since the UK's withdrawal from the European Union, become subject to the screening regime.

Likewise[484], although Switzerland signed the Agreement[485] on the European Economic Area on May 2, 1992, it rejected ratification in the referendum of December 6, 1992. Switzerland is therefore not considered a member of the European Economic Area. As a result, threshold crossings by an investor of Swiss nationality or governed by Swiss law fall within the scope of the French foreign investment screening regime.

*
* *

The second criterion for determining the eligibility of a transaction under the French FDI screening mechanism is that the investment must not only target a French-law entity, but must also result in the acquisition of control over that entity. In this respect, the various developments regarding the definition of control, whether direct or indirect, and the thresholds used to establish it must also be understood as a method for filtering transactions. While this approach is undeniably useful in preventing an administrative overload for the French authorities, it must be recognized that the requirement of control is arguably the criterion most susceptible to circumvention strategies, particularly in terms of the legal and capital structure of the deal. Although such strategies may be legitimate from a business perspective, they are difficult to justify in light of national interest considerations. They will inevitably create the perception that the investor sought to avoid the scrutiny of the FDI screening regime by "neutralizing" this second eligibility criterion.

483. Inserted by Decree No. 2023-1293 of 28 December 2023 on foreign investments in France, Official Journal of the French Republic, No. 0301, 29 December 2023, NOR: ECOT2323089D

484. See Point 1.2.4.2 in Ministry of the Economy, Finance and Industrial and Digital Sovereignty, Directorate General of the Treasury, "Guidelines on the Foreign Direct Investment Screening in France" July 2025, published 30 July 2025, consulted 1 August 2025, available at https://www.tresor.economie.gouv.fr/services-aux-entreprises/investissements-etrangers-en-france

485. European Communities, Council and Commission Decision 94/1/EC, ECSC, of 13 December 1993, concerning the conclusion of the Agreement on the European Economic Area between the EC, their Member States and Austria, Finland, Iceland, Liechtenstein, Norway, Sweden and Switzerland, Official Journal of the European Communities, L 1, 3 January 1994, p. 1, Document 31994D0001

Summary Table – Nature of Qualifying Investment Transactions under the French FDI Screening Regime

<table>
<tr><th colspan="5">Nature of Qualifying Investment Transactions</th></tr>
<tr><td>Target Entity</td><td colspan="4">French-law entity only</td></tr>
<tr><td>Greenfield Investment</td><td colspan="4">Not eligible</td></tr>
<tr><td>Intra-group Transaction</td><td colspan="4">Not eligible</td></tr>
<tr><td>Acquisition of Control</td><td colspan="4">Eligible</td></tr>
<tr><td>—under Article L. 233-3 of the French Commercial Code</td><td colspan="4">Direct or indirect control; de jure or de facto control; exclusive or joint control; by EU or third-country investors unless a previously authorized threshold crossing has already occurred.</td></tr>
<tr><td></td><td>Direct or indirect holding of a capital interest conferring the majority of voting rights</td><td>Holding a majority of voting rights alone (through agreement among shareholders or partners)</td><td>De facto control over corporate decisions via voting rights at general meetings</td><td>Power to appoint or remove the majority of the members of the administrative, executive or supervisory bodies</td></tr>
<tr><td>—of a branch of activity (total or partial)</td><td colspan="4">Eligible for all foreign investors (EU and non-EU)</td></tr>
<tr><td>Threshold Crossing</td><td colspan="4">Eligible</td></tr>
<tr><td></td><td colspan="4">—strict or upward crossing
Constitutes an investment; can be direct or indirect; alone or in concert</td></tr>
<tr><td>—25% threshold of voting rights</td><td colspan="4">Only applicable to non-EU / non-EEA investors EEA investor, unless exclusive or joint control had already been previously acquired and authorized</td></tr>
<tr><td>—10% threshold in listed companies</td><td colspan="4"><u>Only</u> applicable to non-EU / non-EEA investors; subject to fast-track review procedure (10 days)</td></tr>
</table>

Chapter 13

FDI Screening in France ultimately Requires the Presence of a Sensitive Activity

The third cumulative criterion for an investment to fall within the scope of the French FDI screening mechanism is the presence of a sensitive activity. Although this concept is broadly framed, it is objectively defined through a dual-level legal architecture: on the one hand, by statute, which identifies three overarching categories of sensitive activities; and on the other hand, by regulation, which enumerates 22 specific sensitive sectors, themselves grouped into ten critical technologies .

However, the French administration interprets the application of this criterion as subject to two cumulative conditions. According to the government's administrative guidance, only those foreign investments are subject to screening that (i) concern one of the sectors listed in the regulatory annex, and (ii) are likely to affect public order, public security, or national defense interests. Accordingly, the list of 22 sensitive activities serves as the operative reference point for administrative review. That said, the parties to a transaction are well advised to consider the broader categories of sensitive activities as defined in the legislative provisions of the French Monetary and Financial Codein order to understand the underlying rationale and policy objectives of France's FDI screening framework.

Finally, it should be recalled that this activity must be carried out in France. Consequently[486], French-law entities and establishments registered with the Trade and Companies Register (registre du commerce et des sociétés – RCS) that conduct no activity in France and hold no tangible or intangible assets in France as of the date of the transaction do not, by definition, fall within the scope of Article R. 151-3 of the Monetary and Financial Code.

The Legislative Text Identifies Three Categories of Sensitive Activities

The law specifies to the Government a set of sensitive areas of activity that justify the State's right to derogate from the principle of freedom of foreign investment in France. These sensitive areas are three in number.

486. See Point 1.3 in Ministry of the Economy, Finance and Industrial and Digital Sovereignty, Directorate General of the Treasury, "Guidelines on the Foreign Direct Investment Screening in France July 2025, Published July 30, 2025, Consulted August 1, 2025 at https://www.tresor.economie.gouv.fr/services-aux-entreprises/investissements-etrangers-en-france

The first paragraph of Article L. 151-3 of the French Monetary and Financial Code expressly provides that:

"Foreign investments in an activity conducted in France which, even on an occasional basis, involves the exercise of public authority **or** falls within one of the following areas are subject to the prior authorization of the Minister of the Economy:
(a) Activities likely to affect public order, public security, or the interests of national defense;
(b) Activities relating to the research, production, or marketing of arms, munitions, powders, and explosive substances."

Under French law, the term "or" (ou) is generally interpreted in its disjunctive sense, that is, as expressing an alternative between two options. Consequently, it must be understood here that three distinct categories of activities are covered.

A Sensitive Activity May Involve, Even Occasionally, the Exercise of Public Authority

The first category of sensitive activities under the French FDI screening regime includes those that involve the exercise of public authority, even on an occasional basis. This category is established in Paragraph I of Article L. 151-3 of the Monetary and Financial Code (Code monétaire et financier). .

In French administrative law, the concept of public authority (autorité publique) holds particular significance. It generally refers to the set of public bodies, institutions, and officials that exercise powers associated with "puissance publique", the sovereign authority of the State, within the framework of national, regional, or local government, or other public entities. These entities are vested with legal prerogatives, often derogating from ordinary private law, granted by statute in the public interest. Such prerogatives may be regulatory in nature (rulemaking authority) or executive (decision-making powers).

The provision also extends to certain activities that contribute to public authority on a non-permanent basis. Although public authority is structurally distinct from private entities due to the exercise of sovereign powers, private parties may occasionally, incidentally, or subsidiarily act within the framework of public authority, particularly when entrusted with a public service mission.

By explicitly including activities that involve public authority even if only occasionally, the legislature deliberately adopted a broad criterion of applicability, thereby enlarging the scope of transactions potentially subject to the FDI screening mechanism.

A Sensitive Activity May Also Involve Public Order, Public Security, or National Defense Interests

The second category of sensitive activities includes those that are likely to affect public order, public security, or national defense interests. This corresponds to item

(a) of Paragraph I of Article L. 151-3 of the Monetary and Financial Code (Code monétaire et financier). .

The reference to these activities is particularly relevant, as it delineates the continuum between internal and external security, which lies at the heart of a broader concept: national security. It is therefore essential to examine the three components individually.

- Public Order is generally understood in French law as the state of societal peace,, and public hygiene. In the context of FDI screening, this concept should be interpreted narrowly, by reference to applicable legal norms such as Articles 421-1 and 431-13 of the French Penal Code, which invoke disturbances to public order in defining terrorist offenses or unlawful militant groups, as well as Article 78-2 of the French Code of Criminal Procedure, which authorizes identity checks where there is a risk to public order.
- Public Security is addressed in Article L. 111-1 of the Internal Security Code, which states that "security is a fundamental right and one of the conditions for exercising individual and collective freedoms. Accordingly, the State has the duty to ensure security throughout the territory of the Republic, by defending national institutions and interests, enforcing the law, maintaining public peace and order, and protecting persons and property." Article L. 111-2 further establishes the permanent policy objectives of public security, including:
  1° the extension of community policing nationwide to meet the public's security needs;
  2° enhanced cooperation between the police, gendarmerie, and customs authorities;
  3° prioritization of police personnel for missions directly related to maintaining or strengthening security; and
  4° the strengthening of international security cooperation in line with France's international and European commitments.
- National Defense, as defined by Article L. 1111-1 of the Defense Code, seeks to "ensure the integrity of the territory and the protection of the population against armed aggression. It also contributes to combating other threats that may jeopardize national security. It ensures compliance with alliances, treaties, and international agreements, and participates, under current European treaties, in the common security and defense policy of the European Union."

As emphasized by the same article, these three domains, public order, public security, and national defense, collectively fall within the broader framework of France's national security strategy. This strategy is intended to identify all risks and threats that could impact national life, including the protection of the population, territorial integrity, and the continuity of republican institutions, and to determine the appropriate public responses.

Although the term national security is never expressly stated in the FDI screening provisions, it is unquestionably the underlying rationale of the French FDI regime. The mechanism is fundamentally designed to safeguard the national interest.

A Sensitive Activity Also Includes the Research, Production, or Marketing of Weapons, Ammunition, Powders, and Explosive Substances

The third category of sensitive activities encompasses those involving the research, production, or marketing of weapons, ammunition, powders, and explosive substances. This corresponds to item (b) of Paragraph I of Article L. 151-3 of the Monetary and Financial Code (Code monétaire et financier). .

These activities fall under the explosives regulatory regime governed by Articles L. 2352-1 to L. 2353-14 of the Defense Code, and more specifically by Title V of its regulatory part (Articles R. 2351-1 to R. 2353-22). This segment represents the historical core of the French FDI screening regime, as military defense activities have long been excluded from foreign participation. However, because certain explosive-related products were later adapted for civilian and industrial applications, some foreign actors have sought to acquire the associated technologies or patents under the pretense of capital investment or growth financing.

Pursuant to Article R. 2352-1 of the Defense Code, the term explosive products includes all powders and explosive substances, in any form, as well as any processed items containing such materials. The term fixed installations for explosive products refers to sites where such products are manufactured, packaged, cartridge-loaded, stored, distributed, used for industrial purposes (e.g., cutting, forming, stamping, metal plating), or destroyed, as well as depots and retail points for explosive products. Mobile installations are defined as facilities consisting of or mounted on vehicles, designed to operate at multiple locations. These may include mobile depots or mobile manufacturing units. The term use of explosive products is understood to mean any use resulting in detonation.

This category also includes activities involving explosive precursors, i.e., chemical substances used to synthesize explosives by producing highly unstable compounds that release large amounts of energy in a short time. Examples of such precursors include:

- Ammonium nitrate, produced by reacting liquid ammonia with nitric acid;
- Nitroglycerin, made by reacting nitric acid with glycerol (a soap by-product);
- TNT (trinitrotoluene), derived by nitrating toluene with nitric and sulfuric acids;
- RDX and HMX, synthesized by nitration of hexamine with nitric acid;
- TATP (triacetone triperoxide), a homemade explosive formed by oxidizing acetone with hydrogen peroxide.

The manufacture and use of explosive precursors are strictly regulated due to the significant risks associated with handling and deployment. Entities engaged in such activities must comply with stringent safety regulations and often obtain special licenses. These operations require advanced technical expertise to prevent accidents and misuse, and are therefore likely to fall within the scope of the French FDI screening mechanism.

This category also includes explosives intended for military use, as defined in Articles D. 2352-7 to R. 2352-20-1 of the Defense Code. These include:

- All powders (except hunting and mining powders), such as nitrocellulose powders (with or without solvents), black powder, and composite powders;
- Explosive substances including cyclotrimethylenetetranitramine, cyclotrimethylene-trinitramine, pentaerythritol tetranitrate, trinitrotoluene, picric acid, trinitrophenyl-methylnitramine, and other chemicals containing the trinitrophenyl group, as well as any substance composed of more than 50% of any of these compounds;
- Primary explosives and nitrocellulose or other nitric esters with a nitrogen content exceeding 12.6%;
- High-performance explosives, defined by one or more of the following: detonation velocity > 7,500 m/s; thermal stability above 200°C; density > 1.80 g/cm^3; impact sensitivity coefficient < 0.20 kgm; or practical use coefficient > 150.

Lastly, and perhaps most critically, this category covers explosives intended for civilian use, as defined in Articles R. 2352-21 to R. 2352-121-7 of the Defense Code. These products may be vulnerable to misuse by foreign powers or hostile entities. The category includes:
- All explosive products not classified as military-use items; and
- Dual-use items authorized for civilian application by joint ministerial order (Ministries of Defense, Interior, Industry, and Customs), even if originally designed for military use.

This third category is exhaustive and more precisely defined than the previous two. For that reason, the regulatory provisions of the French Monetary and Financial Code provide detailed specifications for these activities, facilitating a clear application of the screening framework.

The regulatory section of the Monetary and Financial Code defines the scope of the twenty-two sensitive activities

To implement its screening authority, the Strategic Information and Economic Security Office (Bureau du CIEF) relies exclusively on Article R. 151-3 of the Monetary and Financial Code. This provision identifies a range of activities that may be grouped into three distinct categories.

The first category consists of activities deemed sensitive by their very nature [487], often referred to as «National:security" activities [488], in the sense that they contribute to a continuum of internal and external security, ranging from the preservation of public order to the protection of national defense. This is the "historical" block, insofar as most of these activities had already been listed in the 2005 decree [489], known as the Villepin Decree, which marked the first significant overhaul of the French foreign

487. France, Ministry of the Economy, Finance and Recovery, Directorate General of the Treasury, FAQ on Foreign Investment Screening in France, January 2025, p. 4, consulted September 1, 2025, available at https://www.tresor.economie.gouv.fr/services-aux-entreprises/investissements-etrangers-en-france
488. Qualification chosen by the author
489. France, Decree No. 2005-1739 of 30 December 2005 regulating financial relations with foreign countries and implementing Article L. 151-3 of the Monetary and Financial Code, Official Journal of the French Republic, No. 304, 31 December 2005, NOR: ECOX0508949D

investment screening regime. A major development was the later inclusion of "data" within this scope, introduced through the PACTE Act reform, in order to take into account the profound transformations brought about by the internet-driven economy.

These activities cover those likely to undermine national defense interests, those involving the exercise of public authority, or those liable to affect public order and public security. In practice, 26% of all authorized foreign investments in 2024 fell within this category [490], representing a slight increase compared to 2023 (22%).

They include [491]:

1° Activities, particularly those listed [492] in Article L. 2332-1 of the French Defense Code, relating to weapons, munitions, powders and explosive substances for military purposes, as well as war materials and related equipment falling under Title III or Title V of Book III, Part II of the same code.
(Examples include: the manufacture of weapons, production of war weapons and military equipment, trading activities such as purchase, sale, import and export of arms, storage and warehousing, maintenance and repair operations, demilitarization activities through destruction or conversion of obsolete weapons, and operations related to export controls.)

2° Activities relating to dual-use goods and technologies as listed in Annex IV of Regulation (EU) 2021/821 of the European Parliament and Council of May 20, 2021, establishing a Union regime for the control of exports, brokering, technical assistance, transit, and transfer of dual-use items [493].
(Examples include: advanced cryptographic equipment, surveillance and communications interception software, advanced imaging sensors and equipment, high-performance composite materials, precision navigation and positioning systems, firearms control devices, and CBRN protection technologies.)

---

490. France, Ministry of the Economy, Finance, Industrial and Digital Sovereignty, Directorate General of the Treasury, Annual Report 2024, "Foreign Direct Investment Screening in France" published 30 July 2025, consulted 31 July 2025, available at https://www.tresor.economie.gouv.fr/Articles/2025/07/30/publication-du-rapport-annuel-sur-le-controle-ief-en-2024

491. The examples provided reflect the author's personal interpretation and do not constitute an official clarification by the administration.

492. France, Defense Code, Article L. 2332-1: I. – Companies engaged in the manufacture or trade of war materiel, weapons, ammunition and their components falling under categories A and B as defined in Article L. 2331-1, or which use or operate such war materiel or equivalent equipment, in the context of the services they provide, as listed in the second paragraph of Article L. 2335-2, may operate, and the activity of their intermediaries or marketing agents may be conducted, only with prior authorization from the State and under its supervision. II. – Any person intending to establish or operate a facility for the manufacture or wholesale trade of war materiel, weapons, ammunition or their components falling under categories A, B, or C, as well as weapons, ammunition and their components falling under category D as listed by decree of the Council of State, or to provide services based on the use or operation of the war materiel and equivalent equipment referred to in paragraph I, must first file a declaration with the prefect of the département in which the facility is located. Termination of the activity, as well as closure or transfer of the facility, must be declared under the same conditions.

493. European Union, Regulation (EU) 2021/821 of the European Parliament and of the Council of May 20, 2021, setting up a Union regime for the control of exports, brokering, technical assistance, transit and transfer of dual-use items (recast), Official Journal of the European Union, L 206/1, June 11, 2021, Document 32021R0821, available at http://data.europa.eu/eli/reg/2021/821/oj (last accessed June 30, 2025); specified in French law by Decree No. 2023-1293 of December 28, 2023, on foreign investments in France, Official Journal of the French Republic, No. 0301, December 29, 2023, NOR: ECOT2323089D

3° Activities [494] carried out by entities entrusted with national defense secrets [495].
4° Activities in the field of information systems security, including those performed as a subcontractor, for the benefit of operators [496] designated under Articles L. 1332-1 [497] or L. 1332-2 [498] of the French Defense Code. (Examples include: cybersecurity audits, incident response, security consulting, secure software development, security training, threat monitoring and mitigation, vulnerability assessments, data encryption and protection, security policy development, identity and access management, log analysis, penetration testing, and secure network and communications management.)
5° Activities carried out by entities having entered into a contract, whether directly or through subcontracting, with the Ministry of Defense for the provision of goods or services falling under items 1°, 2°, 3°, or 6° of this list.
6° Activities relating to cryptographic means and services as referred to in paragraphs III and IV of Article 30 and paragraph I of Article 31 of Law [499] No. 2004-575 of June 21, 2004, on Confidence in the Digital Economy. (Examples include: cryptographic solution development, encryption service provision, cryptography consulting, training, certification of cryptographic products, key management, security analysis and auditing, secure protocol design, etc.)
7° Activities involving equipment or technical devices intended for the interception of communications, or designed for remote detection of conversations or collection of computer data, as defined in Article 226-3 of the French Criminal Code [500]. (Examples include: wireless communicationinterception, wiretapping, Wi-Fi and Bluetooth signal interception, electronic or physical listening devices, audio/video

494. Activities carried out, in particular, under classified national defense contracts or contracts containing security clauses, pursuant to Decree No. 98-608 of July 17, 1998, on the protection of national defense secrets, Official Journal of the French Republic, No. 0165, July 19, 1998, NOR: DEFD9801641D
495. France, Decree No. 2019-1271 of December 2, 2019, on the procedures for classifying and protecting national defense secrets, Official Journal of the French Republic, No. 0280, December 3, 2019, NOR: PRMD1928053D; see also: Prime Minister's Office, SGDSN, Interministerial General Instruction No. 1300/SGDSN/PSE/PSD of August 9, 2021, on the protection of national defense secrets (IGI 1300), which sets out the roles, responsibilities, and requirements for managing the life cycle of classified information and media, available at https://www.sgdsn.gouv.fr/files/files/Nos_missions/igi-1300-20210809.pdf (last accessed September 1st, 2025)
496. These operators are generally entities connected to national defense, internal security, or critical infrastructure, such as nuclear facilities, for example.
497. France, Defense Code, Article L. 1332-1: Public or private operators operating facilities or using installations and structures whose unavailability would likely reduce, in a significant manner, the war or economic potential, the security, or the survivability of the Nation shall, at their own expense and under the conditions defined in this chapter, cooperate in protecting such facilities, installations, and structures against any threat, particularly of a terrorist nature. These facilities, installations, or structures shall be designated by the administrative authority.
498. France, Defense Code, Article L. 1332-2: The obligations set forth in this chapter may be extended to facilities referred to in Article L. 511-1 of the Environmental Code or including a basic nuclear installation as defined in Article L. 593-1 of the Environmental Code, when the destruction or damage of certain installations within these facilities may present a serious danger to the population. These facilities shall be designated by the administrative authority.
499. France, Law No. 2004-575 of June 21, 2004, on confidence in the digital economy, Official Journal of the French Republic, No. 0143, June 22, 2004, NOR: ECOX0200175L
500. France, Criminal Code, Article 226-3: Punishable by five years' imprisonment and a €300,000 fine are:
1° The manufacture, import, possession, display, offering, rental, or sale of devices or technical instruments likely to enable operations that may constitute the offense referred to in the second paragraph of Article 226-15, or designed for remote detection of conversations allowing the commission of the

recording, spyware and malware development, surveillance software, communicationsmonitoring systems, radio signal decoders, GPS tracking devices, online data collection tools, radio frequency analysis, and cryptanalysis.)

8° Activities involving services provided by evaluation centers accredited under the Decree[501] of April 18, 2002, on the evaluation and certification of the security provided by information technology products and systems. (Examples include: security assessments, risk analysis, security testing, security reporting, security certification, consulting services, and ongoing security monitoring.)

9° Activities related to gambling[502] (excluding casinos[503] since 2012). (Examples include: blockchain financial monitoring technologies, financial data analytics tools for detecting money laundering, and AI- or machine-learning-based technologies for analyzing transaction patterns and identifying suspicious activities.)

---

offense provided for in Article 226-1, or intended for the interception of computer data as set out in Articles 706-102-1 of the Code of Criminal Procedure and L. 853-2 of the Internal Security Code and listed under conditions defined by decree of the Council of State, when such acts are committed, including negligently, without the ministerial authorization required under the same decree or without complying with the conditions set by said authorization;

2° The act of advertising a device or technical instrument that may facilitate the commission of the offenses provided for in Article 226-1 and the second paragraph of Article 226-15, where such advertisement constitutes an incitement to commit said offense, or that is intended for the interception of computer data as provided in Articles 706-102-1 of the Code of Criminal Procedure and L. 853-2 of the Internal Security Code, where such advertisement constitutes an incitement to fraudulent use.

This article does not apply to the possession or acquisition by operators referred to in Article L. 1332-1 of the Defense Code, designated as such by virtue of their activity as public electronic communications network operators, of equipment subject to an authorization by the Prime Minister under Section 7, Chapter II, Title I, Book II of the Postal and Electronic Communications Code.

501. France, Decree No. 2002-535 of 18 April 2002 on the evaluation and certification of the security provided by information technology products and systems, Official Journal of the French Republic, No. 0092, 19 April 2002, NOR: PRMX0100183D

502. Gaming regulation and anti-money laundering enforcement

503. DUPEYRAT, op. cit., p. 103: "Before 2012, the scope of control and protection differed depending on the origin of the foreign investment (from within or outside the EEA). However, this list raised concerns within the European Commission, particularly regarding the provisions related to casinos. This is why Decree No. 2012-691 of May 7, 2012, on foreign investments subject to prior authorization, removed casinos from the list of 'activities in the gambling sector' in Article R. 153-2 (investments from third countries) and Article R. 153-5 (intra-Community investments). The purpose of this decree was to bring the original 2005 framework into compliance with the Commission's requirements. In fact, while the Commission's Directorate-General for Internal Market acknowledged that anti-money laundering efforts could justify inclusion within the scope of the decree, it considered that for investments originating within the European Economic Area, such efforts would be more appropriately handled through a sectoral regulatory framework governing licensing and the monitoring of casino shareholders and owners. Thus, the Commission did not oppose investment screening in the casino sector per se, but objected to differential treatment between French and foreign investors. France therefore committed in 2006 to removing casinos from Article R. 153-5 once Directive 2005/60/EC on money laundering had been transposed and a prior authorization regime was established for any investment in a company operating casinos directly or through a holding. The French authorities' position was mainly driven by the need for effectiveness in addressing money laundering strategies involving casinos, an ex ante review of the origin of invested capital being more effective than the ex post withdrawal of an operating license. However, Ordinance No. 2009-104, which transposed the directive, included no provisions on the screening of casino executives or investments in the casino sector. This omission remained problematic in relation to the decree, since even though casinos were indeed removed from the 2005 decree in accordance with France's commitments to the Commission, there was no compensatory measure introduced. Nevertheless, the Government retained a reference to gambling in the screening mechanism in order to account for the possible spin-off of PMU and Française des Jeux's online betting activities. It also intended for the system to accommodate the planned liberalization of the gambling sector, which

10° Activities involving the means and services intended to respond to the unlawful use of pathogenic or toxic agents, or to mitigate the health consequences of such use.
(Examples include: epidemic surveillance, data analysis tools for detecting unusual patterns, bioinformatics techniques for identifying DNA or protein sequences usable for creating pathogens, pathogen detection using mass spectrometry or nuclear magnetic resonance, and activities linked to biosafety in BSL-3 and BSL-4 labs.)
11° Activities involving the processing, transmission, or storage of data whose compromise or disclosure could adversely affect the conduct of the activities listed under items 1° to 10° above (i.e., those relating to national defense, public authority, public order, and public security) or under paragraph II (relating to essential infrastructures, goods, or services).
(Examples include: use of software, algorithms and AI for classification, categorization, forecasting and decision-making; data cleansing, normalization, aggregation, and conversion; use of transmission protocols such as TCP/IP, HTTP, FTP, SMTP; cloud storage services; encryption; and management of storage media such as hard drives, SSDs, and file servers.)

A second category[504] of activities was introduced as part of the regulatory reform[505] initiated by the so-called Montebourg Decree[506] of May 14, 2014, and further reinforced by the Decree of November 29, 2018. This category targets infrastructures, assets, and services that are deemed "essential". In 2024, 37% of

---

was expected to require the revision of around thirty legal texts. The Government therefore maintained the reference to 'gambling' in the current Article R. 152-3 of the Monetary and Financial Code."

504. France, Ministry of the Economy, Industrial and Digital Sovereignty, Directorate General of the Treasury, Annual Report 2024, "Foreign Direct Investment Screening in France," published on June 4, 2024, accessed on June 6, 2024, available at https://www.tresor.economie.gouv.fr/Articles/c7ec36f3-6df0-4cf8-82aa-9c772917afeb/files/249123ae-5a3b-45dd-8f6f-5f84b2fc0c0a

505. As a reminder, it was indeed Decree No. 2014-479 of May 14, 2014, on foreign investments that introduced the notion of "essential activities", which is echoed in the second legislative tier by extending the scope of Decree No. 2005-1739 of December 30, 2005, regulating financial relations with foreign countries, to cover "activities essential to safeguarding the country's interests in terms of public order, public security, or national defense." This approach was carried forward by Decrees No. 2018-1057 of November 29, 2018, No. 2019-1590 of December 31, 2019, and No. 2020-892 of July 22, 2020.
By expanding the scope of the sectors subject to the prior authorization regime for foreign investors to include these essential activities, the Government took the opportunity to significantly broaden the list of strategic sectors. While the term essential activities is never formally defined, the decree aligns with the rationale of Article L. 151-2 of the Monetary and Financial Code, which sets forth the powers of the Minister of the Economy, Industry and Digital Affairs in the defense of «National:interests." In this respect, the concept of essential activities is closely related to the broader notion of "interests of the Nation."
This particular wording is far from incidental, as it serves to meet European requirements, in particular the criteria set by the Court of Justice of the European Union (CJEU), including its March 14, 2000 judgment in Association Église de Scientologie. That decision clarifies that public order and public security justifications may only be invoked in the presence of a real and sufficiently serious threat to a "fundamental interest" of society.
In that same spirit, it must be understood that in the event of litigation, the CJEU's interpretation of these concepts would likely prevail, even in domestic law. The category of essential activities, as framed by the 2014 decree, thus encompasses a wide range of activities and provides the State with a broad margin of discretion.

506. France, Decree No. 2018-1057 of November 29, 2018, on foreign investments subject to prior authorization, Official Journal of the French Republic, No. 0278, December 1, 2018, NOR: ECOT1816712D

authorized investments fell[507] within this sector, representing a slight decrease compared to 2023 (43%).

These activities are intended to ensure, in particular:

1. The integrity, security, or continuity of energy supply (e.g., power generation by electric, nuclear, wind, solar, or hydroelectric plants; electricity transmission and distribution networks via high-voltage lines, substations, and local grids; oil refining and petroleum storage; natural gas storage and pipeline supply; fuel storage terminals and service stations; fuel transportation infrastructure via pipelines);
2. The integrity, security, or continuity of water supply (e.g., water abstraction and treatment facilities for drinking water, pumping stations, water distribution networks via pipelines, storage reservoirs, distribution stations, wastewater treatment plants and sanitation systems, stormwater drainage systems, water resource management services, equipment maintenance and replacement services, protection against sabotage, crisis response to floods or contamination events, etc.);
3. The integrity, security, or continuity of transport networks and services (e.g., road, highway, bridge, tunnel, and railway infrastructure; airports and seaports or inland ports; passenger terminals; public transport networks by bus, tram, or metro; freight transport services; road policing, firefighting, emergency medical services, and other emergency responders; traffic management systems; air and maritime control services; logistics and intelligent transportation systems);
4. The integrity, security, or continuity of space operations within the meaning of Article 1(3) of the French Law[508] of June 3, 2008 on Space Operations (e.g., rocket and launcher-based space vehicle launch services; orbital satellite deployment and maintenance; orbital control and mission command centers; terrestrial communication infrastructure and satellite networks; GPS and satellite navigation constellations; space debris monitoring and collision avoidance systems; rocket propulsion and satellite maneuvering systems);
5. The integrity, security, or continuity of electronic communicationsnetworks and services (e.g., subsea cable networks, telecom towers, data centers, Internet points of presence (PoPs), essential switching and routing equipment, preventive and emergency maintenance, cybersecurity against DDoS attacks and cybercrime, uninterrupted power supply to telecom infrastructure, data management services, signal transmission, service providers for mobile, Internet, and television communications);
6. The performance of missions by the national police, gendarmerie, civil protection services, prison security services[509], as well as the public security missions carried

507. France, Ministry of the Economy, Finance, Industrial and Digital Sovereignty, Directorate General of the Treasury, Annual Report 2024, "Foreign Direct Investment Screening in France," published 30 July 2025, consulted 31 July 2025, available at https://www.tresor.economie.gouv.fr/Articles/2025/07/30/publication-du-rapport-annuel-sur-le-controle-ief-en-2024

508. France, Law No. 2008-518 of June 3, 2008, on space operations, Official Journal of the French Republic, No. 0129, June 4, 2008, NOR: ESRX0700048L, Art. 1, 3°: "Space operation: any activity consisting in launching or attempting to launch an object into outer space, or in exercising control over a space object or a coordinated group of space objects during their stay in outer space, including the Moon and other celestial bodies, as well as, where applicable, during their return to Earth."

509. France, Decree No. 2023-1293 of December 28, 2023, on foreign investments in France, Official Journal of the French Republic, No. 0301, December 29, 2023, NOR: ECOT2323089D

out by customs and licensed private security companies (e.g., secure communications systems for operations coordination; telecom and data networks for emergency services; radio infrastructure; fleets of patrol vehicles, ambulances, and intervention vehicles; transportation logistics; protective gear and safety equipment; weapons and ammunition; specialized firefighting equipment);

7. The integrity, security, or continuity of the operation of a vital[510] infrastructure, facility, or site as defined in Articles L. 1332-1 and L. 1332-2 of the French Defense Code (e.g., protection of production centers, data centers, major distribution hubs, or control centers);
8. The protection of public health (e.g., health services, emergency medical services, infrastructure and services related to clean water supply and sanitation)[511];
9. The production, processing, or distribution of agricultural products listed in Annex I of the Treaty on the Functioning of the European Union, when they contribute to national food security[512] as defined in Article L. 1(I)(1), (17), and (18) of the French Rural and Maritime Fishing Code (e.g., farming activities, food processing plants, agricultural distribution networks, food supply chains[513] in times of crisis, agricultural research, and land[514] preservation[515]);

---

510. France, Secretariat-General for National Defence and Security (SGDSN), "Essential Operators and Vital Importance Sectors - SAIV," consulted on May 9, 2024, available at https://www.sgdsn.gouv.fr/files/files/Nos_missions/plaquette-saiv.pdf
511. France, Senate, Oral Question No. 1394S to the Minister of the Economy and Finance on foreign investments in nursing homes (EPHAD), asked by Senator DEMILLY (Centrist Union Group), Official Journal of the Senate, December 3, 2020, p. 5643; Government reply of December 16, 2020 by the Secretary of State for Digital Transition, Official Journal of the Senate, p. 11933
512. The question of whether food security falls within the broader scope of economic security is a recurring issue in the debate on foreign investment screening. It has been specifically raised by elected officials, notably in the context of foreign acquisitions of agricultural land, as illustrated by Written Question No. 03488 to the Minister of Agriculture and Food submitted by Senator MAUREY (Centrist Union Group), Official Journal of the Senate, March 1, 2018, p. 902.
Land purchases are indeed one of the strategies used by countries to mitigate the risks threatening their food security. Nations invest in foreign farmland either because their food security is directly dependent on imports (e.g., Saudi Arabia, Japan, South Korea, Libya), or because they view such acquisitions as both a means of asserting geopolitical power and a form of strategic food reserve (e.g., China). The topic was discussed during parliamentary debates on the PACTE Law in 2019, particularly in the Senate, which proposed an amendment to Article L. 151-3 of the Monetary and Financial Code aimed at recognizing food security as a component of national security.
DUPEYRAT, op. cit., p. 105.
513. France, Senate, Written Question No. 1417S to the Minister of the Armed Forces, asked by Senator MARCHAND (Renaissance Group), Official Journal of the Senate, December 10, 2020, p. 11926; Government reply of December 16, 2020 by the Minister for Ecological Transition and Transport, Official Journal of the Senate, p. 11926
514. France, National Assembly, Written Question No. 37337 to the Minister of Agriculture and Food, asked by Deputy BAZIN (Les Républicains Group), Official Journal of the National Assembly, March 23, 2021, p. 5798; Government reply of January 4, 2022, Official Journal of the National Assembly, p. 46: "Thus, as soon as land is held by a French legal entity and is targeted by a foreign natural or legal person, the foreign investment screening procedure in France may apply."
515. France, National Assembly, Written Question No. 30301 to the Minister of Agriculture and Food, asked by Deputy MARILOSSIAN (La République En Marche Group), Official Journal of the National Assembly, June 16, 2020, p. 4119; Government reply of September 8, 2020, Official Journal of the National Assembly, p. 5936: "Accordingly, the Government adopted Decree No. 2019-1590 of December 31, 2019, pursuant to the PACTE Law, in order to extend the prior Foreign Direct Investment Screening in France to food security, and therefore to the monitoring of acquisitions of agricultural land."

10. The publishing, printing, or distribution of general political and news publications [516], as defined by Article 4 of the French Law [517] of April 2, 1947 on newspaper and periodical distribution companies, and online press services of general political and news content, as defined in Article 1 of the French Law [518] of August 1, 1986 reforming the legal regime of the press (e.g., news publishing and distribution, press retail outlets, online news services);
11. The integrity, security, or continuity of the extraction, processing, or recycling of critical raw materials [519]. These are materials with significant industrial properties, the scarcity of which may lead to serious economic or industrial risks [520].

A list [521] has been established at the European level, the details [522] of which were recalled by the French administration in its 2025 guidelines. The following raw materials are considered critical :

Antimony, arsenic, bauxite, barite, beryllium, bismuth, boron, cobalt, coking coal, copper, feldspar, fluorspar, gallium, germanium, hafnium, helium, heavy rare earths, light rare earths, lithium, magnesium, manganese, natural graphite, battery-grade nickel, niobium, natural phosphate, phosphorus, platinum group metals, scandium, silicon metal, strontium, tantalum, titanium metal, tungsten, vanadium.

France has become acutely aware, particularly in the wake of the COVID-19 crisis, heightened geopolitical tensions, and its dependence on certain foreign suppliers

---

516. In accordance with the standards set by the EU Regulation establishing a framework for the screening of foreign direct investments into the Union, foreign investments involving press publications and online news services of a political and general nature are subject to screening, with the aim of protecting all French media outlets against any transaction that could jeopardize fundamental principles tied to the exercise of public freedoms, such as media pluralism and independence, and of safeguarding the public from information manipulation by foreign powers. The mechanism also covers critical infrastructure essential to the media sector, such as printing and distribution operations.
517. France, Law No. 47-585 of April 2, 1947, on the legal status of newspaper and periodical grouping and distribution companies, Official Journal of the French Republic, April 3, 1947, No. 81, p. 3126, Art. 4: "The distribution of political and general information press shall be organized in such a way as to ensure its independence and pluralism, as well as readers' freedom of choice. For the purposes of this law, political and general information press refers to newspapers and periodicals that, on a permanent basis, provide news and commentary on local, national, or international political and general current affairs with the aim of informing citizens' judgment, devote the majority of their editorial content to this purpose, and present a clear interest that goes beyond the concerns of a specific readership category. A decree issued by the Council of State shall designate the competent authority responsible for recognizing the political and general information nature of such newspapers and periodicals under conditions of independence and impartiality."
518. France, Law No. 86-897 of August 1, 1986, reforming the legal framework for the press, Official Journal of the French Republic, No. 0178, August 2, 1986
519. France, Decree No. 2023-1293 of December 28, 2023, on foreign investments in France, Official Journal of the French Republic, No. 0301, December 29, 2023, NOR: ECOT2323089D
520. France, Economic, Social and Environmental Council (CESE), Section for Economic Activities, SAINT-AUBIN, Philippe, Opinion No. 2019-03, "Dependence on Strategic Metals: What Solutions for the Economy?," January 22, 2019, DILA, ISBN 978-2-11-152215-2, NOR: CESL1100003
521. European Union, European Parliament and Council, Proposal for a Regulation establishing a framework to ensure a secure and sustainable supply of critical raw materials and amending Regulations (EU) No. 168/2013, (EU) 2018/858, (EU) 2018/1724 and (EU) 2019/1020, Annex II, Critical Raw Materials, Section 1, List of Critical Raw Materials.
522. See Point 1.3 in France, Ministry of the Economy, Finance and Industrial and Digital Sovereignty, Directorate General of the Treasury, Guidelines on the Foreign Direct Investment Screening in France, July 2025, published July 30, 2025, consulted August 1, 2025, available at https://www.tresor.economie.gouv.fr/services-aux-entreprises/investissements-etrangers-en-france

(most notably China), of the need to secure access to critical minerals and strategic metals such as lithium, cobalt, nickel, rare earths, and tungsten. These raw materials are indispensable to key sectors, including the energy transition (batteries, wind, and solar power), digital technologies (semiconductors and electronics), as well as defense and aerospace. In response, a December 2022 decree [523] established the Interministerial Delegation for the Supply of Strategic Minerals and Metals (Délégation interministérielle aux approvisionnements en minerais et métaux stratégiques - DIAMMS), thereby elevating these issues to the highest level of State responsibility.

These infrastructures and activities are protected by the French State on the grounds of their "vital importance." This protection is deeply rooted [524] in France's legal and institutional framework. As early as December 29, 1958, the government adopted an ordinance [525] establishing a policy to that effect, which has been continuously updated by successive interministerial instructions, notably in 1993 [526], 2008 [527], and 2014 [528].

The Decree [529] of May 14, 2014, further reinforced by the Decrees of November 29, 2018 [530], and December 30, 2019 [531], officially recognized these vital sector activities (secteurs d'activités d'importance vitale - SAIV) as part of France's list of "strategic sectors." Their designation remains at the sovereign discretion of the French State, pursuant to a well-defined legal and institutional framework.

A dedicated Interministerial Commission for Defense and Security of Vital Activities [532] (Commission interministérielle de défense et de sécurité des SAIV - CIDS) has been established by decree [533] and codified under Articles R. 1332-10 to R. 1332-12 of the French Defense Code.

---

523. D. n° 2022-1550, 10 déc. 2022, relatif à la délégation interministérielle aux approvisionnements en minerais et métaux stratégiques, JO n° 0287, 11 déc. 2022, NOR : ECOL2221277D
524. DUPEYRAT, op. cit.,
525. France, Ordinance No. 58-1371 of December 29, 1958, aimed at strengthening the protection of vital installations (mandatory cooperation at their own expense by relevant companies, preparation of protection plans, fines for executives in case of non-compliance), Official Journal of the French Republic, December 31, 1958, p. 12064
526. France, Prime Minister, Interministerial General Instruction No. 4600 of February 8, 1993
527. France, Prime Minister, Interministerial General Instruction No. 6600/SGDSN/PSE/PPS of September 26, 2008
528. France, Prime Minister, Interministerial General Instruction No. 6600/SGDSN/PSE/PSN of January 7, 2014, on the security of vital importance activities, NOR: PRMD1400503J, published online on January 21, 2014, accessed on May 9, 2024, available at https://www.legifrance.gouv.fr/download/pdf/circ?id=37828
529. France, Decree No. 2014-479 of May 14, 2014, on foreign investments subject to prior authorization, Official Journal of the French Republic, No. 0112, May 15, 2014, NOR: ERNX1411012D
530. France, Decree No. 2018-1057 of November 29, 2018, on foreign investments subject to prior authorization, Official Journal of the French Republic, No. 0278, December 1, 2018, NOR: ECOT1816712D
531. France, Decree No. 2019-1590 of December 31, 2019, on foreign investments in France, Official Journal of the French Republic, No. 0001, January 1, 2020, NOR: ECOT1932857D
532. France, National Assembly, Written Question to the Prime Minister, asked by Deputy ZUMKELLER (Member of Parliament), Official Journal of the National Assembly, November 13, 2012, p. 6353; Government reply published in the Official Journal of the National Assembly, May 28, 2013, p. 5484
533. France, Decree No. 2006-212 of February 23, 2006, on the security of vital importance activities, Official Journal of the French Republic, No. 47, February 24, 2006, p. 2889, Art. 8

The initial classification of vital sectors was carried out by the Ministerial Order of June 2, 2006, which assigned each sector to a coordinating ministry [534]. Each coordinating minister designates Vital Operators (Opérateurs d'Importance Vitale – OIVs) and notifies them of the relevant National Security Directive (Directive Nationale de Sécurité – DNS), which identifies applicable threats and outlines the sector's overarching security goals.

OIVs are required to draft an Operator Security Plan [535] (Plan de Sécurité Opérateur – PSO), detailing their security policy and outlining response scenarios in line with the threats identified in the DNS. They must also identify their Vital Importance Points (Points d'Importance Vitale – PIVs), which must be approved by the CIDS following submission of a dossier by the coordinating ministry.

For each PIV, the OIV must draw up a dedicated Specific Protection Plan (Plan Particulier de Protection – PPP), subject to validation by the Prefect, who also establishes an external protection plan. According [536] to the General Secretariat for Defense and National Security (SGDSN), France currently has 12 vital sectors, 22 national security directives, 249 designated OIVs, and 1,369 identified PIVs.

The Interministerial Instruction [537] of January 7, 2014 defines a vital sector (SAIV) as a group of activities that:
(i) provide goods or services essential to population survival, the exercise of State authority, the functioning of the economy, the maintenance of defense capabilities, or national security, provided such activities are not easily replaceable or substitutable; or
(ii) pose a serious risk to public safety.

In this context, the Decrees of May 14, 2014 [538], November 29, 2018 [539], and December 30, 2019 [540] also target vital installations and facilities, particularly regarding their secure and continuous operation as defined in Articles L. 1332-1 and L. 1332-2 of the French Defense Code.

534. Civilian activities of the State: Minister of the Interior ; Judicial activities: Minister of Justice ; Military activities of the State: Prime Minister's Office for National Security and Defense (SGDSN or equivalent) ; Food supply: Minister responsible for Agriculture ; Electronic communications, broadcasting and information: Minister responsible for Electronic Communications ; Energy: Minister responsible for Industry ; Space and research: Minister responsible for Research ; Finance: Minister responsible for Economy and Finance ;Water management: Minister responsible for Ecology ; Industry: Minister responsible for Industry ; Health: Minister responsible for Health ; Transport: Minister of Transport

535. DUPEYRAT, op. cit.,

536. France, Prime Minister, Interministerial General Instruction, No. 6600/SGDSN/PSE/PSN, January 7, 2014, on the security of vital importance activities, NOR: PRMD1400503J, published online January 21, 2014, consulted September 1, 2025, available at https://www.legifrance.gouv.fr/download/pdf/circ?id=37828

537. France, Prime Minister, Interministerial General Instruction No. 6600/SGDSN/PSE/PSN of January 7, 2014, on the security of vital importance activities, NOR: PRMD1400503J, published online on January 21, 2014, accessed on September 1st, 2025, available at https://www.legifrance.gouv.fr/download/pdf/circ?id=37828

538. France, Decree No. 2014-479 of May 14, 2014, on foreign investments subject to prior authorization, Official Journal of the French Republic, No. 0112, May 15, 2014, NOR: ERNX1411012D

539. France, Decree No. 2018-1057 of November 29, 2018, on foreign investments subject to prior authorization, Official Journal of the French Republic, No. 0278, December 1, 2018, NOR: ECOT1816712D

540. France, Decree No. 2019-1590 of December 31, 2019, on foreign investments in France, Official Journal of the French Republic, No. 0001, January 1, 2020, NOR: ECOT1932857D

According to Article L. 1332-1, a vital installation is any facility, infrastructure, or site operated by a public or private entity whose loss of availability could significantly reduce France's war potential, economic resilience, security, or national survival, especially in the event of terrorist threats. Article L. 1332-2 adds that this category may include facilities referred to in Article L. 511-1 of the French Environmental Code or those containing a basic nuclear installation within the meaning of Article L. 593-1, where damage to such facilities could seriously endanger the population.

Such facilities are designated by the competent administrative authority and are not made public for national security reasons.

The notion of "non-substitutable or non-replaceable" infrastructure is a key criterion, as reaffirmed by Article R. 1332-2 of the Defense Code.

In practice, knowledge of who qualifies as an OIV is primarily experience-based and not publicly disclosed. Nevertheless, it is possible to identify certain banks as falling within the scope of OIVs even if they are not explicitly named. The Administration has thus reiterated [541] that the list of Operators of Vital Importance (OIVs) is protected under national defense secrecy. Consequently, the State cannot provide confirmation or denial as to whether such an operator is among the French entity's clients.

Sensitive activities also encompass research and development in ten critical technologies

The third category [542] of sensitive activities is set forth under Section III of Article R. 151-3 of the French Monetary and Financial Code. This category includes activities that may pose a threat to national security, whether in relation to national defense, the exercise of public authority, public order, or public safety, when they are intended to be implemented within one of the activities listed in Sections I and II of the same Article.

Foremost among these are research and development (R&D) activities relating to ten "critical technologies," whose scope is defined by order of the Minister of the Economy. In 2024, 14% of authorized investments [543] fell within this sector, a figure that remained stable compared to 2023.

541. See Point 1.3 in Ministry of the Economy, Finance and Industrial and Digital Sovereignty, Directorate General of the Treasury, "Guidelines on the Foreign Direct Investment Screening in France" July 2025, published July 30, 2025, consulted August 1, 2025, available at https://www.tresor.economie.gouv.fr/services-aux-entreprises/investissements-etrangers-en-france

542. France, Ministry of the Economy, Finance, Industrial and Digital Sovereignty, Directorate General of the Treasury, Annual Report 2024, "Foreign Direct Investment Screening in France," published on June 4, 2024, this category accounted for 14.8% of authorized investments in 2023, down from 24.4% in 2022, available at https://www.tresor.economie.gouv.fr/Articles/c7ec36f3-6df0-4cf8-82aa-9c772917afeb/files/249123ae-5a3b-45dd-8f6f-5f84b2fc0c0a (last accessed June 6, 2024)

543. France, Ministry of the Economy, Finance and Industrial and Digital Sovereignty, Directorate General of the Treasury, Annual Report 2024, "Foreign Direct Investment Screening in France," published July 30, 2025, consulted July 31, 2025, available at https://www.tresor.economie.gouv.fr/Articles/2025/07/30/publication-du-rapport-annuel-sur-le-controle-ief-en-2024

An initial list of seven technologies was adopted by Ministerial Order [544] dated December 31, 2019, and includes:

1. Cybersecurity, which involves the protection of computer systems, networks, data, and infrastructures from threats, attacks, and vulnerabilities. Its core objective is to ensure the confidentiality, integrity, and availability of information systems. Given the proliferation of online threats (malware, ransomware, phishing, and advanced cyberattacks), cybersecurity has become essential for individuals, businesses, and governments alike. (Examples of companies concerned: Atos, Thales Group, Sopra Steria, Akka Technologies, Wallix Group, Safe-T Group, Stormshield, etc.)
2. Artificial intelligence, focused on creating machines capable of autonomous reasoning, learning, and decision-making by mimicking certain human cognitive functions. (Examples: Dassault Systèmes, Capgemini, Atos, Sopra Steria, STMicroelectronics, Talend, Robolution Capital (SPAC))
3. Robotics,, encompassing the design, construction, programming, and use of robots capable of performing tasks autonomously or semi-autonomously. (Examples: Balyo, ECA Group, Robolution Capital (SPAC))
4. Additive manufacturing (3D printing), which involves building three-dimensional objects layer by layer using various materials. (Examples: Prodways Group, Solutions 30 SE, Groupe Gorgé, Carboman Group)
5. Semiconductors, relating to the production of electronic chips and integrated circuits that form the backbone of most modern electronic devices, including computers, smartphones, and vehicles. (Examples: STMicroelectronics, Soitec, X-FAB Silicon Foundries SE, Dolphin Integration, Lacroix Group)
6. Quantum technologies, based on principles of quantum mechanics, which enable advanced functionalities that conventional technologies cannot achieve. These technologies leverage the unique behaviors of subatomic particles. (Examples: Atos, Air Liquide, Dassault Systèmes, Quantum Genomics)
7. Energy storage, referring to the capture and retention of energy for later use through technologies such as batteries, supercapacitors, pumped hydro, or thermal storage. This is vital to ensure grid stability and continuous supply in variable production environments. (Examples: Saft, Engie, Schneider Electric, Eramet, Valeo, McPhy Energy)

A second ministerial order [545] dated April 30, 2020, extended the list to include:

8. Biotechnologies, which apply biological organisms or their components to create new products and processes in areas such as genetic engineering, bioproduction, bioremediation, and medicine. (Examples: Genfit, Innate Pharma, Nicox, GenSight Biologics, OSE Immunotherapeutics, Inventiva, AB Science)

A third order [546], dated December 28, 2023, added the final two:

9. Low-carbon energy technologies [547], including but not limited to solar, wind, hydroelectric and nuclear power, energy storage systems, electric vehicle infrastructure,

544. France, Ministerial Order of December 31, 2019, on foreign investments in France, Official Journal of the French Republic, No. 0001, January 1, 2020, NOR: ECOT1937237A

545. France, Ministerial Order of April 27, 2020, on foreign investments in France, Official Journal of the French Republic, No. 0105, April 30, 2020, NOR: ECOT2010256A

546. France, Ministerial Order of December 28, 2023, on foreign investments in France, Official Journal of the French Republic, No. 0301, December 29, 2023, NOR: ECOT2334928A

547. Formerly referred to as "renewable energies" in the Ministerial Order of December 31, 2019, on foreign investments in France

biomass energy, biogas and biofuels, carbon capture and storage (CCS), and green hydrogen production. (Examples include electrolysis-based hydrogen, electric mobility, etc.)

10. Photonics [548], involving the science and technology of light (optics), including optical components, optoelectronic devices, fiber optics, optical communication, lasers, imaging technologies, and quantum photonics, with cross-sectoral applications, including in the energy industry.

Sensitive activities also include R&D related to dual-use goods and technologies

Beyond these ten critical technologies, the third category also captures research and development (R&D) activities, when destined for application in activities listed in Sections I or II, that concern dual-use items and technologies as enumerated in Annex I of Regulation [549] (EU) No. 2021/821 of the European Parliament and of the Council of May 20, 2021.

This includes, in particular:

- Nuclear materials, installations, and equipment;
- Special materials and related equipment;
- Materials processing;
- Electronics;
- Computers;
- Telecommunications and information security;
- Sensors and lasers;
- Navigation and avionics;
- Marine technology;
- Aerospace and propulsion systems.

Additional dual-use items, including related brokering services or technical assistance, are subject to export authorization requirements if they are intended, in whole or in part, for:

- The development or use of chemical, biological, or nuclear weapons;
- Military use in countries subject to arms embargoes;
- Components of military goods previously exported from an EU Member State without proper authorization.

---

548. France, Ministerial Order of December 28, 2023, on foreign investments in France, Official Journal of the French Republic, No. 0301, December 29, 2023, NOR: ECOT2334928A

549. European Union, Regulation (EU) 2021/821 of the European Parliament and of the Council of 20 May 2021 establishing the Union regime for the control of exports, brokering, technical assistance, transit and transfer of dual-use items (recast), Official Journal of the European Union, L 206/1, 11 June 2021, Document 32021R0821, ELI: http://data.europa.eu/eli/reg/2021/821/oj, as further specified under French law by Decree No. 2023-1293 of 28 December 2023 on foreign investments in France, Official Journal of the French Republic, No. 0301, 29 December 2023, NOR: ECOT2323089D (formerly Council Regulation (EC) No 428/2009 of 5 May 2009 setting up a Community regime for the control of exports, transfer, brokering and transit of dual-use items, Official Journal of the European Union, L 134/1, 29 May 2009)

The number of transactions deemed eligible[550] for screening on account of their connection to research and development (R&D)activities in critical technologies has increased steadily, rising from 27 in 2021 to 44 in 2024. Among these transactions, the most represented critical technologies were biotechnology, cybersecurity, and semiconductors, with applications primarily directed toward the health, information technology, and defense sectors.

Moreover, an increasingly significant proportion of the authorizations granted for these research and development (R&D) activities were subject to specific conditions: in 2024, 27 out of the 44 transactions concerned were subject to such requirements. These conditions were designed primarily to ensure the continuity of funding for R&D projects and to safeguard the knowledge and know-how derived therefrom, particularly elements falling within the scope of intellectual property.

The eligibility of sensitive activities is threefold.

In 2025, the administration[551] recalled in its guidelines that three distinct categories of eligibility must be distinguished depending on the nature of the activity carried out by the target entity:

- **Eligibility by nature**: this is the so-called "objective" eligibility (Article R. 151-3, I, Monetary and Financial Code).
- **Eligibility based on a set of indicators**: in this case, activities are subject to a "sensitivity test" to determine whether they are "essential." This test takes into account several factors, tailored to the characteristics of each activity, such as the target entity's clients, the nature, specificity, and applications of its products, services, or know-how, the substitutability of its activities, and the hazardousness of the operations carried out. This list, however, is not exhaustive (Article R. 151-3, II, Monetary and Financial Code).
- **Eligibility by destination**: this category concerns research and development (R&D) activities. Specifically, R&D relating to critical technologies or to dual-use goods and technologies falls within the scope of the FDI screening regime where such R&D is likely to be applied to one of the activities covered by the two categories above. The aim is not to capture mature R&D activities already applied in sensitive sectors (covered by Article R. 151-3, I and II, Monetary and Financial Code), but rather early-stage R&D activities, i.e., before their industrialization phase, where the future applications of such R&D could potentially affect sensitive sectors (Article R. 151-3, III, Monetary and Financial Code).

Accordingly, the determination of sensitivity is made on a case-by-case basis, depending on the characteristics of each transaction (sector concerned, market conditions, etc.).

550. France, Ministry of the Economy, Finance and Industrial and Digital Sovereignty, Directorate General of the Treasury, Annual Report 2024, "Foreign Direct Investment Screening in France," published July 30, 2025, consulted July 31, 2025, available at https://www.tresor.economie.gouv.fr/Articles/2025/07/30/publication-du-rapport-annuel-sur-le-controle-ief-en-2024

551. See Point 1.3 in Ministry of the Economy, Finance and Industrial and Digital Sovereignty, Directorate General of the Treasury, "Guidelines on the Foreign Direct Investment Screening in France" July 2025, Published July 30, 2025, consulted August 1, 2025, available at https://www.tresor.economie.gouv.fr/services-aux-entreprises/investissements-etrangers-en-france

Eligibility of sensitive activities is disconnected from their economic value.

The administration stressed[552] that neither the size of the investment nor the turnover of the French target necessarily constitutes, in itself, a decisive criterion for eligibility under the FDI screening procedure. Activities carried out by a French target may still be deemed sensitive even if they generate only limited revenues, particularly when they involve highly specific services provided to a small number of clients critical to public security, public order, or national defense interests.

The administration therefore strongly recommends that economic operators, in case of doubt as to whether a French entity's activities are sensitive, either file a formal authorization request or make use of the prior review mechanism. This applies, for instance, to subcontracting activities, where, depending on the subcontractor's position in the value chain, the impact on the final output may be difficult for an investor to assess. By contrast, a direct supplier to major defense sector operators is unlikely to be unaware of the ultimate use of its products.

Applications submitted under the French foreign direct investment screening regime must contain a detailed and precise description of the activities carried out, including a description of the services and products provided. Where applicable, such information must be supplied subsidiary by subsidiary.

Finally, it must be emphasized that overly summary descriptions, limited to a short abstract, containing no information on the products or services supplied, or referring only to the target company's corporate communications or website, are deemed insufficient.

Certain "mixed" sectors fall within multiple categories.

Foreign investments classified as "mixed" may fall under two or even three of the aforementioned categories. In 2024, such investments accounted for 22 percent of all reviewed transactions[553], a figure that remained stable compared to 2023. By way of illustration, one may cite French companies engaged in the manufacture of aeronautical components intended for both civilian and military aviation.

Certain sectors or activities are not subject to screening

By contrast, activities that are not expressly covered by Article R. 151-3 of the French Monetary and Financial Code or by the ministerial orders adopted pursuant thereto are de facto excluded from the scope of the French FDI screening mechanism. It is therefore relevant to consider, by way of negative inference, a list of sectors not currently captured by the regime, bearing in mind that the French administration retains wide discretion over the level of granularity with which it assesses eligibility.

552. Ibid
553. ibid

Such a list of non-covered sectors [554] was compiled in 2025 by the Parliamentary Mission on the Evaluation of France's FDI Screening Mechanism. It includes, among others:

- Digital platforms, social networks, and data center activities [555];
- Banking and financial services [556];
- Cultural activities or those relating to the freedom and pluralism of the media,
- Activities connected with real estate;
- Artificial intelligence and new technologies, except where related to research and development (R&D).

Finally, it should not be inferred from this objective situation that public authorities are indifferent to these sectors in terms of safeguarding the national interest. It must be recalled that the Government retains the power to amend, at any time, the regulatory provisions of Article R. 151-3 of the Monetary and Financial Code.

*
* *

While the presence of a "sensitive activity" constitutes the third eligibility criterion for the application of France's FDI screening mechanism, it may not be as readily identifiable as the existence of a formal list might suggest.

Indeed, the activities described in this section are the result of codification efforts undertaken by the French government in order to provide greater predictability to foreign investors. But this codification merely represents the visible tip of the iceberg. It is underpinned by a complex internal analysis conducted by State services to determine whether a given activity may be considered sensitive.

As such, limiting the assessment of whether an activity is sensitive solely to the enumerated list in the Monetary and Financial Code would be a flawed strategy. For the parties to a transaction, it is essential to understand the sectoral analysis carried out by the relevant ministries, which possess the technical and technological expertise necessary to evaluate such matters. This implies, for instance, that due consideration must be given not only to the target's capacity to produce a given technology or service, but also to its global positioning (e.g., whether it constitutes a critical European source), and to the extent to which the acquisition would enable the investor to

554. France, National Assembly, Committee for the Evaluation and Oversight of Public Policies, Information Report No. 1453 by JOLIVET F. and de LEPINAU H., Members of Parliament, on the evaluation of foreign direct investment screening in France, Official Journal of the French Republic, 27 May 2025, text 45 of 69, published on 22 May 2025, available at https://www.assemblee (last accessed 27 May 2025)

555. By way of comparison, the acquisition of a digital platform or a social network already falls within the scope of sectors subject to CFIUS review in the United States. Moreover, activities related to data centers, currently protected only insofar as they are connected to already sensitive operations, but not as such, could benefit from stronger protection against influence operations through an amendment to the relevant paragraph of Article R. 151-3.

556. The evaluation mission notes that, under Article R. 151-3, only those activities involving infrastructure, assets or services essential to ensuring "the integrity, security or continuity of the operations of a facility [...] of vital importance" are afforded protection. This definition refers to the list of Operators of Vital Importance (OIVs), coordinated by the General Secretariat for Defense and National Security (SGDSN), which, in the economic sector, includes 15 major banking and financial institutions. However, this list is by definition restrictive and covers only large institutions, excluding SMEs that may, in the near future, play a strategic role, such as fintech startups.

enhance that technology in ways that could surpass theoretical dual-use performance thresholds.

It is therefore in the interest of all parties to the transaction to assess the sensitivity of the target activity from the viewpoint of the French State, and to consider how public authorities may evaluate the same activity in the context of other national interest protection laws. (See also Chapter 7)

Part Three

Phases of the French FDI Screening Procedure

The implementation of France's foreign direct investment (FDI) screening regime unfolds through several distinct phases, each designed to ensure that foreign investment transactions comply with national security interests and the applicable regulatory framework. This part provides a detailed analysis of the various steps involved in the French FDI screening process, highlighting the formal and informal requirements, procedural stages, and administrative decisions that structure the regime.

Focusing specifically on the sequential phases of FDI screening, this section outlines the key steps to be taken by the parties involved in a covered transaction. The process begins with an internal self-assessment phase, during which the parties must determine whether their transaction falls within the scope of the French screening framework (Chapter 14). At this stage, parties must consider factors such as the structure of the transaction, the character and trustworthiness of the foreign investor, the sensitivity of the French target entity, and the potential obligation to file a declaration in specific circumstances.

The second step consists in engaging in informal pre-filing consultations with the French Treasury at the Ministry of the Economy (Bercy), which, although not legally binding, allow the parties to anticipate any concerns that the authorities may raise and to discuss the contours of the proposed investment in advance (Chapter 15).

A third possible step is the formal pre-filing procedure, designed to clarify whether the contemplated transaction is subject to the French FDI screening regime . This procedure, which may be initiated as soon as the investment project becomes credible, involves submitting a file to the Ministry of the Economy for an initial eligibility review (Chapter 16).

The official review phase begins with the submission of a formal request for prior authorization, which triggers the start of the substantive assessment by the competent authorities (Chapter 17). This review may take the form of a simplified examination (Chapter 18) or a more detailed scrutiny (Chapter 19), depending on the nature and sensitivity of the investment.

Ultimately, during either phase of the official review, the Minister of the Economy may issue a decision declaring the transaction ineligible, authorizing the investment with or without conditions, or refusing it outright.

By way of perspective[557], in 2024 a total of 392 filings[558] concerning foreign investments were submitted to the Directorate General of the Treasury, compared with 309 in 2023 and 325 in 2022.

557. France, Ministry of the Economy, Finance, Industrial and Digital Sovereignty, Directorate General of the Treasury, Annual Report 2025, "Foreign Direct Investment Screening in France," Published 30 July 2025, consulted 31 July 2025, available at https://www.tresor.economie.gouv.fr/Articles/2025/07/30/publication-du-rapport-annuel-sur-le-controle-ief-en-2024

558. This figure encompasses (i) applications for investment authorization filed by a foreign investor, (ii) requests for a prior review of the activities of a French company, which may be submitted either by a foreign investor or by the French company concerned, and (iii) notifications of the crossing of the 10% voting rights threshold in a listed company by a non-European investor.

Chapter 14

An Internal Phase of Due-diligence Between the Parties Is Essential

The existence of a foreign direct investment (FDI) screening mechanism has profoundly reshaped the way parties to an investment transaction must approach the deal. Whereas antitrust and regulatory compliance issues used to dominate transactional analysis, FDI screening has now become a critical, if not the most critical, pillar of the process. The French FDI regime (IEF framework) requires careful consideration of specific legal and strategic aspects.

Accordingly, before any investment transaction is initiated, an internal due-diligence phase between the parties is essential, whether for the target entity or for the prospective acquirer. This internal inquiry should cover a range of issues, including the structuring of the transaction, the reputation and integrity of the foreign investor, the sensitivity of the target's business activities, the potential need for proactive engagement with public authorities, and any complexities arising from multi-jurisdictional transactions.

The IEF Regime Requires the Parties to Understand Certain Specific Features

By establishing a mechanism for the protection of national interests in the context of foreign investments in France, the French FDI screening regime (referred to as the IEF mechanism) results in the State becoming a fully involved stakeholder in the transaction process, solely by virtue of its power to authorize, prohibit, or condition the transaction. The State is not merely overseeing the operation; it becomes a de facto party to it.

This is a key element in understanding the specific nature of M&A transactions involving foreign investments in activities likely to affect national interests.

The dynamic of negotiations between the seller of a French target company and a foreign investor has evolved significantly. What used to be a bilateral negotiation is now a complex process that must incorporate the involvement of the French State. Public authorities thus intervene as active participants in these negotiations. In other words, the State inserts itself into discussions between the foreign acquirer and the French seller.

This context raises a number of complex legal and strategic questions [559] due to the specific nature of the French FDI screening framework. These features include:
—An extensive regulatory scope: "the net is expanding, and the mesh is tightening";
—A fluid and largely unwritten doctrine: the State does not disclose the rationale for its decisions;
—Virtually no case law: parties rarely challenge the State in court;
—Heightened political sensitivity: some transactions become politically emblematic;
—Direct control by the State: no independent administrative or regulatory authorities involved;
—An empirical knowledge of transactions: only the State has a comprehensive view of the cases.

First, these transactions are specific due to the extensive nature of the legal framework. One might summarize the trend by noting that, since the 2005 [560], 2014 [561], and 2019 [562] decrees, and the ministerial orders of 2020 [563] and 2023 [564], the regulatory net has widened while its mesh has become finer.

In the case of sensitive activities, public authorities have continuously broadened the scope of the original list of protected sectors. The initial list of 11 sectors in 2005 has expanded to encompass 22 sensitive activities, supplemented by 10 critical technologies (see Chapter 13). The French government has equipped itself with a strategic tool, the ministerial order, to expand the list of activities subject to screening without resorting to the more burdensome decree procedure. For instance, an initial list of 7 critical technologies was adopted by the ministerial order [565] of December 31, 2019, under Article R. 151-3 III 1° of the Monetary and Financial Code. This was followed by the order [566] of April 30, 2020, which added an eighth technology, biotechnologies, at the height of the COVID-19 pandemic. Most recently, the Ministerial Order of December 28, 2023 added two further critical technologies: low-carbon energy production and photonics.

Another key development concerns the threshold for triggering control in listed companies. The temporary reduction of the threshold from 25% to 10% of voting rights has now become permanent [567], tightening control over minority acquisitions.

559. DUPEYRAT, op. cit.,

560. France, Decree No. 2005-1739 of 30 December 2005 regulating financial relations with foreign countries and implementing Article L. 151-3 of the Monetary and Financial Code, Official Journal of the French Republic, No. 304, 31 December 2005, NOR: ECOX0508949D

561. France, Decree No. 2014-479 of 14 May 2014 on foreign investments subject to prior authorization, Official Journal of the French Republic, No. 0112, 15 May 2014, NOR: ERNX1411012D

562. France, Decree No. 2019-1590 of 31 December 2019 on foreign investments in France, Official Journal of the French Republic, No. 0001, 1 January 2020, NOR: ECOT1932857D

563. France, Ministerial Order of 27 April 2020 on foreign investments in France, Official Journal of the French Republic, No. 0105, 30 April 2020, NOR: ECOT2010256A

564. France, Ministerial Order of 28 December 2023 on foreign investments in France, Official Journal of the French Republic, No. 0301, 29 December 2023, NOR: ECOT2334928A

565. France, Ministerial Order of 31 December 2019 on foreign investments in France, Official Journal of the French Republic, No. 0001, 1 January 2020, NOR: ECOT1937237A

566. France, Ministerial Order of 27 April 2020 on foreign investments in France, Official Journal of the French Republic, No. 0105, 30 April 2020, NOR: ECOT2010256A

567. France, Decree No. 2023-1293 of 28 December 2023 on foreign investments in France, definitively lowering the initial 25% threshold to 10% for acquisitions in listed companies, Official Journal of the French Republic, No. 0301, 29 December 2023, NOR: ECOT2323089D

These transactions are also characterized by a poorly formalized and evolving doctrine. The French approach to FDI screening remains relatively unstructured, despite efforts to balance foreign attractiveness with national sovereignty. Several factors explain this situation. Unlike the United States, France's regulation of foreign investments in strategic sectors is relatively recent, particularly with the major reforms of 2014, 2018, and 2019. Moreover, the French regime has been shaped by a pragmatic, reactive approach, often adjusting legislation in response to European Commission recommendations (see Chapter 1).

Except for a few parliamentary reports [568] or written questions to the Government, the subject received limited attention until the "Alstom affair" in May 2014. That sale triggered significant scrutiny and led to the establishment of a parliamentary fact-finding commission [569], which, for the first time, publicly revealed the reasoning behind the government's application of Article L. 151-3 of the Monetary and Financial Code. Even so, the 2023 guidelines issued by the Directorate General of the Treasury (DGT) offer more insight into procedures than into a substantive doctrine of review.

Another notable feature of the regime is the near absence of case law. Several factors contribute to this: most importantly, the French State exercises broad discretionary power in determining whether a transaction threatens national interests, making its refusals difficult to challenge in court. Even if challenged, judicial review would likely be limited to procedural compliance, not substantive assessment of whether the activity in question endangers public order, public security, or national defense interests.

Moreover, legal challenges are rarely worthwhile: once a transaction is denied, it would be virtually futile to initiate litigation merely to contest a sovereign decision, particularly when any judgment would likely be rendered well after the transaction's contractual deadlines. This leads to a very low rate of appeals, if not a complete absence of litigation, thereby depriving practitioners of insight into the legal reasoning behind government decisions. With the exception of two known cases, one in the administrative courts [570] and one in the civil courts [571] (see Chapter 22), French legal practice lacks case law examples that might clarify the grounds for authorizations or refusals.

FDI screening also makes M&A operations specific due to their heightened political sensitivity. Transactions in strategic sectors, although legally complex in themselves,

568. France, Report to the Prime Minister, CARAYON, Bernard, Intelligence économique, compétitivité et cohésion sociale, 1 July 2003, La Documentation française, 173 pages, accessed September 1st, 2025, available at https://www.vie-publique.fr/files/rapport/pdf/034000484.pdf

569. France, National Assembly, Report No. 897 rect., April 19, 2018, MARLEIX, Olivier, President, KASBARIAN, Guillaume, Rapporteur, Members of Parliament, made on behalf of the Commission of Inquiry tasked with examining the decisions of the State in matters of industrial policy, with regard to recent corporate mergers, in particular in the cases of Alstom, Alcatel and STX, as well as the means likely to protect our national industrial flagships in a globalized trade context, Volume 1, consulted May 9, 2024, available at https://www.assemblee-nationale.fr/dyn/15/rapports/cepolind/l15b0897-ti_rapport-enquete

570. France, Conseil d'État, 6th / 2nd sub-sections (SSR), Decision No. 160550, Société Pathé Holding France, 15 April 1996, published in the Recueil Lebon
France, Conseil d'État, 10th and 9th sub-sections (SSR), Decision No. 262626, 3 November 2004, listed in the tables of the Recueil Lebon

571. France, Paris Court of Appeal, Division 1 – Chamber 5, No. 11/12878, 17 January 2012

are particularly susceptible to political concerns, whether directly related to the transaction or not. Although foreign investment is often sought to foster business growth, fears of offshoring or job losses can provoke broader debates that transcend the strategic or security dimension of the deal.

As a result, a Member of Parliament approached by employees in his district may pressure the government not only on industrial grounds but also on national security if applicable. The Danone case is illustrative: the 2005 decree [572] was cited in response to a potential takeover of Danone by Pepsi, even though dairy products were not covered under the decree at the time.

Similarly, while FDI screening is the exclusive responsibility of the executive branch, the "evaluation" of the Alstom transaction included a hearing of the Minister for Industrial Renewal [573], Arnaud Montebourg, before the National Assembly's Economic Affairs Committee to discuss the application of the May 14, 2014 decree [574]. These concerns were later reiterated during the Parliamentary Committee of Inquiry on Alstom's sale to General Electric.

Beyond the new Article L. 151-7 of the Monetary and Financial Code [575], which authorizes specially mandated parliamentarians to oversee the implementation of Article L. 151-3, other elected officials wrote to the Prime Minister in 2019 to clarify the government's position regarding the protection of national interests in the sale of Latécoère to U.S. fund Searchlight Capital Partners. Similar concerns were raised again in 2023 regarding the sale of Segault [576] and the planned divestiture of Atos [577] (see Chapter 5).

These operations are further distinguished by the fact that control is exercised directly by the State, not through independent administrative authorities, which often serve as a buffer, as is the case in competition law. As such, the parties must engage directly with ministerial authorities, and at times even with the ministers themselves.

572. France, Decree No. 2005-1739 of 30 December 2005 regulating financial relations with foreign countries and implementing Article L. 151-3 of the Monetary and Financial Code, Official Journal of the French Republic, No. 304, 31 December 2005, NOR: ECOX0508949D

573. France, National Assembly, Economic Affairs Committee, 24 June 2014, Minutes No. 96, Public hearing of Mr. Arnaud Montebourg, Minister of the Economy, Industrial Recovery and Digital Affairs, on the future of Alstom, accessed 9 May 2024, available at https://www.assemblee-nationale.fr/14/cr-eco/13-14/c1314096.asp#P2_47

574. France, Decree No. 2014-479 of 14 May 2014 on foreign investments subject to prior authorization, Official Journal of the French Republic, No. 0112, 15 May 2014, NOR: ERNX1411012D

575. Article L. 151-7 of the Monetary and Financial Code : "*The chairs of the committees responsible for economic affairs and the general rapporteurs of the committees responsible for finance in each house of Parliament may, acting jointly, hear the competent ministers, the Strategic Information and Economic Security Commissioner, and the directors of the relevant central government departments, who may be accompanied by staff of their choosing, within the scope of their respective areas of responsibility. These exchanges, which are not made public, may concern information that identifies natural or legal persons subject to the foreign investment prior authorization procedure provided for in Article L. 151-3.*"

576. France, National Assembly, Oral Question No. 712 to the Prime Minister, Official Journal of the National Assembly, 29 March 2023, p. 3169, MARLEIX, Olivier, Member of Parliament, Les Républicains (LR), ministerial reply published in the same issue

577. France, National Assembly, Oral Question No. 1132 to the Prime Minister, Official Journal of the National Assembly, 27 September 2023, p. 8022, MARLEIX, Olivier, Member of Parliament, Les Républicains (LR), ministerial reply published in the same issue, p. 8022

Finally, a crucial feature of the regime lies in the empirical nature of the State's knowledge of reviewed transactions. In practice, public authorities do not disclose the existence of ongoing FDI reviews to protect business confidentiality. However, based on voluntary disclosures by the parties themselves, it is possible to identify a number of examples that illustrate the sectors or technologies attracting regulatory attention under the French FDI regime (see the section on sensitive transactions in Chapter 5).

For this reason, from the outset of any transaction, it is crucial for the parties involved to raise a series of key questions. The following section offers a non-exhaustive selection of the most relevant ones.

Is the structure of the contemplated transaction acceptable under the French FDI screening mechanism (IEF)?

In the context of foreign direct investments (FDI), as with merger control under competition law, the specific features of the French FDI screening regime (IEF) must be taken into account from the very outset of the transaction. For both the parties and their counsel, national interest considerations must be treated with the same degree of importance as compliance or antitrust issues.

It is therefore necessary to conduct an institutional due-diligence that will address not only the likelihood of the contemplated transaction being accepted under the French FDI screening regime, but also the statutory timelines applicable to the review procedure itself. In this regard, the French administration emphasizes that it is the responsibility of the parties to ensure that the regulatory timelines governing the screening process are properly incorporated into the transaction schedule. The Minister of the Economy is not bound by the contractual timetable agreed between the parties. However, insofar as duly substantiated, specific constraints associated with certain transactions (such as insolvency proceedings or cash-flow difficulties) may be taken into account.

More broadly, the parties must also conduct a due-diligence focused on economic security considerations, and, where appropriate, on national security concerns.

Accordingly, such an audit should be initiated as early as possible in the transaction process, in order to avoid exploring divestment options that may ultimately prove unviable in light of what the State is, or is not, prepared to approve. The significant losses that may result from a refusal to authorize an investment, or from an excessively politicized transaction, illustrate the point. In this respect, the case of the divestment of Photonis is instructive (see Chapter 5).

Ideally, the institutional uncertainty arising from the applicability of the French FDI screening mechanism should be addressed at the structuring stage of the transaction, with the same degree of importance as the financial, legal, and operational design of the deal. This form of "institutional due-diligence," both immediate and long-term, must be fully internalized to ensure that the transaction is not only viable for the parties but also acceptable to the public authorities.

Where there is a serious, if not confirmed, risk regarding the prospective position of the public authorities, the parties are strongly advised not to persist along a dead-end path that would inevitably impair the valuation of the transaction.

Finally, this strategic and institutional assessment must also be conducted with a forward-looking perspective, taking into account the eventual divestment or exit of the investment after a few years. This requires a thorough understanding of public policies related to national security and defense, as well as the political calendar and electoral cycles.

Is the foreign investor's reputation and integrity established?

The issue of the investor's honorability lies at the heart of the French government's review when assessing the foreign character and suitability of an investor. The authorities may carry out their own investigation, including through intelligence services, to build a detailed profile of the investor. Nevertheless, the parties should proactively address this issue as soon as initial approaches are made.

A "reputation and integrity due-diligence" becomes crucial in IEF-screened transactions. It aims to thoroughly evaluate the investor's reputation and integrity, whether the investor is a natural person or a legal entity. This involves gathering open-source intelligence as well as human intelligence from local contacts, in order to produce relevant and reliable information.

Pursuant to Article R. 151-10 of the Monetary and Financial Code, an investor's lack of honorability constitutes a serious ground for denial of authorization by the French Minister of the Economy (see Chapter 19 and administrative decisions in Chapter 22).

This assessment serves several objectives:

- Identifying risks related to ethics, integrity, fraud, or corruption within the investing entity;
- Scrutinizing the personal reputation of the company's executives and staff;
- Evaluating the reputation of its business partners, clients, and suppliers;
- Detecting potential smear campaigns or hostile tactics by competitors;
- Anticipating the impact of external risks (e.g. natural disasters, health and safety issues);
- Assessing the quality and reliability of its products or services, which directly affect corporate reputation.

Ultimately, understanding the target company's sector, its competitive landscape, and its key personnel is critical. A robust due-diligence process is essential to foresee and mitigate reputational and compliance-related vulnerabilities.

Is the French target entity's business activity deemed sensitive?

The sensitive nature of the French target's business is a decisive factor. Beyond the legal list of sensitive activities set forth in Article R. 151-3 of the Monetary and Financial Code, the French government supports a number of strategic sectors defined by evolving public policies. These policies often complicate a purely legal interpretation of what constitutes a "sensitive" activity under the IEF framework (see Chapter 7).

Hence, parties must adopt an institutional (rather than merely legalistic) approach to determine whether the target's activities might be perceived as sensitive by French authorities. Understanding the government's policy priorities, or at least its implicit doctrine, is necessary to anticipate how the authorities will assess the transaction.

The proliferation of criteria used to define "strategic" or "sensitive" sectors has led to increasing ambiguity, especially in the wake of systemic crises like COVID-19 or the war in Ukraine. The scope of "strategic," "vital," or "sensitive" activities has gradually expanded to include economic competitiveness and employment issues, in addition to traditional national defense.

Programs such as France 2030 illustrate this expansion. The plan identifies sectors and technologies of high national interest, including the development of small modular reactors (SMRs), green hydrogen, renewable energy, decarbonized industry, and low-carbon aviation. Even if a sector is not yet covered by the IEF regime, its inclusion in such public policy initiatives strongly suggests future eligibility.

Public investments and incentives naturally attract foreign interest, which in turn prompts the government to tighten controls. The decision to add biotechnology[578] during the COVID crisis or low-carbon energy and photonics in 2023 reflects this dynamic.

Anticipation is thus essential, particularly since the French government can extend the scope of the IEF regime via a simple ministerial order, without parliamentary debate.

Should the transaction be notified even if it appears ineligible?

As a matter of legal rigor, a foreign investment that clearly fails to meet the three cumulative eligibility criteria, foreign investor, covered transaction type, and sensitive business activity, should not require formal notification to the Ministry of the Economy.

However, the parties must consider whether it may nonetheless be in their strategic interest to submit a pre-filing request (or even a formal request for authorization).

The pre-filing request, as detailed in Chapter 16, allows the parties to obtain an official position on whether the target's activity qualifies as sensitive. This tool has improved transparency and dialogue between the parties and the administration. It enables the parties to confirm whether the transaction will ultimately fall within the IEF scope once it is fully structured.

Of course, safeguards exist to prevent abuse of this procedure, for example, to avoid overwhelming the administration or, worse, allowing foreign actors to gain intelligence about the sensitivity of specific sectors.

578. France, Ministerial Order of April 27, 2020, on foreign investments in France, Official Journal of the French Republic, No. 0105, April 30, 2020, NOR: ECOT2010256A

Still, the pre-filing process has the clear advantage of resolving eligibility uncertainty early on, thereby derisking the transaction.

Another scenario arises when the transaction seems ineligible, particularly because the operation does not fall under a covered transaction type. A strictly legal analysis might discourage filing.

However, this view ignores the institutional rationale behind IEF. The real question is not whether a filing is legally required, but whether the operation might raise national interest concerns. In such cases, a formal filing, even one that is expected to be rejected, can be a prudent step, both to validate legal assumptions and to detect any red flags that could arise under other sector-specific regulations.

The fear of engaging with the administration, out of concern for "opening Pandora's box", can be short-sighted. A post-closing intervention by the government would carry far more serious consequences.

Though filing entails transaction costs (see Chapter 8), the strategic value of obtaining formal clearance may far outweigh these costs in terms of deal certainty.

Does the transaction require filings in other jurisdictions?

Foreign investment transactions frequently trigger multiple filing obligations in different jurisdictions. This raises the question of filing sequence: in which country should the application be submitted first?

Some practitioners assume that obtaining clearance from jurisdictions with stringent national security reviews (e.g., CFIUS in the U.S.) can serve as a sort of "stamp of approval" that facilitates clearance elsewhere.

This approach is misguided. Each jurisdiction assesses national security through its own lens, and each review is legally and politically autonomous. Moreover, some authorities may resent being presented with "precedents" from other countries, especially if perceived as pressure tactics.

Instead, filing strategies should be based on expected timelines and informational requirements in each country. All filings should be launched as early as possible to ensure all necessary clearances are secured by the closing date.

Within the European Union, this multi-filing reality is integrated into the screening regulation, which provides for intergovernmental information-sharing. France, for example, has extended its own review deadlines to accommodate the time needed for these exchanges.

*
* *

Given its specific features, the French FDI screening mechanism (dispositif IEF) requires the parties to engage in an internal assessment phase as early as possible in the transaction process. Critical questions must be raised at this stage, such as whether the initially contemplated structure of the transaction is acceptable under the IEF framework, whether the foreign investor meets the standard of integrity expected by the French authorities, or whether the target entity operates in a sensitive sector likely to trigger enhanced scrutiny. These issues are not merely procedural, they determine the viability of the transaction in light of the imperative to safeguard the national interest. More importantly, they may have a decisive impact on the valuation of the target company, encapsulated in a fundamental question: what is the value of a company that cannot be sold, or that no one is allowed to buy or sell? The attempted sale of Photonis (see Chapter 5) serves as a striking illustration of this reality.

Chapter 15

An Informal Preliminary Engagement with the French Treasury Is Strongly Advised

Prior to initiating the formal procedure (see Chapter 17), parties to a contemplated foreign investment transaction that may affect France's national interest are encouraged to assess the sensitivity of the operation with the relevant public authorities. This informal engagement, which has become standard practice, is strongly recommended in the interest of all stakeholders involved in a screening procedure under the French FDI regime (IEF). It is incumbent upon the parties to determine whether the Strategic Information and Economic Security Department (SISSE) or the Foreign Investment Screening) Unit (CIEF) is the more appropriate interlocutor for initiating this preliminary dialogue.

The Informal Engagement Phase Is Recognized by the Administration

For a long time, the Foreign Direct Investment Screening in Francein France followed a strictly regulatory and administrative format, with interactions between the parties and the administration limited to the submission of documents and, more rarely, to actual negotiations. The prior authorization regime functioned on a "counter-based" logic: the parties would submit an application, and the administration would approve or reject the transaction.

This approach came to a political halt during the sale of Alstom to General Electric, when then-Minister of the Economy Arnaud Montebourg publicly regretted[579] that the transaction had not been brought to the attention of the government prior to its announcement. Beyond that specific case, public authorities acknowledged the strategic necessity of no longer being presented with sensitive transactions as a fait accompli. At the time, the State often had no other choice but to assess complex transactions within the narrow timeframe of the official review period, frequently resorting to procedural tactics such as requests for additional information to buy time.

579. France, National Assembly, Verbatim Record, No. 37, April 29, 2014, First sitting of Tuesday, 14th Legislature, Ordinary Session 2013–2014, Official Journal of the National Assembly, April 30, 2014, p. 2676: "The Government does not accept being informed on a Friday that one of its national flagships, which lives off public procurement, with €20 billion in turnover and 95,000 employees, would be sold on Sunday evening. No government in any other State would accept being confronted with a fait accompli!"

Since then, the informal preliminary engagement with the Ministry of the Economy (Bercy) has not only been encouraged, it has become a fully integrated practice embraced by all stakeholders. A foreign investor, the target entity, or even the seller will never be penalized for initiating contact with the Treasury's screening authorities. Indeed, it is worth reiterating that the logic of the French FDI screening regime is the protection of the national interest, not an economic or commercial review of the transaction's merits.

This early-stage dialogue is also promoted by public authorities themselves. However, it remains subject to transparency obligations under French public ethics rules (see Chapter 9). Any form of contact, by email, phone, or in-person meeting, with a public decision-maker, namely the Foreign Investment Screening) Unit (CIEF), for the purpose of obtaining an administrative decision (authorization to invest in France), constitutes a lobbying activity and must be declared to the High Authority for the Transparency of Public Life (HATVP) . That said, the HATVP explicitly considers communications with the CIEF, even prior to the formal filing of an application, as part of the standard administrative process and therefore not a form of undue influence, since such contacts are anticipated by law. Conversely, communications with higher-ranking or adjacent authorities outside the CIEF are considered acts of influence, as the legal framework designates the CIEF as the sole interlocutor in the screening procedure.

Informal Discussions Are Primarily Conducted with the Ministry of the Economy (Bercy)

The authority to restrict foreign investment in the name of national interest lies with the French Minister of the Economy, not only for legal reasons but also because he is the natural point of contact for the economic and industrial stakeholders concerned. Accordingly, it is with the services under his authority that the parties to a contemplated transaction are expected to initiate discussions, as early as possible in the deal process.

As the administration emphasizes [580], the provisions governing the review procedure do not preclude an investor or a target entity from contacting the Directorate General of the Treasury (primarily by email at iefautorisations@dgtresor.gouv.fr) prior to a contemplated transaction and even before submitting a formal authorization request. This may be useful, for example, to present a complex or specific proposed transaction and the rationale behind it.

Such a step is not a mandatory prerequisite for filing an application for authorization, a request for prior review, or a prior notification of a threshold crossing. In any event, it cannot predetermine the outcome of the review, which will ultimately be conducted on the basis of the formal application file.

---

580. France, Ministry of the Economy, Finance, Industrial and Digital Sovereignty, Directorate General of the Treasury, "Guidelines on the Foreign Direct Investment Screening in France" July 2025, published July 30, 2025, see Point 2.1.3.1, consulted August 1, 2025, available at https://www.tresor.economie.gouv.fr/services-aux-entreprises/investissements-etrangers-en-france

These initial contacts typically arise when the seller and the prospective foreign investor seek to "test the waters" regarding the strategic nature of the contemplated investment. The parties may use this opportunity to assess whether the transaction falls within[581] the scope of France's foreign investment screening regime and would therefore trigger the requirement to obtain prior authorization (see Chapter 16). They may also seek preliminary feedback on whether the operation might raise concerns in light of France's national interest and, if so, under which specific legal framework or policy (see Chapter 7). Although informal in nature, these exchanges may be documented in writing.

Two interlocutors within the French administration are of particular relevance for such pre-filing engagements: on the one hand, the CIEF (Foreign Investment Control Office), which is responsible for processing authorization requests, and on the other hand, the SISSE (Strategic Information and Economic Security Service), which is charged with protecting France's strategic economic interests[582].

It is up to the parties to determine which authority is the most appropriate to contact depending on the nature of the transaction and their overall strategic approach. The primary objective of such engagement is to obtain a general understanding of how the French administration is likely to view the proposed transaction. It allows the parties to anticipate whether a formal screening procedure will be triggered, assess the risk of a potential denial due to non-compliance with applicable rules, and identify any required changes or commitments that may be necessary to secure approval from the Minister of the Economy.

From the administration's perspective, an early outreach by the foreign investor is viewed as a positive signal, demonstrating a cooperative attitude and a willingness to align with French strategic priorities. To ensure that this proactive step does not adversely affect the transaction or the parties involved, the Minister's services are bound by strict confidentiality obligations with respect to all information provided during these informal exchanges, thereby safeguarding trade secrets and sensitive commercial data.

Importantly, the prospective target company, not just the investor, may also initiate contact with the competent authorities to determine whether the contemplated transaction is subject to prior authorization. This possibility was formalized as part of the 2019 reform, which introduced a preliminary procedure designed to go beyond informal consultations by providing the parties with an official administrative position on whether the regime applies to the deal. (See next chapter)

---

581. As a reminder, prior to the reform introduced by the PACTE Law in 2019, Article R. 151-4 of the Monetary and Financial Code explicitly allowed the foreign investor, before completing an investment, to submit a written request to the Minister of the Economy in order to determine whether the contemplated transaction was subject to prior authorization. The Minister was required to respond within two months; however, the absence of a response did not exempt the investor from filing an authorization request. This provision was subsequently amended and replaced with the so-called "pre-filing review request" (demande préalable d'examen) procedure.

582. France, Senate, Written Question No. 08598 to the Minister of the Economy and Finance, Official Journal of the Senate, January 31, 2019, p. 502, RAVIER S., non-affiliated senator, ministerial reply, April 18, 2019, Official Journal of the Senate, p. 2142. The SISSE may notably be mobilized to counter the destabilization of strategic companies, for instance in the event of predatory action by activist funds.

*
* *

The establishment of a dialogue between the investor and the administration is a critical component of the process. It allows French authorities to assess the foreign investor's readiness to respect the country's fundamental interests. In practice, although the formal authorization request must be filed by the foreign investor, all parties involved in the transaction, including the French target and/or the seller, have a vested interest in initiating this dialogue as early as possible. Failing to do so may expose the transaction to heightened scrutiny or adverse reactions from the French government .

Chapter 16

The Preliminary Review Option as a Tool for Clarifying Regulatory Exposure

With the enactment of the PACTE Act, the French authorities introduced a formalized mechanism known as the preliminary review of an activity, which enables target entities to assess, upstream, the potential sensitivity of their contemplated acquisition by a foreign investor under France's foreign direct investment (FDI) screening regime.

In practice, this preliminary review procedure is initially available to the target company as soon as there is a credible investment project. It may also be initiated by the foreign investor, provided the target company expressly consents to the process. The submission must include only the information strictly necessary for the purpose of the review. Once an acknowledgment of receipt is issued, the Minister of the Economy has two months to respond.

The preliminary review serves to determine whether the contemplated activity falls within the scope of the prior authorization requirement. However, this procedure is not fungible with the formal authorization request: it remains a distinct step in the regulatory process, and the applicant may withdraw the request at any time.

The Preliminary Review Procedure as a Means of Assessing FDI Screening Eligibility

The preliminary review of an activity has been described by the French legislature as a major step forward, as it allows the target entity, and no longer solely the foreign acquirer, to determine whether a contemplated (but not yet finalized) transaction qualifies for review under France's FDI screening regime.

This is not a merely theoretical consideration; it is a practical issue that directly affects the feasibility of the transaction and, by extension, the valuation of the target company. From the perspective of both the parties and the target, the ability to assess whether a sale is possible, or even sellable, is essential. It raises a fundamental question: does the company retain value if it cannot be sold, or if its saleability is uncertain?

From the government's standpoint, the purpose of the preliminary review request is to provide legal certainty for the transaction and, more broadly, to protect French businesses seeking foreign investment. Since the procedure can be initiated as early as the negotiation phase between a French company and a foreign investor, or as soon as the potential opening of the company's capital is under consideration, it offers an early-stage tool to assess the viability of a foreign investment transaction from the standpoint of the applicable regulatory authorization.

As the French administration underscores [583], this is a streamlined process designed to help stakeholders better prepare for an investment transaction. Under Article R. 151-4 of the Monetary and Financial Code, the foreign investor or the French target entity may approach the Ministry early in the investment timeline to determine whether the French entity's activities fall within the scope of France's FDI screening mechanism.

The primary objective of this preliminary review request is to secure transactions and safeguard stakeholders from the outset of negotiations or at the time when the company considers raising capital. For the French entity, it also facilitates early-stage financial planning and helps structure its search for capital more effectively. For both the French business and the prospective investor, it enables early anticipation of any conditions precedent that may be required to complete the transaction.

The Preliminary Review Procedure Is Initially Available to the Target Entity

The procedure for requesting a preliminary review of an activity is set forth in Article R. 151-4 of the Monetary and Financial Code, as introduced by the Decree [584] of December 30, 2019, implementing the PACTE Act [585]. It provides that the Minister of the Economy may be approached by a French-law entity seeking a determination as to whether all or part of its business activities fall within the scope of activities subject to prior authorization under the French FDI screening regime [586].

The purpose of this mechanism is to address issues related to the protection of national interests at a pre-transactional stage, before the investment is actually carried out.

The Procedure Can Be Triggered as Soon as There Is a Credible Investment Project

As clarified by the French authorities [587], unlike a formal request for authorization, which must be submitted once the investment project is sufficiently developed, the

583. France, Ministry of the Economy, Finance and Recovery, Directorate General of the Treasury, "FAQ: Foreign Investment Screening in France," January 2025, p. 12, consulted September 1, 2025, available at https://www.tresor.economie.gouv.fr/Institutionnel/Niveau2/Pages/f149e66d-6df2-4726-a594-3d95409d7a46/files/7d5e95fd-ca16-496d-815a-4242973300f4
584. France, Decree No. 2019-1590 of 31 December 2019 on foreign investments in France, Official Journal of the French Republic, No. 0001, 1 January 2020, NOR: ECOT1932857D
585. France, Law No. 2019-486 of 22 May 2019 on Business Growth and Transformation, Official Journal of the French Republic, No. 0119, 23 May 2019, NOR: ECOT1810669L
586. France, Monetary and Financial Code, Article L. 151-3
587. France, Ministry of the Economy, Finance, Industrial and Digital Sovereignty, Directorate General of the Treasury, "Guidelines on the Foreign Direct Investment Screening in France" July 2025, published

preliminary review request can be filed based on a mere contemplated investment. This option is also available when the target entity is considering opening its capital and has entered into negotiations with one or more potential investors.

Within this framework, the administration accepts that the mere initiation of negotiations, or even the execution of a non-disclosure agreement [588] (NDA), may constitute an investment project sufficient to support the submission of a preliminary review request within the meaning of the applicable regulation.

A statement confirming the existence of such a project must be included in the application file, although no specific formality is required for this particular document. The existence of the project may likewise be substantiated by a written attestation from the parties confirming that discussions are ongoing.

The Procedure Is Also Available to the Foreign Investor with the Target's Consent

Article R. 151-4 of the Monetary and Financial Code further provides that a foreign investor, acting with the consent of the target entity that conducts the relevant activities, may also initiate the same request. In this case, a copy of the Minister's response to the investor must also be sent to the target entity, and the Ministry must provide its opinion within a two-month period.

This constitutes a valuable option for the foreign investor. In addition to offering early-stage visibility into whether the contemplated investment will trigger the requirement for prior authorization, the preliminary review also formalizes the opening of a dialogue with the French authorities. This initial engagement may allow the investor to gain insight into any sensitive issues likely to arise in connection with the proposed acquisition.

The file shall contain only the information strictly necessary

Given that the purpose of the prior examination procedure is to provide a streamlined assessment of whether a contemplated investment qualifies for a formal authorization request, the corresponding submission is limited to the core information required for review by the competent authorities.

In line with this objective, the dossier is intentionally reduced to the bare essentials [589].

July 30, 2025, see Point 2.4.1, consulted August 1, 2025, available at https://www.tresor.economie.gouv.fr/services-aux-entreprises/investissements-etrangers-en-france

588. accord de non-divulgation in French

589. France, Ministry of the Economy, Finance, Industrial and Digital Sovereignty, Directorate General of the Treasury, "Guidelines on the Foreign Direct Investment Screening in France" July 2025, published July 30, 2025, see Point 2.4.2.2, consulted August 1, 2025, available at https://www.tresor.economie.gouv.fr/services-aux-entreprises/investissements-etrangers-en-france

It is compiled in accordance with Article 2 of the Order[590] of 31 December 2019 and must include the following:

, With respect to the French target company:

Information and supporting documents identical to those required in the context of a formal authorization request (see chapter 17);

, With respect to the investment transaction:

A copy of any document[591] evidencing the existence of an investment project, along with:
(i) the written consent of the French target company to the filing of such request, if submitted by the investor; or
(ii) an indication that one or more potential investors are under consideration, if the request is submitted by the French target company[592];

, With respect to the investor (only where the request is filed by the investor):

Investor-related information is required solely when the prior examination request is submitted by the investor.

- If the investor is a natural person:

A copy of any official document showing their full name, date and place of birth, nationality (ies), and tax residence;

- If the investor is a legal entity:

The following documents must be provided:
(i) a certificate of incorporation (or equivalent) stating the corporate name, registered office, registration number (or equivalent), and nationality;
(ii) a corporate structure chart, identifying the individuals or entities within the chain of control who took part in or authorized the decision to invest;
(iii) a detailed description of the investor's business activities, including the nature of the services, products, or operations conducted.

Standard forms and an explanatory memorandum are available on the website of the Directorate General of the Treasury (Direction générale du Trésor)). (See also Annexes C and D of this book.)

Filing with the CIEF and Legal Framework for the Preliminary Examination Procedure

The submission of a preliminary examination request to the French Foreign Direct Investment Screening Office (CIEF) (CIEF – Bureau du contrôle des investissements

590. France, Ministerial Order of 31 December 2019 on foreign investments in France, Official Journal of the French Republic, No. 0001, 1 January 2020, NOR: ECOT1937237A
591. The notion of "any document evidencing an investment project" refers to a less advanced stage of the investment process than that required for a formal authorization request.
592. idem

étrangers en France) triggers an acknowledgment of receipt. The filing procedures are identical to those applicable to formal authorization requests (see Chapter 17).

From a procedural standpoint, the submission of a preliminary examination file gives rise to a formal acknowledgment of receipt confirming the administration has received the documentation. However, the regulatory review period does not begin until the request is deemed admissible. In this regard, the Directorate General of the Treasury (Direction générale du Trésor) verifies whether the applicant is authorized to file an authorization request and qualifies either as a foreign investor or as a target entity. If not, the administration invites the applicant to regularize the situation.

Once the request is deemed admissible, a second acknowledgment of receipt is issued by the Directorate General of the Treasury. This document includes:
—the date the application was received and the statutory deadline beyond which, in the absence of an express decision, the application will be deemed rejected;
—the name, mailing and email address, and telephone number of the CIEF officer assigned to the case;
—where applicable, a list of any missing documents required under the ministerial order[593] of 31 December 2019.

Two-Month Response Time

Pursuant to Article R. 151-4 of the Monetary and Financial Code, the Minister of the Economy must respond to the preliminary examination request within two months. For applicants, this timeframe is nearly identical to that applicable to a formal authorization request. If a preliminary request is submitted in addition to a formal one, this period must be added to the overall timeline, another argument in favor of submitting a direct authorization request.

The administration emphasizes[594] that the regulatory period begins to run on the date the file is physically submitted, provided this occurs on a weekday (excluding holidays) during official business hours (until 5:00 p.m.). It does not begin on the date the acknowledgment of receipt is issued. If the submission occurs during the weekend, on a public holiday, or outside business hours, the period only begins on the next business day.

If the file is incomplete, the timeline is suspended from the date the administration requests additional information until the applicant provides the requested documents and clarifications.

593. France, Ministerial Order of 31 December 2019 on foreign investments in France, Official Journal of the French Republic, No. 0001, 1 January 2020, NOR: ECOT1937237A

594. France, Ministry of the Economy, Finance, Industrial and Digital Sovereignty, Directorate General of the Treasury, "Guidelines on the Foreign Direct Investment Screening in France" July 2025, published July 30, 2025, see Point 2.4.2.1, consulted August 1, 2025, available at https://www.tresor.economie.gouv.fr/services-aux-entreprises/investissements-etrangers-en-france

Purpose of the Preliminary Examination: Determining Eligibility for Authorization

The key objective of the preliminary examination procedure is to determine whether the contemplated investment falls within the scope of the prior authorization regime set out in Paragraph I of Article L. 151-3 of the Monetary and Financial Code, or whether it lies outside the scope of the French FDI screening mechanism.

As clarified in the administrative guidelines [595], the Minister may issue one of two possible decisions:

—an opinion stating that the activities of the target entity fall within the scope of the authorization regime under Article L. 151-3(I) of the Monetary and Financial Code. In this case, the foreign investor must secure a formal authorization from the Minister before completing the transaction. Additionally, if a preliminary examination request has been submitted by the investor and the CIEF determines that the target's activities are subject to the FDI screening regime, the administration may invite the investor to convert the request into a formal authorization application before the preliminary procedure has concluded. The two-month period set out in Article R. 151-6 of the Monetary and Financial Code only begins when the investor formally submits the authorization request.

—an opinion indicating that the activities of the target entity do not fall within the scope of the prior authorization regime. In such case, the investment may proceed without prior approval, provided there are no changes in the law or in the activities of the target entity between the issuance of the opinion and the closing of the transaction.

It is important to note that the Monetary and Financial Code does not set a validity period for decisions issued under the preliminary examination procedure. These opinions are only valid as of the date of the request and in light of the factual and legal circumstances then in effect. Any change in the target's activities or the applicable legal framework may lead to a different conclusion.

Furthermore, the opinion issued during a preliminary examination cannot be disclosed to third parties except under the same confidentiality rules applicable to the formal authorization process (see Chapter 17).

Finally, the administration has made clear that the Minister's silence after the applicable deadline does not constitute an exemption from the requirement to obtain authorization.

• Strategic Use of the Procedure

Given the procedural parallels with the formal authorization process, especially in terms of the file's completeness, applicants must weigh whether a preliminary examination request is appropriate based on their specific timeline.

The added value of the preliminary examination lies in its usefulness at an early stage of the transaction, especially in cases where a subsequent authorization request

595. Ibid, See point 2.4.3

may not immediately follow. It offers the parties legal certainty upstream, without initiating the authorization process prematurely.

The Preliminary Examination Request and Authorization Request Are Not Interchangeable

As the administration has reiterated, the preliminary examination request and the formal authorization request are two distinct procedures that are not interchangeable. A single submission cannot be considered as both a primary preliminary examination request and a secondary authorization request. Investors must clearly choose the type of request they are submitting.

Right to Withdraw the Preliminary Request at Any Time

The filing entity (either the French target company or the foreign investor) may, at any time during the procedure and before the minister issues a decision, choose to withdraw [596] its request for a prior examination .

Such withdrawal must be notified to the Directorate General of the Treasury, either directly by the filing entity or through its duly authorized counsel.

Moreover, the parties remain free to decide whether or not to finalize the contemplated transaction, even after having obtained authorization under the French FDI screening regime . In such cases, if the transaction is not carried out, the Directorate General of the Treasury must be formally notified.

Appeal mechanisms are available.

Decisions rendered by the Minister of the Economy in the context of a prior examination request may be challenged through the same avenues of appeal [597] as those provided in connection with an application for authorization.

*
* *

A major advancement introduced through the successive reforms of France's foreign direct investment (FDI) screening regime, the option of a pre-clearance review ("examen préalable") allows parties to obtain an official determination from the French authorities. In 2024, 73% of the pre-clearance procedures initiated concluded

596. France, Ministry of the Economy, Finance and Industrial and Digital Sovereignty, Directorate General of the Treasury, Guidelines on the Foreign Direct Investment Screening in France, July 2025, published July 30, 2025, Point 2.4.5, consulted August 1, 2025, available at https://www.tresor.economie.gouv.fr/services-aux-entreprises/investissements-etrangers-en-france
597. Ibid, see Point 2.4.4

that the targeted activities did not fall [598] within the scope of the FDI screening framework. In such cases, a foreign investment in the French company carrying out those activities is not subject to prior authorization by the Minister of the Economy.

However, in 2025, the Parliamentary Committee for Evaluation and Oversight [599] (Mission d'évaluation et de contrôle), reporting to the French National Assembly, noted that this procedure remains largely underused in practice. It appears to be little known, even among French companies operating in strategic sectors, including those with regular interactions with the Strategic Information and Economic Security Service (SISSE) .

Yet this pre-clearance mechanism aligns with a broader international trend encouraging early-stage engagement between the target entity and, where relevant, the foreign investor, to assess any potential concerns that the contemplated transaction may raise under national security rules. More fundamentally, the procedure reflects a general policy approach whereby the objective of FDI screening is not to block foreign investment, but rather to ensure that the contemplated transaction does not compromise the national interest. In that respect, any measure capable of addressing potential threats is in the interest of all parties and serves to facilitate the successful completion of the deal.

598. France, Ministry of the Economy, Finance and Industrial and Digital Sovereignty, Directorate General of the Treasury, 2025 Annual Report, "Foreign Direct Investment Screening in France", published July 30, 2025, consulted July 31, 2025, available at https://www.tresor.economie.gouv.fr/Articles/2025/07/30/publication-du-rapport-annuel-sur-le-controle-ief-en-2024

599. France, National Assembly, Committee for the Evaluation and Oversight of Public Policies, Information Report No. 1453, JOLIVET F., de LEPINAU H., Members of Parliament, on the evaluation of foreign direct investment screening in France, Official Journal of the French Republic, May 27, 2025, text 45 out of 69, published on May 22, 2025, accessed on May 27, 2025, available at https://www.assemblee-nationale.fr/dyn/17/rapports/cec/l17b1453_rapport-information

Chapter 17

The Formal Review Phase Begins with the Submission of the Prior Authorization Request

France's foreign direct investment (FDI) screening mechanism operates as a matter of public order, requiring foreign investors to submit a prior authorization request before proceeding with a qualifying investment. This obligation applies as soon as the investor identifies that the proposed transaction falls within the scope of the FDI screening regime . Importantly, failure to submit such a request renders the investment null and void under French law.

The procedural formalities surrounding the submission are critical. The application must be addressed to the competent authority, namely the Foreign Investment Screening) Bureau in France (CIEF). Although the filing procedure is formally unrestricted, it has become increasingly structured, digitalized, and professionalized in recent years, reflecting regulatory developments. All documentation must be submitted in French, the only official language accepted for this purpose.

Submission of the file triggers an acknowledgment of receipt, which marks the official start of the formal review process. A comprehensive list of required documents is defined by regulation, and the completeness of the file is subject to strict assessment. Omitting to file a request can carry severe legal consequences. Furthermore, the determination of a complete application triggers the official instruction timeline, which is governed by Article R. 151-6 of the Monetary and Financial Code and may not exceed 75 business days. The French administration takes into account the complexity of the supporting documents, conducting the review in two phases to ensure efficient processing within the prescribed timeframe.

Filing a Prior Authorization Request Is Mandatory When the Investment Qualifies

Pursuant to Article L. 151-3 of the Monetary and Financial Code, foreign investments in France that fall within certain sensitive sectors are subject to prior authorization by the Minister of the Economy. However, such prior authorization is neither general nor automatic; it applies only when three cumulative conditions, set forth in Articles R. 151-1 through R. 151-3 of the Monetary and Financial Code, are met (see Chapters 10 to 13).

This legal framework carries several important consequences.

First, the obligation to submit a prior authorization request lies with the foreign investor, the entity carrying out the investment operation, not with the target company. This rule is clearly reaffirmed by the French administration in its official guidelines [600]. The duty applies first and foremost to the foreign investor itself but also extends to every entity within its control chain.

The administration specifies that where several foreign entitiesare part of the same control chain, a single filing by one of them is sufficient for the same investment transaction. Conversely, in cases where multiple foreign investors are involved in the same qualifying transaction, such as in a joint control acquisition, each investor must submit an individual request covering its respective investment.

Accordingly, the request for authorization is ratione personae, it depends on the identity and status of the investor. As a result, joint filings are not permitted and must be avoided.

Within this framework, the authorization request may be submitted by any person duly empowered to represent the foreign investor, including external counsel, provided that a valid power of attorney is submitted. This mandate must either be drafted in French [601] or accompanied by a certified French translation if originally issued in another language.

Second, because filing is mandatory [602], the foreign investor is required to carry out a thorough self-assessment of its own situation.

Indeed, the filing obligation is triggered only when the investor has determined that the three legal conditions are met. If the investor, or its advisors, misjudges whether the transaction qualifies under the French FDI screening regime, it may later be required to file retroactively, or worse, risk having the transaction invalidated if it is found to contravene France's national interest. (See next section.)

In light of these risks, the foreign investor has every incentive to file a prior authorization request. Better still, the investor may opt to submit a pre-filing review request (as discussed in Chapter 16), although in practice it may be more prudent to proceed directly with a formal authorization request.

Failure to File a Request Results in Absolute Nullity of the Transaction

Failure to comply with the mandatory filing requirement results in the automatic nullification of the transaction.

600. France, Ministry of the Economy, Finance and Industrial and Digital Sovereignty, Directorate General of the Treasury, Guidelines on the Foreign Direct Investment Screening in France, July 2025, Point 2.2.1, published July 30, 2025, consulted August 1, 2025, available at https://www.tresor.economie.gouv.fr/services-aux-entreprises/investissements-etrangers-en-france

601. France, Ministerial Order of December 31, 2019, on foreign investments in France, Official Journal of the French Republic, No. 0001, January 1, 2020, NOR: ECOT1937237A

602. France, Ministry of the Economy, Finance and Industrial and Digital Sovereignty, Directorate General of the Treasury, Guidelines on the Foreign Direct Investment Screening in France, July 2025, Point 2.2.1,

Article L. 151-4 of the Monetary and Financial Code provides that: "Any commitment, agreement, or contractual clause that directly or indirectly results in a foreign investment within the sectors referred to in paragraph I of Article L. 151-3, without the required authorization having been obtained under that article, shall be null and void."

This absolute nullity is clearly and unequivocally stated by the French administration [603] and must not be taken lightly.

It applies regardless of whether the failure to file was intentional, deliberate, or due to mere negligence or oversight. In addition, the nullity may be coupled with other enforcement measures, including administrative sanctions.

In this context, the Minister of the Economy may order the investor to file a retroactive request for authorization in order to regularize the situation. In cases of good faith, the investor may also take the initiative and approach the Treasury Department (Direction générale du Trésor

) to request such regularization.

When assessing such a request, the administration will apply the three legal eligibility criteria based on the legal and factual circumstances that existed at the date the unlawful investment was carried out, not at the time of the regularization filing.

Regularization may cure the civil nullity, but it does not shield the investor from monetary penalties under Article L. 151-3-2 of the Monetary and Financial Code. (See chapter 21)

Failure to File May Trigger Sanctions and Legal Proceedings

In addition to the nullity of the transaction, the Minister [604] for the Economy is empowered to adopt various enforcement measures, including, where necessary, under penalty payments (astreinte), as well as interim protective measures and administrative monetary penalties, pursuant respectively to Articles L. 151-3-1 and L. 151-3-2 of the Monetary and Financial Code (see Chapter 21).

This enforcement framework applies not only to deliberate or intentional failure to seek prior authorization, but also to cases of mere omission or negligence. The aforementioned enforcement and sanction measures may be imposed cumulatively.

The Minister may, in this respect, order the investor to seek retroactive regularization of the situation by filing an application for authorization. An investor acting in good faith may also, on their own initiative, approach the Directorate General of the Treasury to request the implementation of such a regularization procedure.

---

published July 30, 2025, consulted August 1, 2025, available at https://www.tresor.economie.gouv.fr/services-aux-entreprises/investissements-etrangers-en-france

603. France, Ministry of the Economy, Finance and Industrial and Digital Sovereignty, Directorate General of the Treasury, Guidelines on the Foreign Direct Investment Screening in France, July 2025, Point 2.2.2, published July 30, 2025, consulted August 1, 2025, available at https://www.tresor.economie.gouv.fr/services-aux-entreprises/investissements-etrangers-en-france

604. Ibid, see Point 2.2.2.1

In the context of regularization, the review of the three eligibility criteria is carried out on the basis of the legal and factual circumstances applicable at the date the irregular investment was made, and not at the date of regularization.

The possibility of retroactively regularizing[605] an investment extinguishes the civil nullity of the transaction but does not relieve the investor from potential monetary penalties, as provided for under Article L. 151-3-2 of the Monetary and Financial Code.

The amount of the monetary penalty is determined in proportion to the seriousness of the breach. When deciding which measures to adopt, the authorities also consider the investor's conduct and, more broadly, the circumstances surrounding the failure to file a prior authorization request.

Lastly, such failure may also give rise to criminal proceedings under Article 459 of the Customs Code.

Submission of the Prior Authorization Request Must Be Made to the CIEF

As specified by the administration[606], applications for authorization (or for prior review) must be filed electronically with the Directorate General of the Treasury exclusively via the online portal *plateforme-ief.dgtresor.gouv.fr*. This website constitutes the sole valid means for submitting an application for authorization or prior review.

As made explicit in the 2025 Guidelines, submission through this portal is the only valid method of filing such applications. It is therefore not necessary to duplicate the filing made on the IEF Portal with either a hard copy sent by postal mail or an electronic transmission to the address *iefautorisations@dgtresor.gouv.fr*.

By contrast, advance notifications of the crossing of the 10% voting rights threshold in a French company whose shares are admitted to trading on a regulated market must be submitted electronically to the dedicated address *iefautorisations@dgtresor.gouv.fr*.

Applications are deemed filed as of the business day on which they are received, provided that the filing occurs before 5:00 p.m. If an application is transmitted outside of these hours, acknowledgment of receipt will only be issued on the next business day.

The filing of applications is strictly required to be made in electronic form.

Since 2025, the French government has operated the "FDI Platform" (Plateforme IEF) as the mandatory digital portal[607] for submitting both prior authorization

605. Ibid, see Point 2.1.1.

606. Ibid,

607. France, Ministry of the Economy, Finance and Industrial and Digital Sovereignty, accessed September 1st, 2025, available at https://plateforme-ief.dgtresor.gouv.fr

requests and preliminary review applications. According to the authorities [608], this tool enables any investor or company, as well as their legal advisors, to provide the information required under the Order [609] of 31 December 2019 and to submit it to the Directorate General of the Treasury (Direction Générale du Trésor). It also allows users to communicate directly with Treasury officials and to monitor the progress of the review process step by step.

The FDI Platform is designed to be a user-friendly, secure, and educational interface that helps investors and target companies supply the necessary information during the FDI screening process. It also ensures centralized tracking of all submissions and provides real-time updates on the status of each case, thereby improving the overall transparency and predictability of the review process for all stakeholders.

For the Treasury Department [610], the digital channel provided by the "FDI Platform" is not only a tool for streamlining the filing of authorization requests and activity review applications, but also a structural mechanism for enhancing the accessibility and clarity of the French FDI screening framework.

This digitization effort mirrors the move made by the U.S. Committee on Foreign Investment in the United States (CFIUS), which implemented its Case Management System (CMS) in 2020 via a secure online portal hosted by the U.S. Department of the Treasury.

In addition, the filing process is becoming increasingly professionalized. Although there is no legal obligation to do so, it is now strongly recommended to engage legal counsel, particularly to compile the necessary documentation and to verify the accuracy of the information submitted, especially with respect to the nature of the investment and, more broadly, the overall transaction structure.

The official language for filing is French

As stipulated by the Order [611] of 31 December 2019, the application file for prior authorization, as well as, it should be recalled, for prior examination, must [612] be drafted in French.

608. France, Ministry of the Economy, Finance, Industrial and Digital Sovereignty, Press Release No. 1167, 28 September 2023, consulted on 9 May 2024, available at https://www.tresor.economie.gouv.fr/Articles/257d3b28-f518-4bb3-9bb2-064f4ae0858c/files/612963b3-dca9-4c6d-9a56-95883e29fb79
609. France, Ministerial Order of December 31, 2019, on foreign investments in France, Official Journal of the French Republic, No. 0001, January 1, 2020, NOR: ECOT1937237A
610. France, Ministry of the Economy, Finance and Industrial and Digital Sovereignty, Directorate General of the Treasury, 2024 Annual Report, "Foreign Direct Investment Screening in France," published on June 4, 2024, available at https://www.tresor.economie.gouv.fr/Articles/c7ec36f3-6df0-4cf8-82aa-9c772917afeb/files/249123ae-5a3b-45dd-8f6f-5f84b2fc0c0a (last accessed June 6, 2024)
611. France, Ministerial Order of 31 December 2019 on foreign investments in France, Article 4, Official Journal of the French Republic, No. 0001, 1 January 2020, NOR: ECOT1937237A
612. France, Ministry of the Economy, Finance and Industrial and Digital Sovereignty, Directorate General of the Treasury, Guidelines on the Foreign Direct Investment Screening in France, July 2025, published 30 July 2025, consulted 1 August 2025, see Point 2.1.2, available at https://www.tresor.economie.gouv.fr/services-aux-entreprises/investissements-etrangers-en-france

By way of exception, certain supporting documents such as certificates of incorporation, powers of attorney, and contractual documentation may be submitted in English. However, this general requirement for filing in French implies that, where deemed necessary by the competent administrative authority in charge of the authorization and screening procedure for foreign investments (the Foreign Direct Investment Screening Office (CIEF) – Bureau du Contrôle des Investissements Étrangers en France, or CIEF), a certified translation, carried out, if applicable, by a sworn translator, may be requested for any document or information originally submitted in a foreign language.

One notable exception arises from Regulation (EU) 2019/452 establishing a framework for the screening of foreign direct investments into the Union (see Chapter 6), which requires that the EU notification form, entitled "Request for information from the investor," be completed in English.

Accordingly, it is advisable to provide a full English translation of the authorization application file whenever the contemplated transaction involves an investor from a non-EU country.

Acknowledgment of Receipt of the Filing Package

In any administrative procedure subject to statutory time limits, the acknowledgment of receipt plays a key role in triggering the official start of the process. As confirmed by the French Code on the Relationship between the Public and the Administration (CRPA

(Code des relations entre le public et l'administration), the issuance of such acknowledgment may have significant consequences, notably in terms of the completeness of the application file, the official commencement of the review process, or the admissibility of legal challenges. Accordingly, "any request submitted to the administration shall be subject to an acknowledgment of receipt [613]."

The French foreign direct investment (FDI) screening procedure is no exception. As recalled by the competent authorities [614], the submission of an authorization request file results in the issuance of an acknowledgment of receipt confirming that the request has been duly received.

The administration makes it clear that regulatory timelines begin to run only once the application has been deemed admissible. This step consists in verifying that the applicant is duly authorized to file the request, or that the filing is made by the investor rather than the target entity (except in the case of a request for a prior review of an activity). If this condition is not met, the Directorate General of the Treasury invites the applicant to regularize the filing.

613. France, Code of Relations between the Public and the Administration, Article L. 112-3
614. See Point 2.1.3.2.1 in Ministry of the Economy, Finance and Industrial and Digital Sovereignty, Directorate General of the Treasury, Guidelines on the Foreign Direct Investment Screening in France, July 2025, published on July 30, 2025, consulted on August 1, 2025, available at https://www.tresor.economie.gouv.fr/services-aux-entreprises/investissements-etrangers-en-france

The acknowledgment of receipt specifies:
—the date on which the application was received and the deadline upon which, in the absence of an express decision, the application shall be deemed rejected;
—the name, postal and electronic address, as well as the telephone number of the officer within the Foreign Investment Screening)
—Bureau (CIEF) responsible for reviewing the file;
—where applicable, the missing documents with respect to the list established by the decree of 31 December 2019;
—a statement indicating that the decision may be subject to an implied rejection at the end of the regulatory period.

Regulatory timelines commence only upon the completeness of the file

Regulatory timelines do not begin to run until the application is deemed admissible [615]. This occurs on the day the file is submitted, provided the submission is made on a business day, outside of public holidays, and within the official reception hours (up to 5:00 p.m.), rather than on the date of the acknowledgment of receipt issued by the administration. If the submission takes place during a weekend, on a public holiday, or outside of reception hours, the timeline only begins on the first following business day.

The timeline is suspended when the file is incomplete. In such case, the suspension covers the period between the date on which the administration requests additional documents or information and the date on which the applicant provides the requested material.

The admissibility review also ensures that the applicant is duly authorized to submit a request for authorization and that the filing has been made by the foreign investor rather than the target entity. If this is not the case, the Directorate General of the Treasury will invite the applicant to regularize the situation.

Once the application is deemed admissible, the Directorate General of the Treasury, acting through the CIEF unit, will issue a formal acknowledgment of receipt.

The list of documents that must accompany an application for authorization is precisely defined.

Pursuant to Articles R. 151-5 through R. 151-11 of the French Monetary and Financial Code, as well as the applicable ministerial order [616] setting out the documentation

615. See Point 2.3.2.1 in Ministry of the Economy, Finance and Industrial and Digital Sovereignty, Directorate General of the Treasury, Guidelines on the Foreign Direct Investment Screening in France, July 2025, published on July 30, 2025, consulted on August 1, 2025, available at https://www.tresor.economie.gouv.fr/services-aux-entreprises/investissements-etrangers-en-france

616. France, Ministerial Order of December 31, 2019, on foreign investments in France, Official Journal of the French Republic, No. 0001, January 1, 2020, NOR: ECOT1937237A, as amended by Ministerial Order of December 28, 2023, on foreign investments in France, Official Journal of the French Republic, No. 0301, December 29, 2023, NOR: ECOT2334928A

requirements, a request for prior authorization must include the following documents and information (see Annex D):

I. With respect to the foreign investor [617]:

- If the investor is a natural person: any official document providing proof of identity, including full name, date and place of birth, nationality or nationalities, and tax residence.
- If the investor is a legal entity:

  1. Certificate of incorporation or equivalent, specifying the corporate name, registered office, registration number or equivalent identifier, and nationality.
  2. Organizational chart identifying all entities or individuals in the control chain up to the ultimate beneficial owner (s), within the meaning of Article L. 233-3 of the French Commercial Code [618]. The chart must indicate the percentage of share capital and voting rights held by each controlling entity, as well as the existence, where applicable, of any specific rights granting control within the meaning of Article L. 233-3 or Article L. 430-1(III) of the same code [619]. The filing must also identify the persons or entities within the control chain that authorized or participated in the investment decision.

---

617. France, Monetary and Financial Code, Article R. 151-1, within the meaning of paragraph I of that article

618. French Commercial Code, Article L. 233-3

I. – For the purposes of Sections 2 and 4 of this Chapter, any natural or legal person shall be deemed to control another entity:

1. When such person holds, directly or indirectly, a portion of the capital conferring the majority of voting rights at the general meetings of that company;

2. When such person alone holds the majority of voting rights in that company pursuant to an agreement entered into with other partners or shareholders, provided the agreement is not contrary to the interests of the company;

3. When such person, by virtue of the voting rights held, in fact determines the decisions made at the general meetings of that company;

4. When such person is a partner or shareholder of that company and has the power to appoint or remove the majority of the members of the company's administrative, management, or supervisory bodies.

II. – A person shall be presumed to exercise such control when he or she holds, directly or indirectly, more than 40 percent of the voting rights and no other partner or shareholder holds, directly or indirectly, a greater fraction than his or her own.

III. – For the purposes of the same Sections of this Chapter, two or more persons acting in concert shall be deemed to control another entity jointly when they in fact determine the decisions taken at the general meeting.

619. France, Commercial Code, Article L. 430-1

I. – A concentration shall be deemed to arise:

1° Where two or more previously independent undertakings merge;

2° Where one or more persons already holding control of at least one undertaking, or where one or more undertakings, acquire, directly or indirectly, whether by the acquisition of interests in the share capital or of assets, by contract, or by any other means, control of the whole or parts of one or more other undertakings.

II. – The creation of a joint venture performing on a lasting basis all the functions of an autonomous economic entity shall constitute a concentration within the meaning of this article.

III. – For the purposes of this Title, control shall arise from rights, contracts, or any other means which, either separately or jointly and having regard to the factual or legal circumstances, confer the possibility of exercising decisive influence over the conduct of an undertaking, and in particular:

—ownership or the right to use all or part of the assets of an undertaking;

—rights or contracts which confer decisive influence over the composition, deliberations, or decisions of the organs of an undertaking.

3. Certificates of incorporation or equivalent documents (same requirements as point 1) for each entity listed in point 2.
4. For the entities that ultimately control the investor:
   a. List of members of their management, supervisory, or governing bodies (or equivalent), including their nationalities and tax residencies;
   b. Identity of all shareholders or partners holding more than 5% of the voting rights, with the corresponding ownership percentages.
5. Where the control chain includes one or more investment funds, supporting documentation identifying the fund manager (s) and their own controlling persons or entities.
6. Detailed description of the investor's business activities, including services, products, or operations offered.
7. Disclosure of any equity ties or significant financial support received from a non-EU state or public body during the past five years.
8. Description of the markets on which the investor operates.
9. List of French and foreign competitors.
10. A signed declaration that neither the investor nor any of the entities or individuals identified under point 2 have, in the last five years, been convicted of an offense listed in Article R. 151-10 of the Monetary and Financial Code (see Chapter 21), or of any equivalent offense under foreign law. If the investor is a legal entity, it must also declare, to the best of its knowledge, that none of the members of its management, supervisory, or governing bodies have been convicted of such offenses.
11. The notification form required under Regulation (EU) 2019/452 of the European Parliament and of the Council of 19 March 2019 establishing a framework for the screening of foreign direct investments into the Union (see Annex F: "Request for information from the investor"), if any entity in the control chain is based in a non-EU country.

Note: Items 6 through 9 must also cover the group to which the investor belongs.

II. With respect to the target entity (the French business):

1. Corporate name, registered office, addresses of French operational sites, SIREN number, and codes under the French classification of activities (NAF).
2. Number of employees in France and globally, as well as individual and consolidated net turnover and net income over the past three closed fiscal years.
3. Organizational chart detailing the control chain up to the ultimate beneficial owners, pursuant to Article L. 233-3 of the French Commercial Code.
4. Detailed description of business activities in France and in the European Union, including services, products, and customer data access and management arrangements.
5. List of French and EU-based clients, along with a description of the services, products, or operations performed on their behalf.
6. Markets on which the target operates.
7. List of French or EU competitors, along with market share data by type of service, product, or activity, both in France and in the European Union.
8. Any involvement in projects or programs of interest to the European Union (as defined in Article 8 of Regulation (EU) 2019/452), including any EU funding received.
9. Designation of a contact person, including full name, professional title, business address, and email.

10. Where the transaction involves the acquisition of all or part of a business unit (as defined under Article R. 1151-2 of the Monetary and Financial Code), a list of assets comprising the business unit must be included.
11. List of intellectual property rights (patents, trademarks, licenses) owned or used by the target entity, including their type, duration, and, in the case of licensed or otherwise used IP, identification of the respective owners or licensors.

Note: Items 4 through 7 must also cover the group to which the target entity belongs.

III. With respect to the contemplated investment:

1. A copy of any document evidencing a sufficiently developed investment project.
2. Any option concerning the remainder of the share capital.
3. Amount of the investment, as defined in Article R. 151-2 of the Monetary and Financial Code, and where applicable, the amount of the overall transaction. If the exact figures are not yet known, an estimate must be provided, along with the methodology used to arrive at such estimate.
4. Rationale for the transaction in light of the investor's overall strategy.

4 bis. Description of the investor's general strategy in France and the European Union (e.g., types and duration of past or planned operations).

4 ter. Sector-specific strategy of the investor in the field(s) relevant to the proposed transaction, in France and in the European Union.

5. Financial terms of the deal, including whether payment will be made via capital transfer from abroad or through other arrangements. If final figures are unavailable, an estimate must be provided along with the estimation method.
6. Transaction timeline and any supporting documentation.
7. Where applicable, a list of jurisdictions in which the transaction is or will be notified under foreign investment or merger control rules, including the relevant dates of notification.

The list of documents required for the notification file in cases of crossing the 10 percent threshold is simplified.

As recalled by the French authorities [620], under the amended Order [621] of 31 December 2019, the content of such a notification substantially differs from that of an authorization application and is limited to the transmission of the following information only. The Directorate General of the Treasury (Direction générale du Trésor – DGT) acknowledges receipt of the notification and assesses its completeness under the same conditions.

620. See Point 2.3.2.2 in Ministry of the Economy, Finance and Industrial and Digital Sovereignty, Directorate General of the Treasury, "Guidelines on the Foreign Direct Investment Screening in France" July 2025, Published July 30, 2025, Consulted August 1, 2025, available at https://www.tresor.economie.gouv.fr/services-aux-entreprises/investissements-etrangers-en-france

621. France, Ministerial Order of December 31, 2019, on foreign investments in France, Official Journal of the French Republic, No. 0001, January 1, 2020, NOR: ECOT1937237A

According to the Guidelines [622], the statutory time period applicable to a notification starts running on the date the file is submitted, provided the filing occurs on a weekday, excluding public holidays, and during official business hours (before 5:00 p.m.). The time period does not start running from the date of the acknowledgment of receipt by the administration. If the filing occurs on a weekend, a public holiday, or outside office hours, the period begins on the following business day.

This period is suspended when the file is incomplete. In such cases, the suspension runs from the date on which the administration requests additional information until the date on which the requested documents and information are provided.

Pursuant to the amended Order [623] of 31 December 2019, the content of the notification [624] is limited to the following (see chapter 17):

With respect to the investment transaction:

—the total number of voting rights held by the investor before the investment, and the total number (or an estimate, where the exact number cannot be determined) of voting rights to be held after the investment;

—the number of securities already held by the investor that will give access to shares to be issued, and the voting rights attached thereto;

—the shares already issued and the voting rights attached thereto that the investor may acquire pursuant to an agreement or a financial instrument referred to in Article L. 211-1 of the Monetary and Financial Code;

—the information referred to in Article L. 233-7, VII of the Commercial Code, which must be transmitted to the French Financial Markets Authority (AMF) in the event of a threshold crossing;

—the rationale for the transaction in connection with the investor's overall strategy;

—the investor's overall strategy in France and in the European Union (in particular, the nature of the operations carried out, examples of past transactions, and the typical investment horizon);

—the investor's strategy in the sector(s) of activity concerned by the transaction, in France and in the European Union (in particular, the nature of the operations carried out, examples of past transactions, and the typical investment horizon).

—With respect to the target company :

—a description of the activities carried out in France and in the European Union by the entity subject to the investment, including the description of services or products provided;

622. See Point 2.3.2.1 in Ministry of the Economy, Finance and Industrial and Digital Sovereignty, Directorate General of the Treasury, "Guidelines on the Foreign Direct Investment Screening in France" July 2025, Published July 30, 2025, Consulted August 1, 2025, available at https://www.tresor.economie.gouv.fr/services-aux-entreprises/investissements-etrangers-en-france

623. France, Ministerial Order of December 31, 2019, on foreign investments in France, Official Journal of the French Republic, No. 0001, January 1, 2020, NOR: ECOT1937237A, as amended by Ministerial Order of December 28, 2023, on foreign investments in France, Official Journal of the French Republic, No. 0301, December 29, 2023, NOR: ECOT2334928A

624. See Point 2.3.2.1 in Ministry of the Economy, Finance and Industrial and Digital Sovereignty, Directorate General of the Treasury, "Guidelines on the Foreign Direct Investment Screening in France" July 2025, Published July 30, 2025, Consulted August 1, 2025, available at https://www.tresor.economie.gouv.fr/services-aux-entreprises/investissements-etrangers-en-france

—the markets on which the target entity operates;
—the main clients of the target entity in France and in the European Union.

With respect to the investor:

- where the investor is a natural person: a copy of any official identification document indicating full name, date and place of birth, nationality (ies), and tax residence;
- where the investor is a legal entity:
  i) a certificate of incorporation or equivalent (stating corporate name, registered office, registration number or equivalent, and nationality);
  ii) the investor's corporate structure chart, together with the identification within the chain of control of the entities or individuals who took or authorized the investment decision; and
  iii) a detailed description of the activities carried out, including services or products provided.

As to decisions rendered at the conclusion of the review, the administration recalls [625] that the absence of a response to a prior notification after a period of ten business days implies that a waiver of authorization has been granted, meaning that the contemplated investment does not require prior authorization. However, such a waiver does not constitute a determination of whether the target company's activities fall within the scope of Article R. 151-3 of the Monetary and Financial Code.

If the Ministry of the Economy issues a letter of opposition, the foreign investor must then file a formal authorization request before carrying out the investment. In that case, the time periods set out in Article R. 151-6 of the Monetary and Financial Code begin to run from the date on which the investor files the authorization request.

The waiver of authorization is valid only in light of the circumstances existing on the date of the notification and the applicable legal and factual framework at that time.

With respect to possible remedies, the administration [626] further recalls that decisions by the Minister of the Economy regarding a notification are subject to the same avenues of appeal as other ministerial decisions: either an administrative appeal or judicial review before the administrative courts (see Chapter 22).

Finally, the filing entity may decide at any point in the procedure, and before the Minister's decision, to withdraw [627] its notification. Such withdrawal must be notified in writing to the Directorate General of the Treasury (DGT), either directly by the filing entity or through its duly authorized counsel.

---

625. See Point 2.3.3 in Ministry of the Economy, Finance and Industrial and Digital Sovereignty, Directorate General of the Treasury, "Guidelines on the Foreign Direct Investment Screening in France" July 2025, Published July 30, 2025, Consulted August 1, 2025, available at https://www.tresor.economie.gouv.fr/services-aux-entreprises/investissements-etrangers-en-france
626. Ibid, See Point 2.3.4.
627. Ibid, See Point 2.3.5.

A Standardized EU Screening Form May Be Required for Third-Country Investments

Where a prior authorization request involves a foreign investment originating from a third country (i.e., a non-EU country), the foreign investor must provide a set of information to be shared with other EU Member States participating in the cooperation mechanism. This information must be submitted using a standardized form [628], which is required in addition to the French authorization request. The relevant form is reproduced in Annex E of this book.

As the form itself explains, its purpose is to capture all information that might be necessary for Member States' review. However, the French authorities acknowledge that not all requested data will be available for every transaction. As a result, fields marked with an asterisk [629] (*) are to be completed on a best-efforts basis, taking into account the nature of the transaction and the reasonable cost of gathering the information. If specific data is unavailable or can only be collected at a disproportionate cost, the applicant is instructed to indicate this in the appropriate column of the form.

This flexibility is essential, as the submission of a prior authorization request already entails a significant investment of time and internal resources.

In general, the EU form must be completed in English and requires information on the content of the transaction. This includes general details about the investment, information about the target entity, and, where applicable, data on other legal entities within the target's group that are established in other EU Member States. The form also requires information regarding any planned Greenfield investment, the identityof the investor, the existence of parallel review procedures under EU or national screening rules, and any other information relevant for the assessment of the transaction.

General Information

The following information is required:

—Name and country of incorporation of the direct investor(s) [630];

—Name and country of incorporation of the ultimate global owner of the direct investor(s) [631];

—Name of the target company [632];

---

628. European Union, European Commission, Request for information from the investor for the purposes of notifications pursuant to Article 6 of Regulation (EU) 2019/452, DOCX (Version 1.7), last accessed September 1st, 2025, available at https://policy.trade.ec.europa.eu/enforcement-and-protection/investment-screening_en

629. Complete the following information (= if available). In the same spirit, fields not marked with an asterisk must always be completed.*

630. Indicate the name using the Latin alphabet as well as any local alphabet used in the company's country of origin.

631. Indicate the name using the Latin alphabet as well as any local alphabet used in the company's country of origin.

632. Indicate the name of the entrepreneur or the company to whom the capital is made available in order to carry out an economic activity in a Member State.

—Name and country of incorporation of the group to which the target company belongs.

Information on the Investment

The following information must be provided:

—Description[633] of the investment;
—Approximate value[634] of the investment (in EUR);
—Expected date[635] for completion of the transaction;
—Financing structure[636] and source of funding for the investment;
—Investor's commercial strategy[637] behind the acquisition;
—Financial means ensuring the continued operation and viability of the target company post-acquisition*;
—Actual (direct or indirect) involvement[638] of the investor in the management of the target company;
—Equity interest[639] held by the direct investor and its ultimate global owner in the target company before (if applicable) and after the transaction.

If the post-transaction[640] equity interest is less than 100%, the investor must explain how the ownership stake translates into control or effective participation in the management of the target. A description must also be provided of how control or management is exercised on a joint basis, where applicable.

Furthermore, the applicant must clarify whether any public entity[641] holds shares in, or exercises any form of control over, the investor, including indirect forms of control.

---

633. Describe the structure of the transaction and explain how the change in ownership or control of the target company is implemented, as well as how the newly acquired assets will be integrated into the investor's corporate structure.
634. If the investment subject to this notification is part of a broader transaction, separately indicate the total transaction value and the amount of investment allocated to the company or companies located in the Member State conducting the screening. (Total transaction value and value of the investment allocated to the domestic target company).
635. Provide the information in the form of a specific date or time period, or based on the completion of ongoing authorization processes.
636. Based on the best information available, explain the origin of the funds and the extent to which they originate from external sources. If the investment subject to the notification is part of a broader transaction, specify the financing of the investment in the companies established in the territory of the Member State conducting the screening, as well as the sources of funding for the overall transaction.
637. Explain the reasons for the investor's interest in the investment and the circumstances under which the investment is being made by the target company.
638. If so, explain how.
639. Specify the voting rights attached to the acquired shares as a percentage of the total voting rights, and indicate whether there are any specific provisions regarding voting rights or any arrangements related to effective participation in management, such as veto rights or the right to appoint members of the board of directors, etc. (Both before and after the transaction).
640. Specify the voting rights attached to the acquired shares as a percentage of the total voting rights, and indicate whether there are any specific provisions regarding voting rights, any arrangements relating to effective participation in management, such as veto rights or the right to appoint members of the board of directors, or any other source of influence beyond voting or appointment rights.
641. Specify the voting rights attached to the acquired shares as a percentage of the total voting rights, and indicate whether there are any specific provisions regarding voting rights or any arrangements

Finally, if the transaction has been publicly announced, the investor must provide either a hyperlink to the announcement or a copy of the public statement, if available.

Target Company Information

The investor shall also provide information on the beneficiary company or companies established in the Member State conducting the screening, and where applicable, on the ultimate controlling entity (i.e., the most relevant entity within the ownership structure).

The following information is required (*Mandatory fields) :
—name of the company;
—address/place of residence/registered office of the company;
—national registration number*;
—date of incorporation*;
—annual turnover [642] in euros*;
—total number of employees*;
—stock exchange listing* (trading code, ticker symbol [643], or market identifier);
—website of the target company/companies*;
—role [644] of the company in the transaction;
—economic activity [645] of the company in the Member State where the investment is being screened;
—description of the company's business activity, including NACE codes [646];
—overview of the company's products, services, and activities [647] prior to the transaction;

---

related to effective participation in management, such as veto rights or the right to appoint members of the board of directors, etc.

642. Indicate the amount in euros for the most recent fiscal year and specify if the fiscal year does not correspond to the calendar year.

643. In the stock market sector, the term "ticker" generally refers to the alphanumeric symbol used to identify a stock or a company on a financial exchange. This symbol is typically short and unique to each publicly traded company. Tickers are widely used in stock trading, trading platforms, and financial media to quickly reference a specific company. For example, the ticker for Apple Inc. is "AAPL," and the ticker for Microsoft Corporation is "MSFT," etc.

644. By way of example:
—direct beneficiary of the investment (target)
—material intermediary entity
—ultimate global owner
—corporate group, etc.

645. European Union, Regulation (EU) 2019/452 of 19 March 2019 of the European Parliament and of the Council establishing a framework for the screening of foreign direct investments into the Union, Official Journal of the European Union, L 79I, 21 March 2019, pp. 1–14, Article 2(1): "'Foreign direct investment' means an investment of any kind by a foreign investor aiming to establish or to maintain lasting and direct links between the foreign investor and the entrepreneur to whom or the undertaking to which the capital is made available in order to carry out an economic activity in a Member State, including investments which enable effective participation in the management or control of a company carrying out an economic activity."

646. European Union, RAMON, Eurostat's classification server for NACE codes, accessed May 9, 2024, available at https://ec.europa.eu/eurostat/web/metadata/classifications

647. European Union, Regulation (EU) 2019/452 of 19 March 2019 of the European Parliament and of the Council establishing a framework for the screening of foreign direct investments into the Union, Official Journal of the European Union, L 79I/1, 21 March 2019, Article 2(1): "'Foreign direct investment' means an investment of any kind by a foreign investor aiming to establish or to maintain lasting and direct

—involvement in the development, production, or sale of goods or technologies subject to export control [648] under EU or Member State law [649];
—ownership, production, or sale of technologies or goods subject to export controls under EU law [650] or under the law of any EU Member State from which exports take place;
—list of all items subject to export control in a third country and the third country concerned;
—information* on the sectors [651] in which the target's clients operate within all EU Member States;
—explanations* concerning the products, services, and activities [652] of the company post-transaction;
—products and services offered by the target company with unique selling points*;
—presence [653] of competitors (national, European, global) offering goods and services comparable to those of the target company*;
—existence [654] of patents or other intellectual property rights [655] relevant for security or public order analysis*;
—list of EU Member States in which the company carries out significant business activities (e.g., through subsidiaries or branches), and the names of such entities;
—commercial relationships [656] of the target company with any project or program [657] of interest to the Union;

---

links between the foreign investor and the entrepreneur to whom or the undertaking to which the capital is made available in order to carry out an economic activity in a Member State, including investments which enable effective participation in the management or control of a company carrying out an economic activity."

648. Provide a list of all dual-use items and other goods subject to export control under EU Regulation (EU) 2021/821.
649. Where applicable, indicate the relevant classification of the products supplied by the target, for example:
—the relevant export control code (see Annex I of Regulation (EU) 2021/821 of the European Parliament and of the Council establishing the Union regime for the control of exports, brokering, technical assistance, transit and transfer of dual-use items)
—the relevant military item code pursuant to the Common Military List of the EU (items covered by Council Common Position 2008/944/CFSP defining common rules governing the control of exports of military technology and equipment)
—CN codes pursuant to Annex I of Council Regulation (EEC) No 2658/87 on the tariff and statistical nomenclature and on the Common Customs Tariff.
650. If there is more than one third-country company in the investor chain, provide this information for all foreign investors.
651. Where possible, provide information on all sectors in which the target's clients are active, including indirect clients where such information is available. Otherwise, provide a list of the target's clients (both direct and, where possible, indirect) within the EU.
652. This provision applies to FDI resulting in a change to the activities of the target company.
653. If so, provide information on these competitors.
654. List the patents and, where applicable, other intellectual property rights.
655. These patents or other intellectual property assets may be related to critical infrastructure, critical technologies, or critical inputs. The criticality of a patent may be determined by the degree to which companies rely on the associated licenses.
656. Specify the project, the relevant EU program, and the type of commercial relationship.
657. Explain, for example, whether the target company supplies goods, services, technologies, etc. to the project or program, or to participants in such projects or programs.

—receipt of funding[658] for such projects or programs of Union interest, or direct or indirect participation in their implementation;
—list[659] of natural or legal persons or entities from third countries subject to EU restrictive measures who are involved in the management or control of the EU target;
—shareholding structure of the target company, including information[660] on the ultimate beneficial owner and equity participation prior to the notified transaction.

The following information is required:
—Company name;
—Company address / domicile / registered office;
—Company national registration number;*
—Annual turnover[661] in euros;*
—Total number of employees;*
—Stock exchange listing (trading code, ticker, or stock symbol);*
—Website of the target company / companies;*
—Company's role[662] in the transaction;
—Conduct of economic activity[663] by the company in the Member State where the investment is being reviewed;

---

658. Specify the amount and the relevant EU project or program. The list of projects or programs of interest to the Union is set out in the Annex to Regulation (EU) 2019/452. The Financial Transparency System (FTS) (https://ec.europa.eu/budget/fts/index_en.htm) allows users to search for recipients of funding from the EU budget implemented directly by the European Commission (at headquarters or through EU delegations in third countries) and other EU bodies such as executive agencies ("direct management"), as well as beneficiaries of the European Development Fund. Note that the FTS does not provide information on funding from the EU budget implemented jointly by the Commission and the Member States ("shared management") or implemented indirectly by other international organizations or non-EU countries ("indirect management").

659. The consolidated list of persons, groups, and entities subject to EU financial sanctions can be downloaded from the Financial Sanctions Database (FSF), available at: https://webgate.ec.europa.eu/europeaid/fsd/fsf. Access to this platform requires an "EU Login" account. For more information on ownership and control in the context of EU sanctions, refer to the EU Best Practices for the effective implementation of restrictive measures and the European Commission's Opinion of 19 June 2020 on Article 2 of Council Regulation (EU) No 269/2014. Note that additional sectoral sanctions (not included in the FSF platform) may apply to the proposed transaction. For a complete list of EU sanctions, consult: www.sanctionsmap.eu.

660. A separate table may be provided for each legal entity, as needed.

661. Indicate the amount in euros for the latest fiscal year and specify if the fiscal year does not correspond to the calendar year.

662. By way of example:
—direct beneficiary of the investment (target entity)
—significant intermediary entity
—ultimate global owner
—corporate group...

663. European Union, Regulation (EU) 2019/452 of the European Parliament and of the Council of 19 March 2019 establishing a framework for the screening of foreign direct investments into the Union, Official Journal of the European Union, L 79I, 21 March 2019, pp. 1–14, Article 2(1): *"foreign direct investment" means an investment of any kind by a foreign investor aiming to establish or to maintain lasting and direct links between the foreign investor and the entrepreneur to whom or the undertaking to which the capital is made available in order to carry out an economic activity in a Member State, including investments which enable effective participation in the management or control of a company carrying out an economic activity."*

—Description of the economic activity carried out by the company, including NACE codes[664];
—List of the company's products, services, and activities[665] before the transaction;
—Ownership, production or sale of technologies or goods subject[666] to export control[667] under EU legislation or under the legislation of any EU Member State from which the company exports;
—Ownership, production or sale of technologies or goods subject[668] to export control[669] in the investor's country of origin;
—Information[670] on the sectors in which the target's clients are active across all EU Member States;
—Information[671] on the company's products, services, and activities after completion of the transaction;*
—Existence[672] of unique selling points (USPs) for the products and services offered by the target company;*
—Existence[673] of competitors (national, European, global) that offer goods and services comparable to those of the target company;*

---

664. Provide a brief description of the activities carried out and include the corresponding NACE subcategory at the highest level of detail possible (4-digit code).
NACE is the standard European classification of productive economic activities. It breaks down economic activities in such a way that a NACE code can be assigned to a statistical unit performing them. NACE codes are available in RAMON, Eurostat's classification server.
Description of Activity 1 and NACE code*
Description of Activity 2 and NACE code*
Description of Activity x and NACE code*
665. European Union, Regulation (EU) 2019/452 of the European Parliament and of the Council of 19 March 2019 establishing a framework for the screening of foreign direct investments into the Union, Official Journal of the European Union, L 79I, 21 March 2019, pp. 1–14, Article 2(1): "foreign direct investment" means an investment of any kind by a foreign investor aiming to establish or to maintain lasting and direct links between the foreign investor and the entrepreneur to whom or the undertaking to which the capital is made available in order to carry out an economic activity in a Member State, including investments which enable effective participation in the management or control of a company carrying out an economic activity.
666. Provide a list of all items subject to EU export control.
667. Where applicable, indicate the relevant classification of the products supplied by the target company, for example:
—the relevant export control code (see Annex I of Regulation (EU) 2021/821 of the European Parliament and of the Council establishing the Union regime for the control of exports, brokering, technical assistance, transit and transfer of dual-use items)
—the code for the relevant military items pursuant to the EU Common Military List (items covered by Council Common Position 2008/944/CFSP defining common rules governing control of exports of military technology and equipment)
—the CN codes in accordance with Annex I to Council Regulation (EEC) No 2658/87 on the tariff and statistical nomenclature and on the Common Customs Tariff.
668. Provide a list of all items subject to export control in a third country and specify the third country concerned.
669. If there is more than one third-country company in the investment chain, provide this information for all foreign investors.
670. To the extent possible, provide information on all sectors in which the target's clients are active, including indirect clients where such information is available. Otherwise, provide a list of the target's clients (both direct and, where possible, indirect) in the EU.
671. This provision applies to FDI resulting in a change in the target company's activities.
672. Confirm these points in the affirmative.
673. Provide information on these competitors in the affirmative.

—Ownership [674] of patents or other intellectual property rights [675] relevant for a security or public order assessment;*
—List [676] of EU Member States in which the company carries out significant commercial activities;
—Existence [677] of commercial relationships [678] between the target company and a project or program of Union interest;
—Receipt [679] of funds by the company for projects or programs [680] of Union interest, or direct or indirect involvement in the implementation of such projects or programs [681];
—Involvement of natural or legal persons, or entities from third countries subject to EU restrictive measures [682], in the management or control of the EU target.

Information on Greenfield Investments (where applicable)

It is important to distinguish greenfield investments, which typically involve the creation of a new company, facility, or site abroad, from mergers and acquisitions that result in the transfer of ownership of existing assets to a foreign investor. The standard notification form provides for specific information in the case of greenfield investments, including:
—Name of the new company
—Location/address of the new establishment
—Country in which the new company is incorporated
—Company registration number (if available)

674. List any patents and other intellectual property rights, where applicable.
675. These patents or other intellectual property assets may be related to critical infrastructure, critical technologies, or critical inputs. The criticality of a patent may be determined by the level of dependency of companies on the associated licenses.
676. For example, through subsidiaries or branches, and indicate the names of these entities.
677. Specify the project, the relevant EU program, and the type of business relationship.
678. Explain, for example, whether the company supplies goods, services, technologies, etc., to the project or program, or to participants in such projects or programs.
679. See the Financial Transparency System (FTS) at https://ec.europa.eu/budget/financial-transparency-system/index.html
680. The list of projects or programs of interest to the Union is set out in the Annex to Regulation (EU) No 2019/452. The Financial Transparency System (FTS) (https://ec.europa.eu/budget/fts/index_en.htm) allows users to search for recipients of funding from the EU budget implemented directly by the Commission (either at headquarters or through EU delegations in third countries) and by other EU bodies such as executive agencies ("direct management"), as well as recipients of the European Development Fund. Note that the FTS does not provide information on funding from the EU budget implemented jointly by the Commission and Member States ("shared management"), or indirectly by other international organizations or non-EU countries ("indirect management").
681. Specify the amount and the relevant EU project or program.
682. The consolidated list of persons, groups, and entities subject to EU financial sanctions can be downloaded from the Financial Sanctions Database – FSF, available at: https://webgate.ec.europa.eu/europeaid/fsd/fsf. Access to this platform requires an "EU Login" account. For more information on ownership and control in the context of EU sanctions, see the EU Best Practices for the effective implementation of restrictive measures and the Commission Opinion of 19 June 2020 on Article 2 of Council Regulation (EU) No 269/2014. Note that additional sectoral sanctions (not included in the FSF platform) may apply to the proposed transaction. For a complete list of EU sanctions, consult www.sanctionsmap.eu.

—Incorporation date (if available)
—Description [683] of the company's economic activity, including relevant NACE codes
—Explanation of the company's products, services, and activities after completion of the transaction
—Information on principal competitors (domestic, EU, global) (if available)
—Estimated number of employees (if available)
—Company website (if available)
—Ownership structure [684] of the new entity

Information on the Investor

The notification form also seeks information on the direct investor and, where applicable, on the ultimate beneficial owner, that is, the most relevant entity within the ownership chain. If necessary, each layer of ownership should be disclosed, including the direct investor, intermediary entities, and ultimate investor.

If the investment is carried out by multiple investors, this information must be provided separately for each, including a corporate structure chart illustrating horizontal and vertical relationships between the entities involved. The following information is required:
—Role [685] of the entity in the transaction
—Name
—Address/registered office
—Country of incorporation [686] or equivalent legal organization
—Company registration number (if available)
—Date of incorporation (if available)

683. Provide a brief description of the activities carried out and indicate the corresponding NACE subclassification with the highest possible level of detail (4 digits). Refer to RAMON, Eurostat's classification database, for the relevant NACE codes: https://ec.europa.eu/eurostat/web/metadata/classifications.
NACE is the standard European classification of productive economic activities. It provides a structured framework in which each NACE code may be associated with a statistical unit carrying out the corresponding activities. NACE codes are available in RAMON, Eurostat's classification database: https://ec.europa.eu/eurostat/web/metadata/classifications.
Description of Activity 1 and NACE code*
Description of Activity 2 and NACE code*
Description of Activity x and NACE code*

684. If the ownership structure is complex, provide details on the direct beneficiary, its ultimate owner, and any significant intermediary entities, to the extent that such information is available.
Where possible, include an organizational chart illustrating the horizontal and vertical relationships between the entities concerned and the overall group structure before and after the transaction. The information may also be presented in the form of a diagram (as an annex).

685. If the ownership structure is complex, provide details on the direct investor, any holding company established specifically for the purpose of carrying out the investment, any entity acting as a 100% owner of a holding company without other significant commercial activity, any significant intermediary entity, and the ultimate global owner, to the extent that such information is available.
Where possible, include an organizational chart illustrating the horizontal and vertical relationships between the entities involved and the overall group structure before and after the transaction. This information may also be presented in graphical form (as an annex).

686. If the entity is a natural person, indicate his or her nationality or nationalities.

—Annual turnover [687] (if available)
—Total number of employees [688] (if available)
—Stock exchange listing (trading code, ticker, or symbol) (if available)
—Company website (if available)
—Sector [689] of activity / business activities carried out
—Description of the company's products, services, and activities [690]
—Whether [691] the investor receives significant direct or indirect funding from a non-EU government
—Information on principal competitors (domestic, EU, global) (if available)
—EU Member States where the company conducts significant commercial operations
—Whether the company is subject to EU restrictive financial measures [692] (sanctions)
—Whether the company is subject to sanctions by third countries [693] (if applicable)
—Ownership structure [694] of the investor, including identification of ultimate beneficial owner (s) and shareholding

---

687. Indicate the amount in euros for the most recent fiscal year and specify if the fiscal year does not correspond to the calendar year. If the investor is part of a larger corporate group, also provide the corresponding information for the entire group, if available.
688. If the investor is part of a larger corporate group, also provide the corresponding information for the entire group, if available.
689. Provide a brief description of the activities carried out and indicate the corresponding NACE subclassification with the highest possible level of detail (4 digits).
NACE is the standard European classification of productive economic activities. It provides a compartmentalized breakdown such that each NACE code may be associated with a statistical unit carrying out the corresponding activities. NACE codes are available in RAMON, Eurostat's classification database: https://ec.europa.eu/eurostat/web/metadata/classifications.
Description of Activity 1 and NACE code*
Description of Activity 2 and NACE code*
Description of Activity x and NACE code*
690. Where applicable, explain whether the investment is likely to result in a significant change in the investor's profile or core business activities.
691. For example, also through the contribution of equity capital, subsidies, preferential loans, preferential tax treatment, etc.
692. The consolidated list of persons, groups, and entities subject to EU financial sanctions can be downloaded from the Financial Sanctions Database - FSF, available at the following address: https://webgate.ec.europa.eu/europeaid/fsd/fsf. Access to this platform requires an "EU Login" account.
For more information on ownership and control in the context of EU sanctions, refer to the EU Best Practices for the effective implementation of restrictive measures and to the Commission Opinion of 19 June 2020 on Article 2 of Council Regulation (EU) No. 269/2014.
Note that additional sectoral sanctions (not included in the FSF platform) may apply to the proposed transaction. For a complete overview of EU sanctions, consult the website: www.sanctionsmap.eu.
693. possible source of information on U.S. sanctions is available at the following address: https://sanctionssearch.ofac.treas.gov/
694. If the shareholding structure is complex, provide details on the direct acquirer, the ultimate owner, and any significant intermediary entities.
—Provide a list of all countries involved in the transaction on the investor's side.
—Where possible, include an organizational chart to illustrate the horizontal and vertical relationships among the entities mentioned.
—Where available, the information may also be presented in the form of a diagram (as an annex).

Other Review Procedures under National or EU Law

The form also requires the following:

—Whether the transaction is or will be subject to a merger control review [695] under EU or national law

—Whether the investment [696] is subject to another authorization procedure [697] or inquiry in the Member State conducting the screening, another EU Member State, or a third country (if applicable)

Additional Information Required for the Review

Under the French FDI screening procedure, the Treasury Department (Direction générale du Trésor), through its dedicated unit (CIEF), may [698] request additional information or supporting documentation from the applicant.

Under French administrative law [699], an incomplete application cannot be rejected solely for missing documents. However, if a missing document is essential for the review of the application, the authorization cannot be granted until the relevant document is received by the administration.

The completeness of the application is assessed in accordance with the amended Ministerial Order [700] of 31 December 2019, which establishes the list of documents to be provided for both authorization requests and preliminary review requests.

---

695. If the case has not yet been submitted for merger control, indicate the expected filing date or timeframe. Provide the case number and refer to the "Database for Merger Cases" (Competition Policy).

696. For example, national competition control, prudential supervision, or sector-specific licensing or certification.

697. Specify the type of control and the country responsible for it.

698. See Point 2.1.3.2.1 in Ministry of the Economy, Finance and Industrial and Digital Sovereignty, Directorate General of the Treasury, "Guidelines on the Foreign Direct Investment Screening in France" July 2025, Published July 30, 2025, Consulted August 1, 2025, available at https://www.tresor.economie.gouv.fr/services-aux-entreprises/investissements-etrangers-en-france

699. France, Code of Relations between the Public and the Administration, Article L. 114-5-1:
Where an application submitted to the administration is incomplete, the administration shall inform the applicant of the missing documents and information required under the applicable legislative and regulatory provisions. It shall set a deadline for the receipt of those documents and information.
The time period referred to in Article L. 114-3, upon the expiry of which, in the absence of an express decision, the application is deemed to have been approved, shall begin to run only upon receipt of the required documents and information.
The time period mentioned in the same article, upon the expiry of which the application is deemed to have been rejected in the absence of an express decision, shall be suspended during the time allotted for providing the required documents and information. However, the production of such documents and information before the expiry of the deadline shall end this suspension.
The list of missing documents and information, the deadline for their submission, and a reference to the relevant provisions, either the second or third paragraph of this Article, as appropriate, shall appear in the acknowledgment of receipt provided for in Article L. 112-3. If the acknowledgment has already been issued, these elements shall be communicated to the applicant by letter.

700. France, Ministerial Order of December 31, 2019, on foreign investments in France, Official Journal of the French Republic, No. 0001, January 1, 2020, NOR: ECOT1937237A, as amended by Ministerial Order of December 28, 2023, on foreign investments in France, Official Journal of the French Republic, No. 0301, December 29, 2023, NOR: ECOT2334928A

This assessment involves two criteria:
(i) the material submission of all required documents and information, and
(ii) the sufficiency and quality of the content provided.

As an example, an application that formally includes all required items but fails to detail the target company's activities, by merely stating its business sector or corporate purpose, or listing a few clients without describing the services rendered, will not be deemed complete.

During the review phase, the Treasury Department (CIEF) may request any necessary additional information or documents. The applicant is legally obligated to provide these, and may not invoke [701] legally protected secrecy in response, confirming the overriding public interest in safeguarding national interests.

Such a request suspends regulatory deadlines between the date of the request and the date of receipt of the additional materials.

The CIEF May Request Supplementary Documentation

The review of the application file by the Directorate General of the Treasury, along with any other competent administrative authorities, may give rise to requests for additional information or supporting documents [702].

The completeness of the application is assessed by the relevant government departments based on the Ministerial Order [703] of 31 December 2019, which defines the required contents of both prior authorization requests and preliminary review requests.

This assessment covers both (i) the material submission of the documents and information required, and (ii) the quality and comprehensiveness of the information provided.

During the examination process, the competent unit in charge of the review (the Foreign Direct Investment Screening Office) – CIEF) may also request any further information or documents deemed necessary. The submitting party is required to comply with such requests, and may not invoke legally protected secrecy as a basis to withhold information, in accordance with Article L. 151-5 of the Monetary and Financial Code [704].

701. France, Monetary and Financial Code, Article L. 151-5: "*The investor or the company carrying out the activities referred to in Article L. 151-3 shall, upon request, provide the administrative authority responsible for the authorization and review procedure for foreign investments with any documents and information necessary for the performance of its duties. Legally protected secrets may not be invoked against the authority.*"

702. See Point 2.1.3.2.1 in Ministry of the Economy, Finance and Industrial and Digital Sovereignty, Directorate General of the Treasury, "Guidelines on the Foreign Direct Investment Screening in France" July 2025, Published July 30, 2025, Consulted August 1, 2025, available at https://www.tresor.economie.gouv.fr/services-aux-entreprises/investissements-etrangers-en-france

703. France, Ministerial Order of 31 December 2019 on Foreign Investments in France, Official Journal of the French Republic, No. 0001, 1 January 2020, NOR: ECOT1937237A

704. Monetary and Financial Code, Article L. 151-5: "*The investor or the undertaking carrying out the activities referred to in Article L. 151-3 shall be required, upon request, to provide the administrative authority responsible for the authorization and screening procedure for foreign investments with all docu-*

Completeness of the Application File Triggers the Start of the Review Timeline

As regards the applicable regulatory deadlines, it must be recalled that they are contingent upon the completeness of the application for prior authorization (see above). This completeness is assessed by the French authorities in accordance with the Order [705] of 31 December 2019, which sets out [706] the required content of such application files. (and for requests for a prior review, see Chapter 16).

The administration has clarified [707] that the completeness review covers both (i) the materiality of the documents and elements to be submitted and (ii) the quality, exhaustiveness, and level of detail of the information provided. By way of illustration, a filing that formally includes all the elements required by regulation but fails to provide details regarding the target company's activities, merely stating its business sector or corporate purpose, or listing only a few clients without specifying the services performed for them, cannot be deemed complete.

The administration [708] has also clarified that the regulatory timeline begins on the day the application is received, meaning the day it is filed, provided that filing occurs on a business day (Monday through Friday, excluding public holidays) and within the designated submission window (before 5:00 p.m.). The timeline does not start from the day the administration acknowledges receipt of the application. If the application is submitted on a weekend, a public holiday, or outside business hours, the timeline begins on the next business day

This timeline is suspended if the application is deemed incomplete (see above). In such cases, pursuant to Article L. 114-5 of the Code on Relations Between the Public and the Administration [709], the clock is paused during the period between the date

---

ments and information necessary for the performance of its duties. No legally protected secrets may be invoked against the authority."

705. France, Ministerial Order of 31 December 2019 on foreign investments in France, Official Journal of the French Republic, No. 0001, 1 January 2020, NOR: ECOT1937237A, as amended by Ministerial Order of 28 December 2023 on foreign investments in France, Official Journal of the French Republic, No. 0301, 29 December 2023, NOR: ECOT2334928A

706. Also the one concerning prior review requests.

707. See Section 2.1.3.2.1 in Ministry of the Economy, Finance and Industrial and Digital Sovereignty, Directorate General of the Treasury, "Guidelines on the Foreign Direct Investment Screening in France," July 2025, published July 30, 2025, consulted August 1, 2025, available at https://www.tresor.economie.gouv.fr/services-aux-entreprises/investissements-etrangers-en-france

708. Ibid, See Point 2.2.3.1.2.

709. France, Monetary and Financial Code, Article L. 114-5 – " *Incomplete applications and impact on regulatory timelines When an application submitted to the administration is incomplete, the administration shall inform the applicant of the missing documents and information required under the applicable legislative and regulatory provisions. It shall set a deadline for the receipt of such documents and information.*
The time limit referred to in Article L. 114-3, at the end of which the application is deemed to be accepted in the absence of an express decision, shall run only from the date on which the required documents and information are received.
The time limit referred to in the same article, at the end of which the application is deemed to be rejected in the absence of an express decision, shall be suspended during the period granted for the submission of the required documents and information. However, if the applicant submits the documents and information before the deadline set, the suspension shall end on the date of that submission.
The list of missing documents and information, the deadline set for their submission, and a reference to the provisions applicable, either the second or third paragraph of this article, as the case may be, shall

on which the administration requests supplemental information and the date on which the requested documents or information are provided.

Given that administrative silence constitutes implicit denial under French law, the administration also stresses the importance of promptly submitting any observations or clarifications so that the authorities have sufficient time to consider them within the applicable timeframe.

For prior notifications concerning the crossing of the 10 percent threshold of voting rights in a French-law company whose shares are admitted to trading on a regulated market, the administration recalls [710] that the absence of a response within ten business days from the date of notification implies that a waiver of the requirement to file an authorization request is granted. In such case, the contemplated investment may be completed without prior authorization. This waiver does not constitute a determination as to whether the target company's activities fall within the scope of Article R. 151-3 of the French Monetary and Financial Code.

Conversely, if the Minister issues a letter of opposition, the foreign investor must then file a formal request for authorization with the Minister before completing the transaction. The timelines set forth in Article R. 151-6 of the Monetary and Financial Code begin to run as of the date on which the investor submits its authorization request.

The waiver of the authorization requirement is valid only with respect to the factual and legal circumstances existing as of the date of the request.

It is incumbent upon the transaction parties to account for the FDI screening timelines in the broader deal schedule. The Minister is not bound by the contractual timetable agreed upon by the parties. That said, when duly substantiated, specific constraints, such as pending insolvency proceedings or urgent liquidity issues, may be taken into consideration by the authorities.

The Administration Takes Into Account the Complexity of the Materials to Be Gathered

Completeness of the application file is a key procedural milestone, as it determines whether the legal conditions have been met for the review timeline to commence.

The administration [711] acknowledges that, in certain contexts, particularly transactions governed by foreign legal regimes or those involving hostile public tender offers, investors may face practical difficulties in obtaining all relevant documents and information regarding the target entity or entities.

---

appear in the acknowledgment of receipt provided for in Article L. 112-3. If the acknowledgment of receipt has already been issued, this information shall be provided to the applicant by letter."

710. See Point 2.3.3 in Ministry of the Economy, Finance and Industrial and Digital Sovereignty, Directorate General of the Treasury, "Guidelines on the Foreign Direct Investment Screening in France" July 2025, Published 30 July 2025, consulted 1 August 2025, available at https://www.tresor.economie.gouv.fr/services-aux-entreprises/investissements-etrangers-en-france

711. Ibid, see Point 2.2.3.1.2.

Nevertheless, the French FDI Screening Office (CIEF) requires the investor to submit all documents in its possession or to which it may lawfully gain access. Where appropriate, the CIEF may also request directly from the target entity the production of documents or information necessary for the review. These materials are not intended to be shared with the investor, in order to protect confidentiality and trade secrets.

The Two Review Phases Are Capped at a Maximum of 75 Business Days

The total duration of the FDI review procedure is a critical concern. Beyond a basic administrative requirement, it ensures predictability and enables the parties to manage cross-border timelines, particularly when simultaneous filings are required in multiple jurisdictions.

The length of the review period is also a key indicator[712] of the credibility and reliability of the screening mechanism.

Under Article R. 151-6 of the Monetary and Financial Code, the statutory deadline for the review of FDI applications is 75 business days maximum.

This places France in line with the European average[713] of approximately 3.5 months, comparable to Italy (2.5 months), Denmark and Austria (3 months), and significantly shorter than Germany or Spain, where reviews may take over 6 months.

The review is structured as follows:

- Phase 1: a preliminary review period of up to 30 business days, beginning on the date the application is deemed complete. (See Chapter 18)
- Phase 2: a supplemental review period (also referred to as an "in-depth examination") of up to 45 additional business days, which may be initiated by express decision of the Minister no later than the end of Phase 1. (See Chapter 19)

Notably, the 45-day clock for Phase 2 starts running from the date the investor is notified of the opening of this second phase, regardless of the end date of Phase 1. Parties should plan accordingly, particularly in light of the definition of business days, to avoid undue timing pressure from external transaction constraints.

712. France, National Assembly, Report No. 897 rect., April 19, 2018, MARLEIX O., Chair, KASBARIAN G., Rapporteur, Members of Parliament, submitted on behalf of the fact-finding committee tasked with examining the State's decisions in industrial policy in light of recent corporate mergers, notably in the cases of Alstom, Alcatel and STX, and the tools available to protect France's industrial champions in a globalized trade environment, Vol. 1, see for example Proposal No. 28: "Amend Articles R. 153-7 and R. 153-8 of the Monetary and Financial Code to provide for new instruction deadlines." (a one-month period for the advance ruling procedure; a two-month period for prior authorization requests starting from the submission of a complete file; a two-month period extendable by 30 days at the request of specialized intelligence services if the transaction requires an in-depth review), available at https://www.assemblee-nationale.fr/dyn/15/rapports/cepolind/l15b0897-ti_rapport-enquete (last accessed September 1st, 2025)

713. France, Ministry of the Economy, Finance and Industrial and Digital Sovereignty, Directorate General of the Treasury, Annual Report 2024, "Foreign Direct Investment Screening in France", consulted 1 September 2025, available at https://www.tresor.economie.gouv.fr/Articles/5ed9606f-f37e-4517-ae5d-445dab7ecad0/files/68cd8466-0b98-44d2-9182-777b8768cee0

If additional requests for information are issued during Phase 2, the timeline is not suspended pending submission of those supplemental elements.

The Foreign Investor May Withdraw from the Procedure at Any Time

The foreign investor is free to withdraw its application at any point prior to the Minister's decision [714]. The withdrawal must be formally notified to the French Treasury Department, either directly by the investor or through its duly authorized counsel.

In addition, the parties remain free to abandon the transaction even after having obtained FDI clearance. In such cases, the non-completion of the transaction must be notified to the Treasury Department.

Instruction timelines take into account insolvency and restructuring proceedings

The provisions of the French Monetary and Financial Code do not establish any special fast-track procedure when the French entity concerned is subject to *mandat ad hoc*, conciliation, safeguard, judicial reorganization (*redressement judiciaire*), or liquidation proceedings.

Nevertheless, in the context of such collective procedures, foreign capital contributions are often essential to preserve companies in financial distress [715]. These inflows must therefore be reconciled with France's foreign direct investment (FDI) screening regime in order to safeguard national interests.

Accordingly, the review of FDI filings is adapted to the constrained timetable and specific requirements of the insolvency or restructuring process [716].

To the extent possible, the Minister's decision under the foreign investment regulations is issued prior to the hearing of the Commercial Court that rules on the full or partial sale of the French entity in light of the bids submitted by domestic and foreign acquirers, in accordance with Article L. 631-22 of the French Commercial Code.

---

714. See Point 2.2.3.7 in Ministry of the Economy, Finance and Industrial and Digital Sovereignty, Directorate General of the Treasury, "Guidelines on the Foreign Direct Investment Screening in France" July 2025, Published 30 July 2025, consulted 1 August 2025, available at https://www.tresor.economie.gouv.fr/services-aux-entreprises/investissements-etrangers-en-france

715. In 2024, nearly 65,000 French companies were placed under collective proceedings. Many of them, facing difficulties in securing financing from domestic actors, were therefore compelled to turn to foreign investors. Source: France, Ministry of the Economy, Finance, Industrial and Digital Sovereignty, Directorate General of the Treasury, Annual Report 2025, " Foreign Direct Investment Screening in France," published 30 July 2025, consulted 31 July 2025, available at https://www.tresor.economie.gouv.fr/Articles/2025/07/30/publication-du-rapport-annuel-sur-le-controle-ief-en-2024

716. See Point 2.1.4 in Ministry of the Economy, Finance and Industrial and Digital Sovereignty, Directorate General of the Treasury, "Guidelines on the Foreign Direct Investment Screening in France," July 2025, Published 30 July 2025, Consulted 1 August 2025, available at https://www.tresor.economie.gouv.fr/services-aux-entreprises/investissements-etrangers-en-france

It is strongly recommended that court-appointed administrators (*administrateurs judiciaires*) and potential acquirers contact the Directorate General of the Treasury (DG Trésor) as early as possible, well before the formal submission of offers.

To ensure proper coordination, the Treasury's FDI screening unit works closely with public actors involved in restructuring, namely, the Interministerial Committee for Industrial Restructuring[717] (CIRI), the Interministerial Delegation for Business Restructuring (DIRE), as well as judicial administrators. This cooperation makes it possible to align the FDI review procedure with all stages of insolvency proceedings (conciliation, judicial reorganization, liquidation) and to secure investment decisions.

Although the FDI screening review remains legally independent from proceedings before the Commercial Courts, its timelines are adjusted to the constraints of collective procedures and court hearing schedules. In 2024, for example, the average review period for cases involving judicial reorganization was 20 business days, well below the regulatory deadlines (30 business days for the first phase, and more than 45 business days if a second phase is triggered).

For the administration, the success[718] of this coordination depends on anticipation. Early notification of the FDI screening unit, whether regarding an intended takeover offer by a foreign investor or a request for a preliminary review, improves efficiency, shortens decision-making timelines, and increases the chances of rescuing distressed companies.

*
* *

The official review phase begins with the filing of the prior authorization request. This initiates a process that is governed by clearly defined legal and procedural rules designed to ensure a predictable framework. However, such predictability does not guarantee outcome certainty, the Minister retains broad discretion in rendering the final decision, especially when additional examination is deemed necessary.

---

717. France, Decree No. 2017-1558 of 13 November 2017 establishing an interministerial delegate for corporate restructuring, Official Journal of the French Republic, No. 0265, 14 November 2017, NOR: ECOI1730715D

718. In 2024, 17 decisions were issued in this context, compared to 9 in 2023, underscoring the growing importance of effective coordination between FDI screening and insolvency proceedings. Source: Ministry of the Economy, Finance, Industrial and Digital Sovereignty, Directorate General of the Treasury, Annual Report 2025, "Foreign Direct Investment Screening in France," published 30 July 2025, consulted 31 July 2025, available at https://www.tresor.economie.gouv.fr/Articles/2025/07/30/publication-du-rapport-annuel-sur-le-controle-ief-en-2024.

Chapter 18

The First Phase of the Review: The Initial Screening Procedure

Once all documents required for the foreign investment authorization request have been submitted and the application is deemed complete by the French Foreign Direct Investment Screening Authority (CIEF), the review process conducted by the Ministry of the Economy may begin. This initial review phase is subject to a regulatory deadline of 30 business days.

The initial phase lasts a maximum of 30 business days

Pursuant to Article R. 151-6 of the Monetary and Financial Code, the timeline for the review of a foreign investment authorization request is clearly defined. Within 30 business days from the date the application is received, the Minister of the Economy must inform the investor either that (i) the proposed investment does not fall within the scope of the foreign investment screening regime, (ii) it does, but is authorized without conditions, or (iii) it does, and a further review is necessary to assess whether conditions must be imposed to safeguard national interests [719].

If the administration fails to respond within the 30-business-day period, the authorization request is deemed rejected by default.

More specifically, pursuant to Article R. 151-6 of the Monetary and Financial Code, the Minister of the Economy may choose one of the following three options:

1° The Minister may declare that the investment is not subject to the French FDI screening regime

The Minister may first determine that the transaction does not fall within the scope of France's FDI screening regime and issue a formal non-eligibility decision.

719. as defined under Paragraph I of Article L. 151-3 of the Monetary and Financial Codeand which encompass activities carried out in France that, even on an occasional basis, either involve the exercise of public authority or fall within one of the following areas:
(a) Activities likely to adversely affect public order, public security, or national defense interests;
(b) Activities involving the research, production, or marketing of weapons, ammunition, powders, and explosive substances.

This decision has several legal and procedural consequences.

- First, it enables the investor to obtain an official "out-of-scope" letter, effectively closing the procedure with no further action required.
- Second, it provides the investor with legal certainty. The investor cannot be held liable for carrying out a transaction that may, in retrospect, appear to satisfy the three eligibility criteria, if the State did not identify such eligibility during the review, unless the investor acted fraudulently or deliberately circumvented the authorization process (see Chapter 21).

This safeguard is particularly important in cases where the State may have failed to appreciate the sensitive nature of the target company's activities, especially where these relate to public authority functions or critical technologies (see Chapter 13).

As reiterated by the French administration [720], when at least one of the three cumulative criteria justifying FDI screening (see Chapters 10 et seq.) is not met, the Minister issues a decision declaring that the proposed investment falls outside the scope of the screening regime.

It is important to note that a non-eligibility decision does not imply that the target company's activities are irrelevant to national security interests. Such a decision may be issued even if the target operates in highly sensitive sectors, provided that the foreign investor criterion is not met (e.g., the investor's ownership structure is entirely French), or if the transaction itself does not qualify (e.g., greenfield projects, no change of control, no French entity involved, etc.).

Crucially, a non-eligibility decision does not exempt the investor from all governmental oversight. Investors must consider whether the activity may fall under other sector-specific regulations or raise political sensitivities. Lawmakers, for instance, may view with concern the exclusion of a highly sensitive transaction solely due to a technicality, such as failing to meet the control threshold.

Unlike in the authorization regime, no post-transaction notification is required for non-eligible operations.

2° The Minister may authorize the investment without conditions

The Minister may also conclude that the investment is eligible for screening but does not raise any concerns that would justify a further review or conditional approval. In this case, a simple authorization is issued.

This outcome aligns with the foundational principle of the French FDI framework: foreign investment in France is presumed free and lawful. Restrictions or prohibitions are the exception, not the rule.

---

720. France, Ministry of the Economy, Finance and Industrial and Digital Sovereignty, Directorate General of the Treasury, "Guidelines on the Foreign Direct Investment Screening in France" July 2025, see Section 2.2.3.2.1, published July 30, 2025, consulted August 1, 2025, available at https://www.tresor.economie.gouv.fr/services-aux-entreprises/investissements-etrangers-en-france

Authorized investments must be notified once completed

As the administration emphasizes [721], the completion of an investment transaction that has received ministerial authorization must, pursuant to Article R. 151-11 of the Monetary and Financial Code, be declared to the Directorate General of the Treasury. This declaration is to be made by the investor within two months following the completion of the investment, as defined under Article R. 151-2 of the said Code.

The declaration must be submitted electronically to the address iefautorisations@dgtresor.gouv.fr and must include the information prescribed in Article 3 of the Order [722] of 31 December 2019.

It shall specify:
1. The date the transaction was completed;
2. The ownership structure of the target entity post-transaction;
3. The actual investment amount, if available, or an updated estimate with an explanation of the valuation method;
4. Any changes in the ownership chain of the target company since the date of authorization.

This last point ensures that any minor changes to the investor's acquisition structure, such as the interposition of a new investment vehicle, are disclosed, provided that such changes do not alter the identity of the ultimate controlling entity.

No specific form is required for this post-completion declaration; a simple letter or email is sufficient.

No such notification is required when the transaction was previously deemed non-eligible. Similarly, if the transaction is not carried out (e.g., the deal is abandoned), no formal declaration is required, although notifying the DG Trésor is still recommended.

3° The Minister may initiate a Phase II review

Lastly, the Minister may decide that the proposed investment raises unresolved concerns and requires a Phase II in-depth review (see next chapter). In this case, a formal decision is issued to initiate the complementary phase (also named Phase 2).

This second phase is launched to determine whether the protection of national interests [723] requires the imposition of specific conditions on the transaction. The decision to approve the investment, with or without conditions, will be made at the end of this extended review.

721. See Point 3.1 in Ministry of the Economy, Finance and Industrial and Digital Sovereignty, Directorate General of the Treasury, "Guidelines on the Foreign Direct Investment Screening in France July 2025, Published July 30, 2025, Consulted August 1, 2025, available at https://www.tresor.economie.gouv.fr/services-aux-entreprises/investissements-etrangers-en-france
722. France, Ministerial Order of December 31, 2019, on foreign investments in France, Official Journal of the French Republic, No. 0001, January 1, 2020, NOR: ECOT1937237A
723. France, Monetary and Financial Code, Article L. 151-3, Paragraph I

*
* *

This initial review phase functions as a triage mechanism for foreign investment filings. By the end of the 30-business-day period, the Minister of the Economy may:

- grant a de facto "safe harbor" by declaring the investment outside the scope of the screening regime;
- authorize the transaction outright; or
- proceed to a more in-depth Phase II review if national interests may still be at risk.

In 2024 [724], 390 decisions (eligibility, non-eligibility, in-depth review) were issued in connection with applications for foreign investment authorization, compared to 255 in 2023. A total of 182 foreign investments were authorized under the French FDI screening regime, 98 of which were subject to conditions, representing 54 percent.

724. France, Ministry of the Economy, Finance and Industrial and Digital Sovereignty, Directorate General of the Treasury, Annual Report 2025, "Foreign Direct Investment Screening in France," Published 30 July 2025, consulted 31 July 2025, available at https://www.tresor.economie.gouv.fr/Articles/2025/07/30/publication-du-rapport-annuel-sur-le-controle-ief-en-2024

Chapter 19

The Second Phase of the Screening Procedure: In-Depth Review Process

The launch of an in-depth review, also referred to as supplementary examination, is reserved, according to the French administration [725], for the most sensitive or complex cases. These are situations where either the necessity of imposing conditions to safeguard national interests becomes evident, or the complexity of the transaction requires further examination to assess whether such conditions are needed.

Extension of the second-phase review period by up to 45 business days

Pursuant to Article R. 151-6 of the French Monetary and Financial Code, the final decision, either a refusal or an authorization, with or without conditions, must be issued within 45 business days. This period begins upon the receipt by the investor of the ministerial decision taken at the conclusion of the first phase. The notification is addressed to the investor who filed the authorization request, as well as to any co-investors designated as responsible for complying with the imposed conditions [726].

If no response is issued within the prescribed time limit, the request is deemed rejected by default.

At the conclusion of the in-depth review, the Minister of the Economy has three options:

1. The Minister may grant the authorization subject to conditions

At the end of the in-depth review phase, the Minister may decide to approve the transaction while imposing specific conditions. The imposition of conditions logically

725. See Point 2.2.3.3 in Ministry of the Economy, Finance and Industrial and Digital Sovereignty, Directorate General of the Treasury, "Guidelines on the Foreign Direct Investment Screening in France" July 2025, Published 30 July 2025, Consulted 1 August 2025, available at https://www.tresor.economie.gouv.fr/services-aux-entreprises/investissements-etrangers-en-france

726. France, Monetary and Financial Code, Article R. 151-8, II

results from the inability to render a definitive decision during the first phase, whether to reject the request outright or to grant unconditional approval.

Under the French foreign investment screening framework, conditional authorizations are intended to preserve national interests. Accordingly, the conditions must be justified by the need to protect public order, public security, or national defense, and they must be proportionate to that objective [727].

These conditions are defined under Article R. 151-8 of the Monetary and Financial Code and may notably include:

- Ensuring the continuity and security of sensitive activities conducted on French territory and protecting any related information. For example: ensuring the continuation of a defense production activity in France, in order to prevent the risk that it might be subjected to the laws of a foreign state that could hinder its operation [728].
- Safeguarding the know-how and expertise of the French target entity. For example: ensuring that a patent portfolio originating from a sensitive field of medical research remains owned and operated by a French company [729].
- Restructuring the internal organization or governance of the French entity, as well as regulating the exercise of rights acquired by the investor. For example: establishing within the target entity a security committee responsible for overseeing the implementation of the conditions and subjecting the entity's strategic decisions to the prior authorization of a State representative [730].
- Defining the terms of information-sharing between the transaction parties and the French government . For example: submitting to the State authorities an annual report detailing the measures implemented to ensure compliance with the conditions, and accommodating an on-site inspection by the State authorities at one of the entity's industrial facilities [731].

In addition, the Minister may require the investor to divest part of the acquired capital or one or more business segments of the French target entity to an entity other than the investor and approved by the Minister.

As the administration [732] recalls, the duration of conditions imposed under the French FDI screening regime may range from a few years to the entire period during which the investor holds the rights over the French entity that triggered the screening

727. France, National Assembly, Written Question No. 2307 to the Minister of the Economy and Finance, Official Journal of the National Assembly, October 18, 2022, COLOMBIER, Caroline, Member of Parliament, Rassemblement National (RN); ministerial reply, December 20, 2022, Official Journal of the National Assembly, p. 6470. The Minister of the Economy confirms as soon as possible that "these conditions are still proportionate to the identified risk."

728. France, Ministry of the Economy, Finance and Industrial and Digital Sovereignty, Directorate General of the Treasury, Annual Report 2025, "Foreign Direct Investment Screening in France," Published July 30, 2025, consulted July 31, 2025, available at https://www.tresor.economie.gouv.fr/Articles/2025/07/30/publication-du-rapport-annuel-sur-le-controle-ief-en-2024

729. ibid

730. ibid

731. ibid

732. France, Ministry of the Economy, Finance, Industrial and Digital Sovereignty, Directorate General of the Treasury, "Guidelines on the Foreign Direct Investment Screening in France" July 2025, see Point 2.2.3.3, published July 30, 2025, consulted August 1, 2025, available at https://www.tresor.economie.gouv.fr/services-aux-entreprises/investissements-etrangers-en-france

obligation (e.g., acquisition of control, crossing of a voting rights threshold, or purchase of a business line). However, changes in the economic environment during this period may affect the economic viability of certain conditions imposed by the State, which can lead the investor, despite its prior commitment, to request their revision.

Regarding the duration of ministerial decisions, the administration [733] further specifies that the Monetary and Financial Code contains no provision establishing a validity period for decisions rendered under the FDI screening regime. Such decisions are issued based solely on the circumstances of fact and law existing at the time of the request. Consequently, changes in the target company's activities, the structure of the contemplated transaction, or the occurrence of a similar transaction several years later may lead to a different outcome. Likewise, regulatory changes may also occur. Thus, a finding of non-eligibility by the Minister cannot be interpreted as an absolute guarantee that a future, similar transaction would be deemed non-eligible if the circumstances underlying the initial decision have since changed.

Where an investment transaction has been authorized by the Minister of the Economy, the transaction must be completed within a reasonable period and without any change in fact or law that would alter the initial assessment of the activities or the contemplated transaction. Otherwise, the authorization becomes null and void, and the investor must submit a new application for prior authorization.

In the event of a shift from exclusive to joint control, the investor remains bound by the conditions imposed at the time of its exclusive acquisition of control. Nevertheless, the investor may seek a revision of such conditions on the basis of changes in the ownership structure of the target entity.

The Minister may also take into account any links between the investor and a foreign government or public body. These links may take various forms: ownership (direct or indirect shareholding by public companies or entities, or public controlling influence), financial support (subsidies, loans, grants, or tax exemptions), decisive or political influence (appointment of directors, control over strategic decisions, or determination of the framework of activities), or the investor's submission to a foreign regulatory regime imposing extraordinary obligations toward a foreign State (such as disclosure requirements or prior approval for strategic decisions).

Accordingly, while the FDI screening regime applies without discrimination based on the investor's nationality, the existence of such links with a foreign government or public body is a factor in the risk assessment. Particular scrutiny is given to opaque or complex investment structures and arrangements.

Finally, the ministerial decision must clearly identify the entity or entities within the investor's ownership chain that will be responsible for compliance with the imposed conditions. The designated level is the most relevant one, i.e., the entity possessing the decision-making authority, as well as the human, legal, and financial resources to ensure compliance and, if necessary, to assume the consequences of any enforcement measure in the event of non-compliance. In practice, this cannot, for

733. Ibid, See Point 2.2.3.5.

instance, be the mere investment vehicle created for the transaction; in certain cases, it may be the ultimate controlling entity, though not systematically so.

These conditions are negotiated with the investor, who must sign them prior to receiving formal notification of the Minister's decision. They are binding for the entire period during which the investor exercises control over the French entity, or for a specific duration. Conditions may be revised at the investor's request or on the Minister's own initiative, under the terms set out in Article R. 151-9 of the Monetary and Financial Code.

It should also be noted that the issue of conditional authorizations, and the monitoring of related commitments, is a recurrent topic in public debate. Legislative proposals[734] have been submitted to clarify the criteria applicable to the issuance of prior authorization.

2. The Minister may grant unconditional authorization

At the conclusion of the in-depth review phase, the Minister of the Economy may, as a second option, authorize the investment without attaching any specific conditions. Indeed, where the supplementary review reveals that the imposition of conditions does not appear necessary and proportionate to the protection of the national interests referred to in Article L. 151-3 of the Monetary and Financial Code, the Minister will issue an unconditional authorization.

As in the initial review phase, the decision to authorize the investment transaction without conditions may also be rendered during the in-depth review phase (Phase 2). Although the supplementary review is ordinarily intended to determine the appropriate conditions, it may nevertheless, in certain cases, lead to the granting of an unconditional authorization.

3. The Minister may reject the transaction

Finally, the Minister may choose to reject the investment transaction, either by issuing an express decision or by remaining silent beyond the regulatory deadline (in which case the request is deemed refused).

---

734. France, National Assembly, Bill No. 2857 of April 28, 2020, tabled by Members of Parliament Olivier MARLEIX et al., Les Républicains (LR) group, aiming to better defend France's productive assets in strategic sectors during asset acquisition operations by a foreign investor, proposing to amend Article L. 153-1, II of the Monetary and Financial Code as follows: "II. The authorization granted by the Minister of the Economy is subject to conditions ensuring that the proposed investment does not undermine the national interests referred to in I. The Minister shall ensure, for the activities concerned: the maintenance of production capacities on national territory; the maintenance of sufficient research and development effort to ensure the company's sustainability and performance; the ownership and usage rights of patents; where applicable, the autonomy of management of all or part of the company through a dedicated board of directors appointed with the Minister's approval; the protection of classified defense information."

According to Article R. 151-10 of the Monetary and Financial Code, a refusal may only be based on limited grounds: concerns regarding the investor's integrity (honorabilité), or a finding that no set of conditions would be sufficient to adequately safeguard national interests.

Such a decision is extremely rare and usually reflects an insurmountable deadlock (see also Chapter 5). Nevertheless, it remains possible, as the administration[735] has recorded six refusals over the past three years[736]. Notably, and somewhat unexpectedly, of the two refusals publicly announced, both were made not by the Minister of the Economy but by the Minister of the Armed Forces. These refusals were issued on the grounds that it was impossible to establish conditions capable of ensuring the preservation of national interests.

In addition to these refusals, several authorization requests have, in certain circumstances, been voluntarily withdrawn by the investor before a formal refusal was issued, or when the investor anticipated difficulties in pursuing the transaction under the conditions imposed by the Minister.

Finally, the question arises as to the consequences for the transaction once a refusal has been decided. In practice, a refusal, whether publicly disclosed or not, directly impacts the valuation of the asset, which is de facto deprived of a purchaser. On this point, parliamentary deliberations have led to the proposal to create a strategic holding and investment vehicle that would enable the State to substitute itself for the excluded foreign investor, thereby allowing the seller to dispose of the asset at market value.

*
* *

By establishing a dedicated in-depth review phase, French authorities provide a structured period for resolving any concerns that could jeopardize the protection of national interests. Only when no viable safeguards can be implemented, or when proposed conditions prove unacceptable to the investor, will the Minister issue a refusal. Such decisions remain extremely rare and typically reflect a fundamental, irreconcilable impasse. (See also Chapter 5)

---

735. France, Ministry of the Economy, Finance and Industrial and Digital Sovereignty, Directorate General of the Treasury, Annual Report 2025, "Foreign Direct Investment Screening in France," Published July 30, 2025, consulted July 31, 2025, available at https://www.tresor.economie.gouv.fr/Articles/2025/07/30/publication-du-rapport-annuel-sur-le-controle-ief-en-2024

736. Only two refusals have been officially announced: in 2021, the proposed acquisition of Photonis by the U.S. group Teledyne Technologies, and in 2023, the proposed acquisition of Segault by Velan.

Diagram of the FDI Screening Procedure in France[737]

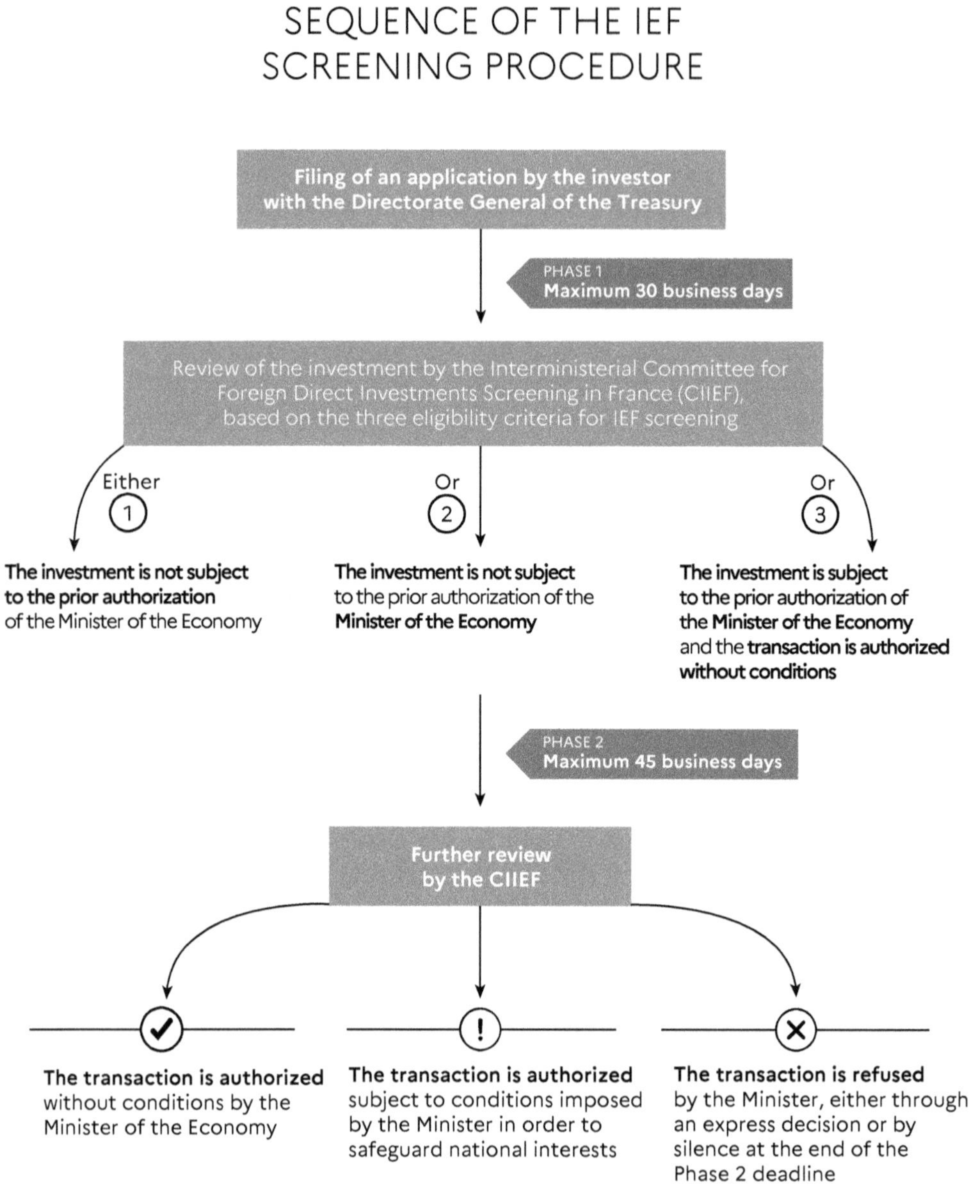

737. Diagram prepared in accordance with Articles L. 321-1 et seq. of the Code des relations entre le public et l'administration (France) (CRPA); source: France, Ministry for the Economy, Finance and Industrial and Digital Sovereignty, Directorate General of the Treasury, Annual Report 2024, *Contrôle des investissements étrangers en France* ("Foreign Investment Screening in France"), published July 30, 2025, available at https://www.tresor.economie.gouv.fr/Articles/2025/07/30/publication-du-rapport-annuel-sur-le-controle-ief-en-2024 (last accessed July 31, 2025).

Part IV

Enforcement of the French FDI Screening Mechanism

This fourth part of the book addresses the enforcement phase of the foreign direct investment (FDI) screening mechanism in France. In this regard, the monitoring of commitments (Chapter 20) is of paramount importance, as it is the fulfillment of these undertakings that allows for the issuance of prior authorization. As binding as they may be, such commitments are not immutable and may be subject to modification. Moreover, because these commitments are known only to the parties involved, any communication concerning them must above all preserve national security interests and the confidentiality of business secrets . Their critical importance warrants regular oversight, and the coordination of this monitoring between the investor and the competent authorities falls under the responsibility of a dedicated operational point of contact.

Furthermore, the issue of non-compliance with obligations and commitments (Chapter 21) is also of significant relevance, particularly in light of the administrative enforcement regime and the Minister of the Economy's power to impose financial or criminal sanctions, especially in cases involving the fraudulent obtaining of an authorization.

Lastly, the question of legal challenges to FDI screening decisions (Chapter 22) deserves to be addressed, as litigation in this field remains rare, but not without legal and strategic significance.

Chapter 20

Monitoring of Commitments: A Critical Element

The monitoring of investor commitments is a critical aspect of the French FDI screening mechanism, as the issuance of prior authorization, granted in the name of protecting national interests, is contingent upon the respect of these undertakings. Under the legal framework [738] governing foreign investments in France, the authorization granted to a foreign investor may, where appropriate, be made conditional upon certain commitments designed to ensure that the contemplated investment does not harm national interests. These commitments are formalized in a letter of undertakings (lettre d'engagement) (see Annex F).

Commitments Arising from Conditions Attached to the Authorization

When prior authorization is granted following the screening procedure, it may be subject to conditions. These conditions are explicitly provided for under French law and further regulated by Articles R. 151-6 et seq. of the Monetary and Financial Code.

In accordance [739] with its role as the interministerial secretariat, the bureau CIEF forwards each application it receives to the ministries likely to be concerned by the contemplated transaction or systematically involved in the review process. Several government departments may be consulted depending on the target company's business activities. In addition to the Ministry of the Armed Forces, this may include, for example, the Ministry of Health, the Ministry for the Ecological and Inclusive Transition, the General Secretariat for Defense and National Security (SGDSN), which oversees the protection of classified information, and the National Cybersecurity Agency of France (ANSSI) . These administrations are consulted on a case-by-case basis.

This in-depth and collective review, often spanning several weeks, is designed first to determine whether the FDI screening procedure applies to the contemplated transaction, based primarily on the nature of the activities carried out by the French target company (ies). Where applicable, the second objective is to define what the State seeks to protect and how it intends to ensure such protection, including the potential imposition of specific conditions.

738. France, Monetary and Financial Code, Article L. 151-3, Foreign investments subject to prior authorization
739. DUPEYRAT, op. cit.,

Where conditions are deemed necessary, the process culminates in the drafting of a letter of undertakings, which is signed by the investor and annexed to the authorization letter issued by the Minister of the Economy. Together, these documents constitute a conditional authorization.

While the specific content of undertakings may vary depending on the characteristics of each investment, in practice they tend to follow recurring [740] patterns. Accordingly, a typology of standard commitments can be established.

Commitments Relating to the Structure and Governance of the Target Entity

A first category of commitments aims to ensure the protection of all sensitive activities carried out by the target entity. These commitments may include the obligation to establish a dedicated legal structure, ideally, a company governed by French law, endowed with legal personality and its own governance bodies vested with autonomous decision-making powers in accordance with French corporate law.

A second set of commitments seeks to secure a certain degree of oversight through the composition of the management bodies of the future entity. The French authorities may, for instance, require that these governing bodies be composed primarily of executives who are either French or nationals of a Member State of the European Union.

Another key point concerns security clearances. The State may require that all legal and regulatory security clearances necessary for the continuation of certain activities carried out by the target entity, whether these concern natural persons or legal persons, be obtained and maintained in accordance with the procedures laid down in Interministerial General Instruction No. 1300 (IGI 1300) on the Protection of National Defense Secrets. Following the 2019 reform [741] of the rules governing the classification and protection of national defense secrets [742], IGI 1300 establishes the roles, responsibilities, and requirements applicable throughout the lifecycle of any classified information or material.

---

740. France, National Assembly, Committee for the Evaluation and Oversight of Public Policies, Information Report, No. 1453, JOLIVET, François, and de LEPINAU, Hervé (Members of Parliament), on the evaluation of foreign direct investment screening in France, Official Journal of the French Republic, May 27, 2025, text 45 of 69, published on May 22, 2025, available at https://www.assemblee-nationale.fr/dyn/17/rapports/cec/l17b1453_rapport-information (last accessed September 1st, 2025) "*Noting the impossibility of tailoring the obligations imposed on companies to the actual sensitivity of the assets concerned, the rapporteurs consider it problematic that the same obligations apply to all FDI projects across the 24 strategic sectors listed in the Monetary and Financial Code. Indeed, weapons manufacturing, cryptology activities, and infrastructures essential to national defense do not raise the same sovereignty concerns, strictly speaking, as other activities.*"

741. France, Decree No. 2019-1271 of December 2, 2019, on the procedures for the classification and protection of national defence secrecy, Official Journal of the French Republic, No. 0280, December 3, 2019, NOR: PRMD1928053D

742. France, Prime Minister, Secretariat-General for National Defence and Security, Interministerial General Instruction No. 1300/SGDSN/PSE/PSD of August 9, 2021, on the protection of national defence secrecy (IGI 1300), which defines the roles, responsibilities and requirements related to the lifecycle management of classified information or media, accessed September 1st, 2025, available at https://www.sgdsn.gouv.fr/files/files/Nos_missions/igi-1300-20210809.pdf

As recalled by ANSSI[743] (National Cybersecurity Agency of France), IGI 1300 applies to all individuals and entities that, in the performance of their duties, handle classified information. This includes not only all government administrations, but also private entities that, due to their status (e.g., operators of vital importance) or by virtue of entering into or performing a contract with the State, may have access to or become aware of classified information or materials. Notably, the instruction provides that any change affecting the holder of a security clearance, whether an individual or a legal entity, must be reported to the competent clearance authority, so that it may reassess the clearance decision.

Lastly, certain commitments may pertain to the preservation of national research and development (R&D) capacities. In this regard, the French authorities may require that R&D centers be maintained on French territory in order to safeguard the national interest.

Commitments Relating to Customer Contracts and Industrial Capabilities

The second category of commitments relates to the target company's customer contracts and industrial capabilities, particularly with regard to the continuity of services and supplies.

First, the commitments may stipulate that, as of the date of the acquisition, the target company complies with all obligations arising from ongoing contracts pertaining to sensitive activities, as well as confidentiality agreements in force with its clients.

The commitments may also require that the target entity continues to provide its clients, on reasonable technical and commercial terms, with access to sensitive products that incorporate technological advancements developed by the company and integrated into those products.

Additional commitments may include ensuring that, for sensitive products already in use by clients as of the acquisition date, such products remain autonomous from the scope of ITAR regulations. As emphasized by the French Secretariat-General for National Defense and Security[744] (SGDSN), U.S. export control laws, particularly the Export Administration Regulations (EAR) and the International Traffic in Arms Regulations (ITAR), have extraterritorial effect. Accordingly, these laws apply to exporters established in France when exporting sensitive goods, services, and technologies, in addition to French and European regulations governing the export of dual-use items, military equipment, and similar goods. Failure to comply with U.S. administrative constraints may lead to significant administrative and criminal penalties for companies and research centers operating in France. U.S. regulations under EAR and ITAR

743. accessed September 1st, 2025, available at https://cyber.gouv.fr/instruction-generale-interministerielle-n1300

744. France, Prime Minister's Office, Secretariat-General for National Defence and Security, "U.S. export control regulations on sensitive goods," January 8, 2021, accessed September 1st, 2025, available at https://www.entreprises.gouv.fr/files/files/entreprises/biens-a-double%20usage/reglementation/guide_de_sensibilisation_aux_lois_americaines_de_controle_des_exportations_sgdsn.pdf

cover not only the export of sensitive goods from the United States but also the reexport of U.S.-controlled items from any other country. Exporters bear the responsibility of ensuring full compliance with these regulations. It is therefore essential to have a clear understanding of U.S. export laws in order to fulfill commitments arising from the import or use of U.S.-origin goods and thereby reduce exposure to potential sanctions. The goods in question may be tangible (such as components or systems) or intangible (such as technology, technical assistance, or even technical discussions).

Commitments may also concern specific expertise or know-how. The State may require assurances that no measures will be taken that could restrict the access or usage rights held by the target company as of the acquisition date regarding know-how and capabilities (including source code) used in the course of its sensitive activities. These commitments may cover associated developments made by the company, whether or not patented or protected by copyright, to ensure they remain available in France and continue to be usable, on at least equivalent terms to those in effect prior to the acquisition, by the company's establishments located in France, for the purpose of carrying out sensitive activities.

This type of commitment may also include giving priority to patent filings in France for inventions resulting from the development and production of sensitive products by the target company, insofar as the company deems such filings to be in its interest. The letter of commitment may specify, for informational purposes, that the company is also authorized to file patents outside of France, either simultaneously with or subsequently to the French filings.

Commitments may also be designed to preserve the competitiveness and innovation capacity of the target company. This typically involves maintaining on French territory the industrial capabilities under the company's control that are necessary to perform, to completion, all contracts in effect as of the acquisition date and relating to sensitive activities, referred to as "industrial capabilities." The term "industrial capabilities" refers to the physical and intangible means and resources required to supply sensitive products and associated services to clients.

Maintaining [745] these industrial capabilities must, for the duration of the commitments, ensure both:

(i) the operational and security maintenance of sensitive products already deployed and in service with the target company's clients; and

(ii) the deployment and subsequent operational and security maintenance of sensitive products covered under legally binding contracts concluded by the company prior to the signature of the commitment letter but not yet implemented.

The French State may further specify that such commitments must be implemented under the following conditions:

(a) execution of such operations by French personnel employed by the French-incorporated target entity (commonly referred to as "intervenants");

(b) prior notification of visits and interventions, including the precise identification of the intervenants, to be provided at least 48 hours in advance in case of planned interventions, or as soon as possible in case of emergencies;

745. DUPEYRAT, op. cit.,

(c) the ability for clients to request that intervenants obtain security clearance at the "Secret" or "Top Secret" level;
(d) the ability for clients to monitor compliance with the security annexes of contracts that were legally concluded by the target company before the commitment letter was signed.

Furthermore, maintaining industrial capabilities may also serve to ensure:
(e) that all supervision, operations, and maintenance activities, regardless of their level, related to sensitive products are conducted in France;
(f) that the supervision, operations, and maintenance centers for sensitive products are located in France.

These provisions may also help shield sensitive products from being subjected to regulations other than those of France or the European Union that apply to sensitive activities.

Commitments Related to the Protection of Information

The third category of undertakings concerns the protection of certain types of information.

In particular, this includes commitments relating to the protection of France's scientific and technical potential (protection du potentiel scientifique et technique de la Nation - PPST[746]). The French State may require the investor to ensure that the target company's industrial sites and information systems used for conducting sensitive activities comply with the regulatory requirements applicable under the PPST framework. (See also Chapter 7.)

In the same vein, the French authorities may require undertakings to the effect that the target company operates a dedicated information system for all applications related to its sensitive activities.

Information and Consultation Commitments to the French State

The fourth category[747] of undertakings concerns obligations related to the duty to inform and/or consult the French State.

First, the investor may undertake to inform the French authorities in writing and with reasonable prior notice of any event, situation, or change that could affect the conduct of the sensitive activities, including any foreseeable or anticipated developments within the Company (such as changes in the ownership chain, disposal of assets related to the Sensitive Activities, etc.).

746. France, Decree No. 2011-1425 of November 2, 2011, implementing Article 413-7 of the Criminal Code and relating to the protection of the Nation's scientific and technical potential, Official Journal of the French Republic, No. 0256, November 4, 2011, NOR: PRMX1118649D
747. DUPEYRAT, op. cit., pp. 121 et seq.

Second, the investor may commit to provide the French authorities, on an annual basis, with the financial statements for the most recently closed fiscal year of the company that was the subject of the investment, along with a report on the implementation of the undertakings. These reports shall include any material changes and developments in the legal or operational control structure of the target company.

Furthermore, the review of these documents by the French authorities, whether at the request of either party, may give rise to a meeting between representatives of the company and the relevant authorities to discuss the contents of the documents.

The French authorities may be represented in this context either by the Ministry of the Armed Forces, in particular the Defence Procurement Agency (Direction générale de l'armement – DGA), or by the Ministry of the Economy and Finance through the Directorate General of the Treasury (Direction générale du Trésor), and more specifically by the Foreign Investment Control Office (CIEF). As such, both entities must receive any correspondence addressed to the French authorities in connection with the undertakings.

The French State may also require that the investor remain bound by the undertakings it has made for as long as it retains direct or indirect control of the company, or until such time as the company ceases to conduct sensitive activities, pursuant to decisions taken in agreement with the French authorities and in compliance with the above-defined undertakings.

Finally, none of these undertakings shall relieve the investor or the target company of their obligations under applicable French or European Union laws and regulations. In particular, should the investor contemplate carrying out one of the transactions referred to in Article R. 151-2 of the Monetary and Financial Code after the acquisition has been completed, it undertakes to inform the prospective acquirer that a prior authorization from the Minister of the Economy may be required in accordance with the Code.

Conditions attached to the authorization may subsequently be amended

Pursuant to Article R. 151-9 of the Monetary and Financial Code, the conditions attached to a prior authorization issued by the Minister of the Economy may be revised after the authorization is granted, under two specific circumstances.

The first scenario applies when the request for revision originates from the investor. The request may be submitted:

1° in the event of an unforeseen change, as of the date of completion of the authorized transaction, in the economic or regulatory conditions under which the activities listed in Article R. 151-3 of the Monetary and Financial Code are carried out by the entity subject to the investment. Example: a persistent disruption in the supply of raw materials preventing the company from ensuring the continuity of the production of sensitive goods.[748]

748. France, Ministry of the Economy, Finance and Industrial and Digital Sovereignty, Directorate General of the Treasury, Annual Report 2025, "Foreign Direct Investment Screening in France," Published July

2° in the event of a change in the shareholding structure of the entity subject to the investment, or a change in the members of the control chain. Example: a reorganization of the investor's group resulting in the integration of the French entity into a new branch of the group's activities, without interrupting sensitive operations [749].
3° pursuant to one of the conditions set at the time of authorization, which may, in certain cases, provide for the possibility of a subsequent revision of the decision.

Example: a decline in the profitability of sensitive activities requiring a reorganization of the entity's industrial sites to ensure their viability [750].

When a request for revision of the conditions is submitted by the investor, it must be accompanied by the documents or information necessary to substantiate the circumstances referred to in items (1), (2), or (3), as well as any additional materials required for the review of such request. The Minister shall render a decision within forty-five (45) business days from receipt of the request.

If no response is issued within that period, the request for revision shall be deemed denied [751].

As the French administration reiterates [752], it is incumbent upon the investor to notify the competent authorities of any development which, during the validity period of the conditions, would in good faith justify a request for revision.

For instance, this may include an evolution in the international context affecting the target's supply chains, thereby preventing the conduct of sensitive activities; a change in the regulatory framework governing the target's sector, significantly undermining the conditions under which the activity is exercised (or even the possibility of conducting the activity itself); or unexpected economic hardships in the sector.

The notification must be accompanied by appropriate supporting materials, such as financial data on the target company, share transfer agreements, updated corporate charts, regulatory or contractual documentation evidencing the change, or independent expert opinions.

The 45-business-day timeline applies to the Ministry's review of the request, starting from the date of receipt. A lack of response within this period results in the automatic rejection of the request.

During this adversarial period, the proposed revised conditions are discussed between the Directorate General of the Treasury (DG Trésor), potentially involving other relevant governmental services, and the investor and their legal advisors. These exchanges, similar to those occurring during the authorization process, allow the investor to present observations and explain any difficulties encountered.

30, 2025, consulted July 31, 2025, available at https://www.tresor.economie.gouv.fr/Articles/2025/07/30/publication-du-rapport-annuel-sur-le-controle-ief-en-2024

749. Ibid,

750. Ibid,

751. See Point 3.4.2 in Ministry of the Economy, Finance, Industrial and Digital Sovereignty, Directorate General of the Treasury, "Guidelines on the Foreign Direct Investment Screening in France" July 2025, published July 30, 2025, consulted August 1, 2025, available at https://www.tresor.economie.gouv.fr/services-aux-entreprises/investissements-etrangers-en-france

752. Ibid, See Point 3.4.1.1.

Throughout this dialogue, the investor is expected to engage in good-faith discussions with the DG Trésor and relevant services, aiming to present the situation and seek agreement on the revision of one or more conditions. The investor may submit proposed amendments to the existing conditions as part of this process.

Once the revised scope has been defined, the amendment is formalized by a decision of the Minister. It may take the form of an amendment to the existing letter of conditions or the execution of a new letter of conditions.

In 2024, eight requests for revision were submitted by investors pursuant to Article R. 151-9 of the Monetary and Financial Code, on average two years and ten months after the completion date of the authorized transaction [753]. Of these requests, seven were granted, while one was denied on the grounds that the proposed revision would have unduly impaired an activity essential to public security.

The second scenario arises where the revision is initiated by the Minister of the Economy, under the circumstances mentioned in points 2° (change in the shareholding structure or control chain of the target entity) and 3° (application of a condition originally imposed under the authorization) outlined above.

In this case, the Minister notifies the investor of the intention to revise the conditions, specifying the grounds supporting such a decision, and invites the investor to submit observations within a 45-business-day period [754]. At the end of this period, the Minister notifies the investor of the amended conditions and their effective date.

The imposition of additional conditions is only permitted if the investor acquires control of the target entity, meaning they had previously crossed either the 25% voting rights threshold under point 3° of Article R. 151-2 of the Monetary and Financial Code, or the 10% threshold in a French company whose shares are listed on a regulated market under point 4° of the same article.

Any newly imposed conditions must meet the requirement of proportionality [755] in light of the national interest at stake. Accordingly, if the risk posed by the investment has diminished compared to the time the authorization was granted, the Minister may, under the principle of proportionality, impose less stringent conditions.

In all cases, whether the revision request originates from the investor or from the Minister, the request has no suspensive effect. The investor remains bound to comply fully with the existing conditions until the Minister of the Economy formally decides whether or not to revise them.

753. France, Ministry of the Economy, Finance, Industrial and Digital Sovereignty, Directorate General of the Treasury, Annual Report 2025, "Foreign Direct Investment Screening in France," published July 30, 2025, consulted July 31, 2025, available at https://www.tresor.economie.gouv.fr/Articles/2025/07/30/publication-du-rapport-annuel-sur-le-controle-ief-en-2024

754. See Point 3.4.1.2. in Ministry of the Economy, Finance, Industrial and Digital Sovereignty, Directorate General of the Treasury, "Guidelines on the Foreign Direct Investment Screening in France" July 2025, published July 30, 2025, consulted August 1, 2025, available at https://www.tresor.economie.gouv.fr/services-aux-entreprises/investissements-etrangers-en-france

755. Principle of proportionality introduced by France, Decree No. 2023-1293 of December 28, 2023, on foreign investments in France, Official Journal of the French Republic, No. 0301, December 29, 2023, NOR: ECOT2323089D

Revised conditions are drafted based on the factual and legal circumstances prevailing at the time the revision decision is adopted. The French Government consistently reaffirms that the principle of proportionality [756] governs the imposition or amendment of conditions.

During the 45-business-day adversarial period, the proposed changes are discussed between the Directorate General of the Treasury (CIEF), other competent government services where applicable, and the investor along with their legal counsel. These discussions, as in the initial authorization process, aim to allow the investor to present arguments and clarify any difficulties encountered.

In 2024, a revision decision [757] was adopted at the initiative of the Minister in a case where a change in the members of the entity's chain of control required an adjustment of the conditions (Section II of Article R. 151-9 of the Monetary and Financial Code).

Certain corporate amendments must be declared

As the French administration emphasizes [758], certain changes occurring during the period in which conditions apply, such as a change of corporate name or legal form, a change in registration, or a modification of the target company's shareholding structure, may affect sensitive activities as well as the investor's ability to comply with the imposed conditions.

In most cases, the conditions attached to an authorization stipulate that the investor must notify the competent authorities of any change in the organization that may impact sensitive activities, as well as of any modification to the legal chain of control of the target entity, prior to implementing such changes, within the time limits set by the Minister in the letter of conditions, and in all circumstances without undue delay.

The competent authorities may object to the implementation of such changes, particularly where they would result in the investor being unable to fulfill the imposed conditions.

756. France, National Assembly, Written Question No. 3493 to the Minister of the Economy, Finance and Industrial and Digital Sovereignty, "Tripartite agreement between the State, Sanofi and CD&R," Official Journal of the National Assembly, No. 4 (Q), January 28, 2025, p. 2307, MARLEIX, Olivier, Member of Parliament, Les Républicains (LR), ministerial reply, Official Journal of the National Assembly, May 20, 2025, p. 3667

757. France, Ministry of the Economy, Finance and Industrial and Digital Sovereignty, Directorate General of the Treasury, Annual Report 2025, "Foreign Direct Investment Screening in France," Published 30 July 2025, consulted 31 July 2025, available at https://www.tresor.economie.gouv.fr/Articles/2025/07/30/publication-du-rapport-annuel-sur-le-controle-ief-en-2024

758. See Point 3.5. in Ministry of the Economy, Finance and Industrial and Digital Sovereignty, Directorate General of the Treasury, "Guidelines on the Foreign Direct Investment Screening in France" July 2025, Published 30 July 2025, Consulted 1 August 2025, available at https://www.tresor.economie.gouv.fr/services-aux-entreprises/investissements-etrangers-en-france

Disclosure of Conditions Must Preserve National Defense and Trade Secrets

As recalled by the French administration [759], the conditions attached to the Minister's authorization may fall within two categories of exceptions to the disclosure of administrative documents under Articles L. 311-1 et seq. of the Code on Relations between the Public and the Administration (CRPA) [760]:

—First, their consultation or disclosure would impair national defense secrecy, State security, public safety, the safety of individuals, or the security of government information systems, pursuant to subparagraphs (b) and (d) of paragraph 2° of Article L. 311-5 of the Code on Relations between the Public and the Administration (CRPA) [761];

---

759. See Point 2.2.3.4 in Ministry of the Economy, Finance and Industrial and Digital Sovereignty, Directorate General of the Treasury, "Guidelines on the Foreign Direct Investment Screening in France" July 2025, Published 30 July 2025, Consulted 1 August 2025, available at https://www.tresor.economie.gouv.fr/services-aux-entreprises/investissements-etrangers-en-france

760. France, Code of Relations between the Public and the Administration, Article L. 311-5, Non-disclosable documents : " *The following documents are not subject to disclosure:*
1° Opinions issued by the Conseil d'État and administrative courts; documents from the Cour des comptes referred to in Article L. 141-3 of the Code of Financial Jurisdictions; documents from the regional chambers of accounts referred to in Articles L. 241-1 and L. 241-4 of the same code; documents prepared or held by the Autorité de la concurrence in the context of its investigative, examination, and decision-making powers; documents prepared or held by the Haute Autorité pour la transparence de la vie publique in connection with the missions set out in Article 20 of Law No. 2013-907 of October 11, 2013, on transparency in public life; documents prepared prior to the drafting of the accreditation report for healthcare establishments under Article L. 6113-6 of the Public Health Code; documents prepared prior to the accreditation of healthcare personnel under Article L. 1414-3-3 of the same code; audit reports on healthcare establishments as provided for in Article 40 of Law No. 2000-1257 of December 23, 2000, on the 2001 Social Security Financing Act; and documents prepared under a service contract performed on behalf of one or more specified persons;
2° Other administrative documents, the consultation or disclosure of which would undermine:
a) The confidentiality of deliberations of the Government and authorities under the executive branch (including Interministerial General Instruction No. 1300);
b) National defense secrecy;
c) The conduct of France's foreign policy;
d) The security of the State, public safety, personal security, or the security of governmental information systems;
e) Currency or public credit;
f) The conduct of judicial proceedings or of preliminary actions relating to such proceedings, unless authorized by the competent authority;
g) The detection and prevention of offenses by competent authorities;
h) Or, subject to Article L. 124-4 of the Environmental Code, other secrets protected by law."

761. France, Article L. 311-6 of the Code of Relations between the Public and the Administration
"Only the person concerned may access administrative documents:
1° the disclosure of which would infringe upon the protection of privacy, medical confidentiality, or trade secrets, including the secrecy of manufacturing processes, economic and financial information, and commercial or industrial strategies, taking into account, where applicable, whether the public service mission of the administration referred to in the first paragraph of Article L. 300-2 is subject to competition;
2° that contain assessments or value judgments concerning a specifically identified or easily identifiable natural person;
3° that reveal the behavior of a person, where disclosing such behavior could cause harm to that person. Medical information shall be disclosed to the person concerned either directly or, if they so choose, through a physician designated by them, in accordance with Article L. 1111-7 of the Public Health Code."

—Second, they are not disclosable to third parties without breaching trade secret protections set forth in paragraph 1° of Article L. 311-6 of the same Code [762]. Such conditions may reveal the target company's financial situation, influence its valuation, and contain elements directly linked to the investor's commercial strategy.

With respect to trade secrets, the notion must be understood in accordance with three cumulative criteria:

—The information is not generally known or readily accessible to persons normally dealing with this type of information within the relevant business sector;
—It holds commercial value due to its confidential nature;
—The lawful holder of the information has taken reasonable steps to preserve its confidentiality.

Accordingly, the communication by the French State of the content of FDI authorization conditions to any party other than the investor responsible for their compliance, the legal representative of the target entity where the conditions will be operationally implemented, and the operational point of contact (POC), must comply strictly with the provisions of the Code on Relations between the Public and the Administration (CRPA).

Furthermore, under Article R. 151-8 of the Monetary and Financial Code, the conditions attached to an authorization may themselves include provisions governing how their content may be disclosed to third parties (e.g., financial service providers, co-controlling shareholders). Such provisions may, for example, require the redaction of sensitive information or the prior approval of the relevant State services.

In any case, the Minister has reiterated [763] the administration's position by stating: "*Beyond the necessary protection of trade secrets and national defense secrecy, this procedure is fundamentally based on the trust of stakeholders in the administration's handling of the information they provide. The Ministry therefore never communicates about individual cases, and the conditions issued by the Minister in connection with foreign investment operations are never made public, except in the very rare cases where another regulation requires it.*"

Nevertheless, some transactions subject to the French FDI screening regime may be subject to public disclosure relating to the transaction itself. For instance, during

---

762. France, Code of Relations between the Public and the Administration, Article L. 311-6 (CRPA): "Administrative documents are only communicable to the person concerned:
1° Where their disclosure would prejudice the protection of privacy, medical secrecy, or trade secrets, which include secrecy of processes, economic and financial information, and commercial or industrial strategies, and are assessed taking into account, where applicable, the fact that the public service mission of the administration referred to in the first paragraph of Article L. 300-2 is subject to competition;
2° That contain an assessment or value judgment concerning a natural person, specifically identified or easily identifiable;
3° That reveal the behavior of a person, where disclosure of such behavior could cause them harm.
Medical information is communicated to the person concerned, at their choice, either directly or through a physician designated by them for that purpose, in compliance with the provisions of Article L. 1111-7 of the Public Health Code."

763. France, Senate, Written Question No. 12963 to the Minister of the Economy and Finance, Official Journal of the Senate, November 7, 2019, p. 5587, VAUGRENARD, Yves, Senator, Socialist, Ecologist and Republican Group (SOCR), Ministerial Reply, August 27, 2020, Official Journal of the Senate, p. 3709

the acquisition of the company Latécoère, one of the conditions imposed on the investor was exceptionally disclosed in order to comply with applicable financial market transparency rules during a public tender offer [764].

Monitoring of Commitments Made by Foreign Investors Is Coordinated by the SISSE

As previously discussed, the monitoring of commitments set at the time of the authorization under the French FDI screening mechanism (procédure IEF) also serves as an opportunity to assess the adequacy of the conditions imposed.

To ensure that commitments made in the interest of national security are not merely symbolic, it is essential that the French State can effectively monitor the implementation of approved investments.

Prior to 2019, this responsibility fell primarily to the relevant sectoral ministries, which oversaw compliance with the commitments they had helped negotiate. The monitoring process, interministerial in nature, began as early as the submission of the FDI application and continued through the enforcement of the related conditions. Once conditions are imposed on an investment transaction, the State has an obligation to monitor their fulfillment, as failure to comply may trigger enforcement action.

As established by the 2018 Parliamentary Committee of Inquiry [765] on the State's industrial policy decisions, monitoring of such commitments was traditionally carried out internally by the administration. The regulatory impact assessment [766] accompanying the 2019 PACTE Law [767] further clarified that "the monitoring of the conditions associated with the authorization is coordinated by the Directorate General of the Treasury (DG Trésor), in association with all relevant government departments." The approach depends on the specific conditions in question and may include: analysis of annual reports, follow-up meetings with the company, inter-agency information sharing, interactions with designated company contact points, implementation of national scientific and technological heritage protection rules, engagement with customers and

764. France, Senate, Written Question No. 13474 to the Minister of the Economy and Finance, Official Journal of the Senate, December 12, 2019, p. 6110, MICOULÉAU, Brigitte, Senator, Les Républicains (LR) Group, Ministerial Reply, February 27, 2020, Official Journal of the Senate, p. 1031

765. France, National Assembly, Verbatim Report No. 14, January 24, 2018, Fact-Finding Committee on the State's Decisions Regarding Industrial Policy in Light of Recent Corporate Mergers, Notably in the Cases of Alstom, Alcatel and STX, and on Possible Means of Protecting France's Strategic Industrial Assets in a Global Trade Context, Wednesday Session, Hearing, Partially Closed-Door, of Ms. Valérie Liang-Champrenault, Head of the Multicom 2 Office "Investments and Rules in International Trade," and Mr. Romain Chambre, Head of the Multicom 3 Office "Fight Against Crime and International Sanctions," accompanied by Ms. Muriel Lacoue-Labarthe, Deputy Director for "Trade and Investment Policy" within the Directorate for Multilateral Affairs and Development of the French Treasury Department, accessed September 1st, 2025, available at https://www.assemblee-nationale.fr/dyn/15/comptes-rendus/cepolind/l15cepolind1718014_compte-rendu

766. France, Regulatory Impact Assessment, Bill on Business Growth and Transformation, NOR: ECOT1810669L/Bleue-1, June 20, 2018

767. France, Law No. 2019-486 of May 22, 2019, on Business Growth and Transformation, Official Journal of the French Republic, No. 0119, May 23, 2019, NOR: ECOT1810669L

prime contractors, and site visits by central administrations or regional services (formerly DIRECCTE[768]).

This administrative oversight was not codified under French law, and was instead described by the government as a "gradually evolving and improvable practice," whose core objective was to "uphold the credibility of the prior authorization regime" and support enforcement where necessary. However, the 2024 reform of Article L. 151-6 of the Monetary and Financial Code introduced the possibility of parliamentary debate on the topic (see Chapter 5).

Competent ministries notify the FDI Screening Unit (CIEF) of their intention to conduct site visits and transmit the corresponding reports. For several years now, companies have been required to submit annual reports on the fulfillment of their commitments. Once these reports are received by the competent administration, follow-up meetings may be scheduled at any time. A designated official within the relevant ministry then circulates the reports to other authorities or to DG Trésor, which ensures broader dissemination.

As emphasized by the administration[769], the State services responsible for monitoring compliance with the conditions are designated in the instrument setting forth the conditions attached to the ministerial authorization. This monitoring is conducted under the terms specified in the letter of conditions itself and may involve both document-based review and on-site inspections.

The investor is subject to disclosure and reporting obligations (submission of annual documents, prior authorizations, notification of specific events) as stipulated in the conditions attached to the minister's authorization. In addition, the Directorate General of the Treasury may request from the investor or the target company any documents necessary to verify proper implementation of the conditions, pursuant to Article L. 151-5 of the Monetary and Financial Code.

Meetings, whether in person or virtual, or site visits may also be required. In such cases, the investor receives prior notice from the competent State services and is obliged to comply. The practical arrangements for such monitoring (date, time, duration, etc.) are determined in consultation with the investor and the target company.

The issue of commitment monitoring remains central to the ongoing debate between the Government and Parliament concerning parliamentary oversight of the FDI screening regime . As described in Chapter 5, a number of investment transactions have been the subject of parliamentary inquiries under traditional legislative oversight powers. In this context, the Government often reiterates[770] its vigilance in ensuring compliance without disclosing specific monitoring outcomes.

768. Acronym of "Regional Directorates for Enterprises, Competition, Consumer Affairs, Labor and Employment"

769. See Point 3.3.2. in Ministry of the Economy, Finance and Industrial and Digital Sovereignty, Directorate General of the Treasury, "Guidelines on the Foreign Direct Investment Screening in France" July 2025, Published July 30, 2025, Consulted August 1, 2025, available at https://www.tresor.economie.gouv.fr/services-aux-entreprises/investissements-etrangers-en-france

770. France, National Assembly, Written Question No. 21540 to the Minister of the Economy and Finance, Official Journal of the National Assembly, July 16, 2019, FIAT, Caroline, Member of Parliament, La France Insoumise (LFI) Group, Ministerial Reply, December 31, 2019, Official Journal of the National Assembly,

Since 2014, for example, the acquisition of Alstom's energy assets by General Electric has been subject to close parliamentary scrutiny and is frequently cited as emblematic of the challenges facing the French FDI screening regime. On this matter, therefore Economy Minister Bruno Le Maire reaffirmed the Government's position [771] and outlined the types of commitments imposed in transactions of such magnitude.

Pursuant to the Decree [772] of March 20, 2019 on the governance of France's economic security policy, the Strategic Information and Economic Security Service (SISSE) was designated to coordinate the monitoring of commitments, in cooperation with the competent ministerial departments or affiliated entities. While DG Trésor remains in charge of investigating potential breaches and enforcing sanctions, SISSE's coordinating role has gained prominence.

Since 2019, SISSE has led the interministerial monitoring of conditions imposed on foreign investors under the IEF framework. Recognizing shortcomings in the system,

---

p. 11529: "Due to the sensitive nature of its activities in relation to national defense, Power Conversion is subject to specific monitoring by the Ministries of the Armed Forces and of the Economy and Finance, within the framework of the foreign investment screening procedure (IEF) provided for under Article L. 151-3 of the Monetary and Financial Code. This monitoring indicates that GE's commitments to the French State are being fulfilled. Should any breach of these commitments occur, all available instruments will be used to ensure GE complies.

771. France, National Assembly, Written Question No. 22084 to the Minister of the Economy and Finance, Official Journal of the National Assembly, July 30, 2019, p. 7026, EVRARD, José, Non-Affiliated Member of Parliament, Ministerial Reply, March 3, 2020, Official Journal of the National Assembly, p. 1690:
"*The energy branch of Alstom was acquired by GE in 2015. It is important to stress that Alstom itself initiated discussions with GE regarding the sale of its activities, with a view to forming a more robust group in the face of global competition. The French State only authorized the transaction after reviewing it under the foreign investment screening procedure (IEF). This authorization was subject to conditions formalized in the agreement and letter of commitment of November 4, 2014, between the State and GE.*
As part of the French foreign investment screening framework (IEF), activities deemed sensitive in terms of national defense, particularly those related to the propulsion systems of the aircraft carrier Charles de Gaulle and submarines, are explicitly covered by GE's commitments and monitored specifically by the Ministry of the Armed Forces. According to this oversight, GE is fulfilling its obligations.
As regards the protection of nuclear-related strategic interests, several mechanisms have been put in place. First, the maintenance activities of the nuclear power plant fleet and the control over Arabelle turbine technology have been consolidated within a subsidiary, GEAST, which is specifically monitored by the French administration. Under the 2014 agreements, the French State holds a seat on the board of directors of this subsidiary, along with veto rights.
The second mechanism is a framework agreement signed in 2014 by the State, GE, Alstom, and EDF regarding the long-term viability of the existing nuclear fleet, in force until the end of the fleet's lifecycle. This agreement is supplemented by a license agreement that grants a dedicated, State-controlled company a license to Alstom's existing and future intellectual property rights, to ensure EDF's continued access in the event of GE's default.
A second framework agreement, this time covering new nuclear projects, was also signed in November 2014 by the State, GE, Alstom, AREVA and EDF. It includes a ten-year renewable commitment. Through this framework, GE committed to developing turbo-generator systems based on Arabelle technology and to submitting competitive offers to EDF for new projects. As with the previous framework, this one is also supplemented by a license agreement with the same parties, granting the same State-controlled company *access to existing and future Alstom IP rights in the event of GE's default. An escrow arrangement is in place to secure this access.*
A dedicated steering committee meets annually to monitor the implementation of commitments set forth in both frameworks. The November 4, 2014, agreement also allows the French State to require the purchaser to commit to maintaining key competencies and know-how."

772. France, Decree No. 2019-206 of March 20, 2019, on the Governance of Economic Security Policy, Official Journal of the French Republic, No. 0068, March 21, 2019, NOR: ECOI1902757D

SISSE established in 2023 a nationwide, interagency mechanism for monitoring commitments. According to the CIEF [773], "the implementation of this monitoring system ensures the long-term credibility of the FDI screening mechanism."

This mechanism includes two key types of control: (i) annual desk audits based on the review of investor-submitted compliance reports, carried out by HFDS services (senior defense and security officials) of the ministries with sectoral jurisdiction; and (ii) on-site inspections.

In the latter case, SISSE aims to audit all active letters of commitment on a rolling five-year basis. This effort comes amid a significant increase in conditional authorizations (+65% in 2024 compared to 2023), with nearly 500 companies expected to be under active commitments by 2025. Accordingly, SISSE conducts around one hundred audits per year, with 90% of the 2024 audits involving on-site inspections led by its 23 regional Strategic Information and Economic Security Delegates (DISSE) . To support this expanded oversight, SISSE added three regional full-time equivalents (FTEs) in 2024.

As noted by the French National Assembly's Evaluation Mission, the annual audit schedule is developed by SISSE in close coordination with competent ministries. Site visits are planned based on objective criteria, including the criticality of the target company's activities, sensitivity of the data processed, past compliance history, and geographic representation.

Notably [774], the Defense Procurement Agency (DGA), under the Ministry of the Armed Forces, conducts its own monitoring independently of SISSE. In 2024, the DGA conducted 70 on-site inspections (out of 1,000 visits to companies in the defense industrial and technological base), covering approximately 200 active letters of commitment. The DGA's deep knowledge of the defense sector and substantial human resources allow for more thorough and frequent checks.

Once letters of commitment are finalized, operational contact points are designated within companies to facilitate ongoing communication with the administration, especially in highly sensitive sectors. In less sensitive areas, monitoring generally centers around the annual report, which becomes a point of engagement [775]. The goal is to foster a relationship of trust enabling the competent ministries to maintain effective oversight of the acquired entity.

Authorities may also engage with the target company's clients, thereby situating the investment within its broader economic ecosystem. Ministries simultaneously conduct sectoral intelligence work that strengthens their understanding of strategic supply

773. France, National Assembly, Committee for the Assessment and Monitoring of Public Policies, Fact-Finding Report No. 1453, JOLIVET, François, and de LEPINAU, Hervé, Members of Parliament, on the Evaluation of foreign direct investment screening in France, Official Journal of the French Republic, May 27, 2025, text 45 of 69, published May 22, 2025, accessed May 27, 2025, available at https://www.assemblee-nationale.fr/dyn/17/rapports/cec/l17b1453_rapport-information

774. ibid

775. France, Ministerial Order of December 31, 2019, on Foreign Investments in France, Official Journal of the French Republic, No. 0001, January 1, 2020, NOR: ECOT1937237A: "9° Designation of a contact person, including full name, professional status, business address, and email address."

chains, particularly for commitments extending over several years. Indicators such as continuity of supply, R&D capabilities, service to the State, and the protection of trade secrets are all quickly assessable in case of breach. In this respect, France has multiple tools at its disposal to enforce compliance.

Regional business, employment and economic development units (Pôles 3E), under the DIRECCTE network, have also been tasked with assisting in monitoring through site visits coordinated with central ministries. Ultimately, however, it is the central administration that retains leadership of the process.

In some cases, letters of commitment waive the requirement for annual reporting to reduce the administrative burden on companies.

Importantly, the PACTE Law[776] marked a turning point in this area. Following the "critical" conclusions[777] of the parliamentary committee of inquiry regarding the monitoring of authorized foreign investments, the law introduced parliamentary oversight through the involvement of qualified individuals tasked with reviewing the Government's actions in connection with the IEF regime . (See chapter 5).

This led to the inclusion of Article L. 151-7 in the Monetary and Financial Code, which requires the Government to submit an annual report to the chairs of the parliamentary economic affairs committees and the finance committee rapporteurs general. The report covers:

- The Government's action to protect and promote France's economic, industrial, and scientific interests, including measures taken to ensure economic security and safeguard strategic enterprises, along with objectives, initiatives, and outcomes; and
- Information on the FDI authorization process, including the number of prior approval requests received, rejections, authorizations granted (with or without conditions), as well as enforcement actions, excluding any identifying details regarding the individuals or entities concerned.

In principle, this parliamentary mechanism should provide for meaningful oversight, as it includes:

- Hearings[778] of relevant ministers, the Strategic and Economic Security Commissioner, and directors of relevant central administrations, accompanied by their staff; and
- Authority to conduct any necessary investigations[779], both on paper and on-site, into the Government's actions in the field of economic security and FDI screening.

Nonetheless, the administration continues to interpret these provisions narrowly, asserting that they do not authorize ongoing oversight of active commitments. As a

776. France, Law No. 2019-486 of May 22, 2019, on Business Growth and Transformation, Official Journal of the French Republic, No. 0119, May 23, 2019, NOR: ECOT1810669L

777. DUPEYRAT, op. cit., p. 236

778. These exchanges, which are not made public, may concern information enabling the identification of natural or legal persons subject to the prior authorization procedure for foreign investments provided for under Article L. 151-3 of the Monetary and Financial Code.

779. *"These investigations may not concern investments that fall within the decision-making authority of the Minister of the Economy. All information and administrative documents requested in the course of such investigations, including any reports prepared by agencies or departments responsible for administrative oversight, must be provided to them, except for information and documents protected by national defense secrecy"*. In DUPEYRAT, op. cit., p. 136

result, the "qualified individuals" appointed under Article L. 151-7 have yet to exercise their formal powers [780].

An operational point of contact coordinates follow-up between the investor and the authorities

As emphasized by the French authorities [781], the operational point of contact (PCO) within the target entity of the investment serves as an intermediary between the target entity, the foreign investor, and the competent government services responsible for monitoring the conditions imposed by the Minister in granting the foreign investment authorization.

The PCO is not responsible for the implementation or compliance with these conditions, which remain the sole responsibility of the investor. Only the investor may face sanctions in the event of a breach of the conditions attached to a foreign investment authorization.

The PCO's role is to assist the investor in the proper implementation of all conditions attached to the foreign investment authorization. To this end, the PCO must have decision-making authority at the level of the target entity and must hold an executive function within that entity, in order to have unrestricted access to any information that could impact the implementation of the conditions. Depending on the nature of the technical or industrial activities concerned, the PCO may also need to have operational responsibilities requiring specific technical qualifications to effectively monitor the implementation of the required commitments.

Depending on the nature of the sensitive activities protected under the authorization conditions, and the sensitivity of the information relating to such activities, the PCO may be required to hold a security clearance under the national defense secrecy regulations.

Lastly, given the PCO's functions within the target entity, they are also responsible for contributing to the preparation of the annual report submitted to the competent authorities, the content of which is defined by the conditions attached to the authorization.

*
* *

In the context of foreign direct investment (FDI) screening, the monitoring of investor commitments is a critical issue for both public authorities and private parties. For

780. France, National Assembly, Written Question No. 6278 to the Minister of the Economy, Finance, Industrial and Digital Sovereignty, Official Journal of the National Assembly, March 14, 2023, p. 2307, MARLEIX, Olivier, Member of Parliament, Les Républicains (LR) Group, Ministerial Reply, Official Journal of the National Assembly, May 16, 2023, p. 4442

781. See Point 3.2 in Ministry of the Economy, Finance and Industrial and Digital Sovereignty, Directorate General of the Treasury, "Guidelines on the Foreign Direct Investment Screening in France" July 2025, Published July 30, 2025, Consulted August 1, 2025, available at https://www.tresor.economie.gouv.fr/services-aux-entreprises/investissements-etrangers-en-france

the former, it is a matter of demonstrating the credibility of their commitment to safeguarding national interests. For the latter, it is a matter of complying with binding conditions, the violation of which may entail serious consequences. Far from being arbitrary constraints, these conditions and undertakings represent a means of enabling foreign investment while preserving the host country's national security interests.

Chapter 21

Breach of Obligations and Commitments Is Subject to Severe Sanctions

The sanctions regime[782] constitutes a core element of the credibility of France's foreign direct investment (FDI) screening framework. It signals to foreign powers the French government's determination to safeguard national interests, particularly the operations of strategic companies engaged in activities pertaining to public order, public security, or national defense.

In addition, the prospect of dissuasive sanctions for foreign investors who fail to comply with the FDI screening rules acts as a powerful incentive for cooperation with the Ministry of the Economy.

The Sanctions Regime Has Been Gradually Developed

Until 2018, the sanctions framework rested primarily on two categories. First, administrative sanctions stemming from the government's exercise of its administrative police powers to enforce the foreign direct investment screening rules in France.

782. *In This Context, the Minister's Injunctive Power Was Strictly Limited. Under the pre-2019 framework, the Minister of the Economy's power of injunction was limited to three types of measures: (i) ordering that the transaction not proceed; (ii) requiring that the transaction be modified; or (iii) instructing that the pre-transaction status quo be restored at the investor's expense. Such injunctions could only be issued after the investor had been formally notified and given fifteen (15) days to submit comments. The deadline for restoring the prior situation was determined by the Minister and could not exceed twelve (12) months. Only in the event of non-compliance with such an injunction could the Minister impose administrative financial penalties, up to a maximum of twice the amount of the unauthorized investment. This rigid framework proved unsatisfactory from a policy standpoint, as it was perceived by the authorities as overly binary, essentially an "all-or-nothing" enforcement logic. In its interpretation of the sanctions regime, the French administration underscored that if a transaction was carried out without prior authorization, the investment was deemed automatically null and void ipso jure, in line with the legislator's express intent. This nullity followed a narrowly defined legal procedure: once a court had declared the investment null and void, the Minister of the Economy had no discretionary power to intervene or reverse the outcome. In such cases, the applicable legal basis was Article L. 151-3, III of the Monetary and Financial Code, as introduced by the 1996 law and reaffirmed by the 2000 ordinance. However, this rule of automatic nullity failed to sufficiently account for economic realities or the interests of the parties involved, including the Minister of the Economy himself, when the primary objective was merely to amend aspects of the transaction that were incompatible with national security. As emphasized in the impact assessment prepared in advance of the PACTE Act, the then-existing police powers were "not fully satisfactory, insofar as the injunctions that the Minister may issue are not sufficiently tailored to each specific situation (e.g., comple-*

In this regard, the Minister of the Economy could principally issue injunctions but did not have the authority to impose fines directly. Administrative sanctions could only be triggered in cases of non-compliance with such injunctions. Second, customs-related sanctions applicable under French customs law, which are discussed in detail further below.

In any case, unauthorized transactions could be subject to absolute nullity, a consequence that, in practice, could appear disproportionate to the nature or gravity of the breaches observed.

For this reason, the sanctions regime underwent a major overhaul in 2019 as part of the Business Growth and Transformation Act (loi PACTE). According to the Minister of the Economy, Mr. Bruno Le Maire, the main shortcoming of the previous framework was its lack of proportionality, which resulted in an all-or-nothing system, either extremely severe penalties, including potential imprisonment and asset confiscation, or virtually no consequence at all. To remedy this, the revised framework introduced a more graduated enforcement mechanism, including the use of financial penalties (astreintes) and corrective measures that can be incorporated directly into the prior authorization process. The revised sanctions now include fixed fines, which may reach up to €5 million or 10% of the target company's annual turnover, in order to avoid situations where the penalty was effectively negligible due to a low business valuation.

The Sanctions Framework Was Gradually Developed

Until 2018, the French sanctions regime for foreign direct investment was essentially structured around two categories. On the one hand, administrative sanctions fell within the scope of the government's regulatory police powers to enforce compliance with France's foreign investment rules. In this respect, the Minister of the Economy's authority was primarily limited to injunction powers[783]: the minister could not

tion of a transaction without prior authorization, or breach of authorization conditions). They also do not adequately allow for emergency response. Furthermore, compliance with the Minister's injunctions is incentivized solely through the threat of financial sanctions (i.e., the Minister may impose a monetary penalty when conditions are not met)." In light of the global nature of foreign investments and the strategic interests at stake, enabling swifter and more graduated enforcement of the FDI rules against foreign investors had thus become imperative."

783. Ibid "*In This Context, the Minister's Injunctive Powers Were Strictly Limited. Under the former regime, the Minister of the Economy's injunctive powers were limited to three options: (i) halting the transaction altogether, (ii) requiring that it be modified, or (iii) ordering the full restoration of the pre-transaction status quo at the investor's expense. Such an injunction could only be issued after the investor had been formally served with a notice to present observations within fifteen (15) days. The deadline for restoring the previous situation was determined by the Minister and could not exceed twelve (12) months. Only in cases of non-compliance with the injunction could the Minister impose an administrative financial penalty, which could amount to a maximum of twice the value of the unauthorized investment. This rigid framework was deemed unsatisfactory by public authorities, who criticized its binary nature, an "all-or-nothing" enforcement approach. In its interpretation of the sanctions regime, the French administration further emphasized that, in cases where the transaction had been carried out without prior authorization, the investment was deemed automatically null and void (nullité de plein droit), in accordance with the express intent of the legislature. This provision reinforced the visibility and seriousness of the prior authorization procedure. Such nullity resulted from a narrowly defined legal process. Once a judge had declared the transaction void ipso jure, the Minister of the Economy had no legal authority to overturn or mitigate the*

impose monetary fines directly. Only non-compliance with an injunction could trigger an administrative sanction. On the other hand, customs-related sanctions applied under the framework of customs law, discussed later.

In any case, an unauthorized investment transaction could be declared absolutely null and void (nullité absolue), a remedy that often appeared disproportionate to the underlying violations or deficiencies.

For this reason, the sanctions framework was substantially revised in 2019 through the Loi [784] relative à la croissance et la transformation des entreprises (the "PACTE Act"). According to the Minister of the Economy [785], Bruno Le Maire, the key weakness of the previous system was its lack of proportionality, which rendered it an "all-or-nothing" mechanism: either extremely severe penalties, including imprisonment and confiscation, or virtually no sanction at all. The 2019 reform therefore introduced a more graduated system of injunction powers, including the ability to impose daily penalty payments (astreintes) and to apply corrective measures as part of the prior authorization process.

The revised regime also provided for fixed fines, which may now reach up to EUR 5 million or 10% of the target company's turnover, in order to avoid situations where a sanction would otherwise amount to "almost nothing" when the company's valuation was very low.

The 2019 PACTE Act [786] thus strengthened the Minister of the Economy's regulatory enforcement authority. The rules governing injunctions and sanctions were clarified in the Decree [787] of 31 December 2019 and are codified in Article L. 151-3-1 of the French Monetary and Financial Code (Code monétaire et financier).

---

consequence. In these cases, the applicable legal framework was set out in Article L. 151-3, III of the Monetary and Financial Code, introduced by the 1996 law and reaffirmed by the 2000 ordinance. However, the application of nullité de plein droit did not sufficiently reflect economic realities or the interests of the parties involved, including those of the Minister of the Economy himself, when the objective was merely to amend specific elements of a transaction that conflicted with national security. As noted in the regulatory impact assessment accompanying the PACTE Act, this enforcement mechanism was "not fully satisfactory, in that the injunctions available to the Minister are not sufficiently tailored to the specific circumstances of each case (whether the transaction was carried out without prior authorization or in breach of the applicable conditions). It does not allow for an adequate response in urgent situations. Moreover, compliance with the Minister's injunctions is incentivized only by the threat of sanctions (the Minister may impose a financial penalty in case of non-compliance)." Given the international nature of foreign investments and the strategic interests protected by the screening procedure, the ability to sanction breaches of the FDI rules more swiftly and with greater proportionality had become a clear necessity."

784. DUPEYRAT, op. cit., pp. 126 et seq.

785. France, National Assembly, Verbatim Record No. 51, April 12, 2018, Fact-finding Committee tasked with examining the State's decisions on industrial policy, in light of recent corporate mergers, including those involving Alstom, Alcatel and STX, as well as the means available to protect France's national industrial champions in a globalized commercial context, Thursday session, Open hearing before the press, of Mr. Bruno Le Maire, Minister of the Economy and Finance, accessed May 9, 2024, available at https://www.assemblee-nationale.fr/dyn/15/comptes-rendus/cepolind/l15cepolind1718051_compte-rendu

786. France, Law No. 2019-486 of May 22, 2019, on Business Growth and Transformation, Official Journal of the French Republic, No. 0119, May 23, 2019, NOR: ECOT1810669L

787. France, Decree No. 2019-1590 of 31 December 2019 on foreign investments in France, Official Journal of the French Republic, No. 0001, 1 January 2020, NOR: ECOT1932857D

Administrative Police Powers of the French Minister of the Economy

The PACTE Law [788] of 2019 aimed to strengthen the administrative police powers of the French Minister of the Economy. These powers are codified in Article L. 151-3-1 of the Monetary and Financial Code. The article distinguishes between two situations.

1) Investments Carried Out Without Prior Authorization (Section I of Article L. 151-3-1)

When a foreign investment is implemented without the required prior authorization, the Minister issue [789] an injunction [790] requiring the investor to:
(i) submit an authorization request for regularization purposes, in which case the same screening procedure applies as for a standard pre-closing review;
(ii) restore, at the investor's expense, the situation that existed prior to the investment;
(iii) modify the transaction.

To ensure compliance with such injunctions, the Minister may impose a daily monetary penalty (astreinte) in all three cases. The injunction must specify the amount and the effective date of the penalty. Under the Decree [791] of December 31, 2019, the daily maximum of this penalty is set at €50,000, with provisions governing its enforcement in the event of full or partial non-compliance or delay.

In addition, where the Minister determines that the investment poses, or is likely to pose, a threat to public order, public security, or national defense, the Minister may adopt precautionary measures (mesures conservatoires) to protect national interests under the French FDI regime. These measures include:
a) suspending voting rights attached to the shares or equity interests whose acquisition required prior authorization;
b) prohibiting or limiting the distribution of dividends or other financial benefits associated with such shares or interests;
c) suspending, restricting, or temporarily prohibiting the free disposal of all or part of the assets related to sensitive activities covered by the screening regime;

788. France, Law No. 2019-486 of May 22, 2019, on Business Growth and Transformation, Official Journal of the French Republic, No. 0119, May 23, 2019, NOR: ECOT1810669L
789. France, Ministry of the Economy, Finance, Industrial and Digital Sovereignty, Directorate General of the Treasury, "The Minister of the Economy's Police Powers," September 10, 2019, explaining that during parliamentary debates, the initial draft was amended to turn the option of issuing an injunction into a mandatory requirement. The administration interprets this mandatory character of injunction measures in cases of unauthorized transactions as granting the Minister the discretion not to systematically regularize the operation but rather, for example, to require the investor to restore the previous situation. Available at https://www.tresor.economie.gouv.fr/services-aux-entreprises/investissements-etrangers-en-france/les-pouvoirs-de-police-du-ministre-charge-de-l-economie (last accessed May 9, 2024)
790. The power to issue injunctions is a significant and particularly dissuasive innovation of the new mechanism.
791. France, Decree No. 2019-1590 of December 31, 2019, on foreign investments in France, Official Journal of the French Republic, No. 0001, January 1, 2020, NOR: ECOT1932857D

d) appointing a trustee [792] (mandataire) responsible for ensuring the protection of national interests within the target company. This trustee may block any corporate decisions that could undermine those interests.

All injunction measures imposed by the Minister of the Economy may be challenged through a full judicial review (recours de plein contentieux) pursuant to Section IV of Article L. 151-3-1 of the French Monetary and Financial Code.

2) Investments Made in Breach of Conditions Imposed by the Prior Authorization (Section II of Article L. 151-3-1)

The second scenario arises when the investment has been carried out with prior authorization but the investor fails to comply with its commitments [793]. In such circumstances, where an investor does not comply with the conditions attached to the authorization, the Minister of the Economy may, on his own initiative, exercise the following powers:

a) the power to withdraw the authorization [794];
b) in addition, the Minister may issue an injunction against the non-compliant investor and, within a time limit that he determines:
   (i) require compliance with the conditions set forth in the authorization; or
   (ii) order the execution of substitute measures for the unfulfilled obligation, including the restoration of the situation that existed prior to the breach, or the divestiture of all or part of the activities subject to the French FDI screening regime ;
   (iii) apply the same interim protective measures available in the case of an investment carried out without prior authorization.

3) Common Provisions Applicable to Both Scenarios

In cases of urgency, exceptional circumstances, or imminent threats to public order, public security, or national defense, the Minister may issue an injunction [795] or adopt a protective measure after having formally requested the investor to submit observations within a shortened period, which may not be less than five business days. At the expiration of this period, the Minister notifies the investor of the decision, specifying the time limit for compliance, which may be subject to a daily penalty (astreinte) set by the Minister.

The regulations [796] further provide that, where the Minister orders [797], under Article R. 151-13 of the Monetary and Financial Code, an investor to file an application to

---

792. His remuneration is set by the Minister of the Economy; it is borne, along with the expenses incurred by the trustee, by the company to which he is appointed.

793. See Point 3.3 in Ministry of the Economy, Finance and Industrial and Digital Sovereignty, Directorate General of the Treasury, "Guidelines on the Control of Foreign Investments in France" July 2025, Published July 30, 2025, consulted August 1, 2025, available at https://www.tresor.economie.gouv.fr/services-aux-entreprises/investissements-etrangers-en-france

794. Unless the foreign investor restores the situation that existed prior to the investment, he must reapply for the investment authorization provided for under the same Article L. 151-3 of the Monetary and Financial Code.

795. Monetary and Financial Code, Article L. 151-3-1, Paragraph I or II

796. Monetary and Financial Code, Article R. 151-13

797. Monetary and Financial Code, Article L. 151-3-1, pursuant to point 1 of Paragraphs I and II of the Article

regularize the investment, the injunction must specify the documents and information required for the review of the application.

Similarly, where the Minister orders an investor to amend [798] the investment or to comply with certain conditions, the injunction must specify the nature of the required modifications or of the new conditions imposed.

The Minister may also order the divestiture of all or part of the shares or equity interests acquired in the capital of the target entity, or of all or part of a business unit [799] operated by the target entity, to an entity distinct from the investor.

As noted above, the daily amount of any penalty (astreinte) imposed [800] may not exceed EUR 50,000 [801]. Such penalties are collected in the same manner as State claims unrelated to taxes or the public domain.

Pecuniary Sanction Powers of the Minister of the Economy

The PACTE Law [802] also reformed [803] the powers of the French Minister of the Economy with respect to pecuniary sanctions. These powers are codified in Article L. 151-3-2 of the Monetary and Financial Code.

Accordingly, in the following circumstances:
(i) where an investment has been carried out without obtaining prior authorization;
(ii) where prior authorization has been obtained by means of fraud [804];
(iii) where the investor has failed to comply with requirements imposed in the national interest;
(iv) where the investor has failed, in whole or in part, to comply with decisions or injunctions issued under the French FDI screening mechanism;

the Minister of the Economy may impose an administrative financial penalty, after granting the investor a minimum period of fifteen (15) days to submit comments regarding the alleged violations.

The amount of the pecuniary sanction may not exceed the highest of the following three thresholds:
(i) twice the amount of the unauthorized investment;
(ii) 10% of the annual net turnover (excluding tax) of the company carrying out the activities covered by the French FDI regime;

798. Monetary and Financial Code, Article L. 151-3-1, pursuant to point 3 of Paragraph I or points 2 and 3 of Paragraph II of the Article
799. Monetary and Financial Code, Article R. 151-3
800. Monetary and Financial Code, Article L. 151-3-1
801. Monetary and Financial Code, Article R. 151-14
802. France, Law No. 2019-486 of May 22, 2019, on Business Growth and Transformation, Official Journal of the French Republic, No. 0119, May 23, 2019, NOR: ECOT1810669L
803. France, Monetary and Financial Code, creation of Article L. 151-3-2, on the implementation of protective measures following the review of a foreign investment
804. The issue also arises as to whether an authorization may be granted in violation of the requirements set out in Law No. 2013-907 of October 11, 2013, on transparency in public life, Official Journal of the French Republic, No. 0238, October 12, 2013, NOR: PRMX1309699L

(iii) EUR 5 million for legal entities and EUR 1 million for natural persons.

The amount of the sanction must be proportionate to the seriousness of the breach. The sanction is recovered in the same manner as debts owed to the State that are not related to tax or public domain revenues.

Finally, any failure by a foreign investor to comply with the requirements of the FDI screening procedure, for example, non-compliance with the conditions imposed by the Minister of the Economy in connection with an authorization, may serve as grounds for the refusal of future authorizations, in addition to the penalties otherwise provided by law.

The Minister of the Economy's Criminal Sanctioning Powers

In criminal matters, the French Minister of the Economy is vested with exceptional powers to safeguard national interests.

Pursuant to Article 458 of the Customs Code [805] (Code des douanes), the Minister holds exclusive standing to file a criminal complaint, meaning that only the Minister or duly authorized representatives may initiate proceedings under this regime.

The Minister may seek the imposition of criminal sanctions that include a five-year prison sentence, the confiscation of the corpus delicti and of any assets or property derived from the offense, as well as a fine ranging from an amount equal to, up to twice the value of, the sum involved in the offense or attempted offense. These penalties are set forth under Article 459 of the Customs Code [806], which is made applicable

805. France, Customs Code, Article 458 : "*Prosecution for violations of the laws and regulations governing financial relations with foreign countries may only be initiated upon a complaint filed by the Minister of the Economy and Finance or by one of his duly authorized representatives.*"

806. France, Customs Code, Article 459:

"1. Any person who has violated or attempted to violate the laws and regulations governing financial relations with foreign countries, whether by failing to comply with reporting or repatriation obligations, by disregarding prescribed procedures or required formalities, or by failing to obtain the necessary authorizations or to comply with the conditions attached to such authorizations, shall be subject to a prison sentence of five years, confiscation of the corpus delicti, confiscation of the means of transport used to commit the offense, confiscation of any property and assets constituting the direct or indirect proceeds of the offense, and a fine of not less than the amount involved in the offense or attempted offense, and not more than twice that amount.

1 bis. The same penalties shall apply to any person who violates or attempts to violate restrictions on economic and financial relations imposed under European Union regulations adopted pursuant to Articles 75 or 215 of the Treaty on the Functioning of the European Union, or under treaties and international agreements duly approved and ratified by France.

1 ter. Legal entities held criminally liable under Article 121-2 of the Criminal Code for the offenses described in paragraphs 1 and 1 bis of this article shall be subject, in addition to the fine determined in accordance with Article 131-38 of the Criminal Code, to the penalties set forth in Article 131-39 of the same Code.

2. If, for any reason, the objects subject to confiscation cannot be seized or are not presented by the offender, or if the Minister of the Budget or his representative so requests, the court shall order the payment of a sum equivalent to the value of such objects in lieu of confiscation.

3. Any person who incites, through writing, propaganda, or advertising, the commission of any of the offenses referred to in paragraph 1 above, whether or not the incitement is followed by action, shall be subject to a prison sentence of five years and a fine ranging from €450 to €225,000.

to foreign direct investment screening by virtue of Article L. 165-1 of the Monetary and Financial Code [807] (Code monétaire et financier).

In its guidelines, the administration clarified that this mechanism applies both to a deliberate or intentional failure to file an authorization request and to an omission or oversight resulting from mere negligence. Police measures and sanctions may be imposed cumulatively.

Sanctions for Fraudulent Procurement of FDI Authorization

The Minister of the Economy may impose a monetary penalty and request the initiation of criminal proceedings in the event of a fraudulently obtained FDI authorization, pursuant to Article 459 of the French Customs Code (Code des douanes).

Fraudulent procurement of an authorization, implying a deliberate intent to mislead, exposes the investor to two categories of consequences [808]:
(i) the withdrawal of the authorization, which may occur at any time under Article L. 241-2 of the Code on Relations between the Public and the Administration (CRPA) (Code des relations entre le public et l'administration – CRPA); and
(ii) the imposition of a monetary penalty under Article L. 151-3-2 of the Monetary and Financial Code (Code monétaire et financier).

Both the withdrawal of the authorization and the imposition of the financial sanction may only occur after due process has been respected, allowing the investor to submit comments, in accordance with Articles L. 121-1 of the CRPA [809] and L. 151-3-2 of the Monetary and Financial Code.

---

4. Persons convicted of offenses under the laws and regulations governing financial relations with foreign countries shall also be declared ineligible to serve as stockbrokers or to vote or stand for election to chambers of commerce, commercial courts, or labor tribunals, for as long as they remain subject to such disqualification.
5. The courts shall also order that their conviction decisions be published, in full or in part, at the expense of the convicted persons, in newspapers designated by the court.

807. France, Monetary and Financial Code, Article L. 165-1 – Applicable Sanctions : "Violations of the obligations set forth in Articles L. 151-2 and L. 151-3 shall be sanctioned in accordance with Article 459 of the Customs Code. Article 451 of the Customs Code shall also apply."

808. France, Ministry of the Economy, Finance and Industrial and Digital Sovereignty, Directorate General of the Treasury, Guidelines on the Foreign Direct Investment Screening in France, July 2025, see Point 2.2.2.2, published July 30, 2025, consulted August 1, 2025, available at https://www.tresor.economie.gouv.fr/services-aux-entreprises/investissements-etrangers-en-france

809. France, Code on the Relations between the Public and the Administration (CRPA), Article L. 121-1 —Prior Adversarial Procedure
Except in cases where the administration is ruling on a request, individual decisions that must be reasoned pursuant to Article L. 211-2, as well as decisions which, although not listed therein, are adopted in consideration of the personal circumstances of the person concerned, are subject to a prior adversarial procedure.
France, Code on the Relations between the Public and the Administration (CRPA), Article L. 211-2 – Statement of Reasons for Adverse Individual Decisions
Natural or legal persons have the right to be informed without delay of the reasons for adverse individual administrative decisions that affect them.
To this end, the following decisions must be reasoned:
1° Decisions restricting the exercise of public freedoms or, more generally, constituting a police measure;
2° Decisions imposing a sanction;

In deciding whether to impose sanctions, the authorities will take into account the factual circumstances surrounding the fraud and its subsequent discovery.

Sanctions Are Governed by Non-Statutable Time Limits

As the administration emphasizes [810], the legal framework governing the minister's police and sanctioning powers under the French foreign investment screening (FDI) regime does not provide for any statute of limitations.

Accordingly, the minister's power to impose sanctions under the FDI regulations is not subject to prescription, and the minister may adopt one or more sanction measures within a reasonable period of time. This reasonable period is assessed by reference, on the one hand, to the date on which the irregularity was committed or ceased, and the date on which it was formally identified, and, on the other hand, to the requirement that the exercise of the minister's powers must follow within a reasonable time after the irregularity has been established. The notion of "reasonable time" is also evaluated in light of the specific circumstances of the case and the complexity of the matter.

The minister's police powers are likewise not subject to prescription, as they embody the authority of the French State acting in its sovereign capacity.

By contrast, criminal sanctions under the Customs Code are subject to the standard six-year statute of limitations running from the date of commission of the offense. Article 351 of the French Customs Code provides that "the action of the customs administration in the repression of customs offenses is subject to the same limitation periods and conditions as the public prosecution of ordinary criminal offenses." In turn, Article 8 of the French Code of Criminal Procedure stipulates that "the prosecution of criminal offenses shall be time-barred after six full years from the day on which the offense was committed."

The investor may regularize its situation under certain conditions

As the administration recalls [811], the Minister may, in cases where the investor has failed to submit an authorization request, whether intentionally, deliberately, or

---

3° Decisions subjecting the granting of an authorization to restrictive conditions or imposing constraints;
4° Decisions withdrawing or repealing a right-creating decision;
5° Decisions invoking a time limitation, foreclosure, or forfeiture;
6° Decisions denying a benefit to which a person is legally entitled if statutory conditions are met;
7° Decisions refusing an authorization, except where disclosing the reasons would likely harm one of the secrets or interests protected under points (a) to (f) of Article L. 311-5, 2°;
8° Decisions rejecting an administrative appeal that must be lodged prior to any judicial remedy pursuant to legislative or regulatory provisions.

810. France, Ministry of the Economy, Finance and Industrial and Digital Sovereignty, Directorate General of the Treasury, "Guidelines on the Foreign Direct Investment Screening in France" July 2025, Point 3.3.1, published July 30, 2025, consulted August 1, 2025, available at https://www.tresor.economie.gouv.fr/services-aux-entreprises/investissements-etrangers-en-france

811. France, Ministry of the Economy, Finance and Industrial and Digital Sovereignty, Directorate General of the Treasury, Guidelines on the Foreign Direct Investment Screening in France July 2025, see Point

through mere negligence or omission, order the investor to seek retroactive regularization of the situation by filing an authorization request (see also Chapter 10).

An investor acting in good faith may also, on its own initiative, approach the Directorate General of the Treasury to request the implementation of this regularization procedure.

In the course of such regularization, the examination of the three eligibility criteria will be carried out on the basis of the legal and factual circumstances applicable at the time the irregular investment was made, and not at the time of its subsequent regularization.

The possibility of retroactively regularizing an investment cures the civil nullity, but does not exempt the investor from the risk of financial penalties provided for under Article L. 151-3-2 of the Monetary and Financial Code.

The amount of the financial penalty is proportionate to the seriousness of the breaches committed. In assessing the measures to be adopted, consideration is also given to the investor's conduct and, more broadly, to the circumstances surrounding the failure to file the required authorization request.

The FDI Sanctions Procedure Includes Adversarial Exchanges

The French authorities have clarified[812] the procedural steps applicable when breaches of the foreign investment screening regime (IEF) are suspected.

The sanctions process begins with a formal finding of non-compliance issued by the Interministerial Committee for Foreign Direct Investments Screening in France (Comité interministériel des investissements étrangers en France – CIIEF).

As a reminder, there are four main types of breaches that may give rise to such a finding:
1. Completion of an investment without prior authorization;
2. Failure to comply with the conditions attached to the Minister's authorization;
3. Total or partial failure to comply with an injunction issued by the Minister;
4. Fraudulent procurement of an authorization.

The finding of non-compliance is reviewed by the Treasury Department (Direction générale du Trésor), specifically by the unit in charge of FDI screening (CIEF), which assesses whether a sanction is warranted.

The finding is then communicated to the investor by mail, which formally notifies the opening of an adversarial procedure.

2.2.2.1, published 30 July 2025, consulted 1 August 2025, available at https://www.tresor.economie.gouv.fr/services-aux-entreprises/investissements-etrangers-en-france

812. France, Ministry of the Economy, Finance and Industrial and Digital Sovereignty, Directorate General of the Treasury, 2025 Annual Report, "Foreign Direct Investment Screening in France", published 30 July 2025, consulted 31 July 2025, available at https://www.tresor.economie.gouv.fr/Articles/2025/07/30/publication-du-rapport-annuel-sur-le-controle-ief-en-2024

The investor is granted a minimum period of fifteen (15) calendar days to respond. Within this timeframe, the investor may submit written comments and explanations to the Treasury Department.

Following review of the investor's observations, the Minister may either render a final decision or decide to continue the adversarial exchanges under the same fifteen-day calendar period if the comments warrant further clarification.

If the investor fails to respond within fifteen days of receiving either the initial or follow-up observations, the Minister may issue a final decision without further delay.

The Minister may not contractually waive the exercise of police powers

The French Government has emphasized[813] that, as a matter of principle, authorities vested with police powers may not relinquish or limit the exercise of such powers through contractual commitments. This rule is firmly established: an administrative authority may neither agree, by contract, to abstain from exercising its police powers, nor bind itself to exercise them in a predetermined manner. Accordingly, even within the framework of a contract concluded with a private party, the government remains free to exercise its police powers whenever necessary to safeguard public order.

This principle ensures that the public authority is not constrained in fulfilling its mission to protect public order or serve the public interest. It guarantees that the State retains the ability to act at any time in light of evolving circumstances, regardless of any prior undertakings.

The issue of non-compliance with obligations is particularly critical, as it directly affects the credibility of the State in enforcing the commitments undertaken by the investor as a condition for authorizing the transaction while preserving the Nation's strategic interests. For this reason, any breach of such commitments is subject to severe sanctions.

813. France, National Assembly, Written Question No. 3493 to the Minister of the Economy, Finance and Industrial and Digital Sovereignty, "Tripartite Agreement between the State, Sanofi and CD&R", Official Journal of the National Assembly, No. 4 (Q), January 28, 2025, p. 2307, MARLEIX O., Member of Parliament, Les Républicains (LR), ministerial reply, Official Journal of the National Assembly, May 20, 2025, p. 3667

Summary Table of Sanctions

Summary Table of Sanctions[814]		
Administrative Sanctions Article L. 151-3-1 of the Monetary and Financial Code		
Powers of the Minister	Section I of Article L. 151-3-1 Investment carried out <u>without</u> prior authorization	Section II of Article L. 151-3-1 Investment carried out <u>with</u> prior authorization but in breach of conditions
Powers of the Minister	Section I of Article L. 151-3-1 Investment carried out <u>without</u> prior authorization	Section II of Article L. 151-3-1 Investment carried out <u>with</u> prior authorization but in breach of conditions
Power of initiative ?	The Minister is required to act but may[815] choose between:	The Minister assesses the nature of the breach and may:
Power of injunction	1° Order the investor to submit an authorization request (for regularization purposes) 2° Order the investor to restore the previous situation at their own expense 3° Order the investor to modify the investment	1° Withdraw the authorization and require the investor to submit a new request 2° Require compliance, within a specified time frame, with the conditions set out in the authorization 3° Impose substitute measures for the unfulfilled obligation: • Restoration of the previous situation • Divestment of all or part of the activities

814. DUPEYRAT, op. cit., pp. 131–132

815. In its 2019 interpretation of the Minister's police powers, the administration had stated that the mandatory nature of the three existing injunction measures applicable when an investment is carried out without prior authorization should be understood together with the Minister's actual discretion not to systematically regularize the operation. This prevented investors from creating a fait accompli and confirmed that the Minister could, in particular, require the investor to restore the situation to its prior state. See France, Ministry of the Economy, Finance, Industrial and Digital Sovereignty, Directorate General of the Treasury, "The Minister of the Economy's Police Powers," 10 September 2019, consulted 1 September 2025, available at https://www.tresor.economie.gouv.fr/services-aux-entreprises/investissements-etrangers-en-france/les-pouvoirs-de-police-du-ministre-charge-de-l-economie. This clarification no longer appears on the same page as consulted on 1 September 2025.

<table>
<tr><td>Power to impose a penalty payment</td><td>Penalty payment, the amount and effective date of which are set by the injunction</td></tr>
<tr><td>Power to adopt protective measures, which may be combined with injunctions, in the event of a potential or actual threat to national interests</td><td>a) Suspend voting rights
b) Prohibit or limit the distribution of dividends or remuneration
c) Temporarily suspend, restrict, or prohibit the free disposal of all or part of the assets
d) Appoint a trustee responsible for ensuring the protection of national interests within the target company</td></tr>
<tr><td>Procedural Safeguards</td><td>A formal notice is sent requesting the submission of observations within fifteen days,
except in cases of urgency, exceptional circumstances, or imminent threat to public order, public security, or national defense.</td></tr>
<tr><td>Legal Remedies</td><td>Full Jurisdiction Appeal</td></tr>
<tr><td colspan="2">Financial Penalties
Article L. 151-3-2 of the Monetary and Financial Code</td></tr>
<tr><td>Power of Initiative</td><td>Yes,
the Minister assesses the situation (after giving the investor the opportunity to submit observations on the alleged facts within a minimum period of 15 days).</td></tr>
<tr><td rowspan="2">In cases of:
• Carrying out an investment without prior authorization
• Obtaining prior authorization by fraud
• Non-compliance with the conditions attached to the prior authorization
• Total or partial non-execution of decisionsor injunctions issued under Sections I or II of Article L. 151-3-1</td><td>Financial penalties, the amount of which may be equal to the maximum of the highest of the following sums:
• Double the amount of the irregular investment,
• 10% of the company's annual pre-tax turnover,
• Five million euros for legal entities,
• One million euros for natural persons.</td></tr>
<tr><td>The amount of the financial penalty is proportionate to the severity of the violations committed.
The penalty amount is collected in the same manner as State claims unrelated to taxes and public property.</td></tr>
<tr><td colspan="2">Criminal Sanctions</td></tr>
<tr><td>Article 458 of the Customs Code
Exclusive right of complaint vested in the Minister of the Economy</td><td>Article 459 of the Customs Code
Imprisonment for 5 years,
Confiscation of the instrument of the offense and of goods and assets that are the proceeds of the offense,
Fine equal to at least the amount and at most twice the amount involved in the offense</td></tr>
</table>

Summary of the IEF Sanctions Procedure[816]

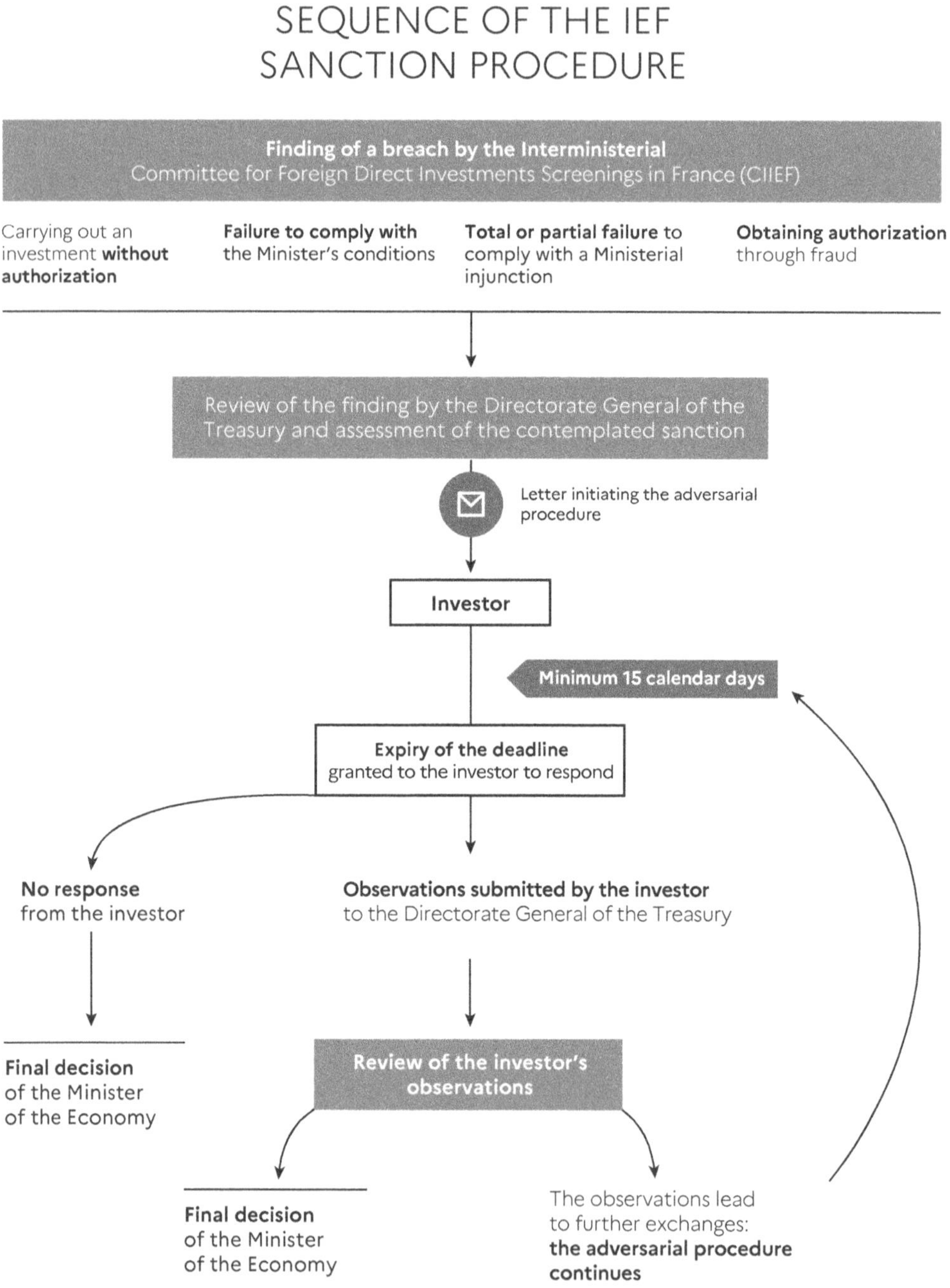

816. France, Diagram established in accordance with Articles L. 321-1 et seq. of the Code on Relations between the Public and the Administration, Ministry of the Economy, Finance and Industrial and Digital Sovereignty, Directorate General of the Treasury, Annual Report 2024, "Foreign Direct Investment Screening in France," Published July 30, 2025, consulted July 31, 2025, available at https://www.tresor.economie.gouv.fr/Articles/2025/07/30/publication-du-rapport-annuel-sur-le-controle-ief-en-2024

Chapter 22

Disputes Arising from the Foreign Investment Control Regime Remain Marginal

As with any administrative decision, the authorization (whether conditional or not) or refusal issued by the Minister of the Economy in the context of foreign direct investment screening is subject to judicial review before the French administrative courts.

In this field, the Minister's decisions, namely, those adopted with respect to requests for prior authorization in both the first and second phases, as well as those taken in response to a preliminary review request, may in principle be challenged through two types of proceedings[817]: an administrative appeal and a full-jurisdiction action (recours de plein contentieux).

However, the legislation creates a degree of ambiguity, as it expressly provides for judicial review (in the form of a full-jurisdiction action) only with respect to the Minister's injunction powers exercised under his administrative police authority (Article L. 151-3-1 of the Monetary and Financial Code).

Finally, beyond the procedural and contentious aspects, any meaningful assessment of these remedies must take into account their practical effectiveness, given the very limited number of court decisionsaddressing foreign direct investment screening, and, more fundamentally, their relevance in light of the sovereign discretion of the French State to safeguard the national interest.

IEF decisions may be challenged through an administrative appeal

First, the investor may lodge an administrative appeal before the Minister of the Economy within two months from notification of the decision at issue, requesting that the Minister reconsider his decision.

An administrative appeal is a procedure by which an individual challenges a decision made by an administrative authority (such as a minister, prefect, mayor, central

817. See Point 2.3.3.6. in Ministry of the Economy, Finance, Industrial and Digital Sovereignty, Directorate General of the Treasury, "Guidelines on the screening of foreign investments in France," July 2025, published on 30 July 2025, consulted on 1 August 2025,, available at https://www.tresor.economie.gouv.fr/services-aux-entreprises/investissements-etrangers-en-france

or local administration, or public institution) without immediately resorting to judicial proceedings. It is therefore a non-contentious mechanism that allows the administration to reassess its own decision before the administrative courts (administrative tribunal, administrative court of appeal, or the Conseil d'État) can be seized.

There are two principal types of administrative appeals. A "recours gracieux" (petition for reconsideration) is submitted directly to the authority that issued the disputed decision, requesting that this authority withdraw, amend, or annul its own decision. A "recours hiérarchique" (hierarchical appeal) is lodged with the hierarchical superior of the authority that issued the decision. These two forms of appeal may be pursued alternatively or cumulatively.

With respect to time limits, an administrative appeal must, in principle, be filed within the same two-month period applicable to judicial review, running from the notification or publication of the contested decision. A recours gracieux or recours hiérarchique suspends the time limit for bringing judicial proceedings. If the administration rejects the appeal, a new two-month period begins to run for filing suit before the courts. If the administration remains silent for two months, this silence is deemed an implicit decision of rejection. The French administration has confirmed this rule, expressly recalling that "failure to respond to such an appeal within two months from the date it was filed shall be deemed a rejection."

In matters relating to the IEF procedure, an administrative appeal may be filed with the Minister of the Economy either by email (iefautorisations@dgtresor.gouv.fr) or by postal mail (Ministère de l'économie, des finances et de la souveraineté industrielle et numérique - Direction générale du Trésor - Bureau CIEF / Télédoc 233 - 139, rue de Bercy - 75572 Paris Cedex 12).

That said, although the theoretical advantage of an administrative appeal is that it gives the administration an opportunity to revisit its decision and spares the investor immediate recourse to the courts, in practice it is a difficult remedy to pursue in the field of IEF control.

Foreign investment control decisions are also subject to judicial review.

Secondly, the investor may file an action for full jurisdiction [818] (recours de pleine juridiction), also referred to as an action for judicial review on the merits. In such proceedings, the administrative judge is not confined to annulling the challenged act but may also modify the contested decision, substitute his or her own ruling, order the administration to pay damages, or even impose new obligations.

818. Whereas an action for annulment (recours pour excès de pouvoir) limits the judge to setting aside an administrative act if it is found to be unlawful, an action for full jurisdiction (recours de pleine juridiction) may result not only in the annulment of the act but also in its modification or in the imposition of other measures (including injunctions). This distinction was first articulated by Edouard Lafferiere, Vice-President of the Conseil d'État, in Traité de la juridiction administrative et des recours contentieux, 1887, Paris, Berger-Levrault et Cie, Libraires-Éditeurs.

The investor must file the action before the competent administrative court within a two-month period. Pursuant[819] to Article R. 312-10 of the Administrative Justice Code, territorial jurisdiction lies with the administrative court having jurisdiction over the seat of the entity that is the object of the investment.

In the specific context of foreign direct investment screening, all ministerial decisions, including[820] those relating to the prior notification of the crossing of the 10 percent threshold, may be challenged before the administrative court[821] within two months.

Furthermore, the administration has clarified[822] that, under Article L. 411-2 of the Code on Relations between the Public and the Administration (CRPA), the filing of an administrative appeal suspends the running of the judicial appeal period, which begins to run anew only upon the explicit or implicit rejection of the administrative appeal.

In practice, legal remedies remain difficult to pursue

The scope of available remedies under the French FDI screening regime should be carefully qualified. From both a legal and policy perspective, the administrative courts are generally reluctant to challenge the State's sovereign assessment of whether a contemplated investment may threaten national interests, namely public order, public security, or national defense.

---

819. Administrative Justice Code, Article R. 312-10
"Disputes relating to legislation governing professional activities, including the liberal professions, agricultural, commercial, and industrial activities, price regulation, labor regulation, and the protection or representation of employees, as well as disputes concerning administrative sanctions imposed under such legislation, fall, where the challenged decision is not regulatory in nature, within the jurisdiction of the administrative court having territorial competence over either the establishment or operation whose activity gave rise to the dispute, or the place where the profession is exercised.
Where, for these same categories of disputes, the contested decision is regulatory in nature and applies only within the territorial jurisdiction of a single administrative court, that court shall have jurisdiction to hear the case.
By way of derogation from the first paragraph, appeals against decisions taken by administrative authorities concerning the composition and election of employee representative bodies, pursuant to Titles I, II, and III of Book III of Part Two of the Labor Code, shall be brought before the administrative court having jurisdiction over the location of the company's registered office."

820. France, Ministry of the Economy, Finance and Industrial and Digital Sovereignty, Directorate General of the Treasury, "Guidelines on the Foreign Direct Investment Screening in France," July 2025, see Point 2.3.4, published July 30, 2025, consulted August 1, 2025, available at https://www.tresor.economie.gouv.fr/services-aux-entreprises/investissements-etrangers-en-france

821. France, Ministry of the Economy, Finance and Recovery, Directorate General of the Treasury, "FAQ: Foreign Investments Screening in France," October 2023, p. 8, consulted May 9, 2024, available at https://www.tresor.economie.gouv.fr/services-aux-entreprises/investissements-etrangers-en-france; the version France, Ministry of the Economy, Finance, Industrial and Digital Sovereignty, Directorate General of the Treasury, "FAQ: Foreign Investments Screening in France," January 2025, consulted September 1, 2025, available at https://www.tresor.economie.gouv.fr/services-aux-entreprises/investissements-etrangers-en-france does not include this mention.

822. See Point 2.2.3.6. in Ministry of the Economy, Finance, Industrial and Digital Sovereignty, Directorate General of the Treasury, "Guidelines on the screening of foreign investments in France," July 2025, published on 30 July 2025, consulted on 1 August 2025,, available at https://www.tresor.economie.gouv.fr/services-aux-entreprises/investissements-etrangers-en-france

That said, in reviewing the State's assessment of the objectives and modalities of an investment transaction, the administrative judge may examine whether the measures imposed by the Minister of the Economy, such as a refusal or a conditional authorization, comply with the principle of proportionality. This control arises under Articles R. 151-8 and R. 151-9 of the French Monetary and Financial Code, which require that any restrictions imposed on a foreign investor must be proportionate to the "seriousness" of the potential threat to the Nation's interests. Such proportionality review is all the more important since prior-authorization requirements constitute a derogation from the fundamental principles of freedom of establishment and free movement of capital. Any restriction of these freedoms must therefore be both legitimate and proportionate.

In this context, one may also envisage that the administrative courts impose on the State an obligation to provide adequate reasoning for its decisions. In particular, restrictive measures must be justified in light of the "seriousness" of the identified threat, and the Minister's decision must be properly reasoned in accordance with Article R. 151-10 of the Monetary and Financial Code.

Thus, the protection of sovereign State interests does not automatically shield the State's assessment of security risks from judicial scrutiny.

Finally, as regards potential litigation before the Court of Justice of the European Union (CJEU), such proceedings are generally ill-suited to the business timeline of cross-border transactions. While they may clarify the scope of the French decree, they would not preclude the State's right to restrict the free movement of capital on grounds of public order or security.

Recourses Remain Limited in Number

In practice, recourses appear of limited utility, as they are difficult to initiate, as demonstrated by the hearings[823] of the Parliamentary Inquiry Commission. It thus emerged that not only are recourses challenging to implement for the parties involved in the transaction, but even more so for third parties, since the procedure is not public[824], nor are the decisions issued[825].

823. French National Assembly, Official Report No. 14, January 24, 2018, Parliamentary Inquiry Commission tasked with examining State decisions regarding industrial policy, particularly in relation to recent company mergers, notably Alstom, Alcatel, and STX, as well as the measures available to protect our national industrial champions within a globalized commercial context, Hearing of Ms. Muriel Lacoue-Labarthe, Deputy Director for "Trade Policy and Investment" within the Multilateral Affairs and Development Department of the Directorate General of the Treasury. "*You can imagine a scenario in which a third party would have grounds to complain about an investment taking place. As soon as, in this context, an investment occurs, it means it has been authorized, with or without conditions. Therefore, I assume, subject to verification, that the classic appeal period would not run because there is no public decision; however, the third party in question could start by asking the minister whether a decision has been made and, if there is no response, possibly contest the minister's failure to respond within the prescribed deadlines, then seek to find out if a decision was made and, if so, initiate an appeal against it. As soon as the investment takes place, it means it has either been authorized or it must be sanctioned.*"

824. It is therefore difficult for a third party to know against what and when to file an appeal.

825. It is therefore difficult for a third party to determine on what grounds, and at what point in time, a challenge may be brought.

From a tactical and opportunistic standpoint, it is furthermore quite unfortunate to challenge the Government's will through litigation in a field, that of protecting the national interest, where it is inherently sovereign. More pragmatically, it is also not sound policy for the investor, the target company, or the concerned third party to confront the State, which they may subsequently encounter again "on their path."

It must therefore be acknowledged that, for the time being, the contentious approach is powerless to resolve the issues faced by the investor or the unsuccessful competitor, as these issues are primarily institutional or political in nature. This remains a distinct feature of this type of operation.

Nonetheless, the deterrent effect of such a context does not preclude the existence of litigation, of which some decisions merit mention.

For instance, in 2004, the Conseil d'État[826] ruled that a decision by the minister in charge of the Economy, determining that the defense of national interests justifies subjecting a person or entity to the prior authorization regime under Article L. 151-2 of the Monetary and Financial Code, is subject to normal judicial review for abuse of power. This does not invalidate the law, which provides that the foreign direct investment screening regime falls under full jurisdiction review.

In 2016, the Conseil d'État[827] addressed the issue of an investor's probity. It recalled that the minister in charge of the Economy may, when assessing the risk posed by a foreign investment project to public order or public security, take into account the conduct of the person benefiting from the investment and the origin of the funds intended to finance the proposed investment. In that case, the file showed that at the date of the challenged decision, the investor's conduct gave rise to serious doubts regarding their probity. Accordingly, the minister was legitimately entitled to rely on facts leading to amnestied convictions or acts of clemency to assess such conduct. Moreover, despite requests for additional information, the company "Pathé France Holding" provided no indication regarding the origin of the funds intended to finance the proposed investment, amounting to over 512 million francs (approximately €140 million). Under these circumstances, the Conseil d'État held that the minister was justified in basing his decision on these elements, which established that the proposed acquisition of the majority of the capital of "Pathé Cinéma" by "Pathé France Holding" posed a threat to public order, thus warranting a decision to defer the investment in question.

In 2020, the Conseil d'État confirmed[828] that, in an investment operation carried out by an investment fund, regarding the identity of the investor in the application file, the administration was entitled to request the identity of the fund manager and those who control it, but not to request the identity of all investors participating in the fund.

826. France, Council of State (10th and 9th Joint Subsections), Decision No. 262626, November 3, 2004, Mentioned in the index of the Recueil Lebon

827. France, Council of State, 6th and 2nd Subsections Specially Reunited, Decision No. 160550 "Société Pathé Holding France," April 15, 1996, Published in the Recueil Lebon

828. France, Council of State, 6th and 5th Chambers Jointly Seated, Decision No. 422580, April 3, 2020, Mr. and Mrs. B... v. FII Co and Warwick Capital Partners, submissions by Stéphane Hoynck, ECLI: FR:CECHR:2020:422580.20200403, Mentioned in the index of the Recueil Lebon

In a ruling[829] by the Court of Cassation, the prior authorization granted under the foreign direct investment screening regime was invoked to dismiss a claim concerning the investor's probity; the foreign investment procedure effectively acting as a clearance in that regard.

Other non-contentious administrative remedies nevertheless exist.

Given the standing requirements to bring actions, the binding nature of defense secrets and business confidentiality, and finally the parties' interest in challenging a decision issued by the Ministry of the Economy against them, legal challenges remain rare.

More specifically regarding third parties' ability[830] to contest decisions of the Minister of the Economy under the foreign direct investment screening regime, such action presupposes the establishment of publicity measures, which currently do not exist.

However, some third parties have genuine motivations to act in the context of a foreign investment transaction. This notably includes trade unions, which may consider themselves entitled to be informed of commitments imposed by the State on the foreign investor as part of the investment authorization.

In this context, it is important to note the use of the administrative document access procedure provided by the Act[831] of July 17, 1978. By invoking the provisions of this Act, any individual or administrative authority that is denied access to an administrative document or that does not receive a response within one month may petition the Commission for Access to Administrative Documents (Commission d'Accès aux Documents Administratifs, CADA) to rule on whether the document is disclosable. The Commission may also be seized when an adverse decision regarding the reuse of public information is issued.

In this regard, attention should be drawn to the 2020 opinion[832] of the CADA, which refers to a petition filed with the Commission in August 2019 following the refusal by the Minister of the Economy and Finance to disclose to a private individual the document(s) indicating the commitments undertaken by Nokia in connection with its acquisition of Alcatel-Lucent by way of a public exchange offer carried out between November 18 and December 23, 2015, an operation subject to an authorization procedure pursuant to paragraph I of Article L. 151-3 of the Monetary and Financial Code.

829. France, Court of Cassation, Decision No. 171 FS-D, February 6, 2019, on the decision of the Grenoble Court of Appeal, Commercial Chamber, Case No. 16/03244, October 12, 2017

830. Publicity of the Procedure (which does not currently exist) is Not Necessarily Incompatible with Business Secrecy : After all, transactions subject to competition authorities are also covered by business secrecy, yet a procedural framework allowing for appeals exists.

831. France, Law No. 78-753 of July 17, 1978, on Various Measures to Improve Relations between the Administration and the Public and Various Administrative, Social, and Fiscal Provisions, Official Journal of the French Republic, July 18, 1978, p. 2851

832. France, Commission for Access to Administrative Documents (CADA), Opinion No. 20194281, February 20, 2020, "Ministry of Economy, Finance and Industrial and Digital Sovereignty," consulted September 1st, at https://www.cada.fr/20194330

In this case, the Commission first recalled, by way of preliminary remark, that it was not competent to rule on the informational rights that employee representatives and trade unions may derive, in their capacity as such, from specific texts. These entities may, however, invoke, like any other citizen, the provisions of Book III of the Code of Relations between the Public and the Administration (CRPA) (Code des relations entre le public et l'administration) and the special regimes enumerated in Articles L. 342-1 and L. 342-2 of that Code to obtain document disclosure. It is on this basis that their request was examined.

The Commission then observed that pursuant to subparagraph (a) of Article L. 151-3 of the Monetary and Financial Code, foreign investments in activities in France that are likely to affect public order, public security, or the interests of national defense are subject to prior authorization by the Minister in charge of the Economy. Among such investments are those concerning the integrity, security, and operational continuity of electronic communications networks and services, as set forth in the combined provisions of Articles R. 153-2 to R. 153-4 of the same Code.

Finally, the Commission concluded that the documents reflecting the commitments made by Nokia in the context of this procedure related to the Alcatel-Lucent acquisition constitute administrative documents within the meaning of Article L. 300-2 of the Code of Relations between the Public and the Administration (CRPA). It specified that their disclosure is governed notably by Article L. 311-5 of the same Code, which provides that documents are non-disclosable if their communication would harm "(b) national defense secrets; (...) (d) the security of the State, public safety, the safety of individuals, or the security of the information (CRPA) systems of administrations; (...)", as well as Article L. 311-6, which limits disclosure solely to the interested party for administrative documents "1° whose communication would harm the protection of privacy, medical secrecy, and business secrets, which include trade secrets, economic and financial information, and commercial or industrial strategies (...)".

In response to the request, the Minister of the Economy and Finance informed the Commission that the letters of commitment contain information protected by national defense secrecy, such as the identification of company activities deemed sensitive, clauses requiring the establishment of restricted and protected zones within Alcatel Submarine Networks and Alcatel-Lucent, information related to a Ministry of Defense contract, or details concerning maintenance and support modalities of defense-related sites. The Minister further indicated that the obligations set forth in these letters of commitment are covered by business secrecy, including clauses requiring the company to comply with specific conditions for appointing executives, provisions regarding the supply of certain services to sensitive clients, obligations to maintain certain sensitive activities and human resources on designated sites, and obligations related to research and development (R&D) of certain activities.

In light of this response, the Commission considered that, given the framework of the authorization within which these commitments were made and to which it was not granted access, these commitments necessarily contain a substantial portion of information the disclosure of which would undermine national defense, State security, public safety, or the security of information systems of administrations. Such information is therefore non-disclosable pursuant to Article L. 311-5 of the Code of Relations between the Public and the Administration (CRPA) .

However, the Commission noted that the request was not limited to the letters of commitment signed by Nokia in order to obtain the authorization provided for by Article L. 151-3 of the Monetary and Financial Code, to which the Alcatel-Lucent acquisition was subject, but concerned "the document(s) indicating the commitments" made by that company in the context of the acquisition, which is an authorized transaction. The Commission also clarified, with respect to business secret provisions, whose disclosure is limited to interested parties, that it considered the company's legal representatives, the representative institutions of its personnel, or its employees to qualify as interested parties with regard to information concerning the company's economic situation, means, organization, and commercial strategy. It deduced that any document relating to commitments made by Nokia on these matters in connection with the Alcatel-Lucent acquisition, and held by the administration, is disclosable to the requester, provided it contains no information the disclosure of which would harm national defense, State security, public safety, or the security of administrative information systems, or if it does contain such information, after redacting those parts if they can be dissociated. Accordingly, the Commission issued a favorable opinion to this extent.

This decision is noteworthy because it establishes that the company's legal representatives, its employee representative institutions, or its employees have an interest in knowing of the existence of commitments made for the preservation of the national interest, but not of their content.

* * *

More generally, litigation concerning foreign direct investment screening remains residual, due both to the limited number of cases and to the lack of interest by parties involved in transactions in contesting the sovereign decisions of the Minister. Similar to parliamentarians who increasingly demand greater transparency and explanations regarding Government decisions taken to protect the national interest (see Chapter 5), the willingness of third parties to the transaction, particularly trade unions, to be informed of these decisions is a factor contributing to a multiplication of challenges.

Conclusion

At the conclusion of this first English edition of the second French version of the work, it becomes clear that the screening of foreign direct investment (FDI) in France has established itself as an essential component of merger and acquisition transactions whenever a foreign investor is involved.

This regime has a dual nature: it is credible and predictable, though not predictive.

It is credible because the statutory framework, the procedures it organizes, and the sanctions it provides ensure an effective and robust screening mechanism.

It is predictable in the sense that the foreign investor is subject to a set of rules and guidelines that guarantee a fair review of the proposed transaction.

However, it cannot be described as predictive. Knowledge of the applicable norms alone does not allow one to anticipate with certainty the Minister of the Economy's final decision. Certain outcomes reflect the inherent margin of discretion in interministerial consultations, and in some cases, even political considerations.

It is precisely because of this institutional uncertainty that a nuanced understanding of the French FDI screening regime becomes an essential condition for success in cross-border transactions. Minimizing this risk is the key to securing the deal, both legally and in terms of economic value.

Thus, it is within this subtle balance between predictability and non-predictability that the freedom to invest in France unfolds, while ensuring the effective protection of the Nation's fundamental interests. This articulation, far from being a contradiction, is instead the guarantee of a system where the public interest and economic initiative can converge, to the benefit of all stakeholders.

Bibliography

Books :

France, AUDIT M., BOLLEE S., CALLE P., Droit du commerce international et des investissements étrangers, LGDJ, 3rd ed., 2019

France, BEGUIN J., MENJUCQ M. (eds.), Droit du commerce international, Lexis Nexis, 23rd ed., 2019

France, CACHARD Olivier, Droit du commerce international, LGDJ, 3rd ed., 2018

France, CARREAU D., JUILLARD P., BISMUTH R., HAMANN A., Droit international économique, Dalloz, 6th ed., 2017

France, DE NANTEUIL A., Droit international de l'investissement, Pedone, 3rd ed., 2020

France, DUPEYRAT P., Le guide des investissements étrangers dans les secteurs stratégiques, Ellipses, 2011

France, DUPEYRAT P., Mondialisation et patriotisme économique, Pref. DUFOURCQ, JM Laffont, 2014

France, DUPEYRAT P. with Houillon Gregory, Lobbying, du déni au défi, Pref. Accoyer Bernard, PresseLittéraire, 2016

France, DUPEYRAT P., Sécurité économique et souverainetés industrielles, Pref. LE MAIRE B., PUF, 2020

France, DUPEYRAT P., CFIUS Le contrôle des investissements étrangers aux États-Unis, Relians, 2022

France, JACQUET J.-M., DELEBECQUE Ph., USUNIER L., Droit du commerce international, Dalloz, 4th ed., 2021

France, JACOMET T., DIDIER E., Les relations financières avec l'étranger, Joly, 1997

France, JUILLARD P., L'évolution des sources du droit des investissements, Brill, 2008

France, HOUET J., « Les Golden shares en droit de l'Union européenne », Études, Larcier, 2015

France, KESSEDJIAN C., Droit du commerce international, PUF, 2020

France, MAUREL R. (ed.), Nouveaux regards sur le droit européen des investissements, Lexis Nexis, 2023

France, ROBERT-CUENDET S. (ed.), Droit des investissements internationaux : Perspectives croisées, Larcier, 2017

France, SYNVET H., « L'impact du droit communautaire sur le droit français des relations financières avec l'étranger », in Mélanges en l'honneur de Yvon Loussouarn, Dalloz, 1994

Reports :

France, NATIONAL ASSEMBLY, Report No. 2492 by the Committee on Finance, General Economy and Planning on Bill No. 2347 amending Law No. 66-1008 of December 28, 1966, regarding financial relations with foreign countries concerning foreign investments, MENUEL G., Deputy, Published January 18, 1996

France, NATIONAL ASSEMBLY, Report No. 807 by the Committee on Finance, General Economy and Planning on the Senate-adopted Financial Security Bill, GOULARD F., Deputy, Published April 10, 2003

France, PRIME MINISTER, CARAYON B., Report on "Intelligence économique, compétitivité et cohésion sociale", La Documentation française, Published July 1, 2003

France, NATIONAL ASSEMBLY, Information Report No. 1664 by the Committee on Finance, General Economy and Planning on the national economic security strategy, CARAYON B., Deputy, Published June 9, 2004

France, NATIONAL ASSEMBLY, Information Report No. 2202 by the Committee on National Defense and Armed Forces on foreign capital participation in European armament industries, DEFLESSELLES B. and MICHEL J., Deputies, Published March 23, 2005

OECD, Directorate for Financial and Enterprise Affairs, Investment Committee, Report "Liberté d'investissement, sécurité nationale et secteurs stratégiques : Fonds souverains et politiques des pays d'accueil", DAF/INV(2008)5/REV, Published April 14, 2008

France, NATIONAL ASSEMBLY, Report No. 2498 by the Special Committee charged with examining under accelerated procedure Bill No. 2447 for growth and activity, FERRAND R., General Rapporteur, Published January 19, 2015

France, NATIONAL ASSEMBLY, Corrected Report No. 897 by the Inquiry Commission on State decisions in industrial policy, regarding recent mergers notably Alstom, Alcatel and STX, and measures to protect national industrial champions in a globalized commercial context, MARLEIX O., President, KASBARIAN G., Rapporteur, Published April 19, 2018

France, MINISTRY OF THE ECONOMY, FINANCE AND RECOVERY, Directorate General of the Treasury, Annual Report 2022, "Contrôle des Investissements Étrangers en France", Published March 17, 2022

[France, MINISTÈRE DE L'ÉCONOMIE, DES FINANCES, DE LA RELANCE, Direction générale du Trésor, Rapport annuel 2022, « Contrôle des Investissements Étrangers en France », publié le 17 mars 2022]

Opinions :

France, ECONOMIC, SOCIAL AND ENVIRONMENTAL COUNCIL (CESE), Economic Activities Section, SAINT-AUBIN Ph., Opinion No. 2019-03, "La dépendance aux métaux stratégiques : quelles solutions pour l'économie ?", DILA, ISBN 978-2-11-152215-2, Published January 22, 2019

France, CESE, COUVERT C. and NIBOUREL Ch., Opinion 2021-09, "Pour une stratégie d'investissements directs étrangers en France soutenables et responsables", DILA, ISBN 978-2-11-155700-0, Published March 23, 2021

Publications / Publications :

ERNST & YOUNG ADVISORY, "Baromètre EY de l'Attractivité de la France 2024 : Attractive un jour, attractive toujours ?", Published May 2, 2024

Journals :

France, CARREAU D. and HURSTEL D., "La Nouvelle Liberté des investissements directs étrangers en France", Recueil Dalloz, 1996, Chroniques, p. 239

France, GUILLEMIN C., LABAUDE H., "La libéralisation des investissements directs étrangers en France", Les Petites Affiches, April 12, 1996, No. 45, p. 12

List of Abbreviations

Meaning (EN)	Abbreviation (FR)	Meaning (FR)
Annex / Appendix	Ann.	Annexe
Article	Art.	Article
Constitutional Law	LC	Loi constitutionnelle
Court of Appeal	CA	Cour d'appel
Court of Appeal of Paris	CA Paris	Cour d'appel de Paris
Court of Cassation	Cass.	Cour de cassation
Court of Cassation, Commercial Chamber	Cass. com	Cour de cassation, chambre commerciale
Court of Cassation, Social Chamber	Cass. soc.	Cour de cassation, chambre sociale
Court of Justice of the European Communities	CJCE	Cour de justice des Communautés européennes
Council of State	CE	Conseil d'État
Delegate Ministry for Industry	Min. dél. Indus.	Ministère délégué à l'Industrie
Defense Code	C. défense	Code de la défense
Decree	D.	Décret
Directorate General of the Treasury	DG Trésor	Direction Générale du Trésor
Directorate of Legal and Administrative Information	DILA	Direction de l'information légale et administrative
Dalloz Collection	D. (Recueil Dalloz)	Recueil Dalloz
Economic, Social and Environmental Council	CESE	Conseil économique, social et environnemental
Editions / Publishing	Ed.	Éditions

Meaning (EN)	Abbreviation (FR)	Meaning (FR)
Electronic Fund Transfer (FMI)	FMI	Fonds monétaire international
European Court of Auditors	C. comptes UE	Cour européenne des comptes
European Parliament	PE	Parlement européen
European Union	UE	Union européenne
General Interministerial Instruction	Instr. gén. intermin.	Instruction générale interministérielle
General Tax Code	CGI	Code général des impôts
Information Report	Rapp. info.	Rapport d'information
Internal Security Code	CSI	Code de la sécurité intérieure
Les Petites Affiches (Legal Gazette)	LPA	Les Petites Affiches
Legislative Proposal (Resolution Proposal)	Proposition res.	Proposition de résolution
Member of Parliament (Deputy)	Dep.	Député / Députée
Ministry of Defense	Min. Def.	Ministère de la Défense
Ministry of Economy, Finance and Industry	Min. Éco. Fin. Ind.	Ministère de l'Économie, des Finances et de l'Industrie
Ministry of Economy, Finance and Privatization	Min. Éco. Fin. Priv.	Ministère de l'Économie, des Finances et de la Privatisation
Ministry of Economy, Finance and Recovery	Min. Eco. Fin. Rel.	Ministère de l'Économie, des Finances, de la Relance
Ministry of Economy, Finance, Industrial and Digital Sovereignty	Min. Éco. Fin. Souv. Ind. Num.	Ministère de l'Économie, des Finances, et de la Souveraineté Industrielle et Numérique
Ministry of Finance and Economic Affairs	Min. Fin. Aff. éco.	Ministère des Finances et des Affaires Économiques
November	Nov.	Novembre
October	Oct.	Octobre
Official Journal of the European Communities	JOCE	Journal officiel des Communautés européennes

Meaning (EN)	Abbreviation (FR)	Meaning (FR)
Official Journal of the European Union	JOUE	Journal officiel de l'Union européenne
Official Journal of the French Republic	JO	Journal officiel de la République française
Official Journal of the National Assembly	JOAN	Journal officiel Assemblée nationale
Official Journal of the Senate	JOS	Journal officiel Sénat
Order / Decree	A.	Arrêté
Oral Question	QO	Question orale
Pages	PP.	Pages
Penal Code	C. pén.	Code pénal
Presidency of the Republic	Pres. Rep.	Présidence de la République
Press Release	Comm. presse	Communiqué de presse
Question to the Government	QAG	Question au Gouvernement
Report	Rapp.	Rapport
Report to the Prime Minister	Rapp. Prem. min.	Rapport au Premier ministre
Regulation	Règl.	Règlement
Resolution Proposal	Proposition res.	Proposition de résolution
Senate / Senator / Senator (female)	Sen.	Sénat / sénateur / sénatrice
State Shareholding Agency	APE	Agence des participations de l'État
Treaty on the Functioning of the European Union	TFUE	Traité sur le fonctionnement de l'Union européenne
Written Question	QE	Question écrite

Appendices

Annex A: Article L. 151-1 and following of the Monetary and Financial Code[833]

Article L. 151-1

Financial relations between France and foreign countries are free.

This freedom is exercised according to the terms provided in this chapter, respecting the international commitments undertaken by France.

Article L. 151-2

Amended by Ordinance No. 2014-158 of February 20, 2014 – art. 1

The Government may, to ensure the defense of national interests and by decree taken on the report of the minister in charge of the economy:

1. Subject to declaration, prior authorization, or control:

a) Foreign exchange operations, capital movements, and payments of any kind between France and foreign countries;

b) The constitution, alteration, and liquidation of French assets abroad;

c) The constitution and liquidation of foreign investments in France;

d) The import and export of gold as well as all other material movements of valuables between France and foreign countries;

2. Order the repatriation of claims on foreign countries outside the European Union arising from the export of goods, the remuneration of services, and more generally from all income or proceeds abroad;

3. Authorize intermediaries to carry out the operations mentioned in 1, a and d above.

Article L. 151-3

Amended by Law No. 2019-486 of May 22, 2019 – art. 152

I. Foreign investments in an activity in France that, even occasionally, participate in the exercise of public authority or fall within one of the following domains are subject to prior authorization by the minister in charge of the economy:

a) Activities likely to harm public order, public security, or national defense interests;

b) Activities of research, production, or commercialization of weapons, ammunition, powders, and explosive substances.

A decree of the Council of State defines the nature of the above activities and the investments subject to authorization.

833. Source: Légifrance, version as of August 12, 2024, available at https://www.legifrance.gouv.fr/codes/section_lc/LEGITEXT000006072026/LEGISCTA000006153982/#LEGISCTA000006153982 (last accessed August 12, 2024).

II. The authorization granted may, if applicable, be subject to conditions aimed at ensuring that the proposed investment will not harm the national interests referred to in I.

The decree mentioned in I specifies the nature and modalities of the review of the conditions that may be attached to the authorization.

Article L. 151-3-1

Created by Law No. 2019-486 of May 22, 2019 – art. 152

I. If a foreign investment has been made without prior authorization, the minister in charge of the economy shall take one or more of the following measures:

1° Order the investor to submit an authorization request;

2° Order the investor to restore the previous situation at their own expense;

3° Order the investor to modify the investment.

The orders referred to in 1° to 3° may be accompanied by a penalty payment. The order specifies the amount and effective date of this penalty. A decree of the Council of State sets the maximum daily amount of the penalty and the modalities according to which, in the event of total or partial non-execution or delay, the penalty is enforced.

The minister in charge of the economy may also, if the protection of the national interests mentioned in I of Article L. 151-3 is compromised or likely to be compromised, take the necessary precautionary measures. In this regard, he may:

a) Suspend voting rights attached to the shares or equity interests whose holding by the investor should have been subject to prior authorization;

b) Prohibit or limit the distribution of dividends or remuneration attached to the shares or equity interests whose holding by the investor should have been subject to prior authorization;

c) Temporarily suspend, restrict, or prohibit the free disposal of all or part of the assets related to the activities defined in the same I;

d) Appoint a representative responsible for overseeing, within the company conducting the activity mentioned in I of Article L. 151-3, the protection of national interests. This representative may block any decision of corporate bodies likely to harm these interests. His remuneration is fixed by the minister in charge of the economy; it is borne by the company to which he is appointed, along with expenses incurred.

II. The minister in charge of the economy, if he deems that the conditions attached to the authorization pursuant to II of Article L. 151-3 have been violated, shall take one or more of the following measures:

1° Withdrawal of the authorization. Unless the previous situation prior to the investment is restored, the foreign investor must request the investment authorization provided for in the same Article L. 151-3 again;

2° Order the investor responsible for the unmet obligation to comply within a fixed deadline with the conditions set out in the authorization;

3° Order the investor responsible for the unmet obligation to comply within a fixed deadline with prescriptions substituting the unmet obligation, including restoring the situation prior to the breach or the disposal of all or part of the activities defined in I of the same Article L. 151-3.

These orders may be accompanied by a penalty according to the modalities provided in I of this article.

The minister in charge of the economy may also take necessary precautionary measures under the conditions and modalities set forth in I above.

III. Decisions or orders taken pursuant to this article may only occur after the investor has been given formal notice to submit observations within fifteen days, except in cases of urgency, exceptional circumstances, or imminent threat to public order, public security, or national defense.

IV. These decisions are subject to full jurisdiction appeal.

V. A decree of the Council of State determines the modalities of application of this article.

Article L. 151-3-2

Created by Law No. 2019-486 of May 22, 2019 – art. 152

In the event of an investment made without prior authorization, obtaining prior authorization by fraud, breach of the provisions of II of Article L. 151-3, total or partial non-execution of decisions or orders taken under Article L. 151-3-1, the minister in charge of the economy may, after giving the investor the opportunity to present observations on the alleged facts within a minimum period of fifteen days, impose a financial penalty of up to the highest of the following amounts: double the amount of the irregular investment, 10% of the annual pre-tax turnover of the company carrying out the activities defined in I of Article L. 151-3, five million euros for legal persons, and one million euros for natural persons.

The amount of the financial penalty is proportionate to the severity of the breaches committed. The penalty amount is recovered as State claims unrelated to taxes and the public domain.

Article L. 151-4

Any commitment, agreement, or contractual clause that directly or indirectly realizes a foreign investment in one of the domains mentioned in I of Article L. 151-3 without having been subject to the authorization required under Article L. 151-3 is null and void.

Article L. 151-5

Amended by Law No. 2019-486 of May 22, 2019 – art. 152

The investor or the company exercising the activities mentioned in Article L. 151-3 shall be required to provide to the administrative authority in charge of the authorization and control procedure of foreign investments, upon request, all documents and information necessary for the performance of its mission, without legally protected secrets being opposable to it.

Article L. 151-6

Amended by Law No. 2024-850 of July 25, 2024 – art. 5

Subject to provisions relating to the protection of national defense secrets, the minister in charge of the economy shall annually publish, in a manner ensuring the anonymity of the natural and legal persons concerned, the main statistical data related to the Government's control of foreign investments in France. The annual publication of this data may give rise to a debate in the National Assembly and the Senate.

Article L. 151-7

Amended by Law No. 2024-850 of July 25, 2024 – art. 5

I. Each year, the Government shall transmit to the chairpersons of the committees in charge of economic affairs and to the general rapporteurs of the committees in charge of finance of each assembly a report concerning the Government's action in protecting and promoting the economic, industrial, and scientific interests of the Nation, as well as on the control of foreign investments under the procedure provided for in Article L. 151-3. This report shall include:

1° A description of the Government's action in protecting and promoting the economic, industrial, and scientific interests of the Nation, notably the measures taken regarding security and economic intelligence and the protection of strategic companies, the objectives pursued, the actions deployed, and the results obtained;

2° Information related to the prior authorization procedure for foreign investments in an activity in France, including detailed elements concerning the number of authorization requests submitted to the minister in charge of the economy, refusals, authorized operations, authorized operations subject to conditions provided for in II of the same Article L. 151-3, as well as elements relating to the exercise by the minister of the sanction power provided in said Article L. 151-3, excluding any information that could identify the natural or legal persons concerned by the prior authorization procedure of foreign investments in an activity in France.

II. The chairpersons of the committees in charge of economic affairs and the general rapporteurs of the committees in charge of finance of each assembly may jointly:

1° Hear the competent ministers, the commissioner for strategic information and economic security, and the directors of the concerned central administrations, accompanied by collaborators of their choice, within their respective fields of competence. These exchanges, which are not public, may concern information allowing the identification of natural or legal persons subject to the prior authorization procedure of foreign investments provided by Article L. 151-3;

2 °Conduct all investigations, on documents and on site, of the Government's action in protecting and promoting the economic, industrial, and scientific interests of the Nation, as well as on the control of foreign investments in France. These investigations cannot concern investments that may be subject to decisions by the minister in charge of the economy. All information and administrative documents they request within the framework of these investigations, including any reports prepared by the bodies and services responsible for administrative control, must be provided to them, subject to information and documents protected by national defense secrecy.

The exercise of the powers mentioned in 1° and 2° gives rise to a public communication by each chairperson and each general rapporteur before their committee, which may be accompanied by the publication of a report. This communication and, where applicable, this report may not mention any information or assessment element allowing the identification of natural or legal persons subject to the prior authorization procedure provided by Article L. 151-3.

Within the framework of their work, the chairpersons and general rapporteurs mentioned in the first paragraph of this II may jointly submit recommendations and observations to the President of the Republic, the Prime Minister, and the competent ministers. They transmit them to the President of the Senate and to the President of the National Assembly.

Each committee chairperson and each general rapporteur mentioned in the first paragraph of this II may delegate to a member of their committee the powers and responsibilities provided in I and in this II. In this case, the committee chairperson or general rapporteur remains the recipient of the report provided in I.

Annex B: Article R. 151-1 and following of the Monetary and Financial Code [834]

Section 1: Definition and Scope (Articles R151-1 to R151-3)

Article R. 151-1

When carrying out an investment referred to in Article R. 151-2, the following constitute an investor within the meaning of this chapter:

1° Any natural person of foreign nationality;

2° Any natural person of French nationality who is not domiciled in France within the meaning of Article 4 B of the General Tax Code;

3° Any entity governed by foreign law;

4° Any entity governed by French law controlled by one or more persons or entities referred to in points 1°, 2°, or 3°.

II. A control chain, within the meaning of this chapter, is composed of an investor referred to in points 3° or 4° of paragraph I and the persons or entities that control it. All persons and entities belonging to a control chain constitute investors within the meaning of this chapter.

III. Control referred to in this article is assessed within the meaning of Article L. 233-3 of the Commercial Code or, if no control can be established on the basis of that article, within the meaning of paragraph III of Article L. 430-1 of the same code.

Article R. 151-2

An investment, within the meaning of Article L. 151-3, is constituted for an investor referred to in paragraph I of Article R. 151-1 by:

1° Acquiring control, within the meaning of Article L. 233-3 of the Commercial Code, of an entity governed by French law or of an establishment registered in the Trade and Companies Register in France;

2° Acquiring all or part of a business branch of an entity governed by French law;

3 °Crossing, directly or indirectly, alone or in concert, the threshold of 25% ownership of voting rights in an entity governed by French law;

4 °Crossing, directly or indirectly, alone or in concert, the threshold of 10% ownership of voting rights in a French law company whose shares are admitted to trading on a regulated market.

Points 3° and 4° do not apply to a natural person holding the nationality of a Member State of the European Union or a state party to the Agreement on the European Economic

834. Légifrance, version as of April 17, 2024, available at https://www.legifrance.gouv.fr/codes/section_lc/LEGITEXT000006072026/LEGISCTA000006140476/2024-04-17/ (last accessed April 17, 2024)

Area having concluded an administrative assistance agreement with France to combat tax fraud and evasion and domiciled in one of these States, nor to an entity whose entire members of the control chain, within the meaning of paragraph II of Article R. 151-1, are subject to the law of one of these States or hold the nationality and are domiciled there.

NOTE: Pursuant to Article 12 of Decree No. 2023-1293 of December 28, 2023, these provisions enter into force on January 1, 2024.

Article R. 151-3

The activities referred to in paragraph I of Article L. 151-3 are as follows:

I. Activities likely to harm national defense interests, participating in the exercise of public authority, or likely to harm public order and public security:

1° Activities, including those referred to in Article L. 2332-1 of the Defense Code, related to weapons, ammunition, powders, and explosive substances intended for military purposes or war materials and equivalents under Title III or Title V of Book III of the second part of the Defense Code;

2° Activities related to dual-use goods and technologies listed in Annex IV of Regulation (EU) 2021/821 of the European Parliament and of the Council of May 20, 2021, establishing the Union regime for the control of exports, brokering, technical assistance, transit, and transfer concerning dual-use goods;

3° Activities carried out by entities holding national defense secrets;

4° Activities carried out in the field of information system security, including as subcontractors, for an operator referred to in Articles L. 1332-1 or L. 1332-2 of the Defense Code;

5° Activities carried out by entities having concluded a contract, directly or by subcontracting, for the Ministry of Defense for the realization of a good or service relating to an activity referred to in points 1° to 3° or 6°;

6° Activities related to cryptology means and services referred to in paragraphs III and IV of Article 30 and I of Article 31 of Law No. 2004-575 of June 21, 2004, on trust in the digital economy;

7° Activities related to equipment or technical devices intended to allow interception of communications or designed for remote detection of conversations or computer data capture, defined in Article 226-3 of the Penal Code;

8° Activities related to services provided by approved evaluation centers under the conditions set out in Decree No. 2002-535 of April 18, 2002, relating to the evaluation and certification of security offered by information technology products and systems;

9° Activities related to gambling, excluding casinos;

10° Activities related to means intended to counter illicit use of pathogens or toxins or to prevent the health consequences of such use;

11° Activities involving processing, transmission, or storage of data whose compromise or disclosure is likely to harm the exercise of the activities referred to in points 1° to 10° of this paragraph I or in paragraph II.

II. Activities likely to harm national defense interests, participating in the exercise of public authority or likely to harm public order and public security, when concerning infrastructures, goods, or essential services ensuring:

1° Integrity, security, or continuity of energy supply;

2° Integrity, security, or continuity of water supply;

3° Integrity, security, or continuity of operation of transport networks and services;

4° Integrity, security, or continuity of space operations referred to in point 3° of Article 1 of Law No. 2008-518 of June 3, 2008, relating to space operations;

5° Integrity, security, or continuity of operation of electronic communications networks and services;

6° Exercise of missions by the national police, national gendarmerie, civil security services, security of penitentiary establishments, as well as public security missions of customs and licensed private security companies;

7° Integrity, security, or continuity of operation of an establishment, installation, or work of vital importance within the meaning of Articles L. 1332-1 and L. 1332-2 of the Defense Code;

8° Protection of public health;

9° Production, processing, or distribution of agricultural products listed in Annex I of the Treaty on the Functioning of the European Union, when these contribute to national food security objectives referred to in points 1°, 17°, and 18° of paragraph I of Article L. 1 of the Rural and Maritime Fishing Code;

10° Editing, printing, or distribution of press publications of political and general information, within the meaning of Article 4 of Law No. 47-585 of April 2, 1947, relating to the status of newspaper and periodical publishing and distribution companies, and online press services of political and general information within the meaning of Article 1 of Law No. 86-897 of August 1, 1986, reforming the legal regime of the press;

11° Integrity, security, or continuity of extraction, processing, and recycling of critical raw materials.

III. Activities likely to harm national defense interests, participating in the exercise of public authority or likely to harm public order and public security, when intended to be implemented in one of the activities referred to in paragraphs I or II:

1° Research and development activities on critical technologies, the list of which is defined by order of the minister in charge of the economy;

2° Research and development activities on dual-use goods and technologies listed in Annex I of the Regulation (EU) of the European Parliament and of the Council of May 20, 2021, cited above.

NOTE: Pursuant to Article 12 of Decree No. 2023-1293 of December 28, 2023, these provisions enter into force on January 1, 2024.

Section 2: Procedure (Articles R. 151-4 to R. 151-11)

Subsection 1: Prior request for examination of an activity (Article R. 151-4)

Article R. 151-4

When seized by an entity governed by French law of a request for an opinion to determine whether all or part of the activity of that entity falls within paragraph I of Article L. 151-3, the minister in charge of the economy shall respond within two months.

Under the same conditions, an investor may, in agreement with the entity exercising the activities subject to the investment, submit the same request to the minister. In this case, a copy of the opinion rendered to the investor shall be sent to the entity exercising the activities subject to the investment.

Subsection 2: Examination of an authorization request (Articles R. 151-5 to R. 151-11)

Article R. 151-5

The authorization request for a foreign investment shall be submitted by the investor.

However, when the envisaged investment concerns one or more investors belonging to a control chain, the request may be submitted by one of the members of that chain on behalf of all the investors who are members of it.

The investor making an investment referred to in point 4° of Article R. 151-2 is exempted from the authorization request provided for in the first paragraph, provided that the investment project has been the subject of prior notification to the minister in charge of the economy. Unless opposed by the minister, the exemption from the authorization request arises at the end of a ten working day period from the notification.

NOTE: Pursuant to Article 12 of Decree No. 2023-1293 of December 28, 2023, these provisions enter into force on January 1, 2024.

Article R. 151-6

Within thirty working days from the date of receipt of an authorization request, the minister in charge of the economy shall inform the investor who submitted the request either that the investment does not fall within paragraph I of Article L. 151-3, or that it falls within it and is authorized without condition, or that it falls within it but a further examination is necessary to determine whether the preservation of the national interests defined in paragraph I of Article L. 151-3 can be guaranteed by attaching conditions to the authorization. In the absence of a response within this period, the authorization request shall be deemed rejected.

The refusal or the authorization, if applicable with conditions, shall be issued within forty-five working days from the date of receipt by the investor who submitted the request of the minister's decision referred to in the first paragraph to that investor as well as to investors designated as responsible for compliance with the conditions pursuant to paragraph II of Article R. 151-8. In the absence of a response within this period, the authorization request shall be deemed rejected.

NOTE: Pursuant to Article 5 of Decree No. 2020-892 of July 22, 2020, these provisions do not apply to investments made within ten working days following its publication.

Article R. 151-7

I. The investor is exempt from the authorization request provided for in this chapter when the ultimate investor in the control chain, within the meaning of paragraph II of Article R. 151-1, had previously acquired control, within the meaning of Article L. 233-3 of the Commercial Code, of the entity subject to the investment.

II. Paragraph I does not apply when:

1° The investment has the effect of preventing an investor from respecting the conditions for which they were made responsible under paragraph II of Article R. 151-8 on the occasion of a previously granted authorization;

2° The investment has as its object the transfer abroad of all or part of a branch of one of the activities listed in Article R. 151-3.

NOTE: Pursuant to Article 12 of Decree No. 2023-1293 of December 28, 2023, these provisions enter into force on January 1, 2024.

Article R. 151-8

I. The conditions referred to in paragraph II of Article L. 151-3 mainly aim, in compliance with the principle of proportionality, to:

1° Ensure the sustainability and security, on national territory, of the activities listed in Article R. 151-3 carried out by the entity subject to the investment, particularly by ensuring that these activities are not subject to the legislation of a foreign State likely to impede them, as well as the protection of information related thereto;

2° Ensure the maintenance of knowledge and know-how of the entity subject to the investment and prevent their capture;

3° Adapt the internal organization and governance methods of the entity, as well as the exercise methods of rights acquired in the entity due to the investment;

4° Establish the methods of informing the administrative authority in charge of control.

To this end, the minister may, in particular, condition their authorization on the transfer of part of the shares or stocks acquired in the capital of the entity subject to the investment or of all or part of a business branch listed in Article R. 151-3 carried out by the entity subject to the investment to an entity distinct from the investor and approved by the minister.

II. When the investment authorization is subject to conditions, it designates among the investors, within the meaning of paragraph II of Article R. 151-1, on whose behalf the authorization was requested, the investor or investors responsible for compliance with these conditions.

Article R. 151-9

I. The conditions set may be revised, at the request of the investor:

1° In case of unforeseeable changes at the time of realization of the authorized operation of the economic and regulatory conditions of exercising the activities listed in Article R. 151-3 by the entity subject to the investment;

2° In case of change in the shareholding of the entity subject to the investment or change in members of the control chain;

3° Pursuant to one of the conditions set at the time of authorization.

When the request for revision of conditions is submitted by the investor, it is accompanied by the documents or information necessary to justify the circumstances mentioned in points 1°, 2°, or 3°, as well as those necessary for the examination of the request. The minister shall decide within forty-five working days from receipt of the request. In the absence of a response within this period, the request for revision shall be deemed rejected.

II. The conditions set may be revised at the initiative of the minister in charge of the economy in the cases mentioned in points 2° and 3° of paragraph I and in compliance with the principle of proportionality.

The minister in charge of the economy shall inform the investor of their intention, specifying the reasons that appear to justify such revision, and shall give the investor the opportunity to present observations within forty-five working days. At the end of this period, the minister shall notify the investor of the modified conditions as well as the date of entry into force thereof.

NOTE: Pursuant to Article 12 of Decree No. 2023-1293 of December 28, 2023, these provisions enter into force on January 1, 2024.

Article R. 151-10

The minister in charge of the economy shall refuse, by reasoned decision, the requested investment authorization if the implementation of the conditions provided for in Article R. 151-8 is not sufficient alone to ensure the preservation of national interests defined by Article L. 151-3. The minister may take into account the fact that the investor maintains links with a foreign government or public body.

They may also refuse, by reasoned decision, the authorization of an investment:

1° If there is a serious presumption that the investor is likely to commit one of the offenses or concealment of one of the offenses referred to in Articles 222-34 to 222-39, 223-15-2, 225-4-1, 225-5, 225-6, 225-10, 313-1, 314-1, 321-6, 324-1, 421-1 to 421-2-6, 433-1, 433-2, 435-3, 435-4, 441-1 to 441-8, 450-1 of the Penal Code, Title I of Book IV of the same code, or in Articles 1741 to 1743, 1746, or 1747 of the General Tax Code;

2° If the investor has been finally convicted on the basis of one of the offenses mentioned in point 1° or for equivalent offenses provided for by the legislation of another State within five years preceding the filing of the authorization request;

3° If the investor has been subject to a sanction pronounced under Article L. 151-3-2 or has seriously and persistently failed to comply with injunctions or precautionary measures pronounced under paragraphs I and II of Article L. 151-3-1 within five years preceding the filing of the authorization request.

Article R. 151-11

The completion of an investment operation authorized under this chapter shall be declared under conditions set by order of the minister in charge of the economy.

Section 3: Police and sanction measures (Articles R. 151-12 to R. 151-15)

Article R. 151-12

In case of urgency, exceptional circumstances, or imminent threat to public order, public security, or national defense, the minister may pronounce a measure provided for in paragraphs I or II of Article L. 151-3-1 after giving formal notice to the investor to present observations within a reduced period not less than five working days.

At the end of this period, the minister notifies their decision to the investor, specifying the deadline to comply, if applicable under penalty, the amount of which is fixed.

Article R. 151-13

When the minister orders an investor, under points 1° of paragraphs I and II of Article L. 151-3-1, to submit a request to regularize their situation, the order specifies the documents and information necessary for the instruction of the request.

When the minister orders an investor, under point 3° of paragraph I or points 2° and 3° of paragraph II of Article L. 151-3-1, to modify the investment or comply with the conditions, the order specifies the nature of the required modifications or new conditions. The minister may prescribe the transfer of all or part of the shares or stocks acquired in the capital of the entity subject to the investment or all or part of a business branch listed in Article R. 151-3 carried out by the entity subject to the investment to an entity distinct from the investor.

Article R. 151-14

The daily amount of a penalty pronounced under Article L. 151-3-1 may not exceed fifty thousand euros.

Penalties are collected as State claims unrelated to taxes and the public domain.

Article R. 151-15

The decision to appoint a representative taken under point d of paragraph I of Article L. 151-3-1 specifies the expected duration of their mission as well as their monthly remuneration, taking into account, in particular, the nature and importance of the mission.

Section 4: Common provisions (Articles R. 151-16 to R. 151-17)

Article R. 151-16

An order of the minister in charge of the economy sets the list of documents and information to be provided in support of the prior request for examination of an activity as well as of the authorization request or notification provided for in Articles R. 151-4 and R. 151-5.

Authorization requests, prior requests for examination of an activity, notifications, declarations provided for in Article R. 151-11, and all correspondence relating to foreign investments in France shall be transmitted electronically according to modalities fixed by order of the minister in charge of the economy.

NOTE: Pursuant to Article 12 of Decree No. 2023-1293 of December 28, 2023, these provisions enter into force on January 1, 2024.

Article R. 151-17

The administrative authorities competent to process the authorization provided for in this chapter may use international cooperation to verify the accuracy of information provided to them by foreign investors, notably concerning the origin of funds.

Annex C: Standard Application Template for a Preliminary Review of an Activity – Required Documents and Information [835]

Introduction

Presentation of the IEF Platform

The IEF Platform is designed as a simple, secure, and user-friendly tool enabling investors and companies to provide the information required in connection with the review of applications under the French foreign investment screening regime. It also allows for centralized monitoring of all submitted applications and real-time updates on the progress of the review, thereby enhancing transparency and clarity of the screening procedure for all stakeholders.

IEF Platform: plateforme-ief.dgtresor.gouv.fr

Information collected from the investor

The Ministerial Order of December 31, 2019 sets forth the list of documents and information to be submitted in support of a prior request for review of an activity as well as in support of an authorization request, as provided for in Articles R. 151-4 and R. 151-5 of the Monetary and Financial Code.

User Guide

This document is intended to provide investors with an overview of the information and materials required for the review of their application, as requested through the IEF Platform.

Legend

* Mandatory field

1. General Presentation

This text field allows you to provide the authorities with any information relating to the proposed transaction: a description of the overall acquisition project, a description of the target company's business sector, and the specific subparagraph of Article R. 151-3 of the Monetary and Financial Code that, in your view, establishes the eligibility of the transaction, among others

---

835. This is an unofficial translation provided by the author and it shall not be considered as an official version.
Official document reproduced for informational purposes.
Source: Ministry of the Economy, Finance, Industrial and Digital Sovereignty, "Submit your application file," Published January 8, 2025, Consulted September 1, 2025, available at https://www.tresor.economie.gouv.fr/services-aux-entreprises/investissements-etrangers-en-france/deposer-votre-dossier-de-demande

[Insert text here]

1. Potential investors

Please specify the identity of the investor(s) interested in the proposed investment project. *

[Insert text here]

Copy of any document evidencing the existence of one or more potential investors *

[You may upload .png, .jpg, .jpeg, .doc, .docx, .xls, .xlsx, .txt, or .pdf files up to 8 MB in size.]

2. Target

a. List of Sellers

Please indicate the sellers holding a pre-closing voting right equal to or greater than 5%.*

Classification	Nationality	Designation	% of the target's pre-closing share capital held	% of the target's pre-closing voting rights held	purpose of the transaction
[Cédant 1]					

b. Subject matter of the investment

General information

Does the entity (or entities) subject to the transaction have subsidiaries within the European Union?*

□ Yes

□ No

If applicable, please list the countries:

[Country 1, Country 2, etc.]

Does the group to which the entity (or entities) subject to the transaction belongs have subsidiaries within the European Union?

* * *

□ Yes

□ No

If applicable, please list the countries:

[Country 1, Country 2, etc.]

Has the direct target entity of the transaction, or any of its subsidiaries, been subject to one or more decisions of the Minister under the French foreign direct investment screening regime? *

□ Yes

□ No

Where applicable, information to be provided for each decision : *

Case/file number	**Subsidiary name**	**Outcome of the decision**	**Date of the decision**	**Additional details / clarifications**
[DN XXXX ou R XXXX]				

Please provide the legal and corporate information of the direct target entity of the transaction.*

Corporate name and legal form	**SIREN number (French company identification number)**	Place of incorporation	Main business sector	Main NAF code (French business activity classification)	Registered office address
[Cible]					

Is there at least one separate operating site located in France ? *

□ Yes

□ No

Name	**Address**
[Site 1]	

Please provide the financial and HR information in the following table for the direct target entity of the transaction.*

Consolidated group figures by year and geographic area

	Worldwide			France		
Numbers	**Turnover (€) / Revenue (€)**	**Net income (€)**	**Workforce / Headcount**	**Turnover (€) / Revenue (€)**	**Net income (€)**	**Workforce / Headcount**
Year N-3						
Year N-2						
Year N-1						

Standalone figures of the investment target entity (France)

	Monde			France		
Numbers	**Turnover (€) / Revenue (€)**	**Net income (€)**	**Workforce / Headcount**	**Turnover (€) / Revenue (€)**	**Net income (€)**	**Workforce / Headcount**
Year N-3						
Year N-2						
Year N-1						

Activities and business environment

Detailed description of the activities carried out in France, including services or products provided.*

[Insert text here]

Description of the activities carried out in the European Union (please specify the country and the relevant services and/or products for each).*

[Insert text here]

Markets on which the company operates in France. *

[Insert text here]

Markets on which the company operates within and outside the European Union. *

[Insert text here]

Market shares*

Business segment	Market share in France (%)	Market share in the EU (%)	Market share outside the EU (%)
[Segment 1]			

Does the entity (or entities) subject to the transaction have clients in France or in the EU? *

□ Yes

□ No

If applicable, please provide the following information for each client :

Corporate name	Service provided	Country
Client 1		

[You may upload .png, .jpg, .jpeg, .doc, .docx, .xls, .xlsx, .txt, or .pdf files up to 8 MB in size.]

Is the entity (or entities) subject to the transaction involved in projects, programs, or financial support of interest to the European Union, or does it receive financial support from EU funds ? *

Where applicable, information to be provided for each decision :

Name / Title	End date (optional)	**Amount (€) (optional)**	**Additional details (optional)**
[**Project / Program / Financial Support 1**]			

Does the entity (or entities) subject to the transaction have partners in France or in the EU ? *

□ Yes

□ No

Where applicable, information to be provided for each decision :

Name / Title	Purpose of the partnership	Country
[Partner 1]		

Does the entity (or entities) subject to the transaction have competitors in France or in the EU ? *

□ Yes

□ No

Le cas échéant, merci de renseigner les informations suivantes : *

Name / Title	**Country**	**Business segment(s)**	**Market share in France (%)**
[Competitor 1]			

Is the entity (or entities) subject to the transaction business units (branches of activity)? *

□ Yes

□ No

List of tangible and/or intangible assets comprising the business unit. *

[Insert text here]

Does the entity (or entities) subject to the transaction have access to French customer data? *

□ Yes

□ No

f applicable, please specify the access and data management arrangements by the investment target entity regarding French customer data.

[Insert text here]

Does the entity (or entities) subject to the transaction hold and/or exploit intellectual property assets ? *

[Insert text here]

If the number of intellectual property assets held or exploited by the target company (or companies) is significant, please provide details of the main IP assets below and include the additional elements in a separate table under the "Other annexes" form. *

Type / Nature	Name / Title	Expiration date (optional)	IP rights holder, if the target is only a licensee (optional)
[Patent, Industrial designs and models, Geographical indications, Trademark, Trade secret]			

c. Subsidiaries

Please provide the following information for each subsidiary of the target. *

Corporate name and legal form	SIREN number (French company identification number)	Place of incorporation	Main business sector	Main NAF code (French business activity classification)	Registered office address
[Target]					

Please provide the financial and HR information for the subsidiary in the following table. *

Subsidiary #1

Does the subsidiary operate at least one separate site located in France ? *

□ Yes

□ No

Name	Address
[Site 1]	

Please provide the financial and HR information for the subsidiary in the following table. *

Figures / Data	Revenue (€) / Turnover (€)	Net income (€)	Workforce / Headcount
Year N-3			
Year N-2			
Year N-1			

Detailed description of the activities carried out in France, including services or products provided.*

[Insert text here]

Description of the activities carried out in the European Union (please specify the country and the relevant services and/or products for each) *

[Insert text here]

Market shares*

Business segment	Market share in France (%)	Market share in the EU (%)	Market share outside the EU (%)
[Segment 1]			

Are the French / EU / foreign markets different from those indicated in the "Investment purpose" section of the form ? *

If applicable, please specify:

[Insert text here]

Are the clients different from those indicated in the "Investment purpose" section of the form? *

□ Yes

□ No

If applicable, please specify the corporate name, country, and services provided by the subsidiary for additional clients. Otherwise, indicate those that should be removed:

[Insert text here]

Are the projects/programs or financial support different from those indicated in the "Investment target entity" section of the form ? *

□ Yes

□ No

If applicable, please specify the name, end date, and possible amount of the additional projects/programs or financial support. Otherwise, indicate those that should be removed :

[Insert text here]

Are the partners different from those indicated in the "Investment target entity" section of the form ? *

□ Yes

□ No

If applicable, please specify the corporate name, country, and purpose of the partnership for additional partners. Otherwise, indicate those that should be removed.

[Insert text here]

Are the competitors different from those indicated in the “Investment purpose” section of the form?*

□ Yes

□ No

If applicable, please specify the corporate name, country, business segment(s), and market share in France (%) for additional competitors. Otherwise, indicate those that should be removed.

[Insert text here]

Does the subsidiary have access to French customer data? *

□ Yes

□ No

If applicable, please specify the access and data management arrangements for French customer data.

[Insert text here]

Does the subsidiary hold and/or exploit intellectual property assets? *

□ Yes

□ No

Please indicate below the characteristics of the intellectual property assets held or exploited by the subsidiary. If the number of intellectual property assets is significant, please provide details of the main IP assets below and submit the additional ones in a separate table under the “Other annexes” form.

Type/Nature	**Name/Title**	**Expiration date / (Optional)**	**IP rights holder, if the target is only a licensee (optional)**
[Patent, Industrial designs and models, Geographical indications, Trademark, trade secret]			

d. Contact person within the investment target entity

Please provide the following information. *

Full name	Position / Job title	Address	Téléphone	mail

e. Organizationnal chart

Organizational chart identifying the entities or natural persons forming the chain of control of the investment target entity up to the entity(ies) or natural person(s) exercising ultimate control, within the meaning of Article L. 233-3 of the French Commercial Code, on the one hand, and the French, European, and foreign subsidiaries of the investment target entity on the other hand.*

Please specify the ownership link between each entity appearing in the organizational chart (percentage of share capital and/or fraction of voting rights expressed in %).

[You may upload files in .png, .jpg, .jpeg, .doc, .docx, .xls, .xlsx, .txt, .pdf formats up to 8 MB]

3. Opération

Please indicate the type of transaction contemplated (Article R.151-2 of the French Monetary and Financial Code): *

- Acquisition of sole control, within the meaning of Article L. 233-3 of the French Commercial Code
- Acquisition of joint control, within the meaning of Article L. 233-3 of the FrenchCommercial Code
- Acquisition of all or part of a business unit
- Direct or indirect crossing, acting alone or in concert, of the 25% threshold of voting rights
- Direct or indirect crossing, acting alone or in concert, of the 10% threshold of voting rights in a listed company

[Insert text here]

Total transaction amount (€)*

If this amount is not determined at the time of filing, please provide an estimate and, if applicable, specify the method used in the box below.

[Amount and, where applicable, the valuation method used]

Valuation of the French target(s) (€) *

You may provide below any useful details regarding the amounts indicated above (enterprise value/equity value, calculation method, reasons why it is impossible to value the French target(s), etc.)

[Amount and, where applicable, the valuation method used]

You may provide below any relevant details regarding the amounts indicated above (enterprise value/equity value, calculation method, reasons for the inability to conduct a valuation of the French target(s), etc.)

[Insert text here]

Document evidencing the target entity's consent to the filing of the request for a prior review of an activity. *

[You may upload .png, .jpg, .jpeg, .doc, .docx, .xls, .xlsx, .txt, or .pdf files up to 8 MB.]

Copy of any document evidencing the investment project (resolution of a governing body, presentation to labor unions, letter of intent, etc.).) *

[You may upload .png, .jpg, .jpeg, .doc, .docx, .xls, .xlsx, .txt, or .pdf files up to 8 MB.]

4. Other annexes

You may upload optional annexes that you consider useful for the review of the application.

[You may upload files in .png, .jpg, .jpeg, .doc, .docx, .xls, .xlsx, .txt, .pdf formats up to 8 MB]

Annex D: Standard Application Form for Prior Authorization – Required Documents and Information [836]

Presentation of the IEF Platform

The IEF Platform is a simple, secure, and educational tool enabling investors and companies to provide the information required for the review of applications under the French foreign investment screening mechanism. It also allows centralized monitoring of all submitted applications and provides real-time updates on the progress of the review, thereby enhancing transparency and clarity of the screening process for stakeholders.

>>> IEF Platform: plateforme-ief.dgtresor.gouv.fr

Information Collected from the Investor

The Ministerial Order of 31 December 2019 establishes the list of documents and information to be provided in support of both the prior review application and the authorization application referred to in Articles R.151-4 and R.151-5 of the French Monetary and Financial Code.

Instructions for Use

This document is intended to provide investors with an overview of the information required to process their application, as requested on the IEF Platform

Legend

* Required field

Prior authorization request

1. General presentation

This text field allows you to provide the competent authority with any information regarding the proposed transaction: description of the overall acquisition project, description of the business sector of the target company, and reference to the specific paragraph of Article R.151-3 of the French Monetary and Financial Code on which you believe the eligibility of the transaction is based, etc.

[Insert text here]

836. Official document reproduced for information purposes. France, Ministry for the Economy, Finance, Industrial and Digital Sovereignty, "Submit your application file," published January 8, 2025, available at https://www.tresor.economie.gouv.fr/services-aux-entreprises/investissements-etrangers-en-france/deposer-votre-dossier-de-demande (last accessed September 1, 2025).

2. Investor

a. Direct investor

The direct investor is the entity that carries out the investment transaction (share purchase, capital increase, etc.) that triggers the foreign investment screening process. If several entities may be considered "direct investors" as defined above, please indicate the main entity and provide details on the other direct investors in the "Control Chain" organizational chart form. *

Investor type

□ Entité financière

□ Financial entity

□ Natural person

Information to be provided for a financial or industrial entity:

[Corporate name, legal form, registration number, nationality, and registered office address]

Information to be provided for a natural person :

[Last name, first name, date of birth, place of birth, nationality, and tax residence]

b. Operating investor

The operating investor is the entity within the control chain that carries out an actual operational activity. If the operating investor is the same as the direct investor, please complete the following fields with the information already provided. *

Investor type

□ Financial entity

□ Industrial entity

□ Natural person

Information to be provided for a financial or industrial entity :

[Corporate name, legal form, registration number, nationality, and registered office address]

Information to be provided for a natural person:

[Last name, first name, date of birth, place of birth, nationality, and tax residence]

c. List of Ultimate Investors

The ultimate investor is the entity that ultimately controls the investor, within the meaning of Article L.233-3 of the French Commercial Code.

If there are multiple ultimate investors, please list all of them below.

If the ultimate investor is the same entity as the direct and/or operating investor, please complete the fields below with the information already provided. *

Investor type

□ Financial entity

□ Industrial entity

□ Natural

Information to be provided for a financial or industrial entity:

[Corporate name, legal form, registration number, nationality, and registered office address]

Information to be provided for a natural person::

[Last name, first name, date of birth, place of birth, nationality, and tax residence]

Table listing (i) the members of its management, supervisory, or any other body performing equivalent functions, and their (ii) nationality and tax residence. *

Last name and first name	Nationality	Tax residence
[Membre 1]		

Table indicating the identity, shareholding percentage, and voting rights held by each shareholder or partner owning more than 5% of the voting rights.*

Identity	Shareholding percentage	Fraction of voting rights held
[Shareholder or partner1]		

d. Control Chain and Investor's Activities

Organizational chart identifying the entities or natural persons forming its control chain up to the entity(ies) or individual(s) ultimately exercising control, within the meaning of Article L.233-3 of the French Commercial Code. *

Please provide, where possible, a clear organizational chart fitting on a single page.

[You may upload 8 MB .png, .jpg, .jpeg, .doc, .docx, .xls, .xlsx, .txt, and .pdf files]

Registration certificates of the entities forming the ownership chain, showing nationality, corporate name, registered office address, and registration number of the entity concerned, as well as official documents proving the identity of natural persons. *

[You may upload 8 MB .png, .jpg, .jpeg, .doc, .docx, .xls, .xlsx, .txt, and .pdf files]

Detailed description of the activities carried out by the investor (the description must highlight the different categories of services, goods, or products provided). *

[You may upload 8 MB .png, .jpg, .jpeg, .doc, .docx, .xls, .xlsx, .txt, and .pdf files]

Has the investor or any entity within the investor's group previously been subject to a decision by the Minister of the Economy under the French foreign investment screening regime? *

If applicable, please provide the following information for each decision:

Case number	**Name of subsidiary**	**Direction of decision**	**Date of decision**	**Details**
[DN XXXX ou R XXXX]				

3. Target

a. List of Transferors

Please indicate the transferors holding at least 5% of the pre-closing voting rights. *

Category	**Nationality**	**Corporate name**	**% of the target's pre-closing share capital held**	**% of the target's pre-closing voting rights held**	**Purpose of the transaction**
[Transferor 1]					

b. Purpose of the Investment

General Information

Do the entity(ies) concerned by the transaction have subsidiaries in the European Union? *

□ Yes

□ No

□ Unkown

If yes, please list the countries:

[Country 1, Country 2, etc.]

Does the group to which the entity(ies) concerned by the transaction belong have subsidiaries in the European Union? *

□ Yes

□ No

□ Unknown

If yes, please list the countries:

[Country 1, Country 2, etc.]

Has the direct target entity, or one of its subsidiaries, been subject to one or more decisions by the Minister of the Economy under the French foreign investment screening regime? *

□ Yes

□ No

□ Unknown

If applicable, please provide the following information for each decision:

Case number	Subsidiary name	Direction of decision	Date of decision	Details
[DN XXXX ou R XXXX]				

Please provide the legal and corporate information of the direct target entity. *

Corporate name and legal form	SIREN number	Place of registration	Main business sector	Main NAF code	Registered office address
[Target]					

Is there at least one separate operating site located in France? *

□ Yes

□ No

Name	Address
[Site 1]	

Please provide the financial and HR information contained in the following table for the direct target entity. *

Consolidated group figures by year and geographical area

	Worldwide			France		
Data	Turnover (€)	Net income (€)	Workforce	Turnover (€)	Net income (€)	Workforce
Y-3						
Y-2						
Y-1						

Individual figures of the target entity (France)

	Worldwide			France		
Data	Turnover (€)	Net income (€)	Workforce	Turnover (€)	Net income (€)	Workforce
Y-3						
Y-2						
Y-1						

Activités et environnement

Activities and Environment

Detailed description of the activities carried out in France, including services, goods, or products provided. *

[Insert text here]

Description of activities carried out in the European Union (please specify the country and the services, goods, and/or products concerned for each). *

[Insert text here]

Markets in which the company operates in France *

[Insert text here]

Markets in which the company operates in the EU and outside the EU * *

[Insert text here]

Market shares*

Business segment	Market share France (%)	Market share EU (%)	Market share outside EU (%)
[Segment 1]			

Do the entity(ies) concerned by the transaction have clients in France or in the EU? **

□ Yes

□ No

If yes, please provide the following information for each client:

Corporate name	Service provided	Country
[Client 1]		

Are the entity(ies) concerned by the transaction involved in projects, programs, or financial support of interest to the European Union, or do they benefit from EU funds? *

If yes, please provide the following information:

Name	End date (optional)	Amount (€), optional	Details (optional)
[Project / Program / Financial support 1]			

Do the entity(ies) concerned by the transaction have partners in France or in the EU? **

□ Yes

□ No

If yes, please provide the following information:

Corporate name	Purpose of partnership	Country
[Partner 1]		

Do the entity(ies) concerned by the transaction have competitors in France or in the EU? **

□ Yes

□ No

If yes, please provide the following information:

Corporate name	Country	Business segment(s)	Market share in France (%)
[Competitor 1]			

Are the entity(ies) concerned by the transaction business units? *

□ Yes

□ No

List of tangible and/or intangible assets comprising the business unit **

[Insert text here]

Do the entity(ies) concerned by the transaction have access to French customer data? *

□ Yes

□ No

Please specify how the target entity accesses and manages data relating to French customers *

[Insert text here]

Do the entity(ies) concerned by the transaction own and/or exploit intellectual property rights? *

□ Yes

□ No

Please provide below the characteristics of the intellectual property rights owned or exploited by the target company(ies).

If the number of intellectual property rights owned or exploited by the target company(ies) is significant, please provide details of the main rights below and include additional rights in a separate table in the "Other Annexes" form.

Nature	Name	Expiration date (optional)	Owner of the IP right, if the target is only a licensee (optional)
[Patent, industrial designs and models, geographical indications, trademark, trade secret]			

c. Subsidiaries

Please provide, for each subsidiary of the target, the following information: *

Corporate name and legal form	SIREN number	Place of registration	Main business sector	Main NAF code	Registered office address
[Target]					

Please provide, for each subsidiary of the target, the following information.

Subsidiary #1

Does the subsidiary have at least one separate operating site located in France? *

□ Yes

□ No

Name	Address
[Site 1]	

Please provide the financial and HR information contained in the following table for the subsidiary. *

Data	Turnover (€)	Net income (€)	Workforce
Y-3			
Y-2			
Y-1			

Subsidiary's Activities and Environment

Detailed description of the activities carried out in France, including services, goods, or products provided *

[Insert text here]

Description of activities carried out in the European Union (please specify the country and the services, goods, and/or products concerned for each) *

[Insert text here]

Market Shares*

Business segment	Market share France (%)	Market share EU (%)	Market share outside EU (%)
[Segment 1]			

Are the French / European / foreign markets different from those indicated in the "Purpose of the Investment" section of the form? *

□ Yes

□ No

If yes, please specify:

[Insert text here]

Are the clients different from those indicated in the "Purpose of the Investment" section of the form? *

□ Yes

□ No

If yes, please specify the corporate name, country, and services provided by the subsidiary to the client for additional clients. Otherwise, please indicate those omitted:

[Insert text here]

Are the projects/programs or financial support different from those indicated in the "Target Entity" section of the form? *

□ Yes

□ No

If yes, please specify the name, end date, and potential amount of additional projects/ programs or financial support. Otherwise, please indicate those omitted:

[Insert text here]

Are the partners different from those indicated in the "Target Entity" section of the form? *

□ Yes

□ No

If yes, please specify the corporate name, country, and purpose of the partnership for additional partners. Otherwise, please indicate those omitted.

[Insert text here]

Are the competitors different from those indicated in the "Target Entity" section of the form? *

□ Yes

□ No

If yes, please specify the corporate name, country, business segment(s), and market share in France (%) for additional competitors. Otherwise, please indicate those omitted.

[Insert text here]

Does the subsidiary have access to French customer data?

□ Yes

□ No

If yes, please specify how the target entity accesses and manages data relating to French customers. *

[Insert text here]

Does the subsidiary own and/or exploit intellectual property rights? *

□ Oui

□ Non

If yes, please indicate below the characteristics of the intellectual property rights owned or exploited by the subsidiary.

If the number of intellectual property rights is significant, please provide details of the main rights below and include additional rights in a separate table in the "Other Annexes" form.

Nature	Name	Expiration date (optional)	Owner of the IP right, if the target is only a licensee (optional)
[Patent, industrial designs and models, geographical indications, trademark, trade secret]			

d. Contact Person within the Target Entity

Please provide the following information. *

Last name and first name	Position	Address	Telephone	Email

e. Organizational Chart

Organizational chart identifying the entities or natural persons forming the control chain of the target entity up to the entity(ies) or individual(s) ultimately exercising control, within the meaning of Article L.233-3 of the French Commercial Code, on the one hand, and the French, European, and non-European subsidiaries of the target entity on the other.

Please specify the ownership link between each entity shown in the organizational chart (percentage of shareholding and/or voting rights expressed in %).

Please provide, where possible, a clear organizational chart fitting on a single page. *

[You may upload .png, .jpg, .jpeg, .doc, .docx, .xls, .xlsx, .txt, .pdf files up to 8 MB]

4. Transaction

Please indicate the type of transaction envisaged (Article R.151-2 of the French Monetary and Financial Code) *:

- Acquisition of sole control, within the meaning of Article L.233-3 of the French Commercial Code
- Acquisition of joint control, within the meaning of Article L.233-3 of the French Commercial Code
- Acquisition of all or part of a business unit
- Crossing, directly or indirectly, individually or in concert, the threshold of 25% of voting rights
- Crossing, directly or indirectly, individually or in concert, the threshold of 10% of the voting rights of a listed company

[Insert text here]

Total transaction amount (€) *

If this amount is not determined at the time of filing, please provide an estimate and, if applicable, specify the method used in the box below

[Amount]

Valuation of the French target(s) (€) *

If this amount is not determined at the time of filing, please provide an estimate and, if applicable, specify the method used in the box below

[Amount]

You may provide below any relevant details regarding the above amounts (enterprise value/equity value, calculation method, reasons preventing valuation of the French target(s), etc.)

[Insert text here]

Document attesting to the agreement of the target entity regarding the filing of the prior review application. *

[You may upload .png, .jpg, .jpeg, .doc, .docx, .xls, .xlsx, .txt, .pdf files up to 8 MB]

Copy of any document evidencing the investment project (resolution of a governing body, presentation to labor unions, letter of intent, etc.) *

[You may upload .png, .jpg, .jpeg, .doc, .docx, .xls, .xlsx, .txt, .pdf files up to 8 MB]

5. **Other Annexes**

You may upload optional annexes that you consider useful for the review of the application.

[You may upoad .png, .jpg, .jpeg, .doc, .docx, .xls, .xlsx, .txt, .pdf files up to 8 MB]

Annexe D : Request for information from the investor [837]

Name of the investor(s):	
Name of the target undertaking *(the entrepreneur to whom or the undertaking to which the capital is made available in order to carry on an economic activity in a Member State):*	

Please complete the following information (* = where available):

1. Information about the investment

Description of the investment *(please explain how the change in ownership or control of the target company is executed and how the new assets will fit into the company structure of the investor)*	
Approximate value of the investment [838] (in €)	
Planned date for completing the transaction *(either as a specific date/period or in function of the completion of ongoing authorisation processes)*	
Funding of the investment and its source [839] *(on the basis of the best information available, cf. Article 9(2)(e)) Please explain the origin of the funds and the degree to which they come from external sources.*	
What is the investor's business strategy behind this acquisition? [840]	
Does the investor appear financially able to ensure the continuity and proper operation of the target undertaking after the acquisition? *	

837. France, Ministry for the Economy, Finance, Industrial and Digital Sovereignty, "Foreign investments in France" information page, available at https://www.tresor.economie.gouv.fr/services-aux-entreprises/investissements-etrangers-en-france (last accessed May 9, 2024). See the source version of "Request for information from the investor for the purposes of notifications pursuant to Article 6 of Regulation (EU) 2019-452.DOCX (Version 1.7)" at https://policy.trade.ec.europa.eu/enforcement-and-protection/investment-screening_en (last accessed May 9, 2024).

838. If the investment subject to this notification is part of a broader transaction, please disclose the total value and the investment provided to the undertaking(s) the territory of the Member State undertaking the screening separately.

839. If the investment subject to this notification is part of a broader transaction, please specify the funding of the investment into the companies established in the territory of the Member State undertaking the screening, as well as sources of funding for the transaction as a whole.

840. Please explain why the investor is interested in making the investment and the circumstances of the investment by the target

Does the investment enable or result in the investor's effective participation in the management of the undertaking subject to screening?	□ No □ Yes, please explain how:
Participation of the direct investor and its global ultimate owner in the capital of the undertaking subject to screening before the transaction (if applicable) and as a result of the transaction *(please specify the votes conferred by the shares purchased as a percentage of the total number of votes, whether there are any specific voting rights arrangements, regime concerning effective participation in the management, etc.)*	Before: As a result of the transaction:
If the ownership is less than 100%, please explain how the ownership shares translate to your control or participation in the effective management. Please describe the modalities of "joint" exercise of control or participation in the effective management.	
Is the investment – in your assessment – likely to affect projects or programmes of Union interest?	□ No □ Yes, please explain which project or programme and how it may be affected:

Has the transaction been announced to the public? If available, please provide a link or attach the text of the announcement.

□ Yes

Link(s) to the source:

□ No

2. Information concerning (A) the undertaking in which the investment is planned or has been completed ("target undertaking") or (B) a greenfield investment

Please indicate, whether the investment concerns a greenfield investment[841]:

□ No

□ Yes

If the answer is "yes", please provide the information in Table B. If the answer is "no", please provide the information in Table A

(* = where available)

Guidelines:

Please complete the table below with information about the beneficiarie(s) of the investment ***established in the Member State undertaking the screening procedure*** *and, if*

841. International greenfield investment typically involves the creation of a new company or establishment or facilities abroad, whereas an international merger or acquisition amounts to transferring the ownership of existing assets to an owner abroad.

applicable, the ultimate controlling entity (most relevant entity within the ownership structure). If required, ***you may add duplicates*** *of the table to capture details for each level of ownership for which information is available.*

In case the beneficiary is part of a larger corporate group not headquartered in the ***Me****mber State undertaking the screening procedure, please provide the information for the other legal entities of the same corporate group situated in other EU Member States,* ***if available****, in the column on the right side.*

If the ownership structure of the target is complex, please provide details on the direct beneficiary, its ultimate owner and any significant intermediate entities to the extent available.

If available, please provide an organigram to explain the horizontal and vertical relationship between the companies referred and the overall structure of the company group before and after the transaction.

Table A

	Company(-ies) subject to the screening procedure	**Other legal entities of the same corporate group situated in other EU Member States (if applicable) ***
Role of the company in the transaction	*For example:* *- direct recipient of the investment (target)* *- significant intermediate entity* *- global ultimate owner* *- company group* ...	
Does this company carry on an economic activity in the Member State where the investment is undergoing screening? [842]		
Name of the company		
Address/domicile/registered office of the company		

842. Art. 2.1: 'foreign direct investment' means an investment of any kind by a foreign investor aiming to establish or to maintain lasting and direct links between the foreign investor and the entrepreneur to whom or the undertaking to which the capital is made available in order to carry on an economic activity in a Member State, including investments which enable effective participation in the management or control of a company **carrying out an economic activity**.

Company's national registration number		
Intra-community VAT number		
Branch of industry/economic activities carried out *Please provide a brief description of the activities being carried out and include the relevant NACE sub-category to the greatest possible granularity (4-digits).*	*Description of Activity 1* NACE code*	*Description of Activity 1* NACE code*
Description of Activity 2 NACE code*	*Description of Activity 2* NACE code*	
Description of Activity 2 NACE code*	*Description of Activity 2* NACE code*	
Please explain the products, services and business operations of the company before the transaction [843]		
Please explain the products, services and business operations of the company after the transaction is completed. * *This is applicable to FDI resulting in a change of operations in the target undertaking*		
Are – to your knowledge – substitute products available on the market? *		
Please provide information about the main competitors (national, European, global) *		
Does the company own any patents or other intellectual property rights relevant for a security or public order analysis? * *Please list them if available.*		
EU Member States in which the company conducts substantive business operations (e.g. through subsidiaries, branches and please provide the name(s) of those undertaking(s)		

843. Art. 2.1: 'foreign direct investment' means an investment of any kind by a foreign investor aiming to establish or to maintain lasting and direct links between the foreign investor and the entrepreneur to whom or the undertaking to which the capital is made available **in order to carry on an economic activity** in a Member State, including investments which enable effective participation in the management or control of a company carrying out an economic activity.

Annual turnover* *(in €, over last fiscal year)* [844]		
Total number of employees*		
Is the company subject to EU financial restrictive measures (sanctions)? [845]		
Is the company subject to restrictive measures by third countries? * [846]		
Has the company received funding from projects or programmes of Union interest or participates directly or indirectly in the implementation of such projects or programmes? [847]	□ No □ Yes, please specify amount and relevant EU project or programme:	□ No □ Yes, please specify amount and relevant EU project or programme:
Does the target undertaking maintain business relations with a project or programme of Union interest? *(e.g. does the undertaking supply goods, technology, etc. to the project or programme?)*	□ No □ Yes, please specify the project, the relevant EU programme and the type of business relation:	□ No □ Yes, please specify the project, the relevant EU programme and the type of business relation:
Listings on stock exchanges*	**Trading code, Ticker or stock symbol**	
1.*Country 1*		
2.*Country 2*		
Website of the target company/-ies*		

844. Please indicate if fiscal year does not correspond to calendar year.

845. The consolidated list of persons, groups and entities subject to EU financial sanctions can be downloaded from accessible via the following address: https://webgate.ec.europa.eu/europeaid/fsd/fsf. In order to access this platform, you need to have an "EU Login" account. For further background on ownership and control in the context of EU sanction, please consult the EU Best Practices for the effective implementation of restrictive measures and Commission Opinion of 19.6.2020 on Article 2 of Council Regulation (EU) No 269/2014. Please note that additional sectorial sanctions (not included in the FSF platform) could apply to the proposed transaction. Please visit www.sanctionsmap.eu for a full list of EU sanctions.

846. Possible source of information for U.S sanctions: https://sanctionssearch.ofac.treas.gov/

847. The Financial Transparency System (FTS) (https://ec.europa.eu/budget/fts/index_en.htm) allows to search the beneficiaries of funding from the EU budget implemented directly the Commission (at Headquarters or in EU delegations to non-EU countries) and other EU bodies such as executive agencies ('direct management'), and beneficiaries of the European Development Fund. Please note that the FTS does not provide information on funding from the EU budget implemented by both the Commission and Member States ('shared management') or implemented indirectly by other international organisations or non-EU countries ('indirect management').

Ownership structure of the target undertaking – information on the ultimate owner and participation in the capital before the notified transaction	• *If the ownership structure is complex, please provide details on the ultimate owner and any significant intermediate entities.* • *When available, the information can also be presented in the form of a chart (as an Annex)*

Table B : Greenfield investment

Name	
Location/Address of the new undertaking	
Country where the new undertaking is headquartered	
Company's national registration number*	
Intra-community VAT number*	
Date of incorporation*	
Branch of industry/economic activities carried out. *Please provide a brief description of the activities being carried out and include the relevant NACE sub-category to the greatest possible granularity (4-digits).*	**NACE codes***
Description of Activity 1	
Description of Activity 2	
Description of Activity X	
Please explain the products, services and business operations of the undertaking after the transaction is completed.	
Please provide information about the main competitors (national, European, global) *	
Estimated total number of employees*	
Website of the company*	

Ownership structure of the new undertaking – information on the ultimate owner and participation in the capital after the notified transaction	• *If the ownership structure is complex, please provide details on the ultimate owner and any significant intermediate entities.* • *When available, the information can also be presented in the form of a chart*

3. Investor

Guidelines :

Please complete the table below with information about the direct investor and, if applicable, the ultimate controlling entity (most relevant entity within the ownership structure). If required, you may add duplicates of the table to capture details for each level of ownership for which information is available (i.e. direct, intermediary, and ultimate investor(s). If the ownership structure is complex, please provide details on the direct acquirer, and where available, the ultimate owner and any significant intermediate entities. If available, please provide an organigram to explain the horizontal and vertical relationship between the companies referred.

In case the investment is made by multiple investors, please provide the information above for each investor separately by multiplying the table hereunder. If available, please provide an organigram to explain the horizontal and vertical relationship between the companies referred.

In case the investor is part of a larger corporate group, please provide the information on "annual turnover of the investor" and "total number of employees" for the entire corporate group as well, if available.

(* = where available)

Role of the company in the transaction	*For example:* *- direct investor* *- holding company created for the purpose of executing the investment* *- 100% owner of a holding company without any other significant business activity* *- significant intermediate entity* *- global ultimate owner* *...*
Name	
Address/domicile/registered office	
Country under whose laws the company is duly constituted or otherwise organised ***If the entity is a natural person, please indicate the nationality/ies of this natural person.***	
Company's national registration number	

Date of incorporation	
Branch of industry/economic activities carried out *Please provide a brief description of the activities being carried out and include the relevant NACE sub-category to the greatest possible granularity (4-digits).*	**NACE code*** [848]
Description of Activity 1	
Description of Activity 2	
Description of Activity X	
Please explain the products, services and business operations of the company. *If available, please explain if the investment is likely to result in a significant change in the profile or main activities of the investor.*	
Please provide information about the main competitors (national, European, global) *	
EU Member States in which the company conducts substantive business operations (*e.g. through subsidiaries or branches and please provide the name(s) of those undertaking(s)*)	*1. Member State / name of undertaking* *2. Member State / name of undertaking* *3. Member State / name of undertaking*
Annual turnover (*in €, over last fiscal year*) [849]*	
Total number of employees*	
Is the company subject to EU financial restrictive measures (sanctions)? [850]	
Is the company subject to restrictive measures by third countries? * [851]	

848. NACE is the European standard classification of productive economic activities. NACE presents economic activities partitioned in such a way that a NACE code can be associated with a statistical unit carrying them out. The NACE codes can be found in RAMON, the Eurostat database for NACE codes.
849. Please indicate if fiscal year does not correspond to calendar year.
850. The consolidated list of persons, groups and entities subject to EU financial sanctions can be downloaded from accessible via the following address: https://webgate.ec.europa.eu/europeaid/fsd/fsf. In order to access this platform, you need to have an "EU Login" account. For further background on ownership and control in the context of EU sanction, please consult the EU Best Practices for the effective implementation of restrictive measures and Commission Opinion of 19.6.2020 on Article 2 of Council Regulation (EU) No 269/2014. Please note that additional sectorial sanctions (not included in the FSF platform) could apply to the proposed transaction. Please visit www.sanctionsmap.eu for a full list of EU sanctions.
851. Possible source of information for U.S sanctions: https://sanctionssearch.ofac.treas.gov/

Listings on stock exchanges*	**Trading code, Ticker or Stock symbol**
1. Country 1	*xxx*
2. Country x	*xxx*
Website of the company*	

Ownership structure of the investor, including information on its ultimate owner(s) and participation in the capital *(cf. Article 9(2)(a))*	• *If the ownership structure is complex, please provide details on the direct acquirer, the ultimate owner and any significant intermediate entities.* • *When available, the information can also be presented in the form of a chart (as an Annex)*

3. Is/was the investment undergoing screening subject to assessment, authorisation, monitoring or other scrutiny pursuant to EU or national rules?

Is (or will) the transaction (be) subject to merger review under the EC Merger Regulation [852]?

□ Yes – case number [853]:

□ Yes, but the case has not been filed for Merger Review yet. Planned date or timeframe of filing: Click or tap to enter a date.

□ No

Is the investment subject to another assessment, authorisation or monitoring in the Member State undertaking the screening, in another Member State or in a third country (*e.g. domestic competition control, prudential supervision, sectoral authorisation or certification*)? *

□ No

□ Yes, please specify type of scrutiny and country undertaking the scrutiny:

4. Any additional information that you wish to disclose for the assessment

852. Council Regulation (EC) No 139/2004 of 20 January 2004 on the control of concentrations between undertakings.

853. Please refer to the database of Merger Cases: https://ec.europa.eu/competition/elojade/isef/index.cfm?clear=1&policy_area_id=2

Annex G – Letter of Undertakings

Foreign Investment Authorization Request under Articles L. 151-3 and R. 153-1 et seq. of the Monetary and Financial Code [854]

From: [•], a company incorporated under the laws of [•], having its registered office at [•]

(hereinafter the "Investor")

To: The French State

Pursuant to Articles L. 151-3 and following and R. 153-1 and following of the Monetary and Financial Code, the proposed acquisition by [•], a company incorporated under the laws of [•], having its registered office at [•], ultimately controlled by [•], residing at [•], is subject to prior authorization from the Minister of the Economy (the "Acquisition").

Immediately upon completion of the Acquisition, [•] will hold, directly or indirectly, [•]% of the share capital of [•], a company incorporated under the laws of [•], having its registered office at [•] (hereinafter, the "Company").

This authorization is subject to the undertakings set out below.

For the purpose of this letter:

—The term "Sensitive Products" means:

• the products (tools, devices, equipment, software) specifically developed or adapted by [•] for defense or national security purposes, used by the French State or its public institutions (directly or through their supply chain) or by public or private operators managing installations as defined in Articles L.1332-1 to L.1332-7 of the French Defense Code (directly or through their supply chain), [as well as for the needs of export clients approved by the French State in the defense sector] (hereinafter, the "Clients");

• the products developed or adapted by [•] that are subject to authorization under Article R. 226-3 of the French Penal Code;

• the products supplied by [•] to other entities of the [•] group for the performance of contractual obligations owed to Clients (excluding generic or standard products).

—The term "Sensitive Activities" means:

research and development, production, implementation, operation, or maintenance of Sensitive Products, as well as technical support services for such products.

854. DUPEYRAT, op. cit., pp. 255–260

—The term "Company" refers to [•], as identified above, as well as any successor legal entity holding all or part of the assets, know-how, or resources, tangible or intangible, necessary for the performance of the Sensitive Activities, following a merger, spin-off, or partial asset contribution.

The undertakings set forth herein are made for a period of [•] years from the effective completion date of the Acquisition.

In consideration of the authorization requested and conditional upon the effective completion of the Acquisition, the Investor hereby undertakes, pursuant to Article R. 153-9 of the Monetary and Financial Code and within the limits defined by that article, to the following:

A. Commitments Relating to the Company's Structure and Governance

1. Ensure, as of the Acquisition date, that all Sensitive Activities remain attached to a company incorporated under French law with legal personality and independent administrative bodies vested with appropriate powers under French law;
2. Ensure that the Company's executive management is composed primarily of French or European senior executives;
3. Ensure that all legally or regulatory required security clearances, whether for natural persons or legal entities, necessary for the continuation of certain Sensitive Activities are maintained and obtained in accordance with applicable procedures under the General Interministerial Instruction No. 1300 on the Protection of National Defense Secrets;
4. Ensure that the R&D center currently located in [•] remains based in France.

B. Commitments Relating to Client Contracts and Industrial Capabilities

5. Ensure that the Company continues to perform all its obligations in effect on the Acquisition date under existing contracts related to Sensitive Activities and under binding confidentiality agreements with its Clients;
6. Ensure that the Company continues to provide Clients with access, under commercially and technically reasonable conditions, to Sensitive Products incorporating technological advancements developed by the Company;
7. Guarantee that Sensitive Products already deployed and in use by Clients as of the Acquisition date remain independent from ITAR regulations;
8. Refrain from taking any action that would prevent the continued availability in France, and the continued use under conditions at least equivalent to those existing prior to the Acquisition, of the rights of access and use held by the Company on the Acquisition date, including know-how, source code, and associated improvements (whether patented or not, whether protected by copyright or not) required for Sensitive Activities, and their use by Company establishments located in France;
9. Prioritize patent filings in France for inventions developed in connection with the design and manufacture of Sensitive Products, provided such filings are in the Company's interest. For the avoidance of doubt, the Company may file related patents outside of France, concurrently or subsequently to the French filing;
10. Help preserve the competitiveness and innovative capacity of the Company and maintain, within France, the Industrial capabilities under the Company's control that are necessary to perform, to completion, all current contracts relating to Sensitive Activities (hereinafter, the "Industrial Capabilities").

These capabilities include all tangible and intangible means and resources required to deliver Sensitive Products and associated services to Clients.

Maintenance of such Industrial Capabilities must ensure, throughout the undertaking period:
—operational availability and security maintenance of Sensitive Products in service with Clients;
—deployment, operational availability, and security maintenance of Sensitive Products not yet delivered but contractually committed before the signature of this letter.

The above shall be ensured through:
—execution of such operations by French personnel of the Company (the "Personnel");
—provision of prior notice (48 hours in advance for scheduled work, or as soon as possible for urgent interventions) including identification of Personnel;
—the ability for Clients to request Confidential Defense-level clearances for Personnel;
—the right of Clients to monitor the enforcement of contract security annexes signed prior to the date of this letter.

These measures shall also ensure that:
—supervision, operation, and maintenance of Sensitive Products (at all levels) are conducted from France;
—supervision, operation, and maintenance centers for Sensitive Products are located in France;
—Sensitive Products are shielded from the application of regulations other than applicable French and EU regulations.

C. Commitments Relating to Information Protection

11. If the Company falls under Decree No. 2011-1425 of 2 November 2011, ensure that its industrial sites and information systems involved in Sensitive Activities comply with the rules on the protection of national scientific and technical potential;
12. Ensure that the Company maintains a dedicated information system for all applications related to its Sensitive Activities.

D. Commitments to Inform and Consult the French Authorities

13. Notify the French authorities in writing, with reasonable advance notice, of any event, situation, or change that could affect the conduct of Sensitive Activities, including any foreseeable changes in the Company (e.g., changes in ownership, divestiture of assets related to Sensitive Activities, etc.);
14. Submit annually to the French authorities:

- the Company's latest annual financial statements; and
- a report on the implementation of the present undertakings, including any significant changes and developments in the Company's legal or operational control structure.

At the request of either party, review meetings may be held between the Company's representatives and the relevant French authorities to discuss the submitted documentation.

The French authorities referenced herein include the French Ministry of Defense (Direction Générale de l'Armement) and the Ministry of the Economy and Finance (Directorate General of the Treasury). Both authorities must be copied on all correspondence related to the undertakings.

The Investor agrees to comply with these undertakings for as long as it maintains direct or indirect control of the Company, or until, by mutual agreement with the French authorities and in compliance with the commitments set forth herein, the Company ceases to carry out Sensitive Activities.

These undertakings do not override any other legal or regulatory obligations applicable to the Investor or the Company under French or European Union law.

In particular, if the Investor contemplates an operation referred to in Article R. 153-1 after the effective completion of the Acquisition, it undertakes to inform the future investor that prior authorization from the Minister of the Economy may be required under the Monetary and Financial Code.

Signed for acceptance:

[•] The Investor

Name:

Title:

Date:

For acknowledgment:

[•] The Company

Name:

Title:

Date:

Annex H – Mandate for Interest Representation in the Context of the French FDI Screening Procedure[855]

Power of Attorney – Authorized Interest Representative

I, the undersigned:

—Mr./Ms.:

—Full name:

—Acting in the capacity of (please specify):

—On behalf of the organization (please specify the type of entity and its legal name):

Organization:

Company registration number (SIREN):

Registered address:

Postal code:

City:

(hereinafter referred to as the "Legal Representative")

Hereby appoint

Mr./Ms. [full name], acting as an interest representative within [organization name], a French law company registered under SIRET number [•], with registered office at [address], and duly listed in the Register of Interest Representatives maintained by the Haute Autorité pour la Transparence de la Vie Publique (HATVP), under the following contact details:

Email address:

Landline:

Mobile phone:

(hereinafter referred to as the "Authorized Representative")

The Authorized Representative is hereby empowered under this instrument to initiate and maintain communication, on behalf of the Legal Representative, in connection with the sale or acquisition of [target company name], a company organized under the laws of [jurisdiction], registered under number [•] and having its principal office at [•], with any public official duly authorized or vested by the laws and regulations of the French Republic

855. DUPEYRAT, op. cit.,

within the framework of the French foreign direct investment screening regime ("FDI screening") as governed by Article L.151-3 et seq. of the French Monetary and Financial Code.

These communications must be conducted in accordance with the provisions of French Law No. 2013-907 of October 11, 2013 on Transparency in Public Life, and Decree No. 2017-867 of May 9, 2017 on the Register of Interest Representatives. Accordingly, the Authorized Representative is subject to the reporting obligations provided for in the digital register of interest representatives managed by the Haute Autorité pour la Transparence de la Vie Publique (HATVP).

The Authorized Representative is hereby further empowered to carry out, on behalf of the organization I represent, any registration required under the law in the Register of Interest Representatives of the HATVP, and to submit to the HATVP the information provided for under Articles 2 and 3 of Decree[856] No. 2017-867 of May 9, 2017.

This power of attorney shall take effect as of the date hereof and shall remain in force until revoked or, in any event, until the termination of my duties as Legal Representative.

Executed in:

On:

Signed by the Legal Representative

(Signature preceded by the handwritten statement: "Read and approved")

Signed in acceptance by the Authorized Representative acting as Interest Representative

(Signature preceded by the handwritten statement: "Read and approved")

856. France, Decree No. 2017-867 of May 9, 2017, on the digital directory of interest representatives, Official Journal of the French Republic, No. 0109, May 10, 2017, NOR: ECFM1706418D

Index

This book was typeset by

<pixellence>